Ramon F. Norris
Novem[illegible] 1970

MODERN TRENDS

IN

PSYCHOSOMATIC MEDICINE

2

Edited by

OSCAR W. HILL

B.A., M.B., M.R.C.P., D.P.M.

Senior Lecturer, Academic Department of Psychiatry, Middlesex Hospital Medical School; Honorary Consultant to The Middlesex Hospital, London

LONDON

BUTTERWORTHS

ENGLAND:	BUTTERWORTH & CO. (PUBLISHERS) LTD. LONDON: 88 Kingsway, WC2B 6AB
AUSTRALIA:	BUTTERWORTH & CO. (AUSTRALIA) LTD. SYDNEY: 20 Loftus Street MELBOURNE: 343 Little Collins Street BRISBANE: 240 Queen Street
CANADA:	BUTTERWORTH & CO. (CANADA) LTD. TORONTO: 14 Curity Avenue, 374
NEW ZEALAND:	BUTTERWORTH & CO. (NEW ZEALAND) LTD. WELLINGTON: 49/51 Ballance Street AUCKLAND: 35 High Street
SOUTH AFRICA:	BUTTERWORTH & CO. (SOUTH AFRICA) LTD. DURBAN: 33/35 Beach Grove

Suggested U.D.C. Number: 616·89: 616

ISBN 0 407 31301 X

Printed in Great Britain by
Western Printing Services Ltd.
Bristol

CONTENTS

PREFACE

So many years have passed since the publication of the first series of *Modern Trends in Psychosomatic Medicine* that no attempt has been made to relate the contents of this present volume to the 1955 collection. At that time the psychosomatic approach was only beginning to gain more general acceptance. In 1955 some 70–80 people attended the annual conference of the Society for Psychosomatic Research; by 1969 the number had grown to 250. Although the great majority of those interested are psychiatrists, there is a growing number of non-psychiatric medical men who accept the need to consider and cater for the psyche in all physical illness. Advocates of the psychosomatic approach will have failed if the subject remains a branch of psychiatry, incomprehensible to the general physician and surgeon. To the extent that a more thorough training in the behavioural sciences is now provided for medical students in the United Kingdom, the general understanding of psychological views will increase. On the other side of the fence, psychiatrists have not always sought to express their views in language that would be generally comprehensible. When psychosomatic medicine was a subject largely for psychiatrists and psycho-analysts, it was appropriate to communicate in technical language, but now that the acceptance of psychosomatic ideas is becoming more general it must be desirable that, where it is possible, our jargon should be avoided.

In this volume, all contributors have attempted to pursue this ideal and it is to be hoped that the contents will appeal to the general physician and surgeon as well as to the psychiatrically trained.

There is a general introduction to current concepts by Schmale and his colleagues from Rochester (New York) where the School, led by Engel and Romano, has made such an outstanding contribution to the understanding and the practice of psychosomatic medicine. There are then a series of chapters on psychophysiological mechanisms, followed by the bulk of the work which is devoted to specific illnesses. The final chapter by Wolff is on the teaching and practice of psychosomatic medicine in the general hospital.

There has been a largely sterile debate on the limits of psychosomatic medicine. The view taken in this volume has been that wherever a psychological approach is relevant to the understanding and treatment of patients with somatic disorders, it is a proper subject for psychological study.

The triumph of psychosomatic medicine will come when the term is dropped, psychopathological mechanisms having become accepted with inflammation, the immune response, neoplastic activity, etc., among the acknowledged basic pathological processes in disease.

Finally, may I say how stimulating and rewarding my contact with all the contributors has been and how easy they have made my task. I would also like to express my thanks to the Editorial Staff of the Publishers who have been extremely helpful in every way during the preparation of this volume.

O.W.H.

CHAPTER 1

CURRENT CONCEPTS OF PSYCHOSOMATIC MEDICINE

ARTHUR H. SCHMALE, JR., SANFORD MEYEROWITZ
and DAVID C. TINLING

INTRODUCTION

The meaning of 'psychosomatic' has evolved over the past 30 years from the specific consideration of a few diagnostic entities to a broad conceptual approach. This approach is based on an understanding of human development and includes consideration of the role of psychological factors in health as well as disease. The influence of psychological factors on changes in health includes consideration of the time and setting of disease onset, disease type and/or location, and the course, duration and termination of the illness. Techniques for eliciting, evaluating and managing these factors are all part of the psychosomatic approach.

The student, investigator and therapist interested in the psychosomatic approach must be prepared to deal with multiple frameworks of reference. This chapter will highlight the approach and concepts which the Medical-Psychiatric Liaison Group at the University of Rochester Medical Center has found helpful in the teaching of medical students, house officers and fellows, in our clinical work as consultants and therapists (medical and/or psychiatric) and in our research (Engel, 1967).

SOMATIC AND PSYCHIC DEVELOPMENT

Somatic and psychic factors which influence the maintenance of health and the occurrence of disease can be pursued in human developmental patterns. The concept of development extends from the genic determinants of physical structure and function, including that of the brain, to the process of maturation, or unfolding of potentials, in the individual's pre- and post-natal environment. The

Work on this chapter was supported by Grant No. MH–11668 from the National Institute of Mental Health and Grant No. MH–7521.

environment of the human infant includes nurturing people, particularly the mother, but also other individuals extending to the culture at large. From the beginning the neonate responds to environmental change, a capacity mediated by the central nervous system. The subsequent nature and variety of responses depends not only upon the maturation of the inherited equipment but also upon cumulative past experiences in interacting with the environment. Although through the pre-natal and newborn period the range of responses is limited, any specific response is not simply a matter of passive or automatic reaction to environmental change. There is a range of options for exploration and ultimately for choice.

Rather than review general developmental issues, we shall attempt here to focus on specific somatic and psychic developmental processes we consider to be the likely determinants of: (1) differential disease susceptibility; (2) the later timing of onset of disease; (3) the later patterning and course of illness; and (4) illness behaviour in the presence or absence of somatic disease.

Genic Influences

Genic influences are crucial in determining the nature of the individual's biological structure and processes. This has been demonstrated in the inherited inborn errors of metabolism (e.g. phenylketonuria) where a clinical syndrome can be correlated with a specific metabolic disturbance, usually the activity of an enzyme, controlled by a defective or mutant gene. Most genic influences operate more subtly to determine the nature and organization of biological structures within a physiological range of variability. Such structural variation, both within and outside the central nervous system, may profoundly influence the potential range of behaviours with which the organism reacts to environmental stimuli. For example, a useful psychosomatic model (Mirsky, 1958) postulates that there are inborn determinants of gastric secretion which, in turn, affect earliest experiences in the mother–child feeding situation as well as later personality development and susceptibility to peptic ulcer. The significance of such correlations involving potentially any physiological system will be discussed in the section on somatopsychic–psychosomatic disease.

Present research with a large variety of species is providing insight into the relationship between genotype and behavioural aspects of phenotype (Hirsch, 1963). However, regarding human development, specific links between genotype, biological structure and organization, and behaviour have been largely conjectural. A few family and twin studies, however, have examined specific relationships between genic influences on behaviour and disease susceptibility in a psychosomatic framework (Meyerowitz, Jacox and Hess, 1968; Greene and Swisher, 1969; Pilot and Spiro, 1958).

Pre-natal Influences

Many inferences have been drawn about special and even critical intra-uterine influences which affect subsequent biological and psychological development. Specific information is available concerning the effects of some drugs, infection and toxins, particularly where the result has been a major detectable biological defect, as with rubella or thalidomide. More inferential and speculative have been statements about possible effects of a range of maternal stimuli upon foetal and post-natal development in both psychological and physiological terms. Included among such stimuli are maternal physiological events such as heart beat, respiration, body movement (Greene, 1958; Sontag, 1963) and patterns of hormone secretion, all of which are influenced by the mother's psychological state during pregnancy.

Experiments with pregnant animals suggest that there is considerable basis for the hypotheses alluded to above. Behavioural and other developmental effects on offspring can be correlated with pre-natal nutritional variables (Dubos, 1969), or with hormone administration to pregnant animals (Valenstein, 1968). Not only does the manipulation of pregnant rats by conditioning techniques or handling affect the emotionality of their offspring, but also such pre-natal variables have been shown to influence plasma corticosterone levels and susceptibility to gastric erosions in the offspring (Ader and Conklin, 1963; Ader and Plaut, 1968).

Infancy

The neonatal period and the first one or two years of life might be described as the most critical developmental period from the viewpoint of delineating psychological and somatic factors which determine later success or failure in maintaining health. The events of this period can be sized up in many ways depending upon the theoretical viewpoint and particular method of observation.

The newborn is a helpless creature whose needs must be met by a mothering figure. Yet each newborn has the biological equipment which, through maturation in an average expectable environment (Hartman, 1958) in which his needs are reasonably met, will eventually ensure biological and psychological autonomy. The inherent equipment of each newborn is unique. This general proposition is being refined through observations of specific differences among neonates in autonomic reactivity (Lipton, Steinschneider and Richmond, 1961) and in spontaneous and responsive behaviours such as rooting, sucking, smiling and perception (Kron, Ipsen and Goddard, 1968; Wolff, 1963; Fantz and Nevis, 1968; Escalona, 1963). How the newborn's needs are met depends upon the style and quality of the mother's responsiveness as well as other environmental variables extending through the whole family setting. The newborn period is one of rapid growth and differentiation, which is seen most clearly in the central nervous system (Conel, 1939–1963; Russell, 1959; Rosenzweig, 1966).

There is evidence for the existence of two basic adaptive responses present at birth in the human as well as other species (Kaufman and Rosenblum, 1967; Engel, 1962). These responses consist of 'fight–flight', a state of sudden arousal, and 'conservation–withdrawal', a state of inactivity and reduced energy expenditure. Both of these basic response patterns which have somatic roots are part of the autonomous psychic structure. They provide the limits within which the infant learns to differentiate and separate (Mahler, 1952) or assimilate and accommodate (Piaget, 1952) in relation to its environment.

From a conceptual viewpoint, in the neonatal period there is initially little distinction between the psychological and physiological. At first, all sensation is influenced by the relative physiological instability of the infant. It is assumed that autonomic sensory and motor pathways are mediating impulses which parallel the increasing capacity to perceive and localize body sensations arising from visceral needs. Concomitantly, the infant develops a repertoire of more discrete responses compared to the initial massive crying fit which occurred when any one of a number of indistinguishable afferent stimuli exceeded threshold. Inherent behaviours such as the cry and smile become communications in a feedback system between mother and child and are also associated with the perceived bodily sensations. Later on, together with gesture and facial expression, these behaviours become manifestations of more discrete affect patterns which have communicative value to self, as well as communicative value to the mother, who reinforces the child's signals through her response.

A pertinent example of the significance of these psychobiological interactions is seen in a detailed longitudinal study of an infant with a gastric fistula (Engel, Reichsman and Segal, 1956) which revealed a correlation between object relating activity, accompanying affective response, and physiological patterns. When the infant was outgoing and relating to persons in the environment the highest levels of gastric secretion were seen. These diminished, however, when she withdrew and was not relating (conservation–withdrawal). High levels were also seen initially when approached by a stranger she could not 'escape' (fight–flight). Psychological processes, involved in object-relating in this infant, paralleled physiological processes. Another inference from these statements is that psychological stress, in which the psychic apparatus is unable to 'deal with' the burden imposed upon it, results in qualitative and/or quantitative shifts in psychological processes. Our later discussion of specific clinical syndromes will indicate that such psychological stress is an important feature of illness setting.

Further glimpses of possible determinants of psychosomatic illness can be gained by again examining the mother–child interaction. We can infer that in this relationship the baby progresses from an original biological dependence on the mother to an emerging psychological dependence as well. Eventually it becomes a completely psychological relationship which serves as a template profoundly influencing all future object relationships. This concept has implications for our later discussion of psychological events which frequently precede illness, i.e. the failure to achieve gratification in an object relationship or the loss of an object leading to a variety of distressing affects. The baby's relationship with the mother profoundly influences the development of the psychic apparatus. It is through repeated perceptions of the mother (initially separate, partial representations of various aspects of the mother) as she cares for him, that the mother achieves representation in the baby's psychic apparatus as a specific differentiated object. Also, these percepts coalesce into the representation of a differentiated object during repeated fluctuations of body tension. Therefore, the object that comes to be represented is associated with tension relief and confidence (as well as degrees of pain and frustration). Such a mental representation facilitates the developing capacity to tolerate frustration and maintain balance.

A critical period for establishing object constancy occurs at about the end of the first year of life when the child normally begins to appreciate his dependence on a mothering-type object for his comfort and protection. In the mother's absence he feels overwhelmed and is immobilized by his sense of deprivation. It is this reaction of helplessness which we interpret to be the first evidence of the infant's intrapsychic awareness of the conservation–withdrawal reaction. We believe this period in development is critical, since the feeling of helplessness, if not effectively dealt with by the environment or if recurring frequently or persisting for any length of time, may lead to an intrapsychic self-representation which is dependent on a mothering object for a sense of well-being and self-esteem. Such an orientation may influence cognitive style, mood pattern and even choice of goals and activities.

While brief repeated separations have positive adaptive implications, prolonged separation has damaging effects. Spitz (1965) called our attention to catastrophic behavioural and somatic sequelae in infants following the loss of the mother and without suitable replacement of a mothering figure. Other studies (Schaffer, 1958; Provence and Lipton, 1962; Heinicke and Westheimer, 1965; Bowlby, 1960) of less total deprivation, involving hospitalized or institutionalized babies, also reveal not only behavioural consequences but an increased incidence of illness. A number of recent studies (Powell, Brasel and Blizzard, 1967) have described reversible syndromes of growth failure in children exposed to chronic maternal deprivation. All these are examples of early psychosomatic illness states related to failures to sustain psychological function because the latter is dependent initially on a consistent mother figure.

The process of psychic representation is a psychological concept, but we assume that it retains some connection to the original somatic processes which entered into it. These include memories of bodily distress and subsequent tension relief in relationship to appearance of the object. These also include memories of various bodily sensations experienced in relationship to the object's activity, i.e. the caretaking activities of the mother, consisting of touching, stroking and stimulation of various sorts. We find here implications for future somatic expression of psychic conflict, whereby a wish or idea, frequently appearing in the context of a disturbance in an object relationship is unable to achieve conscious awareness because of attendant conflict and distressing affects. It is instead represented by a body sensation or a perceived alteration in body function which will be discussed as manifestations seen in the syndromes of conversion and hypochondriasis.

As the psychic apparatus evolves in early infancy, in addition to the representation of the object, there are representations of various parts of self, derived initially from body experience. In this sense, Freud's dictum (1923) 'the ego is first and foremost a body-ego' is pertinent. Unique or idiosyncratic aspects of the body's configuration or functioning tend to be built thereafter into the individual's concept of himself, determining later how he may perceive or respond to illness.

Childhood

Beyond infancy many important developmental issues arise of which we can just mention a few for their relevance to psychosomatic problems. The period of the toddler and school child is characterized by: (1) further development of thinking, including the increasing use of symbols instead of the sensory-motor or action 'thinking' of infancy (Piaget, 1952), and a phase of rapid acquisition of language (Lenneberg, 1967); (2) considerably improved control and co-ordination of muscle activity; (3) establishment of excretory sphincter regulation; (4) the development of an increasingly differentiated role with parents, siblings and playmates, including the 'imprint' of sexual identity.

During early childhood we have an opportunity to follow the further development and differentiation of affects from the aforementioned basic adaptive reactions seen in infancy. In terms of object–self differentiation another critical phase comes during the Oedipal period (age 4–6). The child's conflict with parents who are increasingly perceived as sexually differentiated figures is accompanied by his own perception of maturing body functions. In the case of the boy, during this period of vivid fantasies, a fear of castration may arise in relationship to his own phallic sensations and activities while beginning to experience sexual and aggressive wishes towards the parents. While the boy fears castration, the girl may feel that she has already been damaged.

Thus, the child perceives he has limitations biologically, intellectually and socially about which he can do nothing. When unable to succeed as he thinks others expect, he reacts with feelings of hopelessness.* It is as if there is no further reason to try because no matter how much he does he will never succeed. Such an orientation, if reinforced by subsequent experiences in the latency and adolescent periods will lead to an intrapsychic self-representation which cannot succeed in relation to an overly demanding and unrealistic set of standards and goals.

During the period of childhood and pre-adolescence the continuing differentiation of discrete affects in a widening interpersonal sphere has further significance for psychosomatic problems, the nature of which can only be briefly touched upon. For example, the outcome of the specific developmental issues and conflicts of the childhood Oedipal period will lead in many cases to a tendency to

* The two affective reactions of helplessness and hopelessness called affects of 'giving up' will be discussed again subsequently because of their importance as a permissive or facilitating factor in relation to changes in health.

localize concern about the body to specific regions such as the genitals. There are later clinical implications in relationship to illness behaviour. We see some patients, for example, with an inordinate fear of mutilation and body damage which conditions their response to any proposed medical or surgical procedure. Similarly, we see patients who develop marked anxiety and fear of injury secondary to their perception of any pain or other body distress. Also during this childhood period, idiosyncratic ideas and unrealistic fantasies may arise about body functions and persist in the form of fantasies or conversion symptoms involving notions of pregnancy or of sexual function.

Expression of affect and the perception of body function may become involved in the relationship with the parents under certain circumstances so as to serve as important determinants of specific modes of communication in the adult. For example, certain 'pain-prone' (Engel, 1959) individuals, to be discussed later as presenting with a specific clinical syndrome, have had a childhood history in which there was a preferential reinforcement by the parent for reported pain or body distress rather than for verbalization of other feelings.

Also, during this period of beginning symbolic thinking with little adherence to formal rules of logic and a tendency to vivid fantasy formation, the child's observation of sick or dying individuals may be markedly distorted and may serve later to influence the individual's perception of either his own illness or that of other close individuals. During this period there is also an increasing exposure to the family's values concerning illness behaviour in general and specifically attitudes towards doctors. This extends to the family's broader cultural and social class values concerning doctors and illness which will influence the patient's later attitudes towards medical care and even the pattern of medical care in which he will become involved (Zborowski, 1952; Duff and Hollingshead, 1968).

Adolescence

Adolescence can be briefly summarized as a period of markedly accelerated somatic growth accompanied by differentiation of secondary sexual characteristics. Further cognitive developmental milestones are achieved; formal operational thought (Piaget, 1952) emerges to permit new intellectual accomplishments. Individual identity approaches consolidation during this period in an increasingly wide sphere of objects. In addition to everyday issues and conflicts many adolescents become increasingly absorbed in more abstract, intellectual issues and social values. Intellectual activities will now include new ways of thinking about health and illness in oneself, including at times an intellectualized concept of illness which may characterize later patterns of illness behaviour. Certain special problems of a psychosomatic nature are seen in adolescence. Some of these arise from the great preoccupation and concern many adolescents experience in relationship to a rapidly changing body in conjunction with earlier developmental factors. This may lead to persistent concern about body function as discussed later in terms of hypochondriasis. The preoccupation may centre on body image, weight, eating patterns and food choices; associated phobias may be seen; the syndrome of anorexia nervosa may be one outcome. Special clinical problems may involve adjustment to menarche or conflicts around adolescent masturbation with not only psychological disturbance but also possible impairment of sexual functioning. Once established, the menstrual cycle has mood and object-relating correlates (Benedek, 1963) with clinical implications. This is an example of one of the many biological rhythms influencing psychological functioning.

Implications for Health and Sickness in the Adult

We hope to have conveyed throughout the foregoing the important concept that somatic and psychological functioning, both representing the outcome of genic and developmental factors, are initially indistinguishable one from the other, but continue to influence one another, and determine health and sickness patterns in the adult. The personality of the adult includes characteristic patterns of coping, characteristic vulnerability to experiencing stress and 'giving-up' with certain kinds of life events, characteristic pathways of psychological regression, and a large number of idiosyncratic determinants of illness attitudes. Somatic functioning in the adult is characterized by specific physiological patterns and a predisposition to specific alterations in these which, in turn, may activate disease potentials. The tendency of these psychological and physiological factors to influence one another mutually throughout development, and to interact to allow the emergence of disease underlies the concept of psychosomatic specificity which will be discussed further in the next section.

PSYCHIC AND SOMATIC FACTORS IN CHANGES IN HEALTH

Although we have emphasized the mutually interacting influences of psychological and biological factors during development we think it important to remind the reader that these factors represent two separate abstractions and frameworks of reference. At best we can only hope to demonstrate a co-variance between the two frameworks. Furthermore, all observations of an illness event are relative to the physician-observer, his experience, his techniques of observation and the setting in which he makes his observation. What the patient perceives and reports and what the physician-observer sees, hears and understands to be related to a disease model is what has to be evaluated as a possible change in health. In this sense what the physician usually thinks of as a purely somatic, biochemical, physiological disequilibrium, etc., is no more or less a disease than is a state of psychic disequilibrium. The more we see of patients who come to the general practitioner or the internist, the more we are convinced that the most complete diagnosis of dis-ease* usually includes elements of social, cultural, as well as psychic and somatic factors. Sometimes one seems to predominate or precede the others in time and importance; at other times several or all factors seem to be of equal importance.

There has been a concern about the use of the disease model for categorizing psychological dysfunction. A number of investigators, aware of the importance of social and cultural factors involved with becoming a patient, have preferred sociological models (role playing, game theory) to understand psychological and even somatic dysfunction (Mechanic and Volkart, 1961; Zola, 1966; Kasl and Cobb, 1966). Psychic and cultural factors may play a role in the choice of when in the course of feeling sick the patient seeks medical advice, as well as whom he selects as his physician, or how he follows professional advice. We have difficulty, however, in following the extreme position of those who insist that socio-cultural factors are so overriding that the medical profession sees only a biased sample of those who are ill. More information is needed, however, to delineate what is appropriate for categorization as primary and disease as well as what is secondary and 'illness behaviour'.

Setting of Disease Onset

For the first 20 of the past 30 years the psychological setting of somatic disease onset was said to consist of stress, conflict, anxiety, anger and fear with somatic disease being a result of the biological activity that accompanied these feelings. In the last 10 years the psychosomatic literature has extended the observations and interpretation made in the previous period. However, there has been a

* Concept of dis-ease is derived from a multi-dimensional field theory approach (Grinker, 1956).

focusing on object loss, entrapment, and inability to cope with feelings of depression, sadness, or despair reported as the final psychological reaction prior to the onset of somatic disease (Thurlow, 1967). From our clinical studies we have come to refer to the combination of an unresolvable object loss (actual, threatened or symbolic) and its accompanying affects of helplessness or hopelessness as the 'giving-up' reaction. The reaction includes not only feelings of deprivation and despair but loss in self-esteem, a disinterest in relating to objects, a lack of motivation to change what seems to be unchangeable and a recall of similar feelings experienced in the past. Associated with the giving-up reaction is the whole spectrum of diseases from the traditional medical to the psychosomatic and psychiatric (Schmale, 1958; Adamson and Schmale, 1965).

We postulate that the giving-up reaction acts as a facilitating factor which permits disease to appear when it does. The reaction, however, has little or nothing to do with the choice of the disease which may ensue. The individual's specific somatic and psychic predispositions as well as the then current environment and its pathogens will influence the actual chance for disease to occur as well as the type of disease which may ensue (Schmale and Engel, 1967).

There are individuals who have a high predisposition for experiencing helplessness and others who carry a high predisposition for experiencing hopelessness. The former are constantly exposed to what they feel are external sources of deprivation while the latter perceive they are personally responsible for all that goes wrong as a result of internal defects. These extreme orientations have already been delineated as developmentally related to differences which have resulted from relationship experiences and expectations. We think our identification of helplessness and hopelessness predispositions relate to differences in cognitive style as described by such investigators as Witkin *et al.* (1962), who used the terminology of field and body orientation, and Rotter (1966), who has studied preferred patterns of cognitive control in terms of external and internal reinforcement.

Disease Specificity and Location

At one time psychosomatic disease was thought to represent a group of specific diseases, each of which had its own psychodynamic constellation. We now recognize a psychological specificity which is more general and linked in some cases to a number of different dysfunctions within an organ or system. Some studies suggest that all 'psychosomatic patients' regardless of bodily disorders have some personality characteristics in common (Nemiah and Sifneos, 1968).

The anatomical or topographic location at which a change in health may occur is probably not only determined by somatic predisposition but also by the individual's attitude and fantasies about various bodily parts and their functioning as already noted in our discussion of development. The cognitive and physiological set of the individual, the dynamics of the psychological conflict, and the habitual style and/or current use of the body may determine the site and system which will be involved in the dysfunction.

Specific Clinical Syndromes

Somatopsychic–Psychosomatic Disease

A broad notion of psychosomatic specificity as well as specific formulations for particular psychodynamic constellations in a handful of diseases derives from the work of Alexander (1968) in progress since the early 1930s. Previous clinical impressions of a number of observers led to the choice of a group of specific diseases, each of which was thought to have its own constellation of psychological factors. The diseases originally considered psychosomatic are: bronchial asthma, rheumatoid arthritis, ulcerative colitis, essential hypertension, neurodermatitis, thyrotoxicosis, and peptic ulcer. Other investigators have since delineated attitudes and personality profiles associated with a number of additional diseases too numerous to mention.

Alexander's specificity hypothesis has been broadened by Mirsky (1958) and Engel (1962). A conceptual model of somatopsychic–psychosomatic disease has been elaborated by Engel. This states that there is a genically and/or a developmentally determined biological predisposition to a disease which is insufficient in itself to produce disease. The biological predisposition, however, influences the psychic development of the individual in such a way that certain personality characteristics result. At some later point in time disease will occur when the personality characteristics are found inadequate to cope actively with a then existing conflict. Weiner *et al.* (1957) presented a classical test of this hypothesis by predicting on the basis of a known biological predisposition to peptic ulcer (high pepsinogen levels) and the known associated psychological pattern of predisposition (Alexander's formulation for peptic ulcer) who of a group of Army recruits would develop an ulcer in the setting of basic training. (This setting was considered to be the kind of setting in which the ulcer personality would not be able to cope.)

Mirsky (1958) has elaborated the above peptic ulcer model to include the idea that the somatic potential for ulcer exists at birth as a result of the infant's elevated pepsinogen. He postulates that such an elevation must have its influence on the psychological development of the infant which in turn leads to the personality characteristics that make up the psychological profile of the ulcer-prone individual. This model applies not only to the original small group of 'psychosomatic' diseases but potentially speaks to the factors operative in a number of diseases in which there are predisposing somatic influences such as the extremes of endocrine secretion, autonomic and metabolic imbalances, chronic infections and tissue hypersensitivities.

Psychic Syndromes which Present with Somatic Complaints

This is an area of confusion for many interested in psychosomatic phenomena. Many reports are unclear as to what, if any, are the differentiating characteristics of these several syndromes. Some lump them in with the somatopsychic–psychosomatic diseases and psychophysiological reactions and call them all psychosomatic. It is also of importance to recognize that while observing the patient, a psychic symptom expressed in somatic terms may change in its descriptive characteristics so that it appears as a new symptom or as a fantasied new site of involvement.

Somatic conversion symptom.—Conversion reactions are recognized to occur in other than the dramatic forms of paralysis, blindness, deafness and in women with a hysterical character structure. A conversion reaction can occur along with almost any psychic or somatic dysfunction or it may appear all by itself at any age and even in 'essentially healthy' people. It is postulated that the conversion process is an intrapsychic compromise process which prevents a conflict, usually thought of in terms of a basic wish (instinctual drive) and a counteracting prohibition against the wish, from becoming conscious. It is of diagnostic interest that the individual frequently cannot at first remember what was happening at the time the symptom appeared and, more specifically, cannot report the nature of the underlying psychic conflict. (This is in contrast to the style of reporting hypochondriacal preoccupations which will be described in the next section.) The somatic conversion symptom usually represents the sudden and fortuitous identification with an observed symptom of someone the individual has known or heard about or a previously experienced symptom of the individual himself. The developmental aspects of such somatic identifications have been discussed in the first section of this chapter. The symptom usually comes on suddenly and at a time when an underlying wish or impulse threatens to break through to consciousness because it has been reawakened by recent events or sudden associations to past events. It is postulated that the symptom occurs because it has the capacity to express symbolically both the wish and its prohibition without allowing the conflict to become conscious.

In this regard, then, any memory of a previously experienced symptom or the memory of the symptoms of someone else can be recalled and used as a conversion symptom. There is no mysterious or puzzling 'leap' from the psyche to the soma as postulated by Freud (1909) nor is there any restriction of conversion symptoms to the voluntary neuromuscular or sensory perceptive systems as postulated by Alexander (1948) and others. Memories or fantasies of symptoms such as feeling nauseated, breathless, feverish or injured, for example, may occur as conversion reactions as well as the more traditional symptoms of pain, paralysis, anaesthesia and aphasia. Engel (1970b) has catalogued some 109 different symptoms with fantasied involvement of almost every system in the body.

It is important to recognize that an actual somatic or bodily reaction may follow a conversion symptom. Furthermore, a somatic complication may result from a reaction to the fantasied symptom: e.g. vomiting in response to nausea may persist until electrolyte imbalance occurs; hyperventilation in response to breathlessness may lead to respiratory alkalosis; and a local inflammatory reaction followed by a secondary infection may occur in response to a fantasied local injury (Schmale, 1969). Of final importance is the finding that somatic disease has been observed to have had its onset in a location where a conversion reaction was first experienced. This has been reported, for example, with patients who ultimately have developed such diseases as rheumatoid arthritis (Schmale, 1969), multiple sclerosis (Langworthy, 1948; Mei-Tal, Meyerowitz and Engel, 1970), cancer (Ludwig, 1959), herpes (Blank and Brody, 1950), and erythroid autosensitivity (Ratnoff and Agle, 1968).

Hypochondriasis.—There are some who feel hypochondriasis does not exist as an entity and others use it as a wastebasket to label all patients who are resistive to any kind of therapeutic intervention—psychic or somatic. In our experience, a hypochondriacal symptom represents an increased focusing of attention on actual somatic functioning. Underlying the somatic preoccupation is usually a long-standing psychic discomfort for which there has been no relief. In contrast to the conversion reaction the individual with a hypochondriacal reaction can talk freely of his emotional difficulties; however, he does not link up his somatic preoccupation with these problems. They are kept separate (isolated). The focusing of attention on to bodily activity leads to a full time preoccupation with the details of one or another aspect of somatic control. The functioning of the gastro-intestinal, respiratory, cardiovascular, visual, auditory and reproductive systems are favourite sources of such hypochondriacal complaints as spasm, burning, photophobia, hyperacusis, hypersecretion, pulsations, etc. The hypochondriacal symptom may appear at any age and, as indicated in the section on development, some of the earliest experiences with the mothering object may influence the focused awareness of particular bodily functioning as a means to achieve or avoid interpersonal activities. Frequently, the somatic preoccupation will have its onset at the time of a somatic illness and the preoccupation will linger on, e.g. cough, after the 'flu, changes in bowel or urinary habits after immobilization, pain or aching following trauma (see the section on pain-prone). The hypochondriacal symptom is usually difficult to remove. This can be understood in terms of the control the symptom gives the patient not only over himself but also his previous psychic discomfort. The symptom also is reinforced inadvertently by the physician's examinations and tests undertaken to find something 'organically' wrong and by the generous trials of drugs for symptomatic relief. Actual somatic complications may occur as a result of the medications and manipulations used.

Somatic delusion.—Delusional symptoms can be seen as representing the individual's inability to tolerate the awareness of primitive sexual or aggressive impulses or fantasies over which he has no intrapsychic control. These impulses may be expressed in symbolic terms involving fantasied somatic functioning. In contrast to hypochondriasis in which the symptom is limited to specific organ functioning, the delusional symptom has but a fantasied relationship to actual bodily processes. The preoccupation with the fantasied functioning of the body may have familial and cultural determinants as was alluded to in the section on early development. Delusional symptoms are frequently expressed in terms of one part of the body attacking another or the body being taken over or invaded by an outside or foreign substance. These symptoms may be seen as isolated and self-limited symptoms at times of acute and sudden threats to bodily parts and life itself or at times of sudden metabolic disequilibrium (open heart surgery, amputation, renal dialysis, cataract or breast surgery). At other times these symptoms may initiate or be part of a more generalized and chronic psychotic reaction. In the latter case bizarre, self-mutilating behaviour may occur in response to the intensity of the somatic delusion.

Psychophysiological Reactions

These reactions have been variously called vegetative neuroses (Alexander, 1948), actual neurosis, depressive equivalents, neurasthenia, effort syndrome, vasodepressor syncope (Engel, 1959), etc. They are developmentally related to the adaptive processes which initially prepared the body for fight–flight or conservation–withdrawal as described in the section on early development. Later in life these same physiological reactions may be experienced as symptoms when action does not follow the wish to act based on the perception of threat and the recall of past danger. These symptoms of arousal or withdrawal are mediated through endocrine as well as autonomic pathways and begin as acute reactions but may become chronic by means of the learning that takes place (Miller, 1969). In a somatically vulnerable person such excessive or diminished activity can lead to malfunctioning of the same or other systems, e.g. cardiac arrhythmia leading to failure, pylorospasm with secondary obstruction, diarrhoea with bleeding, and vasodepressive reaction with syncope. The symptoms may respond to beta-adrenergic blocking agents, anticholinergic drugs or sedatives. In more chronic situations conditioning techniques may offer hope for relief.

Differential Diagnosis of Pain and the Pain-prone

A frequent request for psychosomatic consultation by medical and surgical practitioners is for a differential diagnosis of pain. The question asked is whether the pain is primarily of peripheral and tissue origin or of central and psychological origin. Engel (1970a) has defined pain as a 'psychological experience involving the concepts of injury and suffering, but not contingent on actual physical injury'. Thus, there is always a compounding of factors which influences the character and intensity of the pain and which determines whether pain is felt and/or reported at all, even with injury. By the time a consultation is requested the picture usually is complicated by the chronic nature of the pain, the many diagnostic and therapeutic interventions, and by the reactions of family, friends and frequently a number of physicians from whom the patient has sought advice. The picture becomes even more complex when the pain has a traumatic setting for its beginning and possible financial compensation for injury or work lost.

The criteria for the differential diagnosis of pain include considerations of the patient's cultural and experiential background. It has been well documented by Petrie (1963) and others that there are some individuals who tolerate very little pain and others who, consistent over many years of measurement in various settings, tolerate a lot of pain. There are still other individuals who fluctuate in their tendency to perceive peripheral stimuli as pain, depending on the life setting and their expectations and psychological needs at the time of the experience. Thus, one cannot evaluate the nature of pain without a complete history of the individual, focusing particularly on his previous experiences of pain and the current life situation in which he finds himself at the time the pain is experienced. Pain has great value as a signal of danger and in eliciting help from others. It is also frequently experienced as a way of avoiding conflict, of reducing activity, of atoning for wrong doing and of alleviating or preventing feelings of guilt. As previously mentioned in the section on psychic syndromes with presenting somatic complaints, pain may represent a conversion, hypochondriacal or a delusional reaction. Furthermore, pain can also occur as a result of a prolonged psychophysiological reaction. If the psychological price the pain-prone individual (Engel, 1959) is paying through suffering is not too great it may be difficult to reduce his discomfort. Tinling and Klein (1966) have described the role of pain in controlling aggression in a group of solitary hunters.

Oral Somatic Syndromes

The syndromes of obesity, anorexia nervosa, alcoholism and drug addiction make up a group which are very difficult to treat because they involve immediate forms of gratification which are under the individual's control. It gives the individual a detachment or a sense of independence from events or people in his environment who are depriving or inconsistent in their responses. The individual does not have to anticipate or wait to see what the environment is willing to give and does not have to conform or perform according to the wishes of someone else. It is possible that each of these diseases may have an underlying biological defect, perhaps even genically determined. The defect may, in turn, influence psychic as well as somatic development and relationships. In any case, it is becoming evident that these individuals reinforce the patterns of their disease by their perceptions of themselves and their environment. The therapeutic challenge is to break through the pattern of distorted beliefs and perceptions. For some the postponement of gratification is more than they can tolerate. Thus, the physician must begin by manipulating and substituting other gratifications. The ultimate goal in therapy is to convince the patient that he has means of controlling himself and his environment other than by means of food, alcohol or drugs.

Delirium and Dementia

The group of disorders classified as the organic brain syndromes, including delirium and dementia, are often omitted when discussing or considering psychosomatic relationships. This is so in spite of a demonstrably more direct relationship between psychic and somatic factors. As pointed out in a recent comprehensive review by Lipowski (1967), delirium can be understood as a psychosomatic condition which highlights the dependence of psychological activity upon intact cerebral functioning. Cerebral functioning, in turn, may be influenced by a wide variety of metabolic disturbances, toxins, drugs and alteration in stimulus input from the environment. The psychological response to any of these somatic factors will be determined to an extent by antecedent personality variables and the nature of the current setting, including psychological stress, but invariably a specific defect in attention, orientation and memory is found. Engel and Romano (1959) contributed in a major way to a definition of this syndrome, calling it cerebral insufficiency and relating the above psychological characteristics to specific physiological insufficiency. (The latter is manifested by relative electroencephalographic changes which require serial observations.)

Drugs and Placebos

The literature now extensively documents the variability of reaction to sedatives, stimulants and placebos. We have learned that much depends on what the individual expects or wants to be the result. Those individuals who in general are most suggestible seem to get the greatest response. As indicated earlier the cognitive style and the anticipation of reward or punishment may influence an individual's physiological as well as psychological response. It is generally recognized that to achieve reduction in somatic discomfort from a placebo does not differentiate the malingerer from the individual with a psychic syndrome or from the individual with peripheral somatic dysfunction.

Effects of Psychological Factors on the Course and Treatment of Disease

As indicated in the section on pain, the patient may find that being sick provides a more comfortable adaptation than was possible when not sick. The unconscious preoccupation and interest in being sick in such patients can lead to a change in the self-image and the use of various psychic defence mechanisms to restrict interests and activities. Actual symptom reinforcement may occur by means of unconsciously determined acting out behaviours which may include not following the regime prescribed and the drugs necessary to control symptoms as with arthritis, diabetes, peptic ulcer, heart failure, hypertension, etc. There are others who are frightened by somatic symptoms and cannot tolerate the immobility imposed by the symptoms or the treatment. Patients with myocardial infarction, for example, have notorious difficulty in observing bed rest. At such times greater physiological stress and complications occur as a result of the patient's psychic conflict over following the programme of inactivity than would follow from being allowed a minimal amount of activity.

We have come to recognize that much of the practice of medicine involves making the patient more comfortable and productive while he and his body reach new levels of adaptation during various phases of growth and ageing. Our therapeutic zeal to cure 'the disease' must be tempered by our understanding of the many levels at which each patient experiences 'dis-ease'. Although we have outlined a perspective we think important in understanding psychic and somatic functioning, the application has to depend on the individual physician's sensitivity and experience with specific patients and their problems (Romano, 1963). The fascination in medicine is that there are no two patients who will perceive and react in the same way regardless of the similarity of the apparent pathology.

TRENDS IN PSYCHOSOMATIC RESEARCH

Many disciplines are concerned with the concomitant study of behaviour, central nervous system activity and psychological aspects of illness. As a consequence we are faced with the challenge of using and understanding two broad vocabularies, one for biological phenomena and one for psychosocial events. This does not mean that we have to see some kind of theoretical interface operating between our vocabularies. It is not our purpose to review all of the work relating to the co-variance of behaviour and physiology, but only some selected samples of what appear to be important trends.

An area with prospects for future research is the relationship of perceptual style to early life experience and its effect on health. From our previous discussion the mutual influencing of the two should be apparent. Witkin *et al.* (1962) have developed a technique which differentiates perceptual style along a spectrum according to how an individual can disembed an object from its context. The individual's position in the resultant continuum of field orientation may, in correlative studies, relate to a number of variables (Pillsbury *et al.*, 1967), including differential susceptibility to specific disease (Silverstone and Kissin, 1968; Karp and Pardes, 1965; Fishbein, 1963; Karp, Winters and Pollack, 1969). Similarly, Petrie, Holland and Wolk (1963) have demonstrated that many people tend to augment painful stimuli while others tend to diminish painful stimuli and that such augmented perception of pain co-varies with a more externally derived perception of object size through touch. These observations are consistent with our aforementioned discussion of the clinical problem of pain and may help us in our diagnostic work.

Rotter (1966) and his colleagues have demonstrated that people differ in terms of how they view the control of their reinforcement in any situation. Some people see and expect environmental factors to be the determining and controlling force in their lives and decisions. Other people feel that environmental responses are inconsequential while their own decisions are most important. Rotter finds that learning behaviour differs depending upon how people view the control in a situation. This may have significance for psychosomatic medicine regarding the nature of the conditioning of physiological responses, the differential effect of stressful situations among individuals, and, again, in relationship to disease susceptibility.

Delgado (1966) has experimented widely with central nervous system stimulation in animals and in humans. Electrical stimulation of the human brain has evoked a variety of behaviours including complex motor responses, aggressive behaviour, and the inhibition of activity. Mason's (1968) psycho-endocrine research demonstrates the multi-potency and overlapping of hormone effects that may be additive, synergistic, permissive or antagonistic. His work indicates the importance of the endocrine system 'as the third effector system of the brain, along with the skeletal-muscular and the autonomic systems'.

The clinical work of Sachar, Mackenzie and Binstock (1967) has demonstrated correlations between psychological and behavioural events and adrenal corticosteroid functioning. The adrenal appears to respond to disequilibrium with an increase in corticosteroid production. Sachar has demonstrated that as long as people are functioning in a stable system, healthy or psychotic, they will not increase their steroid output. However, it is with change such as occurs during the event of hospitalization, a confrontation, a particular stress, or an imposed environmental event, that patients demonstrate increased steroid production.

Using instrumental techniques Miller (1969) and his associates have been able to condition autonomic responses involving all major areas of functioning which were traditionally thought not to be subject to classical conditioning. We now have the potential not only for conditioning and shaping autonomic responses which have control over the viscera, but also for using such techniques to extinguish aberrant autonomic patterns in patients.

Several laboratories are currently studying sleep. Behaviour patterns such as dreaming, enuresis, somnambulism and night terrors are related to different EEG levels of sleep (Broughton, 1968). Sleep and dream deprivation has been an intriguing model of psychic disruption for some workers (Dement, 1960).

The importance of awake–sleep cycles, light–dark cycles, temperature cycles, fluctuating cycles of important metabolites in the serum, etc., all seem highly relevant to current psychosomatic research (Stroebel, 1967). Almost all biological events appear to have a pattern or rhythm; researchers are beginning to learn that their results may vary considerably according to where in a cycle they study a biological pattern.

We have offered a few examples of promising approaches to the study of the co-variance between behaviour and biological phenomena. The complexity of this co-variance is difficult for researcher and clinician. But we believe such is the path to more insight into how man integrates and organizes function, and how when significantly stressed from either external or internal factors, he may utilize a pattern of adaptation which will lead to a state that may be diagnosed as disease.

REFERENCES

Adamson, J. D. and Schmale, A. H. (1965). 'Object Loss, Giving Up, and the Onset of Psychiatric Disease.' *Psychosom. Med.*, **27,** 557.

Ader, R. and Conklin, P. M. (1963). 'Handling of Pregnant Rats: Effects on Emotionality of Their Offspring.' *Science, N.Y.*, **142**, 411.

— and Plaut, S. M. (1968). 'Effects of Prenatal Maternal Handling and Differential Housing on Offspring Emotionality, Plasma Corticosteroid Levels and Susceptibility to Gastric Erosions.' *Psychosom. Med.* **30**, 277.

Alexander, F. (1948). *Fundamentals of Psychoanalysis*, p. 245. New York: Norton.

— (1968). *Psychosomatic Specificity.* Chicago: University of Chicago Press.

Benedek, T. (1963). 'Investigation of the Sexual Cycle in Women.' *Archs gen. Psychiat.*, **8**, 25.

Blank, H. and Brody, M. W. (1950). 'Recurrent Herpes Simplex.' *Psychosom. Med.*, **12**, 254.

Bowlby, J. (1960). 'Grief and Mourning in Infancy and Early Childhood.' *Psychoanal. Study Child*, **15,** 9.

Broughton, R. J. (1968). 'Sleep Disorders: Disorders of Arousal?' *Science, N.Y.*, **159,** 1070.

Conel, L. J. (1939–63). *The Postnatal Development of the Human Cerebra Cortex*, Vols. I–VI. Cambridge: Harvard University Press.

Delgado, J. M. R. (1966). 'Emotions.' In *Self-Selection Psychology Textbook*, pp. 1–56, Ed. by J. A. Vernon. Dubuque, Iowa: Brown.

Dement, W. (1960). 'The Effect of Dream Deprivation.' *Science, N.Y.*, **131,** 1705.

Dubos, R. (1969). 'Lasting Biological Effects of Early Influences.' *Perspect. Biol. Med.*, **12,** 479.

Duff, R. S. and Hollingshead, A. B. (1968). *Sickness and Society*. New York: Harper & Row.

Engel, G. L. (1959). ' "Psychogenic" Pain and the Pain-Prone Patient.' *Am. J. Med.*, **26,** 899.

— (1962). *Psychological Development in Health and Disease*. Philadelphia: Saunders.

— (1967). 'Medical Education and the Psychosomatic Approach. A Report on the Rochester Experience 1946–1966.' *J. Psychosom. Res.*, **11,** 77.

— (1970a). 'Pain.' In *Signs and Symptoms. Applied Pathology, Physiology and Clinical Interpretation*, 5th ed., Ed. by C. M. MacBryde. Philadelphia: Lippincott.

— (1970b). 'Conversion Symptoms.' In *Signs and Symptoms. Applied Pathology, Physiology and Clinical Interpretation*, 5th ed., Ed. by C. M. MacBryde. Philadelphia: Lippincott.

— and Romano, J. (1959). 'Delirium. A Syndrome of Cerebral Insufficiency.' *J. chron. Dis.*, **9,** 260.

— Reichsman, F. and Segal, H. L. (1956). 'The Study of an Infant with a Gastric Fistula. I. Behavior and the Rate of Total HCL Secretion.' *Psychosom. Med.* **18,** 374.

Escalona, S. K. (1963). 'Patterns of Infantile Experience and the Developmental Process.' *Psychoanal. Study Child*, **18,** 197.

Fantz, R. L. and Nevis, S. (1968). 'Pattern Preferences and Perceptual-Cognitive Development in Early Infancy.' In *Annual Progress in Child Psychiatry and Child Development*, p. 22, Ed. by S. Chess and A. Thomas. New York: Brunner Mazel.

Fishbein, G. M. (1963). 'Perceptual Modes and Asthmatic Symptoms: An Application of Witkin's Hypothesis.' *J. consult. Psychol.*, **27,** 54.

Freud, S. (1909). *Notes Upon A Case of Obsessional Neurosis*, Standard Edition, Vol. 10, p. 157. London: The Hogarth Press.

— (1923). *The Ego and the Id.* Vol. XIX. London: The Hogarth Press.

Greene, W. A. (1958). 'Early Object Relations, Somatic, Affective and Personal.' *J. nerv. ment. Dis.*, **126,** 225.

— and Swisher, S. (1969). 'Psychological and Somatic Variables Associated with the Development and Course of Monozygotic Twins Discordant for Leukemia.' Presented at the New York Academy of Sciences Second Conference on Psychophysiological Aspects of Cancer, May 1968.

Grinker, R. R. (Ed.) (1956). *Toward a Unified Theory of Human Behavior.* New York: Basic Books.

Hartman, H. (1958). *Ego Psychology and the Problem of Adaptation.* New York: International Universities Press.

Heinicke, C. M. and Westheimer, I. (1965). *Brief Separations.* New York: International Universities Press.

Hirsch, J. (1963). 'Behavior Genetics and Individuality Understood.' *Science, N.Y.* **142,** 1436.

Karp, S. A. and Pardes, H. (1965). 'Psychological Differentiation (Field Dependence) in Obese Women.' *Psychosom. Med.,* **27,** 238.

— Winters, S. and Pollack, I. W. (1969). 'Field Dependence Among Diabetics.' *Archs gen. Psychiat.,* **21,** 72.

Kasl, S. and Cobb, S. (1966). 'Health Behavior, Illness Behavior and Sick Role Behavior.' *Archs Environ. Health,* **12,** 531.

Kaufman, I. C. and Rosenblum, L. (1967). 'The Reaction to Separation in Infant Monkeys: Anaclitic Depression and Conservation Withdrawal.' *Psychosom. Med.,* **29,** 649.

Kron, R. E., Ipsen, J. and Goddard, K. E. (1968). 'Consistent Individual Differences in the Nutritive Sucking Behavior of the Human Newborn.' *Psychosom. Med.,* **30,** 151.

Langworthy, O. R. (1948). 'Relation of Personality Problems to Onset and Progress of Multiple Sclerosis.' *Archs Neurol. Psychiat.,* **59,** 13.

Lenneberg, E. H. (1967). *Biological Foundations of Language.* New York: John Wiley.

Lipowski, Z. J. (1967). 'Delirium, Clouding of Consciousness and Confusion. *J. nerv. ment. Dis.,* **145,** 227.

Lipton, E. L., Steinschneider, A. and Richmond, J. B. (1961). 'Autonomic Function in the Neonate: V. Individual Differences in Cardiac Reactivity.' *Psychosom. Med.,* **23,** 473.

Ludwig, A. O. (1959). 'The Role of Identification in the Conversion Process.' In *On the Mysterious Leap from the Mind to the Body: A Workshop Study on the Theory of Conversion,* p. 105, Ed. by F. Deutsch. New York: International Universities Press.

Mahler, M. S. (1952). 'On Child Psychosis and Schizophrenia: Autistic and Symbiotic Infantile Psychoses.' *Psychoanal. Study Child,* **7,** 286.

Mason, J. W. (1968). 'Organization of Psychoendocrine Mechanisms.' *Psychosom. Med.,* **30,** Pt. II.

Mechanic, D. and Volkart, E. (1961). 'Stress, Illness Behavior, and the Sick Role.' *Am. Soc. Rev.,* **26,** 1961.

Mei-tal, V., Meyerowitz, S. and Engel, G. L. (1970). 'The Role of Psychological Process in a Somatic Disorder: Multiple Sclerosis. I. The Emotional Setting of Illness. II. The Role of the Conversion Process in the Prelude of Illness.' *Psychosom. Med.* In Press.

Meyerowitz, S., Jacox, R. F. and Hess, D. W. (1968). 'Monozygotic Twins Discordant for Rheumatoid Arthritis: A Genetic, Clinical and Psychological Study of 8 Sets.' *Arthritis Rheum.,* **11,** 1.

Miller, N. E. (1969). 'Learning of Visceral and Glandular Responses.' *Science, N.Y.,* **163,** 434.

Mirsky, I. A. (1958). 'Physiologic, Psychologic and Social Determinants in the Etiology of Duodenal Ulcer.' *Am. J. dig. Dis.,* **3,** 285.

Nemiah, J. C. and Sifneos, P. E. (1968). 'A Study of the Specificity of

Current Psychological Factors Involved in the Production of Psychosomatic Disease in Patients Each Suffering From Two Psychosomatic Illnesses' (Abstract). *Psychosom. Med.*, **30,** 553.

Petrie, A., Holland, T. and Wolk, I. (1963). 'Sensory Stimulation Causing Subdued Experiences: Audio-Analgesia and Perceptual Augmentation and Reduction.' *J. nerv. ment. Dis.*, **137,** 312.

Piaget, J. (1952). *The Origins of Intelligence in Children.* New York: International Universities Press.

Pillsbury, J. A., Meyerowitz, S., Salzman, L. F. and Satran, R. (1967). 'Electroencephalographic Correlates of Perceptual Style: Field Orientation.' *Psychosom. Med.*, **29,** 441.

Pilot, M. L. and Spiro, H. M. (1958). 'The Use of Monozygous Twin Cases in the Study of Psychosomatic Concepts.' *Yale J. Biol. Med.*, **31,** 92.

Powell, G. F., Brasel, J. A. and Blizzard, R. M. (1967). 'Emotional Deprivation and Growth Retardation Simulating Idiopathic Hypopituitarism.' *New Engl. J. Med.*, **276,** 1271.

Provence, S. and Lipton, R. C. (1962). *Infants in Institutions.* New York: International Universities Press.

Ratnoff, O. D. and Agle, D. P. (1968). 'Psychogenic Purpura: A Reevaluation of the Syndrome of Autoerythrocyte Sensitization.' *Medicine,* **47,** 475.

Romano, J. (1963). 'Requiem or Reveille: The Clinician's Choice.' *J. med. Educ.*, **38,** 584.

Rosenzweig, M. R. (1966). 'Environmental Complexity, Cerebral Change and Behavior.' *Am. Psychologist,* **21,** 321.

Rotter, J. B. (1966). 'Generalized Expectancies for Internal Versus External Control of Reinforcement.' *Psychological Monographs: General and Applied,* Vol. 80, No. 1, Whole No. 609.

Russell, W. R. (1959). *Brain, Memory, Learning—A Neurologist's View.* Oxford University Press.

Sachar, E. J., Mackenzie, J. M. and Binstock, W. A. (1967). 'Corticosteroid Responses to Psychotherapy of Depression: I. Evaluation During Confrontation of Loss.' *Archs gen. Psychiat.*, **16,** 461.

Schaffer, H. R. (1958). 'Objective Observations of Personality Development in Early Infancy.' *Br. J. med. Psychol.*, **31,** 174.

Schmale, A. H. (1958). 'Relationship of Separation and Depression to Disease.' *Psychosom. Med.*, **20,** 259.

— (1969). 'Somatic Expressions and Consequences of Conversion Reactions.' *N.Y. St. J. Med.*, **69,** 1878.

— and Engel, G. L. (1967). 'The Giving Up–Given Up Complex Illustrated on Film.' *Archs gen. Psychiat.*, **17,** 135.

Silverstone, S. and Kissin, B. (1968). 'Field Dependence in Essential Hypertension and Peptic Ulcer.' *J. psychosom. Res.*, **12,** 157.

Sontag, L. W. (1963). 'Somatopsychics of Personality and Body Function.' *Vita Humana,* **6,** 1.

Spitz, R. A. (1965). *The First Year of Life.* New York: International Universities Press.

Stroebel, C. F. (1967). 'Behavioral Aspects of Circadian Rhythms.' In *Comparative Psychopathology*, Ed. by J. Zubin and H. F. Hunt. New York: Grune and Stratton.

Thurlow, H. J. (1967). 'General Susceptibility to Illness: A Selective Review.' *Can. med. Ass. J.*, **97,** 1.

Tinling, D. C. and Klein, R. F. (1966). 'Psychogenic Pain and Aggression: The Syndrome of the Solitary Hunter.' *Psychosom. Med.*, **28,** 738.

Valenstein, E. S. (1968). 'Steroid Hormones and the Neuropsychology of Development.' In *The Neuropsychology of Development*, Ed. by R. L. Isaacson. New York: John Wiley.

Weiner, H., Thaler, M., Reiser, M. F. and Mirsky, I. A. (1957). 'Etiology of Duodenal Ulcer: I. Relation of Specific Psychological Characteristics to Rate of Gastric Secretion.' *Psychosom. Med.*, **19,** 1.

Witkin, H. A., Dyk, R. B., Faterson, H. F., Goodenough, D. R. and Karp, S. A. (1962). *Psychological Differentiation.* New York: John Wiley.

Wolff, P. H. (1963). 'Observations on the Early Development of Smiling.' In *Determinants of Infant Behaviour*, Vol. II, p. 113, Ed. by B. M. Foss. New York: John Wiley.

Zborowski, M. (1952). 'Cultural Components in Responses to Pain.' *J. soc. Issues*, **8,** 16.

Zola, I. K. (1966). 'Culture and Symptoms.' *Am. Soc. Rec.*, **31,** 615.

CHAPTER 2

AFFECT AND FANTASY IN PATIENTS WITH PSYCHOSOMATIC DISORDERS

JOHN C. NEMIAH and PETER E. SIFNEOS

BACKGROUND TO THE STUDY

At a time when the clinical investigation of psychosomatic disorders was focused on elucidating the specificity of personality patterns for the various disease entities under study, Ruesch (1948) called attention to the fact that certain personality traits were common to all patients suffering from psychosomatic illness. In particular he noted that 'verbal, gestural, or other symbols are not connected with affects and feelings' and that 'signs used for self-expression originate in the somatic sphere or are related to action'.

A year later, in an important publication suggesting that the psychological manifestations of patients with psychosomatic diseases were related to the function of the rhinencephalon, MacLean (1949) cited the clinical observation that the patient with such a disease had 'an apparent intellectual inability to verbalize his emotional feelings', with the result that 'instead of finding expression and discharge in the symbolic use of words and appropriate behavior, (they) might be conceived as being translated into a kind of "organ language"'.

Although great strides were made during the years following MacLean's publication in the elucidation of the physiology of the limbic system (as the rhinencephalon came to be called), the clinical observations to which he had called attention lay fallow. It was not until the early 1960s, when Marty and de M'Uzan (1963) and Marty, de M'Uzan and David (1963) summarized their clinical experience with psychosomatic patients in France, that attention was focused on the phenomenological aspects of the mentation of patients with psychosomatic disorders.

Marty and de M'Uzan made the striking observation that psychosomatic patients were apparently incapable of producing fantasies.

The work reported in this chapter was supported in part by a National Institute of Mental Health Research Grant, Project No. M–626 (c).

During interviews the content of their associations reflected and was determined by everyday events in their lives, particularly activities in which they were engaged. Unlike ordinary fantasy, which through its imagery symbolizes and expresses drive tensions, the thought content of their patients with psychosomatic disorders was mundane, restricted in time, unimaginative, tied to reality, and utilitarian. To this latter kind of mentation the authors gave the name 'pensée opératoire'.

In 1967, Sifneos (1967) presented his 'preliminary psychological observations on randomly selected patients' with psychosomatic disorders. A striking characteristic of some of the patients in this group was 'their marked difficulty to find appropriate words to describe how they feel. Their vocabulary is limited . . . They give the impression that they do not understand the meaning of the word "feeling".'

GENESIS OF THE STUDY

Some 15 years ago one of us (Nemiah, 1964) conducted a study of specificity in psychosomatic disease which involved the tape-recording of psychiatric interviews of patients with two psychosomatic disorders* aimed at eliciting the psychodynamic and situational factors related to the onset or exacerbation of each disease. Thirty-eight patients (17 women and 21 men) were seen, each of whom gave a current or past history of two of the following illnesses: duodenal ulcer, rheumatoid arthritis, asthma, ulcerative colitis and atopic dermatitis. It was noted that in the group as a whole (regardless of which diseases each patient manifested) their personality structure was characterized in the majority by the presence of marked reaction formation against aggression and dependency, and in almost half of the patients by the frequent use of suppression, repression or denial of affects.

Inspired by the observations of Marty and de M'Uzan, and those of Sifneos summarized earlier, we decided to re-examine the available typed protocols of their interviews, with a view to determining the nature of the patients' thought content and expression of affects. There were three reasons for turning to the productions of these patients recorded so long ago:

(1) The findings concerning the personality structures of patients in this group suggested that they might have restrictions in their fantasy and affective life similar to the patients observed by Marty

* Drs. Frances J. Bonner and Gardner C. Quarton collaborated in interviewing these patients.

and de M'Uzan, and by Sifneos. However, in the earlier study the use of summarizing analytic terms (e.g. 'reaction formation', 'repression') to categorize them involved an inference from more basic clinical phenomenological observations, and a valid comparison of these patients with those of other investigators required looking directly at their actual productions.

(2) The interviews had been carried out with a view to stimulating the patients' free associations, and it could therefore be anticipated that the material elicited from them would adequately reflect the characteristics of their mental functioning.

(3) The interviews had been completed long before either of us had become familiar with the concept of the 'pensée opératoire' or had formulated our own more recent notions of the expression of affects by patients with psychosomatic disorders. We could accordingly be confident that the interviewing of this group of patients had not been influenced by any bias resulting from such concepts and notions.

OBSERVATIONS

The protocols of 20 patients (8 women and 12 men) were available for this study. As manifested in their interviews, 16 of the 20 showed: (1) a marked difficulty in verbally expressing or describing their feelings; and (2) an absence or striking diminution of fantasy, and the frequent production of the kind of mental content delineated by Marty and de M'Uzan (the 'pensée opératoire').

Expression of Affect

In discussing situations in which they might normally have been expected to experience affect, these patients manifested either a total unawareness of feelings or an almost complete incapacity to put into words what they were experiencing. On those occasions where they were aware of a vague, usually unpleasant affect, or where they would state that they were 'mad' or 'angry' or 'sad', the attempts of the interviewer to get them to elaborate on their experience or to describe it further usually ran into an impenetrable mental blankness. When thus pressed, the patients would respond, 'I can't say', 'I can't tell you anything more', 'I can't express it', 'I can't put it into words'.

This phenomenon had no consistent relation to their verbal facility (many patients were very voluble as will be seen shortly), to their educational level or to their sophistication about psychological procedures and functioning. Two examples must suffice by way of demonstration:

(1) A professional woman of 38 with duodenal ulcer and asthma had completed three years of college followed by further training in a professional school. With reference to feeling angry the following interchange occurred:

Patient: 'It gives me some physical disagreeable feeling.'

Doctor: 'Can you explain it?'

P. 'Well, it seems to me that I get sort of a tightness in my chest and throat. I feel inarticulate when I come here and try to explain my feeling to you.'

D. 'I think it's very hard for you to talk about feelings.'

P. 'I don't know why it is. I used to be considered a pretty articulate person, but I noticed it at the other session too at the other hospital. When it comes to describing feelings, I seem to be at a loss for words.'

(2) Two years before being interviewed in this investigation, a woman of 42 with duodenal ulcer and rheumatoid arthritis had completed a $3\frac{1}{2}$ year analysis in the course of a psychoanalytic research study of arthritis. She confessed to having always found it difficult to talk freely to the previous analyst and during the series of five investigative interviews in the later study still remained inarticulate about her feelings. When asked to elaborate on feelings of sadness and anger which she reported she had experienced as a response to a disappointment in marriage plans, she replied:

P. 'I don't seem to think straight. I just go around in circles.'

D. 'I wonder what the feeling of sadness is that you have. Is there any way you can describe it?'

P. 'No, I really can't. You don't mean my physical feeling?'

D. 'Not necessarily. But are there physical feelings that go with the sadness? Do you feel it anywhere?'

P. 'Oh, I have a sort of dead feeling.'

D. 'Where?'

P. 'Oh, right through my stomach. That's not a very full explanation.'

D. 'When you feel angry, do you have any physical feelings anywhere? Do you feel that in any part of your body?'

P. 'No, Oh. I can't say that I do. I don't really know now. I guess I get warm.'

The 'Pensée Opératoire'

The patients varied in regard to the freedom with which they would talk with the interviewer. A few tended to be laconic in their remarks and to require the constant stimulation of questions to keep them going. Many, on the other hand, spoke very freely, some to the point of marked garrulousness. The spontaneous associations of the great majority of them was characterized by: (1) a nearly total absence of fantasy or other material related to their inner, private mental life of thoughts, attitudes and feelings; and (2) a recounting, often in almost infinite detail of circumstances and events in their environment, including their own actions. It was noteworthy that in some of these patients a question by the interviewer regarding their feelings about some seemingly disturbing event in their lives would produce such a response.

The following patients exemplify this kind of mentation (pensée opératoire):

(1) Some 30 years before the interview, a man of 70 with a long history of duodenal ulcer and rheumatoid arthritis had received from a local doctor a series of 'serum shots' in his right arm (the nature and purpose of which could not be determined), which had resulted in a stiffness in the elbow and a partial crippling of that extremity. When asked by the interviewer, 'How did you feel about this crooked arm the doctor gave you?', the patient replied:

'Well, when I went back the next week (he was giving me a shot a week)—when I went back the next week he gave me a double shot—well, I came right home. My wife could drive the car. I was perspiring and everything. How I got up in the morning with my arm like that—I was going to say something to him, but before I could do it, he had my sleeve up and said, "Can't you straighten that arm out any more than that?" I said, "No." "Oh, isn't that a shame." He never made any attempt to straighten that arm. I believe that's the last time I went to him. The way I felt—well—the way he talked, and I was supposed to be that way all my life. But you know, of course, when you have anything like that, you always hope that eventually you'll be all right again. And I worked with that arm quite a lot. I mean, around the house.'

D. 'You were going to say something to him about it, though?'

P. 'Yes, I don't know just what, now. I was going to inquire as to what happened and what the results would be. But when he said to me, "Oh, my goodness! You can't straighten that arm out any better than that?" he said, "Isn't that a shame! Don't ever let anybody put weights on it." So, it was quite a blow, but still I held hopes that—sometimes you have faith or something that you're going to snap out of it. But that's been that way for years and years.'

D. 'But how did you feel about his giving it to you?'

P. 'Well, I didn't think much about it. I wasn't—a professional man should know what he was doing. He should know what he was giving me. He even mentioned, "I'll give you a double shot" (I think he said), "and we'll drive that out of you". And it's a funny thing (I don't think I've told you this), this arm—when I played ball in Chelsea, the last year I played, a fellow by the name of Morgan and I were throwing the ball. We were throwing it too hard to start; we weren't just lobbing it around. We were throwing it too hard, and I got this terrible sore right elbow from it. I was practically no good all season. I stayed with the team, but I didn't play my regular position. I was on the reserve.'

(2) A man of 37 with duodenal ulcer and ulcerative colitis mentioned that his troubles had started after his marriage had brought upon him the responsibility of a wife and family. When the doctor asked him, 'How did you feel about this responsibility?', the patient responded:

'I don't know what you mean. What do you mean how I'd feel about it?'

D. 'What did you think about it? How did you feel about it?'

P. 'It was hard, the responsibility. That's how I figured it. I don't know how you do, but it was just hard on me.'

D. 'Hard on you?'

P. 'Because I wasn't making much money driving a cab, you know what I mean? She was hollering "You're not making enough money to feed the kids". You know what I mean?'

D. 'Your wife would holler at you like that?'

P. 'It's true enough. I wasn't making much money—forty-five, fifty dollars sometimes. Sometimes I'd go in the garage for a day. I don't get paid for that. The cab breaks down or the night man breaks down in the night time and leaves me a note. I got to go into the garage with it. You know what I mean? But I could try to take it out for the day, try to make my day's pay with it. But at night time—a guy's going to lose his money at night. And the boss says "What's the story? Couldn't you go into the garage today?" And the cab would get fixed about two or three o'clock. What am I going to make till five o'clock? So I leave the cab there till the night man comes in and lose the whole day's pay. We don't get paid for that, you know. So I'm just wanting to wait till I get on my feet and get good and strong, that's all. I don't want to try anything yet. I'll go on my own afterwards. If I tried to do something now, then I got to come back again. There's no such thing as you're not going to be as good as you were. If I'm having trouble with it now, I think I'll have trouble with it always.'

In each of these two patients it is to be noted that there is an apparent wealth of mental content which they pour out in detail in response to a question about their feelings. For the most part, however, the content of their thoughts does not express their feelings, or contain fantasies associated with and determined by their affect. On the contrary, it dwells primarily on events in their surroundings, including their own actions as well as that of others. As one considers the events they describe, one can easily understand how these events might act as a stimulus to unpleasant feelings. The patients, however, focus on the facts of their environment, not on their fantasies and related affects. Their thoughts are stimulus-bound rather than drive-directed.

Manifestations of Affect

In our broader clinical experience with patients with psychosomatic disorders we have been struck by the frequency with which there is a paucity of external, observable manifestations of affect. They frequently talk in an even, monotonous voice, and in their often long monologues there is little in the way of emotional emphasis to indicate which of the topics they are talking about are important, which unimportant. This flat, lifeless, emotionally shallow quality to their productions not uncommonly makes these patients appear dull and boring.

There is, however, one exception to this general rule. In some patients evidence of emotion, especially tears, may appear with a sudden abruptness for which one is unprepared. This was evident in the first three of the patients quoted above. The first would begin to cry whenever she talked about the fact that because of her divorce her daughter had grown up without a father; the second whenever she discussed the dependency forced on her by her crippling arthritis; the third whenever he mentioned his mother, who had died 60 years before, when he was ten.

What is particularly to be noted is that the show of emotion comes on suddenly as an immediate response to the stimulus topic, that it disappears equally rapidly when the patient or the interviewer switches to another subject, and that generally it is not accompanied by an elaboration of appropriate fantasies or thought. It appears to be an isolated, discontinuous response, bound to the stimulus, but without connection with what has gone on before or after. It is as if a valve were suddenly opened, then closed.

DISCUSSION

From our observations derived from the group of patients specifically focused on in the earlier part of this chapter, as well as from our wider clinical experience, we believe that we have further evidence for a form of mentation characteristic of many psychosomatic patients that has escaped the explicit attention of all but a few investigators. In short, these patients: (1) usually have a disturbance in affective functioning characterized by an incapacity to describe or express their feelings in words; and (2) there is generally a striking absence of drive-directed and affect-directed fantasy; instead their thought content often appears to reflect and to be determined by the events occurring in their surroundings.

The explanation for these phenomena is not as yet clear, but their elucidation can be conceptualized in at least three different ways:

(1) In psychological terms, one may invoke the psychodynamic concept of ego defences (e.g. reaction formation, repression) erected to keep affects and fantasies from reaching conscious awareness.

(2) In developmental terms, one may conceive of a disturbance in early learning processes, such that the individual has failed to develop the usual connections between words and emotions, with a consequent deficit in the capacity to discern the qualities of emotions or to express them verbally or in fantasy.

(3) In neurophysiological terms, one may think (as MacLean long ago suggested) of a lack of connection and communication between the limbic system (the substrate of emotion) and the neocortex (underlying the capacity for critical evaluation and for the creation of complex systems of associations).

Presumably each explanation will be more applicable to one group of patients than to another. It is certainly reasonable to raise the question whether the disturbance in affective expression and the absence of fantasy is the result only of the operations of psychic functions in an anatomically and physiologically normal brain, or whether in some patients there may be an actual absence of anatomical connections between neocortex and limbic system, either as the result of a hereditary deficit or of a failure to learn and develop in the early months of life.

Only further investigation aimed at testing these hypotheses can determine their validity, and it is not our purpose here to provide evidence in support of any particular theoretical scheme, but rather to suggest that at present the scientific explanation of psychosomatic disorders must employ concepts from a number of possible theoretical frameworks. An initial conceptual approach that is too narrow may blind the investigator to new and significant observations; it is possible, in our opinion, that the too ready explanation of the disturbance of affective expression in psychosomatic patients as being the result of specific psychic defence mechanisms has prevented most investigators from more closely defining the phenomenological characteristics of that disturbance.

Furthermore, it has not been our intention in this chapter to provide a detailed statistical presentation of the psychological patterns that characterize and distinguish patients with psychosomatic disorders. Our material permits us only to define certain striking phenomena in our patients that coincide with the as yet isolated findings of two or three other investigators, and that, in our opinion, are important in their own right. We hope that our observations will sound a responding chord in the experience of yet other clinicians, and will induce them in turn to test the validity of these concepts on their patients. A much larger body of observations is needed before the concepts can be further refined and before their actual significance for psychosomatic processes can be determined.

REFERENCES

MacLean, P. D. (1949). 'Psychosomatic Disease and the "Visceral Brain".' *Psychosom. Med.*, **11,** 338.

Marty, P. and de M'Uzan, M. (1963). 'La "pensée opératoire".' *Rev. Franc. Psychanal.*, **27,** Suppl. 1345.

— — and David, C. (1963). *L'investigation psychosomatique*. Paris: Presses Universitaires de France.

Nemiah, J. C. (1964). Final Report on NIMH Project No. M-262 (c). 'A Study of the Specificity of Current Psychological Factors Involved in the Production of Psychosomatic Disease in Patients, Each Suffering from Two Different Psychosomatic Illnesses.' (Submitted in 1964.)

Ruesch, J. (1948). 'The Infantile Personality: The Core Problem of Psychosomatic Medicine.' *Psychosom. Med.*, **10,** 134.

Sifneos, P. E. (1967). 'Clinical Observations on Some Patients Suffering from a Variety of Psychosomatic Diseases.' *Acta med. psychosom.* (Proceedings of the 7th European Conference on Psychosomatic Research, Rome, September 11–16, 1967.)

CHAPTER 3

PSYCHOSOMATIC AND PSYCHOPHYSIOLOGICAL ASPECTS OF ANXIETY

MALCOLM LADER

INTRODUCTION

The topic of anxiety is one in which the problems of the psychosomatic approach and its underlying epistemology are well illustrated. Wittkower (1969) has stated: 'In fact, by its very nature psychosomatic medicine is one of the few areas in the field of psychological medicine in which to some extent, criteria of biological research can be successfully employed.' In general the trend of psychosomatic research is away from clinical observations towards basic psychophysiological research (W.H.O., 1964). In this review I shall discuss a few aspects of biological research into morbid anxiety and also some psychophysiological studies of relevance to the psychosomatic approach.

Definition of Anxiety

It is impossible to give a scientific definition of anxiety because, as it is essentially an introspective experience, it is an irreducible concept. However, it can be usefully described thus (Lewis, 1967):

1. It is an emotional state, with the subjectively experienced quality of fear or a closely related emotion (terror, horror, alarm, fright, panic, trepidation, dread, scare).
2. The emotion is unpleasant.
3. It is directed towards the future.
4. There is either no recognizable threat, or the threat is, by reasonable standards, quite out of proportion to the emotion it seemingly evokes.
5. There are subjective bodily discomforts during the period of the anxiety.
6. There are manifest bodily disturbances.

Anxiety may exist as a transient emotion, as a more chronic mood state, as a life-long personality trait or as a morbid state of illness. Concepts such as 'unconscious anxiety' may be found useful by some clinicians but are of dubious scientific value as anxiety, being an emotion, must be experienced in consciousness.

The physiological changes which accompany the affect of anxiety are widespread and obvious. Anxiety provides a fascinating study of the interplay between the psychological and somatic spheres of human activity. The physiological changes provide a tool by which the measurement of the somatic changes may (with certain precautions) give useful estimates of the morbid affective state. Thus, the dual nature of the phenomena of anxiety is of great theoretical interest for clinicians and research workers professing a psychosomatic approach to the problems of physical illness.

SYMPTOMS AND SIGNS OF ANXIETY

The patient complaining of anxiety may proffer his symptoms in psychological terms, e.g. as feeling 'anxious', 'tensed up', 'jittery', 'panicky', 'feeling of something terrible going to happen'. Alternatively, he may describe his feelings solely in somatic terms such as 'butterflies in the stomach', 'tightness in the chest', 'difficulty in swallowing'. Most commonly, anxious patients have both types of complaint. Many aspects of bodily function are disturbed. A widespread feeling of tension may be commented upon or the tension may be localized such as a tension headache or 'rheumaticky' aches and pains in the limbs or trunk. Tremor is very common and may be associated with generalized weakness or episodes of 'collapse' due to weakness in the legs. The patient may complain of his restlessness and will show fidgety movements and even agitation. Tic-like movements may occur or the patient may bite his nails or fiddle with an object such as a button or pencil. Respiration is deeper, more rapid and may take on a sighing quality; the patient may feel that he cannot get enough air and that he is suffocating or feel a sense of constriction in his chest.

The disturbance in autonomic activity is widespread and gives rise to a variety of symptoms. Marked increases in heart rate commonly occur and are perceived as palpitations; peripheral vasoconstriction is noted as cold extremities, and an increase in pulse pressure occurs. Hollow organ activity is generally increased with frequency of defaecation and micturition, looseness of motions, increased belching and borborygmi. Gastric discomfort or pain is complained of on occasion and repeated vomiting may occur. Glandular activity is altered so that the patient may note dryness of the mouth although sweat-gland activity is usually markedly augmented, sometimes to the extent of hyperhidrosis.

Sleep is disturbed with an inability to fall promptly asleep followed by fitful and unrefreshing sleep. Appetite is usually diminished with subsequent loss of weight. However, some patients find eating alleviates their anxiety and rapidly become obese. Libido is sometimes diminished and potency impaired.

PSYCHOPHYSIOLOGY OF ANXIETY

Techniques

The widespread symptoms of anxiety are mirrored by marked physiological changes in many systems of the body. Careful and detailed studies of these changes, their characterization, quantification and inter-relation, are the particular concern of psychophysiologists. Psychophysiology has been defined as 'the science which concerns those physiological activities which underlie or relate to psychic functions' (Darrow, 1964). This wide area of research endeavour would designate psychophysiology as basic to psychosomatic medicine in the way that neurophysiology is fundamental to clinical neurology. However, the links between psychophysiology and psychosomatic medicine are still surprisingly tenuous and fragile. Moreover, in practice, clinical psychophysiologists have generally restricted their efforts to the elucidation of the physiological concomitants to one aspect of psychic function—the emotions. Anxiety with its protean physiological changes has been intensively studied.

Of the large number of techniques used in psychophysiology, many are autonomic (Brown, 1967; Venables and Martin, 1967). Cardiovascular measures include blood flow through various regions of the body, the finger-tip and the forearm being most commonly used; the former reflects skin blood flow, the latter muscle blood flow. Pulse rate, often finely analysed as beat-to-beat interval, is widely employed as is blood pressure. Salivary secretion may be measured in several ways and other autonomic measures include the assessment of pressures and movement in hollow organs such as the bladder and stomach and estimation of pupil size.

The most widely used autonomic measure is palmar sweat-gland activity measured indirectly as the electrical resistance (or conductance) of the skin. The palmar sweat-glands are not thermoregulatory but probably serve to optimize tactile sensitivity and grip. Alterations in skin resistance in response to stimuli—auditory, visual, tactile, etc.—always take the form of transiently increased sweat-gland activity (lowered resistance) and are termed galvanic skin responses (GSR's) or psychogalvanic reflexes (PGR's). Spontaneous fluctuations in the skin resistance are a usual feature of the tracings and take the form of small diminutions in resistance in the absence of any apparent external stimuli.

Among somatic measures surface electromyography has yielded much useful information as it facilitates the assessment of activity from a substantial mass of muscle such as the forearm extensors or posterior cervical muscles. The psychophysiologist is interested in the activity found in muscles supposedly at rest and the amplified and integrated action potentials from these muscles provide an estimate of 'tension'.

Respiration may be assessed in several ways but the most convenient technique, such as a strain-gauge detecting chest movements or temperature-sensitive devices monitoring nasal air flow, are only semi-quantitative. Estimates of respiratory efficiency have also been used.

The electroencephalogram has been used in a psychophysiological context, the usual variable being the percentage alpha time. Recently the advent of on-line laboratory computers has rekindled interest in this aspect of the EEG as sophisticated mathematical analyses of the complex waveforms are at last feasible.

Two general experimental strategies have been used. First, stimulation or 'stress' procedures have been applied to subjects in order to induce anxiety, the consequent physiological changes being recorded. This is a useful technique in normal subjects but is less appropriate to anxious patients who are already experiencing the emotion the stress procedure is supposed to engender. The second approach is to study a group of patients with anxiety states and a group of normal subjects matched at least for sex and age; in this case, there is no necessity to induce anxiety. Indeed, a profitable method is to encourage both groups of subjects to relax, a difficult undertaking for an anxious patient.

Findings

Many physiological measures are elevated in anxious patients as compared with normal subjects. Respiration is more rapid (Goldstein, 1964) with impaired respiratory efficiency (Coppen and Mezey, 1960) and palmar sweating is increased (raised skin conductance) (Lader and Wing, 1966). In the cardiovascular system, heart rate is elevated (Lader and Wing, 1966; Tan, 1964; Wing, 1964), forearm blood flow is increased (Kelly, 1966) and blood-pressure (especially systolic) tends to be raised (Goldstein, 1964; Malmo and Shagass, 1952). The above changes also occur when normal subjects experience marked anxiety (Ira, Whalen and Bogdonoff, 1963; Blair *et al.*, 1959). Electromyographic activity has been reported to be increased in anxious patients but this appears to depend on the recording site (Goldstein, 1964).

Reactivity studies have yielded conflicting results. Some researchers have found patients to be *less* reactive than controls (Kelly, 1966; Lader and Wing, 1966; Wing, 1964; Wishner, 1953) whereas others have found them to be *more* reactive (Davis, Malmo and Shagass, 1954; Goldstein, 1964; Malmo and Shagass, 1952; Martin, 1956). The reasons for these discrepancies are complex (Lader, 1969) but very often the 'pre-stimulus' levels are already raised in the patients as a response to the general experimental conditions so that further stimulation will produce little further rise. Nevertheless, it is an over-simplification to assume that anxious patients or any other neurotics are emotionally and physiologically over-reactive.

Another facet of psychophysiological research in anxiety has provided consistent results. *Anxious patients demonstrate an impaired ability to adapt to the demands of the experimental situation.* For example, they continue to show elevated physiological activity long after a stimulation procedure has ceased whereas normal subjects quickly return to resting levels. This phenomenon has been described for skin conductance (Lader and Wing, 1966), forearm blood flow (Kelly, 1966), pupil size (Rubin, 1964), blood-pressure (Innes, Millar and Valentine, 1959) and electromyogram (Martin, 1956; Wing, 1964).

Similarly, if a stimulus is repeated, normal subjects show a decrement in response often to the point of extinction. This is termed habituation and is the simplest form of learning—learning not to respond to an irrelevant stimulus. Anxious patients show impaired habituation with respect to the electromyogram (Davis, Malmo and Shagass, 1954) and sweat-gland responses (Lader and Wing, 1966). Severely anxious patients continue to give responses as long as the stimuli are repeated or may even *increase* the size of their responses—a grossly abnormal and maladaptive occurrence.

Summarizing, anxious patients are characterized by abnormally high levels of physiological activity even when they are ostensibly at rest. Their reactivity to extraneous stimuli is, in general, diminished because they are already responding to the general experimental situation. They show impaired powers of adaptation to a changing environment. The abnormalities are not specific to morbid states of anxiety but occur to a greater or lesser extent during episodes of transient anxiety in normal subjects.

PROBLEMS IN PSYCHOPHYSIOLOGY

After outlining the most consistent psychophysiological findings in anxious patients, the wider implications are usefully examined. These relate to some of the basic problems in psychophysiology, to some of its working concepts and to their relevance to psychosomatic research. First, all too commonly, psychophysiological techniques are used and the resulting data interpreted as if the measures reflected psychological factors alone. These measures subserve primarily physiological functions and the physiological needs of the body take priority. For example, if a subject exercises, his pulse rate rises: no conclusions can be drawn regarding any changes in his psychological status. In laboratory practice, the somatic changes which occur as a concomitant of psychic changes in the subject, e.g. emotions such as anxiety, can only be accurately studied when the somatic needs of the subject are kept constant.

Despite methodological problems in experimentation, some concepts and theories in psychophysiology have been developed and have been heuristically fruitful. Of these concepts, 'response specificity', 'arousal' and 'stress' are of great importance to psychosomatic theory and research and will be discussed from the viewpoint of psychophysiology.

Concept of Stimulation

In practically all psychophysiological research, the physiological measures are recorded during some sort of stimulation procedure. Even if the subject is left at 'rest' it is highly probable that, unless he is a very sophisticated individual who has participated in many such experiments, the general experimental situation acts as a powerful stimulus. In effect, recordings can only very rarely be regarded as 'base-line' or 'at rest'.

The superadded stimulation may take many forms. The simplest consist of auditory tones or clicks, flashes of light or moving patterns, or standard mild electric shocks. These stimuli are definable solely in physical terms: e.g. 70 dB of 'white noise' of 5 sec. duration. Such stimulation has the virtues of reproducibility, standardization between subjects and psychological neutrality: a flash of light of moderate intensity is not usually emotive. This method of approach is time-honoured by physiologists as it facilitates the study of responses and intermediary processes in the central nervous system.

The second approach is far more complex. Stimulation procedures are used which produce a series of responses in the subject depending on his interpretation of his situation. The stimuli may be definable in physical terms but they are not neutral in emotional content. Most are carefully chosen to elicit emotions in which the experimenter is interested. Real-life situations may be exploited such as parachute jumping (Basowitz *et al.*, 1955), presenting cases at formal case conference (Ira, Whalen and Bogdonoff, 1963), facing major surgery (Janis, 1958), speaking before large audiences, and taking examinations. Artificial situations include mental arithmetic tests with or without harassment, painful thermal or electric shock stimulation (Hardy, Wolff and Goodell, 1952; Malmo *et al.*, 1948), presenting the patient with insoluble tasks, showing him films of Australian Aboriginal circumcision rites (Lazarus *et al.*, 1962) or with exciting cliff-hanger films (Clemens and Selesnick, 1967; Levi, 1969). With these forms of stimulation certain problems arise. First, a wide range of emotions may be elicited in quickly changing proportions. Secondly, different emotions may be elicited in different subjects. I have found that mental arithmetic under harassment produces anger, resentment, anxiety, embarrassment, amusement and indifference in different subjects as judged from their verbal reports afterwards. Consequently, the investigator may find himself side-tracked into attempting to delineate the factors in the subject (personality, previous experience, expectancy, etc.) which determine the dominant emotion evoked rather than in studying the physiological changes accompanying that emotion.

One attempted solution to this problem has been to devise stimulation procedures tailored to the individual patient. For example, Grinker *et al.* (1957) attempted to induce anxiety by means of an interview dealing with topics especially upsetting to the patient. To their dismay they found that 'paradoxical reassurance from the stimulus interviews was a surprisingly common occurrence'. However, such a technique has been used with some apparent success by Malmo, Shagass and Davis (1950). The disadvantage of this type of approach is that it yields detailed information about only one patient which is not generalizable to any other patient; it is too limited for general use but it may provide pointers towards the design of more standardized techniques. A second disadvantage is that it is not easily applicable to normal subjects for control purposes.

Concept of 'Stress'

Selye, in his well-known and voluminous studies on the effects of intense stimuli, designated the pathological anatomical and physiological changes in the organism as the stress response. The stimuli producing the changes have been termed the 'strain' (following the practice in physics) or the 'stressors'. Unfortunately, confusion has arisen because common parlance refers to stress as both the external forces and the internal responses (Kollar, 1961).

The concept of 'psychological stress' appears to have become firmly established in the past few years. Stimuli utilized to induce 'stress' are characterized primarily by their intensity in psychological terms and sometimes in physical terms as well, e.g. painful electric shocks. The second characteristic which is supposed to be present is 'the intervening variable of *threat*, a state in which the individual anticipates harm' (Lazarus and Opton, 1966). In real-life situations involving hazard, threat would undoubtedly be present to a varying extent in every subject. In the laboratory, within the bounds of ethical permissibility, threat may be nugatory. On the response side, no characteristic 'stress' response has ever been described, the reaction being that accompanying emotion. Again, the emotion evoked will vary both qualitatively and quantitatively from subject to subject.

Psychological stress should be viewed as an intense emotional response to powerful stimulation procedures, its nature varying from subject to subject. Allotting 'stress reactions' a pivotal role in the genesis of psychosomatic conditions attributes a specificity to the responses which occur which is not justified by the experimental evidence. Nonetheless, the study of extreme emotional responses and the 'coping processes' by which the subject deals with the putative threat will continue to be a fruitful line of enquiry (Lazarus, 1966; Levi, 1967; Tong and Murphy, 1960).

The extrapolation to psychosomatic medicine has resulted in a further diffusion of the concept of stress (Wolff, 1968). Stress in this context becomes so ubiquitous a concept that it suggests not only marked stimulation but also retains its special connotation as an abnormal response.

The Concept of Arousal

The difficulty of interpreting physiological changes in psychological terms overshadows much of psychophysiology. We can work in empirical terms up to a point, i.e. we can compareg roups of patients with respect to a physiological variable or note the changes in that measure in response to stimulation. But eventually we need to interpret the findings in terms of central processes. It is an over-facile simplification to assume that the physiological variables 'measure' anxiety. Although the experiencing of anxiety is regularly accompanied by increased levels of these variables other intense affects, such as rage, ecstasy and revulsion, are also accompanied by such changes. Attempts have been made to distinguish different patterns of physiological responses accompanying different affects such as anxiety and anger and some contrasts were found (Ax, 1953; Schachter, 1957). Arguing teleologically, it is probable that wide but subtle differences do exist as it would be maladaptive for an organism to show stereotyped response patterns to stimuli of differing affect-producing properties.

From these considerations has arisen the concept of 'arousal', 'activation', or 'energy-mobilization' (Malmo, 1966; Lindsley, 1951; Duffy, 1962). This is generally regarded as a behavioural continuum ranging from deep sleep to lighter stages of sleep, to drowsiness and an inalert state through normal levels of alertness and wakefulness. Higher levels of arousal are represented by edginess, disquiet and uneasiness and then by affective states such as anxiety, anger, disgust, pleasure and resentment. At the upper extreme of the continuum are the over-arousal states such as terror, horror, rage and ecstasy. Martin (1961) regards anxiety as just one of the over-arousal states which becomes distinct as arousal heightens. The concept of arousal enables the insertion of a construct between the physiological measures and the concomitant affect: one regards the measure as reflecting arousal level rather than the emotion. Inasmuch as heightened arousal is a necessary condition for the experience of an emotion then the measure will reflect the emotional intensity. But one must ask the subject which emotion he is experiencing before confidently ascribing a change in a physiological measure to a change in the level of any particular emotion such as anxiety.

It is generally assumed that if these various physiological measures are all indicators of the one level of arousal then high correlations between the measures across subjects should be found. In general, inter-correlations of this sort have been disappointingly low and doubts have been cast on the validity of the concept of arousal as a unitary factor. Thus, there has been a division of the concept into many components such as 'autonomic' arousal, 'cortical' arousal, etc. This process can be taken to its extreme by postulating as many levels of arousal as there are apparently appropriate psychophysiological measures. It is interesting, in this respect, that Sherrington, and especially Head (1925), used the idea of 'vigilance' of the central nervous system to refer to its degree of integrative function and preparedness; vigilance was not a unitary concept but could be applied to anatomical or functional divisions of the central nervous system, e.g. 'vigilance level of the spinal cord'.

Undue fragmentation of the concept of arousal would result in its debasement as it does serve some heuristic value as the summary of results in studies of anxiety shows. All in all, then, the view that anxiety both in its normal and its morbid form is related to a substrate of high arousal in the central nervous system is a useful summary of the present position.

Response Specificity

This phenomenon is of much importance to psychosomatic medicine as it provides some experimental support for the notion that the degree of vulnerability of the physiological systems of the body varies from subject to subject.

The first form of 'response-specificity' is termed 'intra-stressor stereotypy': each individual subject shows a reproducible pattern of response to a repeated stimulus situation. For example, one subject might show a marked heart-rate response and a minimal electromyographic response to a stimulus and will demonstrate the same preponderance of heart-rate response whenever the stimulus is repeated. The hypothesis is supported by the results of two studies in which the patterns of autonomic responses to repeated stimuli remained stable (Lacey, 1950; Lacey and Van Lehn, 1952). In two further studies (Lacey, Bateman and Van Lehn, 1952; Lacey and Lacey, 1958), an attempt was made to extend the concept by examining the patterns of response to different stimulation procedures. However, whereas some subjects gave reproducible response patterns ('inter-stressor stereotypy'), others were more variable. Schnore's (1959) experiments supported Lacey's findings but Wenger *et al.* (1961) thought that the similarity between the stimuli used and their temporal proximity could account for the similarities of response.

A different view was put forward by Davis (1957) who showed that response patterns appeared to depend more on the nature of the stimulus than on the idiosyncrasies of the subject. This is termed 'situational stereotypy'. Other investigators have concluded that both individual and stimulus factors are important in determining the pattern of a response (Engel, 1960; Engel and Bickford, 1961). In a revision of his original views, Lacey (1967) has proposed that different somatic processes have different roles to play in the execution of different types of behaviour: in other words, situational stereotypy is acknowledged to be important. This is certainly in accord with general physiological principles regarding the adaptive and integrative nature of bodily responses.

A related principle of direct relevance to psychosomatic research is that of 'symptom specificity' which proposes 'that in psychiatric patients presenting a somatic complaint, the particular physiological mechanism of that complaint is specifically susceptible to activation by stressful experience'. A group of patients were divided into those with cardiovascular complaints and those with head and neck pains. The former sub-group had a higher mean heart rate and heart-rate variability while the other sub-group had higher mean electromyographic levels in the neck muscles (Malmo and Shagass, 1949). A further study showed relationships between electromyographic activity recorded during an interview from different sites of the body and the patient's symptoms (Malmo, Shagass and Davis, 1950). Supporting evidence may be adduced from Sainsbury and Gibson's (1954) investigation. They divided their anxious patients into a group with aching of the limbs or rheumatic pains and a group complaining of headache. The former group had higher forearm electromyographic levels whereas the headache group had higher frontalis tension.

An interesting study was that reported by Graham, Kabler and Graham (1962) who induced hypnotically suggestions of unjust treatment (postulated as common in patients with hives) or of being on guard against bodily assault (believed to be the characteristic attitude in hypertensives) in 20 normal subjects. The hives suggestion induced a marked rise in skin temperature, the other suggestion a rise in diastolic blood pressure. Despite the problems in interpreting studies using hypnosis, itself an ill-understood phenomenon, this type of experiment is important in the testing of hypotheses linking emotional states and attitudes to morbid physiological changes.

Specificity has long been a key concept in psychosomatic medicine although the nature of the specificity has been disputed. Alexander's (1950) theory postulates that 'physiological responses to emotional stimuli, both normal and morbid, vary according to the nature of the precipitating emotional state'. Whenever attempts have been made to correlate psychological events with specific psychosomatic conditions, over-ambitious aetiological theories have been constructed and disillusionment with 'specificity' has set in. The psychophysiological concept of patterns of response which depend partly on the stimulation situation and partly on individual idiosyncrasies enables a more flexible experimental approach. Nevertheless, for the concept to retain its usefulness, the factors governing the individual patterns must be elucidated. Whether these are related to specific attitudes induced in the individual is still to be confirmed.

COGNITIVE FACTORS

If terror, rage, ecstasy, revulsion and other intense affect states are all high arousal states, what factors govern which particular emotion is experienced? Some light has been shed on this problem by the ingenious experiments of Schachter (1966). He demonstrated that although a high arousal state, as produced by an adrenaline injection, enhances the intensity of introspected emotion or of emotional behaviour, the type of emotion felt was dependent on the situation in which the subject was placed, i.e. on his cognitive clues. If, however, the subject was told exactly what to expect as a result of the adrenaline injection he was more difficult to manipulate into experiencing specific emotions. Thus, to experience an emotion a high arousal state has to be induced and the appropriate cognitive clues provided.

There is another way in which cognitive factors play an important part. Peripheral physiological changes can be perceived by the subject and may reinforce his emotional feelings. Such autonomic feedback or, at least, the perception of it often appears to increase as a patient continues to experience a morbid anxiety state. He offers increasingly detailed accounts of his physical symptoms and if the anxiety is episodic, the onset of a bout may be presaged by subtle, minimal physiological changes. It may be seen that a 'vicious circle' or positive feedback system becomes established in that an anxious patient's awareness of marked peripheral physiological changes such as palpitations increases his anxiety.

AUTONOMIC CONDITIONING

The simpler studies of anxiety have used unconditioned stimulation procedures but there has also been much work using more complex conditioning procedures. Physiological responses can certainly be conditioned as the host of studies following Pavlov's have shown. Autonomic responses may be linked to a wide variety of conditioned stimuli. Furthermore, anxiety responses can be conditioned and form the basis of some phobic reactions. In a similar manner, excessive physiological responses could become conditioned so that they are elicitable by stimuli of a usually innocuous nature. It has been generally believed that autonomic responses can only be conditioned using classical, Pavlovian conditioning techniques (Kimble, 1961).

Very recently, a series of fascinating experiments have been carried out by Miller and his associates which will necessitate a re-examination of present ideas regarding physiological responses and will affect theorizing about anxiety and psychosomatic conditions (Miller, 1969). They have shown that autonomic responses can be modified by operant conditioning techniques, i.e. rewards applied contingent upon the appropriate autonomic response will result in the 'shaping up' of that response. Thus, thirsty dogs could be trained to decrease or *increase* their salivation rate by giving them water as a reward for the appropriate spontaneous response. Using various reinforcers, the heart rates of rats could be increased or decreased, their intestinal activity augmented or abolished, their glomerular filtration rate and renal blood flow increased or decreased, their electroencephalograms increased or decreased in voltage, their gastric or tail blood flow raised or lowered, their blood pressures increased or decreased. Each physiological response could be modified independently of the others. Indeed, one ear of a rat could be made to vasodilate without affecting the other one. These experiments in animals were all elegantly controlled and add up to an impressive volume in support of the instrumental modification of autonomic activity.

The evidence for human instrumental conditioning is still inconclusive but attempts have been made not only to operantly condition responses such as the GSR and heart rate but to suppress abnormal paroxysmal discharges in epileptics and to treat organic cardiac arrhythmias.

Miller is fully aware of the implications of his work for psychosomatic research and theory. The evidence that visceral responses are no different from musculo-skeletal responses in their susceptibility to instrumental conditioning 'removes the main basis for assuming that the psychosomatic symptoms that involve the autonomic nervous system are fundamentally different from those functional symptoms, such as hysterical ones, that involve the cerebrospinal nervous system' (Miller, 1969). Furthermore, Miller speculates that if a child experienced anxiety due to any cause (e.g. going to school) together with its autonomic symptoms, the mother could reinforce one of the symptoms, say gastric distress, by drawing attention to it and keeping the child from school. As a wide variety of rewards may theoretically exist, many new possibilities for the reinforcement of psychosomatic symptoms are opened up.

A SYNTHESIS

A model of the psychophysiological basis for psychosomatic symptoms can be drawn up using the experimental evidence obtained from studies of anxiety. The extrapolation from the laboratory to real-life situations is always daunting but at the present time the type of model which could be set up would be thus:

The environment provides sensory stimuli which interact with factors in the subject such as previous experience and personality and result in a non-specific general arousal state. The cognitive factors are simultaneously interpreted so that a specific emotion is experienced. The interactive process between sensory stimuli and intra-personal factors may occur at the conscious level, or at the subconscious symbolic level. At the former level, the emotional experience will appear appropriate to the subject or, if inappropriate, the reasons for the irrationality will be apparent. If the interaction is at a symbolic level then the emotion will appear irrational. It may be noted that these interactions govern both the intensity and the quality of the affect. Also the stimuli may not be primary but may have been secondarily conditioned.

As a concomitant to the emotion, physiological changes occur. Here, four factors operate to allow differing individual patterns of response: (1) The emotion produced depends to some extent on the particular individual and physiological patterns vary according to the emotion. (2) Individual variations in response to affectively neutral stimuli would suggest that at least equal variability is present in responses to emotion-evocative stimuli. (3) The intensity of response varies and various systems of the body would be differentially involved at the various levels of response. (4) Awareness of peripheral autonomic changes varies from system to system so that differential feedback could occur.

This stimulus-response model provides the classical paradigm for psychosomatic medicine. Environmental influences of a severe, chronic or abnormal nature interact with factors in the subject such as personality, previous experience, expectations, etc., to produce a high arousal state. This is accompanied by an emotion if the arousal state is of sufficient intensity. However, even if an emotion is not evoked, physiological changes will occur. These changes may be morbidly severe in one particular system of the body if the subject has a diathesis towards excessive responses in that system. In time, the function of this system will break down or be permanently impaired—hypertension, peptic ulcer, asthma and other 'psychosomatic conditions' will result.

A second element in the paradigm is loss of adaptation. Under conditions of high arousal the ability of the subject to adapt to a continuing or repetitive intense stimulus is greatly impaired. Consequently once a high level of arousal has been attained the condition tends to become self-perpetuating. At the upper extreme adaptation becomes negligible and untrammelled rises in physiological activity can occur (Lader and Mathews, 1967). It should be noted that the responses induced are normal in quality but abnormal in intensity and duration.

This very wide model has much basic evidence to support it.

Physiological changes accompanying high arousal states have been studied in detail; each subject tends to show some individuality of pattern of response; adaptation is slow in intense arousal states; cognitive clues are important in the elicitation of emotion, etc. However, the extrapolation from responses in normal subjects to those in patients with psychosomatic conditions has not been easy. The findings that the malfunctioning system in patients with a particular complaint is abnormally reactive is inconclusive evidence: the abnormal reactivity might be secondary to the illness, not a cause of it. Secondly, it is well known that physiological systems which are already functioning at a high level may show little further response on stimulation (so-called 'law of initial values'—Wilder, 1962). Consequently, it would be predicted that patients with psychosomatic conditions would be *less* reactive. The problem, therefore, is that this model in psychosomatic terms is difficult to approach experimentally. The only rigorous proof would be to test a large group of normal subjects to determine their hierarchy of reactive physiological systems and then to follow them up studying their life-situations, prevalent emotional state and illnesses, both physical and mental.

CONCLUSIONS

The term 'psychosomatic' may be used in two main ways. It may refer to all illnesses in that every type of illness has psychological concomitants; this connotation is merely eclecticism regarding aetiology. The more narrow use is to refer to certain specific illnesses in which psychological factors are thought aetiologically important —asthma, peptic ulcer, hypertension, etc. It has been urged that the psychosomatic approach should 'focus on the relationship between specific psychological variables—such as affects—and specific physiological functions and processes rather than disease entities' (Lipowski, 1968). The psychophysiology of affects, especially anxiety, demonstrates ways in which this approach appears profitable. Nevertheless, the time may be ripe for psychosomatic medicine to finally discard the tattered shreds of Cartesian dualism as evidenced by the notion that a 'psychosomatic sequence' is 'a process in which psychological events are followed by organic changes' (World Health Organization, 1969). Instead it could concentrate on the relationships between events occurring at the highest levels of central nervous system activity and changes in visceral and musculo-skeletal functions in the body, healthy and diseased.

REFERENCES

Alexander, F. (1950). *Psychosomatic Medicine*. New York: Norton.

Ax, A. F. (1953). 'The Physiological Differentiation Between Fear and Anger in Humans.' *Psychosom. Med.*, **15,** 433.

Basowitz, H., Persky, H., Korchin, S. J., and Grinker, R.R. (1955). *Anxiety and Stress. An Interdisciplinary Study of a Life Situation*. New York: McGraw-Hill.

Blair, D. A., Glover, W. E., Greenfield, A. D. M. and Roddie, I. C. (1959). 'Excitation of Cholinergic Vasodilator Nerves to Human Skeletal Muscles during Emotional Stress.' *J. Physiol.* (*Lond.*), **148,** 633.

Brown, C. C. (Ed.) (1967). *Methods in Psychophysiology*. Baltimore: Williams & Wilkins.

Clemens, T. L. and Selesnick, S. T. (1967). 'Psychological Method for Evaluating Medication by Repeated Exposure to a Stressor Film.' *Dis. nerv. Syst.*, **21,** 98.

Coppen, A. J. and Mezey, A. G. (1960). 'The Influence of Sodium Amytal on the Respiratory Abnormalities of Anxious Psychiatric Patients.' *J. psychosom. Res.*, **5,** 52.

Darrow, C. W. (1964). 'Psychophysiology, Yesterday, Today, and Tomorrow.' *Psychophysiology*, **1,** 4.

Davis, J. F., Malmo, R. B. and Shagass, C. (1954). 'Electromyographic Reaction to Strong Auditory Stimulation in Psychiatric Patients.' *Can. J. Psychol.*, **8,** 177.

Davis, R. C. (1957). 'Response Patterns.' *Tr. N.Y. Acad. Sci.*, **19,** 731.

Duffy, E. (1962). *Activation and Behavior*. New York: John Wiley.

Engel, B. T. (1960). 'Stimulus-response and Individual-response Specificity.' *Archs gen. Psychiat.*, **2,** 305.

— and Bickford, A. F. (1961). 'Response Specificity. Stimulus-response and Individual-response Specificity in Essential Hypertensives.' *Archs gen. Psychiat.*, **5,** 478.

Goldstein, I. B. (1964). 'Physiological Responses in Anxious Women Patients. A Study of Autonomic Activity and Muscle Tension.' *Archs gen. Psychiat.*, **10,** 382.

Graham, D. T., Kabler, J. D. and Graham, F. K. (1962). 'Physiological Response to the Suggestion of Attitudes Specific for Hives and Hypertension.' *Psychosom. Med.*, **24,** 159.

Grinker, R. R., *et al.* (1957). 'Use of an Anxiety-producing Interview and its Meaning to the Subject.' *Archs Neurol. Psychiat.*, **77,** 406.

Hardy, J. D., Wolff, H. G. and Goodell, H. (1952). *Pain Sensations and Reactions*. Baltimore: Williams & Wilkins.

Head, H. (1925). 'The Conception of Nervous and Mental Energy. II. Vigilance: a Physiological State of the Nervous System.' *Br. J. Psychol.*, **14,** 126.

Innes, G., Millar, W. M. and Valentine, M. (1959). 'Emotion and Blood-pressure.' *J. ment. Sci.*, **105,** 840.

Ira, G. H., Whalen, R. E. and Bogdonoff, M. D. (1963). 'Heart Rate Changes in Physicians during Daily "Stressful" Tasks.' *J. psychosom. Res.*, **7,** 147.

Janis, I. L. (1958). *Psychological Stress*. New York: John Wiley.
Kelly, D. H. W. (1966). 'Measurement of Anxiety by Forearm Blood Flow.' *Br. J. Psychiat.*, **112,** 789.
Kimble, G. A. (1961). In *Conditioning and Learning*, Ed. by E. R. Hilgard and D. G. Marquis, 2nd ed. New York: Appleton-Century-Crofts.
Kollar, E. J. (1961). 'Psychological Stress: a Re-evaluation.' *J. nerv. ment. Dis.*, **132,** 382.
Lacey, J. I. (1950). 'Individual Differences in Somatic Response Patterns.' *J. comp. physiol. Psychol.*, **43,** 338.
— (1967). In *Psychological Stress*, Ed. by M. H. Appley and R. Trumbull. New York: Appleton-Century-Crofts.
— Bateman, D. E. and VanLehn, R. (1952). 'Autonomic Response Specificity and Rorschach Color Responses.' *Psychosom. Med.* **14**, 256.
— and VanLehn, R. (1952). 'Differential Emphasis in Somatic Response to Stress. An Experimental Study.' *Psychosom. Med.*, **14,** 71.
— and Lacey, B. C. (1958). 'Verification and Extension of the Principle of Autonomic Response-stereotypy.' *Am. J. Psychol.*, **71,** 50.
Lader, M. H. (Ed.) (1969). In *Studies of Anxiety*. London: Royal Medico-Psychological Association.
— and Mathews, A. M. (1967). 'A Physiological Model of Phobic Anxiety and Desensitization.' *Behav. Res. Ther.*, **6,** 411.
— and Wing, L. (1966). *Physiological Measures, Sedative Drugs, and Morbid Anxiety*. London: Oxford University Press.
Lazarus, R. S. (1966). *Psychological Stress and the Coping Process*. New York: McGraw-Hill.
— and Opton, E. M. (1966). 'The Study of Psychological Stress: a Summary of Theoretical Formulations and Experimental Findings.' In *Anxiety and Behavior*, Ed. by C. D. Spielberger. New York: Academic Press.
— Speisman, J. C., Mordkoff, A. M. and Davison, L. A. (1962). 'A Laboratory Study of Psychological Stress Produced by a Motion Picture Film.' *Psychol. Monogr.*, **76,** No. 34, Whole No. 553.
Levi, L. (Ed.) (1967). 'Emotional Stress.' *Försvarsmedicin*, **3,** Suppl. 2.
— (1969). In *Studies of Anxiety*, Ed. by M. H. Lader. London: Royal Medico-Psychological Association.
Lewis, A. J. (1967). 'Problems Presented by the Ambiguous Word "Anxiety" as used in Psychopathology.' *Israel Ann. Psychiat. rel. Discip.*, **5,** 105.
Lindsley, D. B. (1951). In *Handbook of Experimental Psychology*, Ed. by S. S. Stevens. New York: John Wiley.
Lipowski, Z. J. (1968). 'Review of Consultation Psychiatry and Psychosomatic Medicine. III. Theoretical Issues.' *Psychosom. Med.*, **30,** 395.
Malmo, R. B. (1966). In *Anxiety and Behavior*, Ed. by C. D. Spielberger. New York: Academic Press.
— and Shagass, C. (1949). 'Physiologic Study of Symptom Mechanisms in Psychiatric Patients under Stress.' *Psychosom. Med.*, **11,** 25.
— — (1952). 'Studies of Blood Pressure in Psychiatric Patients under Stress.' *Psychosom. Med.*, **14,** 82.

Malmo, R. B., Shagass, C. and Davis, F. H. (1950). 'Symptom Specificity and Bodily Reactions during Psychiatric Interview.' *Psychosom. Med.*, **12,** 362.

— *et al.* (1948). 'Standardized Pain Stimulation as Controlled Stress in Physiological Studies of Psychoneurosis.' *Science, N.Y.* **108,** 509.

Martin, B. (1961). 'The Assessment of Anxiety by Physiological Behavioural Measures.' *Psychol. Bull.*, **58,** 234.

Martin, I. (1956). 'Levels of Muscle Activity in Psychiatric Patients.' *Acta psychol. (Amst.)*, **12,** 326.

Miller, N. E. (1969). 'Learning of Visceral and Glandular Responses.' *Science, N.Y.*, **163,** 434.

Rubin, L. S. (1964). 'Autonomic Dysfunction as a Concomitant of Neurotic Behavior.' *J. nerv. ment. Dis.*, **138,** 558.

Sainsbury, P. and Gibson, J. G. (1954). 'Symptoms of Anxiety and Tension and the Accompanying Physiological Changes in the Muscular System.' *J. Neurol. Neurosurg. Psychiat.*, **17,** 216.

Schachter, J. (1957). 'Pain, Fear, and Anger in Hypertensives and Normotensives. A Psychophysiological Study.' *Psychosom. Med.*, **19,** 17.

— (1966). 'The Interaction of Cognitive and Physiological Determinants of Emotional State.' In *Anxiety and Behavior*, Ed. by C. D. Spielberger. New York: Academic Press.

Schnore, M. M. (1959). 'Individual Patterns of Physiological Activity as a Function of Task Differences and Degree of Arousal.' *J. exp. Psychol.*, **58,** 117.

Tan, B. K. (1964). 'Physiological Correlates of Anxiety. A Preliminary Investigation of the Orienting Reflex.' *Can. psychiat. Ass. J.*, **9,** 63.

Tong, J. E. and Murphy, I. C. (1960). 'A Review of Stress Reactivity Research in Relation to Psychopathology and Psychopathic Behaviour Disorders.' *J. ment. Sci.*, **106,** 1273.

Venables, P. and Martin, I. (Eds.) (1967). *Manual of Psychophysiological Methods.* Amsterdam: North-Holland Press.

Wenger, M. A., *et al.* (1961). 'Autonomic Response Specificity.' *Psychosom. Med.*, **23,** 185.

Wilder, J. (1962). 'Basimetric Approach (Law of Initial Value) to Biological Rhythms.' *Ann. N.Y. Acad. Sci.*, **98,** 1211.

Wing, L. (1964). 'Physiological Effects of Performing a Difficult Task in Patients with Anxiety States.' *J. psychosom. Res.*, **7,** 283.

Wishner, J. (1953). 'Neurosis and Tension: an Exploratory Study of the Relationship of Physiological and Rorschach Measures.' *J. abn. soc. Psychol.*, **48,** 253.

Wittkower, E. D. (1969). 'A Global Survey of Psychosomatic Medicine.' *Int. J. Psychiat.*, **7,** 499.

Wolff, H. G. (1968). *Stress and Disease*, 2nd ed. Springfield, Ill.: Thomas.

World Health Organization (1964). 'Psychosomatic Disorders.' *Wld Hlth Org. techn. Rep. Ser.*, No. 275.

— (1969). 'Biochemistry of Mental Disorders.' *Wld Hlth Org. techn. Rep. Ser.*, No. 427.

CHAPTER 4

PSYCHOLOGICAL INFLUENCES ON THE CARDIO-VASCULAR SYSTEM

JAN BROD

That psychological factors have a profound effect on the cardiovascular system is commonplace knowledge. This is proved by expressions such as 'heart-breaking', 'the blood is up', 'the blood is boiling', and also 'the heart is smiling', 'pleasing to the heart', etc., which occur in various languages. The layman must have observed the fast-beating heart in the course of an anxious expectation, the pallor of the face of somebody who was deeply distressed or the red cheeks of a person who was either ashamed or greatly pleased, connecting emotions of all kinds—pleasant or unpleasant—with a changed function of the heart and of the circulation. Most of the scientific interest has been concentrated on unpleasant emotional states. Pleasant emotions, however, may have a circulatory effect, Levi (1965) having found an increased catecholamine excretion in the urine under such circumstances.

HAEMODYNAMIC CHANGES ASSOCIATED WITH MUSCULAR EFFORT

In his famous book *Wisdom of the Body* Cannon (1932) pointed out that, during the millions of years of life on the earth and of the phylogenesis, the organisms in their fight for survival had to develop mechanisms which would enable them to cope at a moment's notice with the possible enemies represented by the various animals of prey. They had to be equipped for fight or for flight. However, the same is true for the animals of prey themselves to enable them to get their proper share of the victim captured by the pack. Thus, the ability to carry out strenuous muscular work belonged and belongs to the basic mechanisms which make survival possible. Without muscular activity the animal and even a primitive human being would be lost, as it would be unable to provide for itself the necessary nutrition and would sooner or later be devoured by its luckier adversary. It can be stated that the survival of its species would be impossible without muscular action as the sexual partners could never meet. Muscular action is, of course, impossible without the necessary energy and this depends on the circulation. Although the muscle can work for a short period of time anaerobically, i.e. with an oxygen debt, it would soon fatigue with the accumulation of the metabolic products, and anaerobic work for more than a limited length of time is impossible. The circulatory changes occurring in the body during muscular exercise are well known. They consist of an increase in the cardiac output, deepening of the respiration supplying the blood with more oxygen, constriction of the vessels in the kidneys, splanchnic region and at the start of the exercise also in the skin, with a shift of the cardiac output to the working muscles, to the myocardium and to some extent also to the brain. This demonstrates a perfect adaptation to the requirements of the organism in the course of an increased demand for oxygen and for the energetics during muscular works. However, the situation may demand an immediate maximum activation of the muscles for defence, for the flight or for the fight. It would therefore appear advantageous if a preparatory state of the circulation with a shift of the blood to the muscles could occur during a signal of a potential danger or prey. This is possibly the biological explanation for such psychological states as fear, anxiety, rage, anxious expectation, etc. An unusual sound in a quiet isolated room, the rasping of grass in a dark forest, the smell of the prey—all these and many others may be such signals which may necessitate within the next second a strenuous muscular action for the sake of survival. It is very likely that the originally conditioned connections between such external signals and the circulatory readjustment to a maximal muscular exertion became throughout the ages unconditioned attributes of these emotional states.

HAEMODYNAMIC CHANGES ASSOCIATED WITH 'EMOTIONAL' STRESS IN ANIMALS

Compared with the wealth of information concerning the details of the haemodynamic changes during strenuous muscular exercise in animals, less work has been devoted to the haemodynamic changes during emotional stress in animals. That fear may lead to vasoconstriction in dogs has been demonstrated by the study of changes of the renal volume for the first time by Handovsky and Samaan (1937). Friedman (1947) found that careless handling of experimental rats may produce a vasoconstriction in their kidneys. Bing and Knudsen (1954) have observed blanching of the exposed surface of rat kidneys under stressful experimental situations. Rabbits react by protracted renal vasoconstriction to a multitude of disturbing stimuli from their environment which may even induce a temporary anuria (Brod and Sirota, 1949). A shutdown of the cortical renal vessels and a diversion of the blood from the renal cortex to the juxtamedullary vessels of the cat in whom a typical rage reaction has been produced when it was attacked in the laboratory by a dog, has been demonstrated by Lüvgren (1952). Also the orientation reflex appears to be accompanied by marked haemodynamic changes. This name was given by Pavlov (1949) to the behavioural changes of a dog (and possibly of any other animal) under circumstances when an unusual or unaccustomed stimulus such as a hissing sound of gas escaping from the tubing in a quiet experimental room, a strange light, etc., reaches the organism. The animal is visibly aroused and it turns the sensory organs to the stimulus to explore it. Madlafousek (1957) found that in a dog under such circumstances vasoconstriction takes place in the skin but not in the muscular part of the extremity, to which the cardiac output thus appears to be preferentially directed.

Hess (1928) established that by an electrical stimulation of a certain area in the hypothalamus a typical rage reaction can be produced. Eliasson *et al.* (1951) found that when stimulating a widespread hypothalamic area in acute experiments in cats the blood pressure rises and this is accompanied by a vasoconstriction in the splanchnic area and by a vasodilatation in the muscles. This vasodilatation can be partly blocked by atropine, which suggests that it is mediated by the cholinergic sympathetic fibres that Bülbring and Burn (1937) showed supply the vessels of the skeletal muscles. That a close connection exists between this reaction and the haemodynamic response accompanying muscular exercise seems to follow from the fact that a similar haemodynamic pattern can be also elicited from the motor cortex (Green and Hoff, 1937). Abrahams, Hilton and Zbrozyna (1960), working on cats with chronically implanted electrodes into the hypothalamic area—studied by Eliasson *et al.* (1951)—found that the stimulation with a current of low intensity produced, in addition to the rise in blood pressure with visceral vasoconstriction and muscular vasodilatation, a pattern of behaviour typical of an orientation reflex: the animal becomes alerted and directs its sensory organs as if searching for a possible enemy. An intensification of the stimulating current produces a typical rage reaction with the same haemodynamic changes as discussed previously. The authors speak of a defence reaction, although it appears that this reaction can be biologically as useful for defence as for attack. By shifting the raised cardiac output to the muscles during a situation which may be potentially dangerous, the necessity is obviated of pumping blood to the muscles after they already had to be activated to a maximum and forced to work under anaerobic conditions. It thus makes the animal fit for fight or flight at once should the danger prove real.

HAEMODYNAMIC CHANGES ASSOCIATED WITH EMOTIONAL STRESS IN MAN

The biological necessity for the strenuous muscular action, for fight or flight under emotional situations in civilized man does not exist any more under most circumstances. It can still be found, of course, in a child who will fight or run away from a real or imaginary enemy. However, in adults, under circumstances connected with fear, anxiety, anger or anxious expectations, any muscular action is absent or will be suppressed by social inhibitions. The question may therefore be asked whether the circulatory changes, which—as mentioned at the beginning—are known even to the layman to take place, are analogous to those in the animal and whether they can also be considered preparatory to muscular action. Tachycardia is the rule under such conditions, but occasionally the heart rate may slow down markedly and heralds a vaso-vagal syncope (Boas and Goldschmidt, 1932), which is known to occur occasionally under conditions of acute mental distress. That the emotional tachycardia leads to a marked increase in the cardiac output has been demonstrated by modern techniques for the first time by Grollman (1929), using his acetylene method, and confirmed using the Fick technique by Stead *et al.* (1945) and by Hickham, Cargill and Golden (1948), who observed that subjects who were tense during the heart catheterization had higher cardiac outputs than those who were relaxed. As the oxygen consumption is only slightly raised, the arterio-venous oxygen difference is diminished. This observation has been confirmed since then by everybody who has used this technique and even the application of the dye-dilution method can lead to falsely high values of the cardiac output, if the measurement is carried out under conditions of unrest in the laboratory or if the patient is tense for some reason. The rise of the blood pressure under states of tension, emotional stress, etc., is well known, as also is the pallor of the skin observed in some people during conditions of fear. A drop in skin temperature in affective states has been actually observed by Mittelmann and Wolff (1939), and Fencl *et al.* (1959), using the 'Wärmeleitmesser' of Hensel and Bender (1956), found a decrease in skin blood flow during stressful mental arithmetic. In view of the increase in blood pressure this finding points to a vasoconstriction in the skin.

Vasoconstriction in the kidneys in man during an emotional upset had been found by the clearance technique (Smith, 1940) and confirmed by Pfeiffer and Wolff (1950). Even a short cold stimulus connected with a feeling of pain in the extremity may lead to a vasoconstriction in the kidneys (Brod *et al.*, 1954). Using the local thermodilution technique in the renal vein Brod, Hornych and Šlechta (1969) came to the same conclusion.

On the other hand, an increase in blood flow through the extremity during an emotional stress in man has been found by Wilkins and Eichna (1941). As vasoconstriction takes place in the skin under such circumstances, this result is suggestive of an increased blood flow through the muscles during emotion. This has been directly demonstrated by Golenhofen and Hildebrand (1957) and Blair, Golenhofen and Seidel (1959) using Hensel's thermoprobe, and Brod *et al.* (1958, 1959) using the occlusion plethysmography of Barcroft and Swan (1953) and later of Whitney (1953) for the study of total forearm blood flow and Hensel and Bender's (1956) 'Wärmeleitmesser' to differentiate the skin and the muscle. Ganz (1965), measuring the outflow from the coronary sinus by the thermodilution catheter (Froněk and Ganz, 1960), found a rise in the coronary blood flow and a drop in the coronary vascular resistance under conditions of stressful mental arithmetic. Applying the same technique to the jugular bulb, draining over 90 per cent of the cerebral venous outflow in man, Brod *et al.* (1966a) found that during stressful mental arithmetic cerebral blood flow as a rule increases by some 20–30 per cent, the rise being due in most instances to the increase in blood pressure, but exceeding it in about one-fifth of the observations. The increase in the cerebral blood flow is accompanied by a parallel rise in the cerebral oxygen consumption (*Figure 1*).

REGIONAL DIFFERENCES IN THE HAEMODYNAMIC RESPONSE TO EMOTION

In order to get a better overall view of the emotional haemodynamic changes Brod *et al.* (1959) studied the redistribution of the cardiac output to the various organs and the changes of the regional vascular resistances in an experimental set-up which permitted a simultaneous recording of the cardiac output by the dye-dilution technique, a continuous measurement of the systolic, diastolic and mean blood pressure, the follow-up of renal haemodynamics by the PAH clearance technique, of the total forearm blood flow by occlusion plethysmography, of the skin blood flow by the Hensel and Bender's (1956) 'Wärmeleitmesser', forearm muscle blood flow being calculated from the difference of the total forearm and skin blood flow.

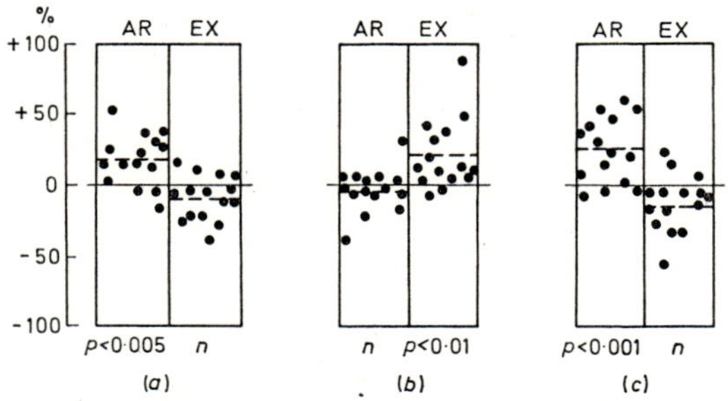

Figure 1. Summary of the changes of (a) cerebral blood flow, (b) cerebral vascular resistance and (c) cerebral oxygen consumption during stressful mental arithmetic (AR) and during muscular exercise (EX) (pedalling on a bicycle ergograph in a lying position) in a group of normotensive subjects. As in the majority of instances cerebral blood flow increased only in proportion to the rise of the blood pressure, the cerebral vascular resistance did not change in 80 per cent of the observations, decreasing in the remaining 20 per cent (*Brod* et al., *1966a*)

An indicator of the splanchnic blood flow was obtained from the slope of the disappearance curve of the Rose Bengal or later of the cardio-green. They attempted also to check the same parameter from the ratio

$$\frac{\text{extrarenal vascular resistance}}{\text{forearm muscle vascular resistance}}$$

The ratio should remain unchanged, if the vascular resistance in the other important extrarenal vascular area, namely in the splanchnic region, behaved in the same way as in the muscles. A marked rise of the ratio is suggestive of a splanchnic vasoconstriction, a marked drop of a splanchnic vasodilatation, the extrarenal vascular resistance being calculated from the difference of the reciprocals of the total peripheral vascular resistance and of the renal vascular resistance (in analogy with Kirchhoff's law).

The result of such a typical experiment is shown in *Figure 2*. The emotional stress was produced by mental arithmetic consisting of the subtraction of a difficult number (e.g. 17) every two seconds from a previous result starting with a difficult four figure number (e.g. 3194), with a permanent harassing of the subject to whom all the mistakes were pointed out while a metronome was beating the time. This raised the systolic, diastolic and mean blood pressure by 25 mm. Hg. This was entirely accounted for by a steep increase in the cardiac output from 5·5 to 9·1 while the calculated total peripheral vascular resistance dropped slightly. However, the regional vascular resistance in the kidneys increased markedly, and there was also an

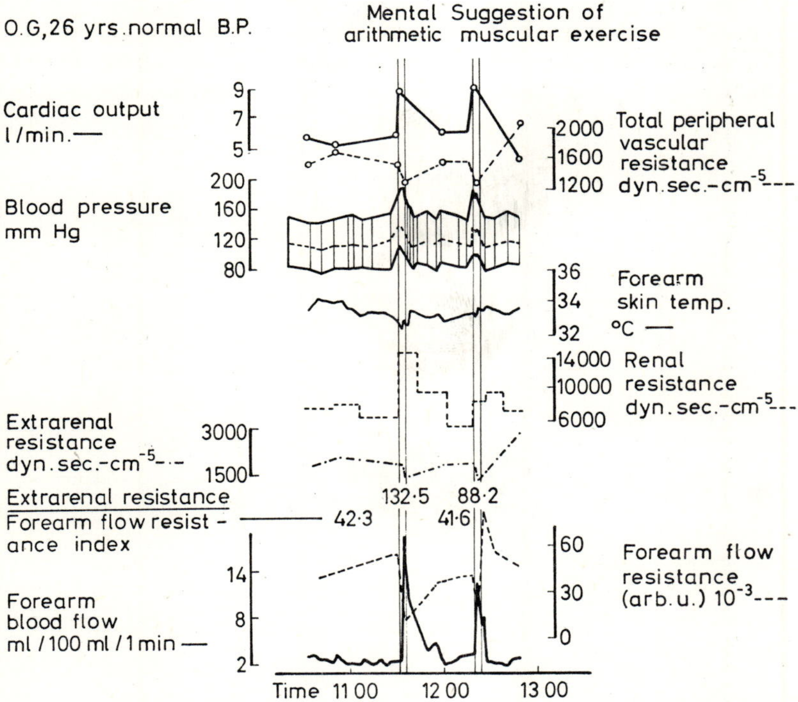

Figure 2. General and regional haemodynamic changes during stressful mental arithmetic and during a verbal suggestion of strenuous muscular exercise. The vascular resistances were calculated in arbitrary units as $\frac{\textit{mean BP}}{\textit{blood flow ml./min.}}$

The ratio $\frac{\textit{extrarenal vascular resistance}}{\textit{forearm muscle vascular resistance}}$

should not change, if all the vascular resistance outside the kidneys changes in parallel. A rise in ratio suggests a vasoconstriction in some large area, while the muscular vessels were dilating, and points to the splanchnic region. It is obvious that the emotional stress and the suggested muscular exercise produced similar haemodynamic changes (*Brod* et al., *1959*)

increase in the ratio of the extrarenal vascular resistance to the forearm vascular resistance, suggesting a vasoconstriction in the splanchnic area, and a drop of the skin temperature in the face of a rise in blood pressure could be accounted for only by a vasoconstriction in the skin. On the other hand, there was a very marked increase in the blood flow in the forearm muscles from an average of 2 ml./100 g. forearm muscle per minute to 17 ml. The calculated forearm vascular resistance decreased steeply.

Another type of emotional haemodynamic reaction, produced this time by the immersion of a leg into ice-cold water, is reproduced in *Figure 3*. Here the systolic, diastolic and the mean blood pressure rose by about 20 mm. Hg, but this time this was due exclusively to a

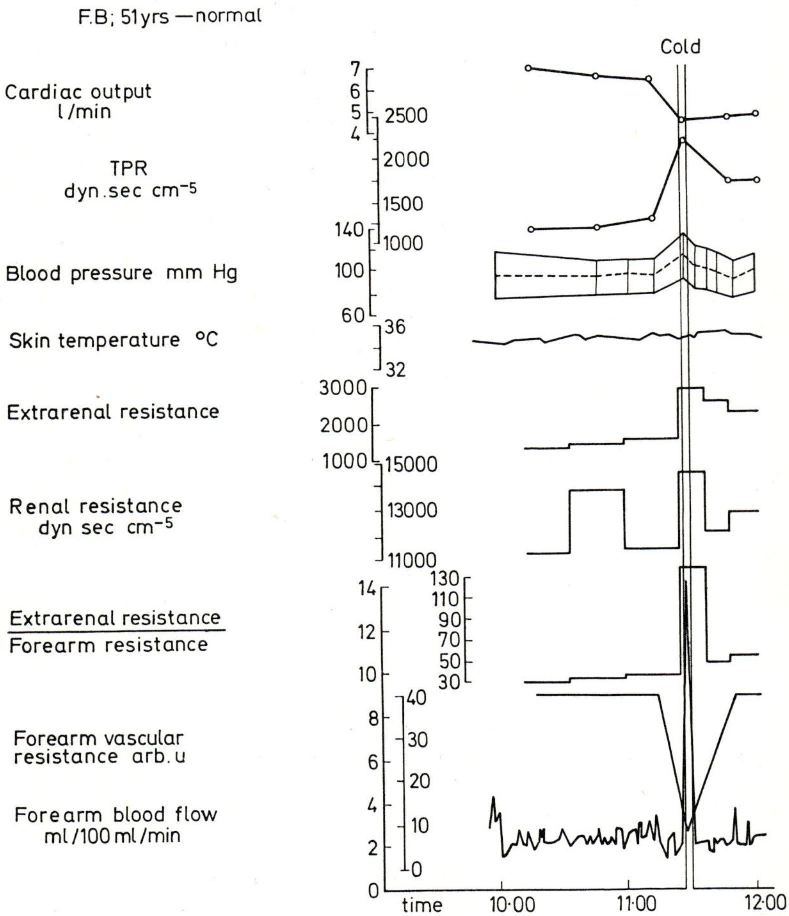

Figure 3. General and regional haemodynamic changes during a cold pressor stimulus. For explanation see legend to Figure 2 (*Brod* et al., *1959*)

marked increase in the total peripheral vascular resistance, while the cardiac output decreased. In spite of this opposite change of the general haemodynamics underlying the rise of the blood pressure, the regional haemodynamic changes were analogous as in the previous experiment. The renal vascular resistance rose, the indicator of the splanchnic vascular resistance pointed to a vasoconstriction in this large area and the slight drop in skin temperature also suggested a vasoconstriction. On the other hand, there was again a marked rise in the forearm muscle blood flow with a drop of the forearm muscle vascular resistance.

All the experimental data are summarized in *Figure 4*. Each line indicates the percentage change of the parameter studied in an individual subject. The division into the three columns is made according to the general haemodynamic changes: in the first column those experiments are summarized where the blood pressure rose by an increase in the cardiac output while the total peripheral vascular resistance remained unchanged or decreased. The second column summarizes those studies where the blood pressure rose by an increase in the total peripheral vascular resistance while the cardiac output decreased. In the third column those few observations are summarized in which both the cardiac output and the total peripheral vascular resistance rose. However, in all these three seemingly different patterns of the overall haemodynamics the renal vascular resistance always rose, the indicator of the splanchnic vascular resistance practically always suggested a vasoconstriction in this area and there was always a tendency to cutaneous vasoconstriction, while the vascular resistance in the forearm muscles and in the myocardium decreased and the vascular resistance in the brain (*see above*) exhibited little change. It is clear that the change of the total peripheral vascular resistance depends on the mutable balance of these vasoconstrictions and vasodilatations occurring simultaneously in the various vascular regions of the body. The total peripheral vascular resistance decreased if the vasodilatation in the muscles and myocardium outweighed the vasoconstriction in the viscera and skin, while a rise in the total peripheral vascular resistance suggested that the vasoconstriction in the viscera and skin had the upper hand. In a few experiments where the vasoconstriction and vasodilatation kept a perfect balance, the total peripheral vascular resistance remained unchanged. A rise of the cardiac output even in these instances suggested that this was not a secondary consequence of a falling peripheral vascular resistance, but that this increase in cardiac output formed an integral part of the response of the organism to emotional stress. The same change took place even if the total peripheral vascular resistance

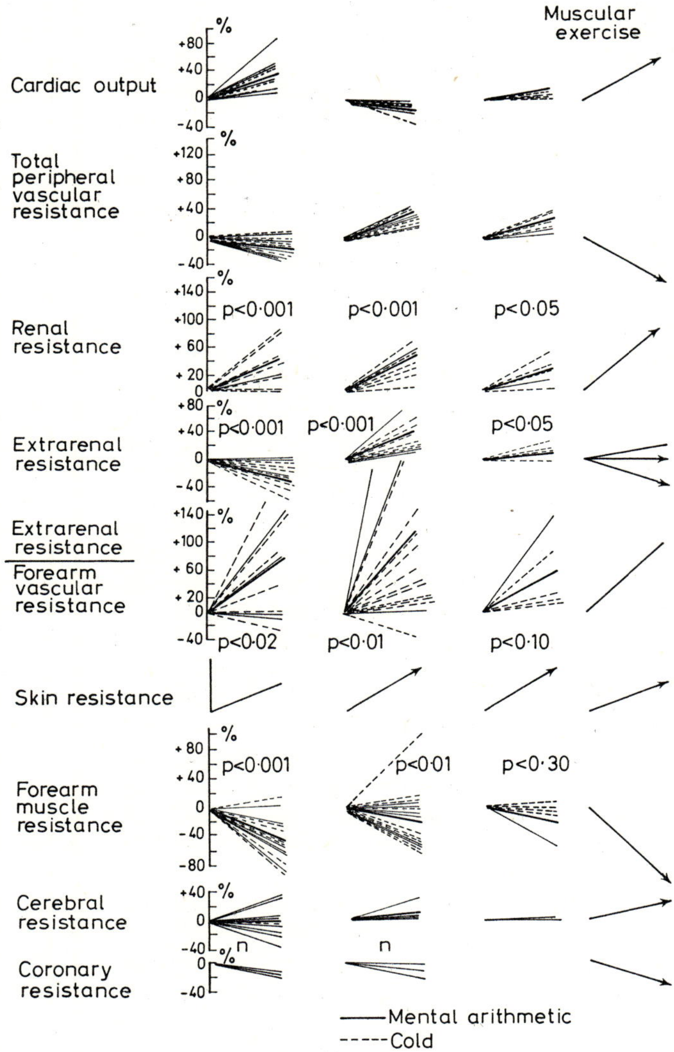

Figure 4. Summary of the general and regional haemodynamic changes produced by stressful mental arithmetic and by the cold stimulus. Each line indicates the results in one subject. The arrows in the line of the skin resistance indicate the general trend found in another series of subjects. The arrows in the right column indicate changes known to occur during strenuous muscular exercise (*Brod* et al., *1959*)

increased slightly, but if this rise exceeded some 20 per cent of the original level the cardiac output started to fall, perhaps by some reflex connections known to exist between the peripheral vascular bed and the heart (Warren and Stead, 1947; Aviado *et al.*, 1950). It is obvious that by these regional haemodynamic changes the cardiac output is shifted from the viscera and from the skin to the muscles, to the myocardium and passively also to the brain. Thus the vascular reaction occurring in animals during an emotional stress is present also in humans under conditions of tension, fear and anger (all these subjective feelings were reported in this investigation).

It has been pointed out that this haemodynamic response with the redistribution of the cardiac output in favour of the muscles and myocardium is preparatory to strenuous muscular exercise. The increase in muscle blood flow during actual muscle exercise is assumed by Krogh (1929) to be produced by the accumulation of muscle metabolites opening up the capillaries, especially relaxing the precapillary sphincters. Kjellmer (1965) has recently provided evidence that some two-thirds of this vasodilator action is due to the accumulation of potassium ions in the interstitial fluid of the muscles. However, neither a visible muscular activity nor any increase in the tension of the muscles took place in the majority of the investigated subjects. Thus the problem of the mechanism of the emotional vasodilatation in the muscles requires an explanation. One possibility would be that the oxygen requirement of the muscles rises during emotion even without any visible muscular action, Bykov (1947) claiming that it is possible to condition the increase in oxygen consumption produced by muscular exercise. This was, however, disproved. During actual exercise of the forearm muscles produced by opening and closing of the fist Barcroft *et al.* (1960) found an increase in the oxygen consumption in the forearm muscles (recorded from the changes of the oxygen saturation of the blood collected from a deep forearm vein), which markedly exceeded the increase in the forearm blood flow so that the oxygen utilization increased as evidenced by the rise of the arterio-venous oxygen difference. On the other hand, an increase in forearm blood flow during an emotional stimulus (mental arithmetic) of the same degree exceeded the small rise (or there was no change at all) in the oxygen consumption of the forearm muscles, with a subsequent drop of the forearm oxygen utilization (*Figure 5*). Thus the emotional hyperaemia of the muscles is out of proportion to their metabolic demands and cannot be accounted by them.

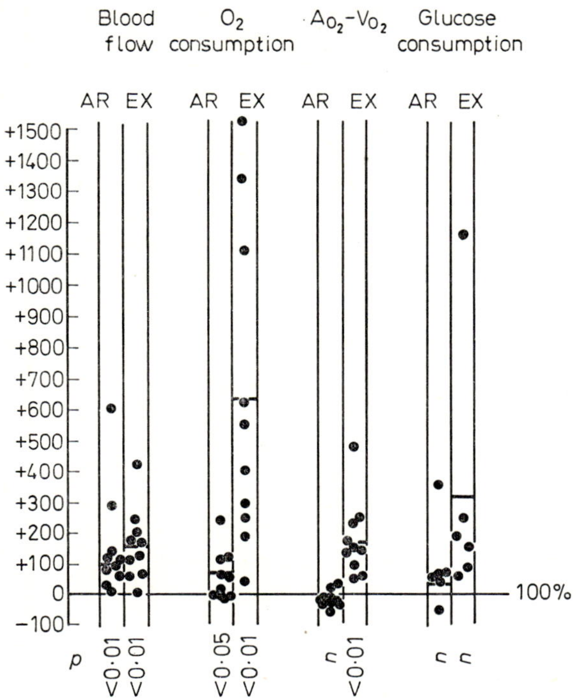

Figure 5. Summary of the changes of forearm muscle blood flow, oxygen consumption, oxygen utilization and glucose consumption during stressful mental arithmetic (AR) and during forearm muscle exercise (opening and closing of the fist—EX) (Barcroft et al., *1960)*

THE MECHANISM OF EMOTIONAL VASODILATATION

The metabolic factors opening the capillaries being absent, what is then the mechanism for the emotional vasodilatation in the muscles? The uptake of radioactive substances injected into the muscle depends on the size of the capillary surface. The increase in blood flow during exercise of the forearm muscles leads to a marked steepening of the disappearance slope of the radioactive ^{131}I or xenon. However, muscular hyperaemia of the same degree produced by an acute emotional stress leaves the disappearance slope of ^{131}I or xenon unaffected and suggests that the extra blood entering the muscle flows either faster through the previously available capillaries or traverses them through some other functional by-pass. As the problem of vascular shunts in the muscles is still a matter of dispute

(Barlow, Haigh and Walder, 1961), Brod *et al.* (1966b) studied the capillary filtration coefficient of Folkow *et al.* (1964) during the emotional stress of mental arithmetic and during the opening and closing of the fist, producing a similar degree of increase in forearm blood flow. The capillary filtration coefficient indicates how much tissue fluid is being produced per minute in 100 ml. of forearm muscle by an increment of the capillary pressure by 1 mm. Hg. It depends obviously on the size of the capillary surface. It may be seen from *Figure 6* that the coefficient increased steeply during muscular

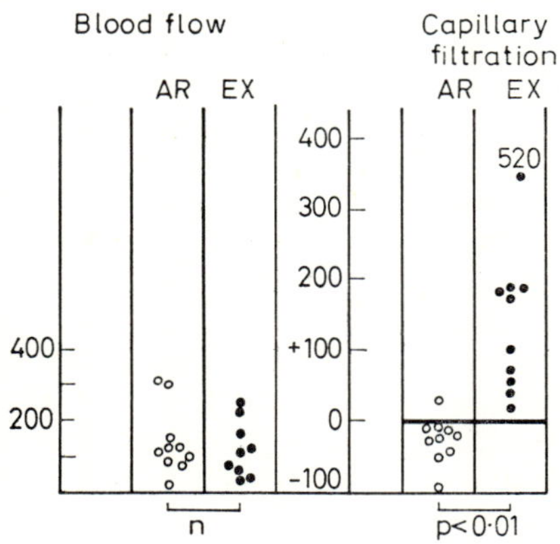

Figure 6. Summary of the changes of the forearm blood flow and the coefficient of the capillary ultrafiltration during stressful mental arithmetic (AR) and during forearm muscle exercise (opening and closing of the fist—EX)

exercise corresponding to the well-known increase in the number of opened capillaries. During the emotional hyperaemia of the same degree there was, however, no change at all of the coefficient, confirming once more the previous conclusion that during emotional hyperaemia of the muscles new capillaries are not opened up.

As local factors cannot obviously account for the vasodilatation in the muscles during emotion, reflex or humoral mechanisms (or both) are to be considered. It is well established that vessels in the muscles normally possess a vasoconstrictor sympathetic tone (Barcroft and Swan, 1953) and that a vasodilatation in the muscle can be produced either by a decrease in this vasoconstrictor tone or by the activation of the sympathetic cholinergic vasodilator fibres (Bülbring and Burn, 1937). Among the humoral agents, the vasodilator properties of adrenaline in the muscle have been recognized by Grant and Pearson (1938) and confirmed by Allen, Barcroft and

Edholm (1946). That both the adrenaline and the acetylcholine may mediate this response follows from the fact that both these agents produce a vasodilatation in the forearm without changing the capillary filtration coefficient (Brod *et al.*, 1966b).

A release of the sympathetic vasoconstrictor tone is an unlikely explanation, as vasoconstriction occurs at the same time in the kidneys and in the other organs and is obviously mediated by an increased vasoconstrictor sympathetic tone. The high renal vascular resistance can be reduced by the α-blocking agent dibenamine along with the reduction of the emotionally increased blood pressure (Brod and Fejfar, 1954).

The study of the delay of onset of the muscular vasodilatation following the beginning of the emotional stimulus admits both a reflex and a humoral mechanism. The vasodilatation may occasionally start at once but at the other extreme it was delayed by 35 seconds, suggesting the release of a humoral agent, which had to be carried to the muscular vessels by the blood stream (Barcroft *et al.*, 1960). The attempt to block the presumed sympathetic pathway by anaesthesia of the stellate ganglion gives equivocal results. The decrease in the emotional vasodilatation in the muscles following such an anaesthesia may only mean that the limits of the vasodilatation were already approached by the previous release of the vasoconstrictor sympathetic tone by this procedure. Also, the interpretation of the diminution of the emotional vasodilatation in the muscles after intravenous atropine is made difficult by the fact that the heart action speeds up and thus the whole circulation is markedly changed. However, the degree of the emotional vasodilatation could be reduced by some 20 to 30 per cent in 15 out of 20 experiments in which atropine has been injected into the brachial artery, prior to the emotional stimulus. This result is suggestive of activation of the sympathetic cholinergic fibres in man in the course of emotional stress. However, this mechanism accounts only for one part of the emotional vasodilatation and is analogous in this respect to the partial blockade by atropine of the vasodilatation in the muscles in cats, produced by the hypothalamic stimulation (Eliasson *et al.*, 1951).

That the residual component of the vasodilatation is due to circulating adrenaline is suggested by the experiments of Holmberg *et al.* (1965) and Konzett, Strieder and Ziegler (1968) who succeeded in removing a large part of the emotional vasodilatation by β-blocking agents.

We may thus conclude that the same mechanisms which are responsible for the haemodynamic response accompanying fear and rage in animals are also responsible for the resetting of the circulation during an emotional stress in man. This analogy suggests that we are dealing with the same reaction which has been developing throughout the whole long phylogenesis and which could not be extinguished during the 30 to 50 generations of civilized human life, which made this haemodynamic accompaniment of the emotional upset superfluous and perhaps even harmful as it may lead to acute vascular accidents. It is even possible that a faulty regulation of this important haemodynamic reaction may be the basis of some pathological states, such as essential hypertension (Brod, 1960).

SUMMARY

The survival of the individual and of the species depends on the ability to activate at a moment's notice the muscles for the sake of defence, of attack, of prey. This necessitates the resetting of the circulation to satisfy the increased metabolic demands by an increased cardiac output and its redistribution to the active muscles and the myocardium. This haemodynamic response is co-ordinated by a well-defined hypothalamic area. The efferent pathways to the viscera lie in the vasoconstrictor sympathetic fibres, to the muscles and myocardium in the vasodilator cholinergic sympathetic fibres. Adrenaline is released at the same time. The reaction is preserved even in humans, in spite of the fact that its biological value is lost.

REFERENCES

Abrahams, V. C., Hilton, S. M. and Zbrozyna, A. (1960). 'Active Muscle Vasodilatation Produced by Stimulation of the Brain Stem: its Significance in the Defence Reaction.' *J. Physiol.*, **154**, 491.

Allen, W. J., Barcroft, H. and Edholm, O. G. (1946). 'On the Action of Adrenaline on the Blood Vessels in Human Skeletal Muscle.' *J. Physiol.* (*Lond.*), **105**, 255.

Aviado, D. M., Lu, T. H., Kalow, W., Peskin, G. W., Turnbull, G. L. and Hess, M. E. (1950). 'Circulatory and Respiratory Reflexes from the Perfused Heart of the Dog.' *Am. J. med. Sci.*, **220**, 707.

Barcroft, H. and Swan, H. J. C. (1953). *Sympathetic Control of Human Blood Vessels*. London: Edward Arnold.

— Brod, J., Hejl, Z., Hirsjärvi, E. A. and Kitchin, A. N. (1960). 'The Mechanism of the Vasodilatation in the Forearm Muscle during Stress (Mental Arithmetic).' *Clin. Sci.*, **19**, 577.

Barlow, T. E., Haigh, A. L. and Walder, D. N. (1961). 'Evidence for Two Vascular Pathways in Skeletal Muscle.' *Clin. Sci.*, **20**, 367.

Bing, J. and Knudsen, P. J. (1954). 'Effects of Severe Hypoxin Fright on the Renal Blood Flow of Normal and Shocked Mice.' *Acta path. microbiol. scand.*, **35**, 39.

Blair, D. A., Glover, W. E., Greenfield, A. D. and Roddie, I. C. (1959). 'Excitation of Cholinergic Vasodilator Nerves to Human Skeletal Muscles during Emotional Stress.' *J. Physiol.* (*Lond.*), **148,** 633.

— Golenhofen, K. and Seidel, W. (1959). 'Muscle Blood Flow during Emotional Stress.' *J. Physiol.* (*Lond.*), **149,** 618.

Boas, E. P. and Goldschmidt, E. L. (1932). *The Heart Rate.* Springfield, Ill.: Thomas.

Brod, J. (1960). 'Essential Hypertension. Haemodynamic Observations with a Bearing on its Pathogenesis.' *Lancet,* **1,** 773.

— and Fejfar, Z. (1954). 'The Role of Neuro-humoral Factors in the Genesis of Renal Haemodynamic Changes in Heart Failure.' *Acta med. scand.,* **148,** 273.

— Fencl, V., Gerová, M., Hejl, Z., Jirka, V., Kotanová, E., Prát, V., Seidlová, P. and Zajíc, F. (1954). 'Changes of Renal Haemodynamics and Function following a Cold Stimulus in Normal Subjects and in Hypertensive Disease.' In *Hypertensivní choroba,* p. 73. Prague: State Medical Publishing House.

— — Hejl, Z. and Jirka, J. (1958). 'The Changes of Muscle and Skin Blood Flow during Emotional Stimuli.' *Čslká Fysiol.,* **7,** 437.

— — — (1959). 'Circulatory Changes Underlying Blood Pressure Elevation during Acute Emotional Stress (Mental Arithmetic) in Normotensive and Hypertensive Subjects.' *Clin. Sci.,* **18,** 269.

— Ganz, V., Ulrych, M. and Froněk, A. (1966a). 'Changes of Cerebral Haemodynamics and Metabolism during Emotional Pressor Reaction and Muscular Exercise.' In *L'hypertension artérielle,* International Club on Arterial Hypertension, Paris 1965, p. 427. Paris: L'expansion scientifique française.

— Hornych, A. and Šlechta, V. (1970). 'The Effect of Emotion on the Renal Blood Flow.' *Nephron.* (in press).

— Přerovský, I., Ulrych, M., Linhart, J. and Heine, H. (1966b). 'Changes in the Capillary Filtration in Muscles during Muscular Hyperaemia Accompanying Emotion, Exercise and Adrenaline, Acetylcholine and Isopropyladrenaline Intra-arterial Infusion.' In *L'hypertension artérielle,* International Club on Arterial Hypertension, Paris, 1965, p. 433. Paris: L'expansion scientifique française.

— and Sirota, J. H. (1949). 'Effect of Emotional Disturbance on Water Diuresis, and Renal Blood Flow in the Rabbit.' *Am. J. Physiol.,* **157,** 31.

Bülbring, E. and Burn, J. H. (1937). 'Sympathetic Vaso-dilator Fibres in the Hare and Monkey Compared with Other Species.' *J. Physiol.* (*Lond.*), **88,** 341.

Bykov, K. M. (1947). *Cerebral Cortex and Internal Organs.* Moscow: Medgiz.

Cannon, W. B. (1932). *The Wisdom of the Body.* New York: Norton.

Eliasson, S., Folkow, B., Lindgren, P. and Uvnäs, B. (1951). 'Activation of Sympathetic Vasodilator Nerves to the Skeletal Muscles in the Cat by Hypothalamic Stimulation.' *Acta physiol. scand.,* **27,** 18.

Fencl, V., Hejl, Z., Jirka, J., Madlafousek, J. and Brod, J. (1959). 'Changes of Blood Flow in Forearm Muscle and Skin during an Acute Emotional Stress (Mental Arithmetic).' *Clin. Sci.*, **18**, 491.

Folkow, B., Lewis, D. H., Lundgren, O., Mellander, S. and Wallentin, I. (1964). 'The Effect of the Sympathetic Vasoconstrictor Fibres and the Distribution of Capillary Blood Flow in the Intestine.' *Acta physiol. scand.*, **61,** 458.

Friedman, M. (1947). 'The Creatinine, Inulin and Hippurate Clearance in the Rat.' *Am. J. Physiol.*, **148,** 387.

Froněk, A. and Ganz, V. (1960). 'Measurement of Flow in Single Blood Vessels Including Cardiac Output by Local Thermodilution.' *Circulat. Res.*, **8,** 1751.

Ganz, V. (1965). Unpublished Data.

Golenhofen, K. and Hildebrandt, G. (1957). 'Psychische Einflüsse auf die Muskel-durchblutung.' *Pflügers Arch.*, **263,** 637.

Grant, R. T. and Pearson, R. S. B. (1938). 'The Blood Circulation in the Human Limb: Observations on the Differences between the Proximal and Distal Parts and Remarks on the Regulation of Body Temperature.' *Clin. Sci*, **3,** 119.

Green, H. D. and Hoff, E. C. (1937). 'Effects of Faradic Stimulation of Cerebral Cortex on Limb and Renal Volumes in Cat and Monkey.' *Am. J. Physiol.*, **118,** 641.

Greenfield, A. D. M. (1962). 'The Effects of Emotional Stress on the Circulation through Voluntary Muscles. Shock, Pathogenesis and Therapy.' *Ciba International Symposium.* London: Churchill.

Grollman, A. (1929). 'The Effect of Psychic Disturbances on the Cardiac Output, Pulse Rate, Blood Pressure and Oxygen Consumption in Man.' *Am. J. Physiol.*, **89,** 366.

Handovsky, H. and Samaan, A. (1937). 'Observations on the Renal Circulation and Secretion in the Dog, with Special Reference to the Effect of Pituitary (Posterior Lobe) Extract., *J. Physiol.* (*Lond.*) **39,** 14.

Hensel, N. and Bender, F. (1956). 'Fortlaufende Bestimmung der Hautdurchblutung am Menschen mit einem elektrischen Wärmeleitmesser.' *Pflügers Arch.*, **263,** 603.

Hess, W. R. (1928). 'Stammganglien-Reizversuche.' *Ber. ges. physiol.*, **42,** 554.

Hickam, J. B., Cargill, W. H. and Golden, A. (1948). 'Cardiovascular Reactions to Emotional Stimuli. Effect on the Cardiac Output, Arteriovenous Oxygen Differences, Arterial Pressure and Peripheral Resistance.' *J. clin. Invest.*, **27,** 290.

Holmberg, G., Levi, L., Mathe, A., Rosen, A. and Scott, H. M. (1965). 'Comparison of the Plasma Catecholamine Levels and the Influence of Propranolol on Peripheral Hemodynamic Manifestations of Emotional Stress in Labile Hypertensive and Normal Subjects.' *Circulation*, **32,** (suppl. 2), 11.

Kjellmer, I. (1965). 'The Potassium Ion as a Vasodilator during Muscular Exercise.' *Acta physiol. scand*, **63,** 460.

Konzett, H., Strieder, N. and Ziegler, E. (1968). 'Die Wirkung eines β-Receptorenblockers auf emotionell bedingte Kreislaufreaktionen, insbesondere auf die Durchblutung des Unterarms.' *Wien klin. Wschr*, **80,** 953.

Krogh, A. (1929). *The Anatomy and Physiology of the Capillaries.* Yale University Press.

Levi, I. (1965). 'The Urinary Output of Adrenaline and Noradrenaline during Pleasant and Unpleasant Emotional States.' *Psychosom. Med.*, **27,** 80.

Lüvgren, quoted by Franklin, K. J. (1952). 'Aspects of the Renal Circulation and its Regulation. Visceral Circulation.' *Ciba International Symposium*, p. 187. London: Churchill.

Madlafousek, J. (1957). 'Orientation Reflex as an Initial Part of the Defensive Adaptative Equipment of the Organism.' *Čslká Psychol.*, **1,** 39.

Mittelmann, B. and Wolff, H. G. (1939). 'Affective States and Skin Temperature: Experimental Study of Subjects with "Cold Hands" and Raynaud's Syndrome.' *Psychosom. Med.* **1,** 231.

Pavlov, I. P. (1949). 'Lectures on the Work of the Hemispheres of the Brain.' *Izdaŭ. Akad. Nauk. SSSR, Leningrad.*

Pfeiffer, J. B. and Wolff, H. G. (1950). 'Studies in Renal Circulation during Periods of Life Stress and Accompanying Emotional Reactions in Subjects with and without Essential Hypertension; Obervations on the Role of Neural Activity in Regulation of Renal Blood Flow.' *J. clin. Invest.*, **29,** 1227.

Smith, H. W. (1940). 'The Physiology of the Renal Circulation.' *Harvey Lect.*, **35,** 166.

Stead, E. A., Warren, J. V., Merrill, A. J. and Brannon, E. S. (1945). 'The Cardiac Output in Male Subjects as Measured by the Technique of Right Arterial Catheterization. Normal Values with Observations on the Effect of Anxiety and Tilting.' *J. clin. Invest.*, **24,** 326.

Warren, S. V. and Stead, E. A. (1947). 'Control of the Cardiac Output in Man: Studies on Reactive Hyperemia.' *Fedn. Proc.*, **6,** 223.

Whitney, R. J. (1953). 'The Measurement of Volume Changes in Human Limbs.' *J. Physiol.* (*Lond.*), **121,** 1.

Wilkins, R. W. and Eichna, L. W. (1941). 'Blood Flow to the Forearm and Calf. I. Vasomotor Reactions: Role of the Sympathetic Nervous System.' *Bull. Johns Hopk. Hosp.*, **68,** 425.

CHAPTER 5

THE PSYCHOSOMATIC EFFECTS OF BEREAVEMENT

C. MURRAY PARKES

INTRODUCTION

Most of those phenomena which are classed as stressful can be construed as losses or threats of loss. However, the great variation in intensity, duration and character of events so classified must lead us to be wary of broad generalizations about the effects of loss.

Losses of one sort or another are common in the lives of us all and it is tempting to blame them for any illnesses which follow them even when these too are common occurrences.

Several authors have described psychosomatic conditions which they attribute to bereavement but such anecdotal accounts must be set against others in which bereavement may actually be followed by improvement in health. Wear (1963), for instance, has described two patients with psychosomatic symptoms (flexural eczema in one case and rheumatoid arthritis with duodenal ulcer in the other) which rapidly disappeared after the death of a spouse.

In this chapter attention will be mainly confined to systematic studies of the psychosomatic effects of bereavement by death in which some sort of comparison or control is attempted and in which sufficient numbers of cases were studied to make generalization possible. Studies of hypochondriacal and other purely psychological reactions to bereavement will not be included.

These studies fall into two categories: studies of sickness rates in bereaved populations, and studies of loss rates in sick populations.

STUDIES OF SICKNESS RATES IN BEREAVED POPULATIONS

A number of important studies of bereaved populations have been carried out in recent years. Bereaved populations have proved readily identifiable and in such studies it can seldom be supposed that the bereavement was the direct consequence of the behaviour of those who survive. Hence it seems reasonable to conclude that major changes in survivors which occur in close time relationship to the bereavement are causally related to it (even though the nature of this causal relationship may not be clear).

A methodological difficulty has been that of obtaining the co-operation of newly bereaved people. Whilst those who agree to take part in such studies usually seem grateful for the opportunity to discuss the events and feelings which are preoccupying them, there is an understandable suspicion of all who intrude into a situation of mourning and most investigators report that about a quarter of bereaved subjects refuse to be interviewed. Other sampling difficulties result from the tendency of bereaved people to move away from home for a time after bereavement so that difficulty may be found in tracing them.

Reassurance that such sampling difficulties do not constitute major sources of error come from two studies (Parkes, 1970; Parkes and Brown, 1970) which made use of information from general practitioners and telephone follow-up of subjects who had refused an interview to assess the subsequent health and psycho-social adjustment of 'refusers'. They revealed no major differences between those who refused and those who accepted an interview in terms of the limited information obtainable in these ways.

There are many operational indices of 'sickness', none of them very satisfactory. In the studies to be described these include subjective evaluations of 'health', counts of the frequency of utilization of medical services, counts of reports of symptoms, and mortality figures.

Assessments of 'General Health'

Among the 72 unselected London widows whom Peter Marris (1958) interviewed on average two years after bereavement 43 per cent thought that their health was worse since bereavement. In a comparable study of 40 widows in a midland market town Hobson (1964) reported that 42 per cent thought their health had deteriorated. In my own study of 22 unselected London widows whom I interviewed at intervals throughout their first year of bereavement (Parkes, 1970) 9 (41 per cent) thought their general health was worse during the first month of bereavement and in 6 cases (27 per cent) deterioration in health was still thought to be present a year later. (None thought their health better than it had been before the illness and death of their spouse.)

But what is meant by 'general health?' Is health, in fact, a unitary concept which, like intelligence, is capable of general assessment? Do subjective measurements of general health constitute valid indicators of somatic pathology?

One means of answering these questions is to study how closely subjective measures of general health correlate with other health measures. Among my 22 London widows a health score based on the widow's assessment of her own general health made at each of five interviews showed little correlation with a count of the number of symptoms from a check list which she reported at each interview ($r = 0{\cdot}07$). On the other hand it did correlate, at a statistically significant level, with a score based on the interviewer's observation of anger or irritability at the time of the interview ($r = 0{\cdot}60$, $t = 3{\cdot}39$, $p < 0{\cdot}01$). It seems that for these London widows complaints of ill health are a better indicator of irritability and anger than they are of somatic dysfunction.

In view of these findings we must hesitate to accept 'general health' estimates as evidence of psychosomatic disorder.

Utilization of Medical Services

Counts of the frequency of utilization of medical services have been used as an index of 'health' in several studies. In Britain, under the National Health Service, almost all members of the population are registered with a general practitioner and he is responsible for most of the referrals that are made to other medical agencies. It follows that G.P. consultation rates should give a fair idea of the amount of use which bereaved people made of medical services.

With the assistance of eight London general practitioners who were chosen for the accuracy of their case records it was possible to study the consultation rates of unselected London widows during 2 years before and 1½ years after bereavement (Parkes, 1964a). There was a sharp rise from 2·2 consultations per patient per six-month period during the pre-bereavement period to 3·6 consultations during the first six months of bereavement and 2·6 and 3·0 consultations in the next two six-month periods ($Z = 5{\cdot}7$, $p < 0{\cdot}001$, Wilcoxon matched-pairs signed-rank test). Furthermore, when consultations in which psychiatric symptoms were recorded or psychotropic drugs prescribed were excluded from consideration there was still a significant difference between the consultation rates during the pre- and post-bereavement periods ($Z = 3{\cdot}96$, $p < 0{\cdot}001$ Wilcoxon test).

Although there was a 240 per cent increase in consultations for depression, insomnia and other psychiatric symptoms ($p < 0{\cdot}001$) in the under-65 age group there was no such increase in the over-65 group. On the other hand, there was a significant increase in consultations for somatic symptoms in the over-65 age group ($p = 0{\cdot}05$) and a smaller increase in the younger widows which did not reach significant levels.

When individual disease categories were studied the numbers were mostly too small for statistical analysis but the increase in the group of consultations for muscle and joint conditions did reach the 0·05 level of significance in the younger age group.

Whatever the explanation of these findings it is clear that bereavement commonly causes the widow to seek help from her general practitioner.

In a comparable American study 69 Boston widows and widowers under the age of 45 (Parkes and Brown, 1970) were compared 14 months after bereavement with a carefully matched control group of 69 married people of the same age; 34 per cent of bereaved and 17 per cent of controls answered 'yes' to the question 'during the past year have you seen anyone such as a minister, social worker, psychologist or psychiatrist, about any emotional problems?' (Chi-squared 10·9, $p < 0{\cdot}001$). But there was very little difference between the number of individuals in the two groups (23 and 20) who visited medical clinics.

It may be that differences in the utilization of medical services between British and American widowers reflect the difference between a 'free' health service and one whose cost is likely to tax the reduced financial resources of the newly bereaved.

Frequency of Individual Symptoms

Counts of the frequency of individual symptoms have been made in several studies. The largest are those carried out by Maddison on widows in Boston, Massachusetts and Sydney, Australia (1967 and 1968). A comprehensive health questionnaire was sent to Boston widows between the ages of 45 and 60 years and to Sydney widows under 60: 375 completed questionnaires were obtained from 66 per cent of those approached, and these were compared with identical questionnaires from 199 married control subjects.

Out of 57 questions concerned with health over the period from 2 to 13 months after bereavement 33 were found to distinguish the bereaved from the control groups at the 0·05 level of significance (and 20 at the 0·01 level).

Using a complicated system of weighted scores Maddison claimed that marked deterioration in health was found in 21 per cent of the Boston and 32 per cent of the Sydney widows. Comparable figures for the control groups were 7·2 per cent and 2·0 per cent. These differences are significant at the 0·01 level. Many of the symptoms which distinguish the bereaved and control groups in Maddison's study, however, are psychological symptoms of the type which one expects to find in newly bereaved women.

Confining attention to psychosomatic symptoms he found the following to be complained of more frequently by bereaved than by non-bereaved women (all are significant at the 0·05 level, those marked * at the 0·01 level): headache*, dizziness, fainting spells, blurred vision, skin rashes, excessive sweating, indigestion*, difficulty in swallowing, vomiting*, excessive appetite*, anorexia*, weight loss*, menorrhagia, palpitations*, chest pain*, dyspnoea*, frequent infection*, general aching*. Among these symptoms only four were reported by more than 10 per cent of the widows—these were headaches (18 per cent), blurred vision (14 per cent), weight loss (14 per cent) and anorexia (13 per cent).

No serious physical conditions occurred with sufficient frequency to distinguish the two groups but it is worth noting that 47 per cent of Maddison's widows reported a reduction in work capacity and 13 per cent had sought medical treatment for depression.

In a much smaller sample of 68 widows and widowers under the age of 45 studied by Parkes and Brown there were few physical symptoms a year after bereavement which occurred with sufficient frequency to permit statistical analysis. Exceptions were various measures of sleep, appetite and weight disturbance which were all significantly greater in the bereaved group. An 'autonomic disturbance score' was obtained by counting the number of symptoms (from a list of 12 symptoms of this type) which had occurred for the first time or became worse during the period from 2 to 13 months after bereavement. Bereaved subjects had a mean score of 1·53 on this scale compared with a mean of 0·88 in the non-bereaved control group ($t = 2{\cdot}42$, $p < 0{\cdot}02$).

Similar figures showing the incidence of particular symptoms in bereaved subjects have been given by Hobson (1964) and Parkes (1970), but since these studies lack comparison groups and add little to other studies they will not be described here. Similarly, the systematic study by Imboden, Canter and Claff (1963) of the health of 117 Fort Detrick employees who had suffered separations and losses during a one-year period will not be detailed here because the losses studied include no major bereavements (death of spouse or child). Suffice it to say that the 'separation group' showed no more clinic visits than non-separated employees but that they did obtain higher scores on the Cornell Medical Index.

Physiological Functions

Only one study of physiological functions following bereavement is known to the writer. Wolf and Wolff (1943) studied the gastric activities of 'Tom', a man with a gastric fistula, over a long period of time. Following the death of his favourite nephew Tom showed some resentment and blamed the doctors who had attended the deceased. But his main emotion was one of dejection. He looked pale and haggard, lost his appetite and complained of a feeling of 'fullness' in the stomach, symptoms which are common in bereaved subjects.

During this period his gastric mucosa was relatively pale and flattened, acid secretion was diminished and salivary secretion was a third of the usual amount. The writers found gastric changes of this type on other occasions when Tom had felt depressed and defeated. Engel and Reichsman (1956) have observed similar changes during periods of depression and withdrawal in a 22-month-old child with a gastric fistula.

These findings may throw some light on the frequency of anorexia, indigestion, difficulty in swallowing and weight loss reported in several studies of bereaved subjects.

Mortality Rate

Studies of mortality rate following bereavement have only been made in recent years although the tradition that one might die of a 'broken heart' goes back to biblical times.

It has been known for some time that widows and widowers have a higher mortality rate than married persons of the same age, but it was a study by Young, Benjamin and Wallis (1963) which revealed that the greatest change in mortality is found during the first six months of bereavement.

They found a mortality rate 40 per cent higher than the rate for married men of the same age among 4,486 widowers, a total sample of all widowers over the age of 55 in England and Wales whose wives died during two months of 1957. A further study of this sample by Parkes, Benjamin and Fitzgerald (1969) revealed that the greatest increase in mortality took place in the widowers certified as dying from 'coronary thrombosis and other arteriosclerotic and degenerative heart diseases' ($p < 0{\cdot}01$). This accounted for 77 of the 213 deaths during the first six months of bereavement.

When deaths from all other causes were combined the 99 per cent confidence interval for expected deaths was 77–137 and the actual deaths numbered 136. The excess in the bereaved group is therefore only just short of significance at the 1 per cent level and it seems justifiable to conclude that heart disease is not the only cause of the increased mortality which follows bereavement.

Confirmation of the effects of recent bereavement upon mortality come from studies by Cox and Ford (1964) and by Rees and Lutkins (1967). The former relies on the widow having applied for a contributory pension and since this may well not take place among widows who die within six months of their husbands their figures for this period must be discounted. During the second half of the first year of bereavement, however, Cox and Ford did find a rise in mortality rate which declined thereafter.

Rees and Lutkins compared the death rate among 903 relatives of persons dying in a semi-rural area of Wales with a control group of non-bereaved persons. No less than 4·8 per cent of the bereaved group died within a year compared with only 0·68 per cent of the non-bereaved ($p < 0.001$). After this time the mortality rate in the bereaved group fell off sharply and was not significantly higher than that of the control group.

Among the various types of relative who were included in this study it was widows and widowers who showed the greatest increase in mortality. Where the death had taken place at home there was a smaller increment in mortality among the surviving relatives than there was if the death had occurred in hospital or elsewhere.

These studies show a clear association between recent bereavement and increased mortality but one can only speculate as to the causal explanation for this association.

STUDIES OF BEREAVEMENT RATE IN SICK POPULATIONS

In the various studies which have been carried out into loss rates in sick populations bereavements by death constitute a minority of the losses reported. This is hardly surprising when one recalls the relative frequency of losses of one type or another in the lives of all of us.

Schmale (1958), who studied an unselected series of patients admitted to the medical wards of an American general hospital, found evidence of loss or threat of loss in the recent history of 41 out of 42 patients. But he admits that only 30 of these actually reported having experienced a loss or threat of loss and in 11 cases this was inferred by the investigator from 'non-verbal evidence'.

Studies such as that by Parkes (1964b) which show an increased rate of bereavement by death of a spouse among unselected psychiatric admissions will not be detailed here. But it is worth noting that Morrison, Hudgens and Barchka (1968), who compared rates of separation and bereavement among 100 non-psychiatric and 100 psychiatric patients in a general hospital, found no differences between the two groups. They conclude that life stresses of this kind may be as important a factor in the causation of physical illness as they are in mental illness.

Several studies have focused on loss rates in particular illnesses. Some of the more important are a series of studies of reticuloses and cervical cancer by workers at the Strong Memorial Hospital, Rochester, New York (*see* Chapter 1).

Other reports occurring in particular diagnostic groups are mostly anecdotal. Exceptions are Lindemann's (1945) study of 46 patients with ulcerative colitis, 57 per cent of whom were said to have lost an important person in close time relationship to the onset of the illness; McDermott and Cobb's (1939) study of 50 patients with asthma, in 6 of whom (12 per cent) it came on following the death or severe illness of a loved person; and a study by Knapp and Nemetz (1960) who found evidence of 'actual or immediately threatened losses' preceding 110 of 406 (27 per cent) acute asthmatic attacks in 9 patients. None of these studies includes a comparison group and none is confined to bereavements by death.

One of the few studies of this type which gives figures for losses by death and does include a comparison group is Kissen's (1958) study of emotional factors in pulmonary tuberculosis. He compared the incidence of a variety of supposed psychological stressors in 64 tuberculosis patients and 134 other attenders at a chest clinic. Although he found a larger proportion of 'loss of loved persons' among the tuberculous patients the incidence of bereavement by death was not significantly greater in this group (12·5 per cent) than it was in the non-tuberculous group (11·2 per cent).

What conclusions can be drawn from these studies? It seems that there is now good evidence that major bereavements, and particularly the death of a spouse or child, are potential causes of ill health. Some deterioration in health can be expected in about a quarter of men and women under the age of 65 during the first year after the death of a spouse, although further work is needed to determine how long this is likely to continue and to what extent deterioration in health also occurs in older widows and widowers.

Most of the deterioration in health is attributable to minor digestive upsets and other ailments attributable to psycho-physiological dysfunction but there is also evidence that more serious physical illnesses, such as coronary thrombosis, ulcerative colitis, asthma and certain neoplastic conditions, are occasionally related to bereavement. The nature of this relationship is still obscure.

Bereavement emerges from these studies as an important area for further research. Not only is it one of the few life events whose pathogenic potential has been established but its clear-cut occurrence at a particular time and place, the existence of national statistics relating to it and the frequency with which medical practitioners are in touch with survivors at the time it occurs make bereavement an eminently suitable subject for research by the medical profession.

Particular questions which such research could answer are: What distinguishes bereaved persons who become sick from others who do not? What can be done to prevent or ameliorate the pathological consequences of bereavement? Is it possible to predict outcome following bereavement and to reduce pathology by focusing preventive intervention services on those at high risks of pathology?

Studies of the psychological reaction to bereavement have already gone a long way towards establishing grief as a key concept in psychopathology. It may be that bereavement studies will eventually become equally important in leading to an understanding of psychosomatic relationships.

REFERENCES

Cox, P. R. and Ford, J. R. (1964). 'The Mortality of Widows Shortly after Widowhood.' *Lancet*, **1,** 163.

Engel, G. L. and Reichsman, F. (1956) 'Spontaneous and Experimentally Induced Depressions in an Infant with a Gastric Fistula: A Contribution to the Problems of Depression.' *J. Am. Psychoanal. Ass.*, **4,** 428.

Hobson, C. J. (1964). 'Widows of Blackton.' *New Society*. **24** (Sept.), 13.

Imboden, J. B., Canter, A. and Claff, L. (1963). 'Separation Experiences and Health Records in a Group of Normal Adults.' *Psychosom. Med.*, **25,** 433.

Kissen, D. M. (1958). *Emotional Factors in Pulmonary Tuberculosis*. London: Tavistock Publications.

Knapp, P. H. and Nemetz, S. J. (1960). 'Acute Bronchial Asthma: I. Concomitant Depression and Excitement and Varied Antecedent Pattern —in 406 Attacks.' *Psychosom. Med.*, **22,** 42.

Lindemann, E. (1945). 'Psychiatric Factors in the Treatment of Ulcerative Colitis.' *Archs Neurol. Psychiat.*, **53,** 322.

McDermott, N. and Cobb, S. (1939). 'Psychogenic Factors in Asthma.' *Psychosom. Med.*, **1,** 204.

Maddison, D. C. and Walker, W. L. (1967). 'Factors Affecting the Outcome of Conjugal Bereavement.' *Br. J. Psychiat.*, **113,** 1057.

— and Viola, A. (1968). 'The Health of Widows in the Year Following Bereavement.' *J. Psychosom. Res.*, **12,** 297.

Marris, P. (1958). *Widows and their Families*. London: Routledge & Kegan Paul.

Morrison, J. R., Hudgens, R. W. and Barchka, R. G. (1968). 'Life Events and Psychiatric Illness: A Study of 100 Patients and 100 Controls.' *Br. J. Psychiat.*, **114,** 423.

Parkes, C. M. (1964a). 'Effects of Bereavement on Physical and Mental Health: a Study of the Medical Records of Widows.' *Br. med. J.*, **2,** 274.

Parkes, C. M. (1964b). 'Recent Bereavement as a Cause of Mental Illness.' *Br. J. Psychiat.*, **110**, 198.

— (1970). *Grief: Studies of Bereavement*. In preparation.

— Benjamin, B. and Fitzgerald, R. G. (1969). 'Broken Heart: A Statistical Study of Increased Mortality among Widowers.' *Br. med. J.*, **1**, 740.

— and Brown, R. (1970). 'Physical and Mental Health after Bereavement. A Controlled Study.' In preparation.

Rees, W. D. and Lutkins, S. G. (1967). 'Mortality of Bereavement.' *Br. med. J*, **4**, 13.

Schmale, A. H. (1958). 'Relationship of Separation and Depression to Disease. I. A Report on a Hospitalized Medical Population.' *Psychosom. Med.*, **20**, 259.

Wear, L. E. (1963). 'Disorders of Communion—Some Observations on Interpersonal Tensions in General Practice.' *Lancet*, **1**, 103.

Wolf, S. and Wolff, H. G. (1943). *Human Gastric Function*. Oxford University Press.

Young, M., Benjamin, B. and Wallis, C. (1963). 'The Mortality of Widowers.' *Lancet*, **2**, 454.

CHAPTER 6

CHILDHOOD ASTHMA

PHILIP PINKERTON and CORINNA M. WEAVER

INTRODUCTION

The Psychosomatic Prototype

Asthma is perhaps the example *par excellence* of psychosomatic illness, the clearest demonstration of that complex inter-relationship of body, intellect and emotion, which links patient, family, doctor and nurse in the elusive quest for aetiology and therapeutic efficacy.

In recent years there have been rapid advances in respiratory physiology, reflected in the work of Palmer and Diament (1967a,b, 1968a,b, 1969a,b), Rees, Millar and Donald (1967), Tai and Read (1967), and others. Such studies of ventilatory function, blood gastensions, ventilation-perfusion ratios etc., have greatly clarified our understanding of the respiratory abnormalities resulting from asthma.

Similarly, the immunological mechanisms involved have become somewhat clearer, although correct evaluation and connotation of these developments is more difficult. Ishizaka, Ishizaka and Hornbrook (1966) and Johannson (1967), for example, have described an hitherto unrecognized immunoglobulin (IgE) in asthmatic patients whose allergen history is clear cut. The successful introduction of a new immunosuppressive drug, disodium cromoglycate, has also yielded concrete evidence for the immunological processes in asthma and provides stimulus for further research. Comparable advances in psychosomatic research, however, are infinitely more open to debate so that while 'it is more important to know what sort of person has a disease than to know what sort of disease a person has' (Hippocrates), data in the latter category lend themselves to objective study much more readily than in the former; hence the perpetuation of diametrically opposed viewpoints on psychosomatic aetiology with evidence in support of each.

Classification

There have been many attempts both to define and to classify asthma, but none is entirely satisfactory since the basic lesion

The work described in this chapter was supported by the Medical Research Committee of the United Liverpool Hospitals, Research Scheme No. 103.

remains unknown. Even the standard division into extrinsic and intrinsic types, whilst useful, can be misleading since they are indistinguishable pathologically and physiologically. The intrinsic almost certainly has an immunological basis, even though allergens cannot be identified, and paradoxically, an 'allergic' subject may experience attacks unrelated to allergens.

Attempts have been made to differentiate 'organically' determined asthma from the so-called 'psychogenic' variety (Mitchell, Curran and Myers, 1947; Rees, 1956a,b; Block *et al.*, 1964). This popular misconception has been challenged in turn by McDermott and Cobb (1939) and Dekker, Barendregt and de Vries (1960). Such studies yield no evidence of negative correlation between allergy and neurosis and therefore no grounds for any such differentiation. On the contrary, the dichotomy so implied can be exceedingly dangerous. There is, in fact, no evidence for primary psychogenesis in asthma.

While it is true that asthmatics do not form a homogeneous population, and some patients undoubtedly experience more trouble than others in relation to psychological factors, it is now well accepted that there must first exist a somatic substrate for bronchial hyper-reactivity before psychosomatic mechanisms can act (Peshkin, 1963; Freeman *et al.*, 1964; Feingold *et al.*, 1966; Aas, 1969).

Bruce Pearson (1968), in an excellent review of 611 cases, has been able to distinguish asthma of onset under 30 years of age 'as a single disease partly dependent on the inheritance of some factor not essentially a predisposition to allergy.' He declares this factor to be an unstable bronchial tract which readily contracts in response to many stimuli acting directly, indirectly or through allergic mechanisms. This concept is much the most satisfactory one and recent physiological advances are in keeping with it.

Leigh and Marley (1967), in their meticulous epidemiological survey, support the view that asthma is a genetically determined condition with probably a multifactorial mode of inheritance. Schwartz (1952) suggested a dominant inheritance with incomplete penetrance.

Childhood asthma, therefore, must be viewed primarily as an inborn lesion causing hyper-reactivity in the bronchi. Airways obstruction, the *sine qua non* of asthma, is the resulting functional abnormality. It can be measured by means of spirometry (forced expiratory volume in one second) or with the flow meter (peak flow rate) and it prompts a pragmatic definition '. . . dyspnoea caused by extensive narrowing of peripheral airways which is partially or totally reversible either spontaneously or in response to treatment' (Scadding, 1963).

Classification of childhood asthma is based most usefully upon ventilatory function measured at rest, with exercise and in response to bronchodilator drugs (Jones, Wharton and Buston, 1963).

PHYSIOLOGY AND SYMPTOMATOLOGY

Ventilatory Function

The normal bronchial tract is remarkably stable, so that alteration in the FEV_1 with various stimuli is negligible. Asthmatic bronchi, on the other hand, are highly reactive, both to bronchoconstricting and bronchodilating agents.

Using exercise and nebulized isoprenaline as standard stimuli, it is possible on the basis of FEV_1 measurements to distinguish normal from asthmatic subjects, and further, to demonstrate a range of severity among the latter.

Prolonged exercise (eight minutes or more) produces bronchoconstriction, whilst isoprenaline dilates the bronchi. Both these effects are minimal in the normal person. The extent to which the FEV_1 alters when expressed as a percentage of predicted normal gives an indication of the degree of bronchial lability in that patient—the lability index (*see Figure 1*).

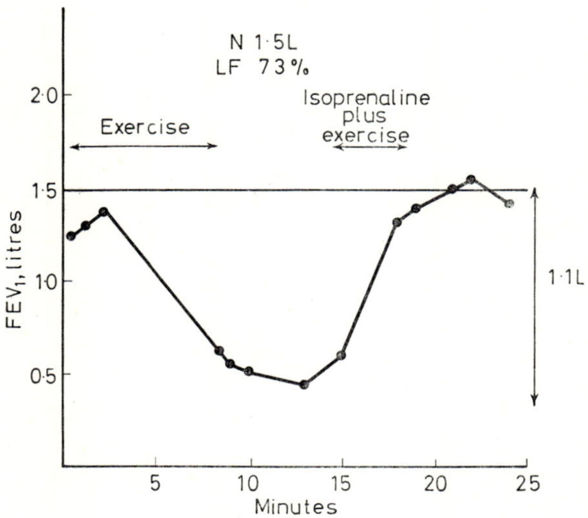

Figure 1. The lability index

Normal subjects have a lability index of less than 15 per cent of predicted normal FEV_1. Outside this range, asthmatics fall into three broad categories (Jones, 1966) (*see Figure 2* and Table 1).

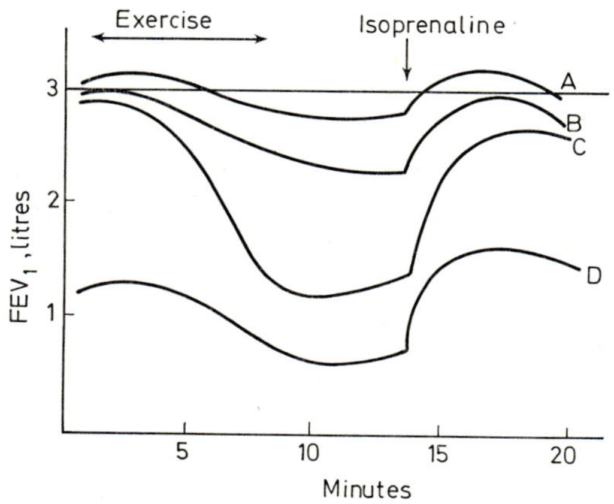

Figure 2. The effects on the FEV_1 of brief exercise, prolonged exercise and isoprenaline on: (a) normal subject; (b) Group I; (c) Group II; (d) Group III asthmatic children. Lability index: normal 10 per cent, Group I 23 per cent, Group II 66 per cent, Group III 33 per cent

TABLE 1

Physiological Classification of Childhood Asthma

Group	*Resting FEV_1*	*Lability index*	*Response to isoprenaline*
I	Normal	15–30%	FEV_1 reaches normal
IIA	Usually normal	30–85%	FEV_1 reaches normal range
IIB	Usually below normal	30–85%	FEV_1 reaches normal range
III	Always below normal	Usually 20–40%	FEV_1 fails to reach normal range

Group I

Children with normal resting function whose lability index is between 15 and 30 per cent.

Group II

More labile asthmatics who may have a lability index as high as 85 per cent. This group can be further subdivided on the basis of their resting ventilatory function: *Group IIA* in whom FEV_1 at rest is usually within the normal range; *Group IIB* in whom resting FEV_1 is below normal but does respond to a bronchodilator.

Group III

Children who, by contrast, cannot achieve normal spirometric readings even with isoprenaline, probably because of a more 'fixed' (mucosal) component of airways obstruction (Jones, 1966). The bronchi here show reduced lability compared with Group II, but corticosteroids will usually reverse this resistance, at least temporarily thereby 'unmasking' the underlying reactivity. They then behave more like Group II subjects.

There is, therefore, a range of severity in childhood asthma as judged by this particular physiological parameter, Group I being the mildest, Group III the most severe. The majority of cases, as one would expect, fall into Group II. A recent study (Jones and Jones, 1966) showed that young adults who have 'outgrown' their asthma nevertheless continue to have demonstrable bronchial lability. This confirms the clinical view that most children lose their symptoms as they mature (Rackeman and Edwards, 1952; Peshkin, 1960), but continue to be asthmatic subjects.

Clinical Course of Asthma in Relation to its Physiology

Although physiological tests provide a valid indication of the severity of bronchial abnormality and form an essential part of the assessment of asthma, they do not necessarily reflect the patient's symptomatic experience. Many children troubled to the extent of significant school loss despite medical help are found to be at the milder end of the physiological spectrum. Conversely, children known to be severely affected may cope more adequately on therapy with minimal invalidism.

Asthmatic symptoms, and therefore the FEV_1 are known to be greatly influenced by a multiplicity of factors, so that ventilatory function should always be viewed in the light of prevailing circumstances. In many asthmatics with an inordinate amount of trouble clinically, environmental change commonly produces improvement not only in symptoms (Peshkin, 1959; Munro Ford, 1968) but even in ventilatory function (Buston, 1966), so that to achieve true assessment of severity, as opposed to 'trouble', temporary admission may be necessary in order to stabilize the setting, including withdrawal of drugs known to affect the bronchi. Such a standardizing procedure ensures evaluation of the disorder in its natural state.

In appraising severity, a history of status asthmaticus, the presence of cyanosis or unconsciousness during attacks, demonstrable hypoxaemia, or stunted growth are important additional clinical pointers. Conversely, frequent attacks, excessive school loss, repeated visits to general practitioner or hospitalizations, though possibly alarming, are not in themselves comparably valid indicators of severity. They tend mainly to characterize Groups I and IIA, whereas the former are frequent concomitants of Group III cases and more faithfully reflect true severity. This distinction between 'severity' and 'trouble' is important both therapeutically and prognostically, although 'trouble' remains the chief preoccupation of most practitioners, particularly family doctors.

Many attempts have been made to devise some standard grading of symptomatology, particularly in evaluating response to therapy (Falliers *et al.*, 1966; Walsh and Grant, 1966; Howell and Altounyan, 1967; Morrison Smith and Devey, 1968). Keeping a diary or score chart, accounting for tablets taken or weight of aerosol inhaled, time lost from school and restriction of physical activity etc., have all had their place in the Asthma Clinic records. No scheme satisfies everyone since it is impossible to be entirely objective.

Grading of trouble is necessarily arbitrary but must be based in some way upon the degree to which the asthma interferes with daily living. The following broad outline indicates the type of criteria included in any single scheme:

Grade 1. No school loss; mild attacks; occasional need for bronchodilator.

Grade 2. Days off school; mild to moderate attacks; need for regular bronchodilator.

Grade 3. Weeks off school; more prolonged and severe attacks; need for steroid in addition to bronchodilator.

Grade 4. More than 50 per cent school loss; persistent symptoms; need for special schooling; need for regular steroid therapy.

A severe asthmatic will hardly qualify for Grade 1, yet children with far less severe physiological impairment often qualify for Grade 4, thereby indicating a disproportionate degree of disablement. Children whose symptoms fail to respond to standard therapy (Grades 3 and 4) are regarded as intractable asthmatics.

Intractable Asthma—Parentectomy

The great majority of these children, including the more severe cases, improve symptomatically away from home (Peshkin, 1959; Bernstein *et al.*, 1960). It has been the tradition to incriminate prevailing allergens (spores, pollens, mites etc.), or climatic and geographic factors, to account for this phenomenon, but in a classic experiment, Long *et al.* (1958) collected dust samples from the homes of asthmatic children known to be sensitive to house dust and deliberately exposed them in the symptom-free state within the hospital setting. Failure to provoke asthmatic attacks under these circumstances suggested that sensitivity to house dust was not the only factor involved.

In practice, the scientific evaluation of any one factor is exceedingly difficult because there are so many other variables which defy control, but Tuft (1957), in a detailed analysis of 500 cases at the Children's Asthma Research Institute, Denver (perhaps the largest institution of its kind in the Western hemisphere), was able convincingly to dismiss the role of infective, allergenic and atmospheric influences in the development of refractory asthma. He concluded that emotional influences were paramount.

The experience of Lask (1966) in the field of general practice, and Leigh and Marley (1967) in the field of epidemiology, both support the same conclusion.

Reversal of intractability with change in the emotional milieu led Peshkin in 1930 to advocate long-term residential care for asthmatic children. Unfortunately, his term 'parentectomy' has been widely misunderstood with resulting over-simplification of the emotional factors involved in intractability. This, in turn, has led to indiscriminate separation of children from their homes, which is a potentially harmful practice.

Pinkerton (1967), while indicting psychopathology as the main factor in intractability, insisted that emotional concomitants must be linked with physiological assessments to ensure their proper evaluation, thereby echoing Peshkin's premise (1964) that, '. . . intractability is essentially a *secondary* psychogenic application of a primary immunologic process'. However, there is urgent need to define exactly what we mean by significant emotional concomitants in the field of childhood asthma.

PSYCHOLOGICAL CONSIDERATIONS

Many areas have been explored in the quest for clearer understanding of the intricate relationships involved. They include the personality characteristics and behaviour patterns of the patient (Rogerson, 1937; Dunbar, 1938; Leigh and Rawnsley, 1956; Herbert, 1965); the relationship of asthma to psychoses (Appel and Rosen, 1951; Leigh and Doust, 1953); the association of asthma with psychiatric illness generally (Leigh and Marley, 1967); the emotional precipitation of attacks (French, 1939); the EEG abnormalities of allergic diseases (Rubin and Moses, 1944; Panzani, Boyer and Turner, 1956); the allergic aspects of behaviour disorders (Dees and Lowenbach, 1948), and so on. As always, the truth is not confined to any single area but drawn from overlapping spheres.

Psychoanalytic Concepts

Maurer (1965) presents a brief review of psychoanalytic thought in this field. Asthmatic symptoms are interpreted as the symbolic somatization of emotional conflicts stemming from early life, i.e. as an 'organ neurosis'. Disturbances in the mother–child relationship have attracted frequent comment; for example, the classic monograph by French and Alexander (1941) describing asthma as the 'repressed cry' of the child in response to maternal irritation and even rejection. Separation anxiety inhibits the cry which is replaced by an alternative respiratory response, namely wheezing. This 'approach-avoidance' conflict has been similarly highlighted by Miller and Baruch (1957) and Alcock (1960), while Turnbull (1962) conceived asthma as a learned response conditioned by traumatic early experience.

Implicit in these formulations is the concept of an ambivalent aura. Fenichel (1945) speaks of asthma as the outcome of the patient's conflict in trying to remain part of his 'good' mother, yet rid himself of the 'bad' mother. Abramson (1954) described 'mutual engulfment' of mother and child; Mitchell, Curran and Myers (1947) referred to alternating extremes of maternal over-concern and rejection. Alexander (1950) saw the attack as expressing opposite tendencies, the wish to separate and the wish to remain dependent. Coolidge (1956) and Monsour (1960) both regarded asthma as a 'special type of inter-communication' between mother and child. Burton (1968) linked asthmatic children with two other groups, juvenile victims of sexual assault, and accident-prone cases, regarding all three as 'children in conflict'. Saul and Lyons (1954) interpreted the syndrome as a return to the intra-uterine form of breathing symbolic of passive dependence.

These studies forfeit their claim to validity through failure to acknowledge the somatic substrate which is fundamental to our understanding of the asthmatic state. Manifestly, no analytic construct can ever be said to produce the asthmatic's labile bronchus, yet by emphasizing ambivalence and early childhood experience as factors influencing the course of the illness—the way the labile bronchus behaves—psychoanalytic theory does tie in with data from other disciplines and, therefore, does retain some relevance though not in any causal sense. In short, asthma is not an organ neurosis but a truly psychosomatic disorder. Early childhood experience does seem the probable foundation for subsequent psychopathology, be it intrapsychic or interpersonal, which may serve to aggravate and perpetuate the asthmatic illness granted its specific basis of physiological vulnerability. Without that substrate, however, no matter what disorders are evoked by corresponding conflict, the subject will not wheeze.

Behavioural and Personality Studies

Although the search for a specific personality structure in asthmatic patients continues, there is now impressive evidence that this is non-existent (Dubo *et al.*, 1961; Graham *et al.*, 1967). Indeed there seems no logical reason why this genetically transmitted and organically based disorder should be associated with any particular personality features, although it is true that the course of the disease may be materially affected by the kind of person who has it. Knapp and Nemetz (1957) found no single personality type characteristic of childhood asthma but rather a range of disturbance, the severity of which was positively correlated with clinical severity. Alcock (1960) found the asthmatic personality to be characterized by inner conflict, weak ego defence mechanisms and a tendency to self-punishment. In a valuable study by Neuhaus (1958), asthmatic children and children with cardiac disease were individually and strictly matched with normal controls, using the Brown Personality Inventory for Children, the Despert Fables and the Rorschach. Both the asthmatic and the 'cardiac' children were shown to be more disturbed than the normal subjects (over-dependent, neurotic, maladjusted etc.) and furthermore the siblings of the sick children proved to be equally disturbed. The implication is that children with any chronically disabling illness will show similar deviations in personality adjustment which will, in turn, affect their immediate interpersonal milieu.

The experimental approach, though valid statistically, ignores the whole reality of the illness. The clinical approach, by contrast, is arraigned as too discursive and subjective. The first is too narrowly specific, the second too broadly diffuse. Irrespective of methodology, however, the dichotomy continues between the views exemplified by Groen *et al.* (1965), who still regard the patient's personality as the predisposing factor in the genesis of asthma, and the mounting evidence of more recent work (Leigh and Marley, 1967) that while asthmatics present certain personality traits, there is no clear-cut specificity of asthmatic personality.

Parental Attitudes in Asthma

Using personality and attitude inventories, Fitzelle (1959) found no significant differences in personality or child-rearing attitudes between parents of asthmatic and non-asthmatic children.

Block *et al.* (1966) used the Q-sort rating system to identify three types of asthmatogenic mother from among clinicians' concepts—the 'deprived', the 'achievement-orientated' and the 'assertive' mother. Morris (1961) found the mothers of asthmatic children to be over-controlling and over-ambitious.

Such studies are inconclusive. To the extent that they generate tension, parental attitudes will be relevant to the course of the disorder but this is far from claiming that certain maternal prototypes may actually 'cause' or 'exacerbate' the child's asthma.

Of more serious import, papers have been published by the Denver team claiming differences in parental attitude among sub-groups of the asthmatic population (Purcell, Bernstein and Bukantz, 1961). On the basis of their symptomatic response to hospitalization, children were placed in one of two groups, the steroid-dependent (SD) or the rapidly-remitting (RR). Using the Parental Attitude Research Instrument (PARI), together with self-rating questionnaires for the children, these authors claim a greater incidence of psychopathology in the RR group with the greater tendency for asthma to 'function' as a neurotic expression of conflict than in the SD children. However, this is not to decry the importance of psychopathology among steroid-dependent cases, although its significance may be different. Pinkerton (1967) was able to show, in fact, that emotional factors operate throughout the whole range of physiological severity in childhood asthma with a definite tendency for the more negative or rejective attitudes to be correlated with the severe end of the physiological spectrum, where the steroid-dependent cases are located.

PSYCHODYNAMICS IN PERSPECTIVE

What holds good for personality and attitude factors in childhood asthma is almost equally apposite for other chronic illnesses—with one fundamental difference. Although these factors determine overall adjustment and invalidism in every illness, it is in truly psychosomatic conditions alone that they will actually affect the physical manifestations and course of the disease. For example, the tension evoked by an over-anxious mother is hardly likely to produce cyanotic attacks or cardiac decompensation in a child with congenital heart disease, whereas equivalent tension accorded to an asthmatic child may well aggravate or even produce serious bronchoconstriction.

The essential unpredictability of the syndrome, its capricious nature, inevitably gives rise to mercurial emotions and attitudes. At the height of an attack a bewildered parent may be distracted with fear, yet when the doctor arrives, her child may be already symptom-free and she therefore feels castigated as unduly fussy at the very least, or at worst mendacious. In these circumstances, some degree of hostility must inevitably colour the mother–child relationship, however warmly concerned she may be. Alternatively, an aggrieved parent may accuse the child of 'bringing on the asthma to get his own way', which tempers her anxiety for his life with exasperation at his behaviour. It is the more annoying that once induced, attacks can be exaggerated volitionally. Ambivalence, therefore, pervades most attitudes at some stage and in some form in childhood asthma so that in practice 'pure' attitudes are almost never encountered.

We are essentially concerned with the orientation of parents and child towards the disease and towards one another, so that by adopting a small number of broadly descriptive terms to designate the interaction between child, family and doctor, we avoid the pitfalls of specificity and can draw the relevant areas together in a dynamic formulation, thereby approaching the problem holistically.

ANALYSIS OF 206 CASES OF CHILDHOOD ASTHMA

The applicability of these dynamic concepts can best be illustrated through detailed analysis of the child asthmatic population seen in our department for assessment and study over a four-year period.

The Sample

Two hundred and six children and their families were investigated; 84 per cent within a large children's hospital, 16 per cent in a residential 'open-air' school (ROAS). In all cases the asthma had been sufficiently troublesome to warrant hospital consultation, or admission, or special school placement.

The age range of the sample was 2 to 16 years with the typical 2 : 1 ratio of boys to girls (Siegel and Lovin, 1960; Dawson *et al.*, 1969). In each case, physiological and psychological assessments were undertaken.

The youngest child able to co-operate with ventilatory function testing was 5 years old, so that 94 per cent of the total sample could be assessed by spirometry and classified accordingly. As expected, the majority (55·6 per cent) belonged to Group IIA, that is, labile asthmatics with good resting function.

Psychopathology

As in any field of human relationship, it is extremely difficult to evaluate attitudes objectively. Therefore, each method has its limitations. The PARI, for example, is limited by acquiescence-response bias (Margolis, 1961) and is perhaps more suitable as a group-testing instrument than for individual cases (Schubert and Weaver, 1970). A similar criticism applies to Osgood's semantic differential. According to Lindt and Goldman (1961) the so-called one-shot method (single interview or battery of tests) is unreliable. Like Abramson and Peshkin (1960, 1961) they claim that clinical or therapeutic interviewing is the most satisfactory way of defining attitudes and family dynamics. Rutter and Brown (1966) have shown this procedure to be both reliable and valid as a research tool, with the interviewing team itself acting as the measuring instrument. Rutter and Graham (1968) extended the technique to psychiatric assessment of the child, and this in fact was the means adopted for assessing family dynamics in the present series.

Acceptance

If the optimum attitude towards childhood asthma is defined as realistic acceptance, with all that this implies in terms of intellectual understanding, emotional insight and overall adjustment, then the psychodynamics of all cases may be classified according to deviations from this ideal. In this way, it is possible to recognize an attitude spectrum ranging from 'over-acceptance' with warm, benign, fostering of invalidism, through 'realistic acceptance' to the opposite extreme of 'non-acceptance' where there is intolerance of illness. A further distinction may be made between attitude to asthma and attitude to the child. Parental intolerance of the disease usually involves a lesser degree of negative aura than where the child himself is unacceptable to the parent. This latter situation is the most inimical of all and may indeed prove positively dangerous.

As for the child, his attitude to himself and to his handicap is determined largely by his parents' feelings but also by his own personality structure; for example, a sensitive and immature child of vulnerable personality is likely to 'over-accept' his disability, i.e. remain within the 'chrysalis' of dependent invalidism. The child of more robust and mature personality may, conversely, resent his asthma and protest denial of handicap, especially if he senses non-acceptance by his parents. The obstructive child with negativistic traits, or the histrionic child, may show fluctuating attitudes, tending to manipulate or exploit the situation with alternating acquiescence and non-acceptance (Pinkerton, 1969).

The parents and children in our series were respectively rated 'accepting', 'over-accepting' or 'non-accepting' according to these criteria and an appropriate positive or negative 'score' allotted, with ambivalence rating as negative.

The factors which contribute to these overall attitudes, both in parent and child, derive from two main sources—the personality make-up and the life circumstances obtaining (Pinkerton, 1965). In practice, of course, there is enormous interplay between personality traits, attitude, and life situation, which in themselves are meaningless until they are related dynamically to each other and to the underlying pathophysiological substrate (*see Figure 3*). It is for this reason

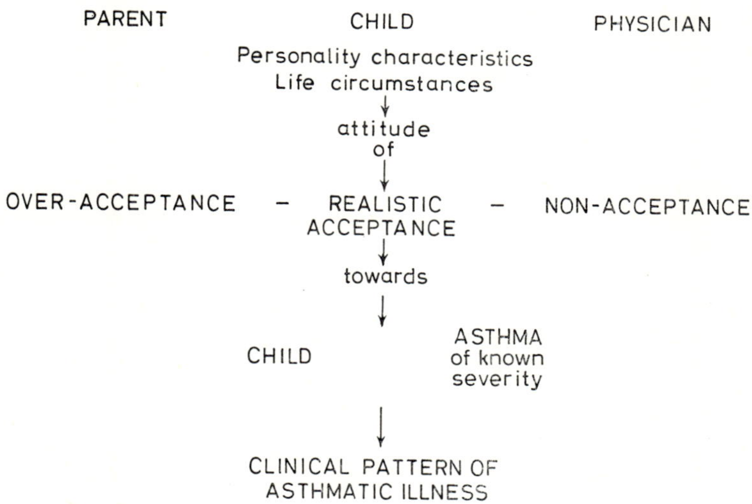

Figure 3

that the various objective techniques available are largely inadequate. The 16 Personality Factor Questionnaire (IPAT), for example, was found to yield excellent personality profiles both of parents and children in this series but the only valid conclusion to be drawn was that neither the asthmatic children nor their parents differed significantly from the normal population (Macdonald and Weaver, 1970). In short, while they measure static factors admirably, such procedures fail to demonstrate dynamic interplay; yet the outcome in asthma is not affected by a particular entity but by conflict in interpersonal relationships (Lask, 1966) which, to date, defy objectification. It is the tension engendered by such conflict which primes the already unstable bronchus to react more precipitately to bronchoconstricting stimuli (Pinkerton, 1969).

Motivation

An additional facet, equally germane, is motivation to improve. On the one hand, the powerful desire to be rid of asthma, attendant upon non-acceptance, produces so much tension as to defeat its own ends. Conversely, over-investment in invalidism, whether by parent or child, induces ambivalent motivation. This, though different, exerts equivalent intensity of effect. In our series, motivational intensity was taken into account by allotting an appropriate supplementary 'score'.

From among the many psychodynamic formulations of potential significance, we were now in a position, utilizing this single composite parameter, to condense the complexities operating individually in each case. In 182 cases (88 per cent) there was significant deviation in attitude; 107 were of the over-accepting, cosseting type; 75 demonstrated non-accepting intolerant attitudes.

Relationship of Psychopathology to Physiology

A statistically significant relationship emerged between type of deviation and physiological grouping. The more negative, critical, rejective aura was associated with Groups IIB and III; the over-protective type of aura with Groups I and IIA (*see* Table 2).

TABLE 2

Relationship of Physiological Groups to Attitude

Group	*Attitude deviation*		
	0	+	–
I	1	5	2
IIA	19	58	32
IIB	2	27	14
III	1	11	12

$\chi^2 = 21{\cdot}18$ df = 6 p = 0·01

This association has been noted previously (Pinkerton, 1967) and is of major import both therapeutically and prognostically. While there is no evidence that the true physiological status of asthma is dependent upon psychological factors, it seems both pointless and fruitless to argue over 'cause' and 'effect' in this relationship. What is important to recognize is that the child with severe impairment of ventilatory function needs all the therapy we can muster to stabilize his bronchi, including psychotherapeutic intervention, which, if anything, is a more vital indication for the serious asthmatic. It is tempting for physicians to applaud the 'sensible' or 'healthy' attitude of non-acceptance of disability while failing to recognize that such stoicism may well have a fatal outcome.

Relationship of Psychopathology to Discrepancy in Trouble Score

As anticipated from the explicit referral of these children for help, the majority (85 per cent) were experiencing more trouble than one might reasonably expect from a detailed clinical and physiological knowledge of the case.

There was a highly significant relationship between this discrepancy in trouble score and psychopathology. All intractable cases (whatever their physiological status) were seen to have unsatisfactory attitudes, while children whose asthma was not disproportionately troublesome, equally had no outstanding emotional problems (*see* Table 3). The small number who did have psychopathology, but

TABLE 3

Relationship of Discrepancy to Psychopathology

	Psychopathology	*No psychopathology*
Discrepancy	174	0
No discrepancy	8	24

relatively little trouble asthma-wise, had presented with some alternative complaint—behaviour disorder, eczema, bronchiectasis—i.e. they appeared to be expressing tension through channels other than their asthma, which was consequently reasonably controlled.

Sociopathology

This term was applied wherever gross social factors were operative, such as broken home, extreme overcrowding and/or insanitary conditions, immoral behaviour, delinquency etc. Forty-four per cent of the special school children were deemed to have a positive 'index' of sociopathology, compared with only 15 per cent of the hospital group—a statistically significant difference all the more pertinent in that no equivalent differentiation emerged between the two populations either in respect of trouble-score discrepancy or in the proportions of constituent physiological grades (*see* Table 4).

This means that unequivocal sociopathology can be regarded as a variant of psychopathology in the genesis of intractability and should properly represent the main indication for residential school placement. In practice, many asthmatic children are accommodated in residential schools for other reasons both inappropriate and of doubtful long-term advantage (Weaver and Pinkerton, 1970).

TABLE 4
Proportions of Constituent Physiological Groups

Group	*Hospital*		*ROAS*	
		%		%
I	6	(3·7)	2	(5·8)
IIA	86	(53·4)	23	(67·6)
IIB	39	(24·2)	4	(11·7)
III	30	(18·6)	5	(14·7)
	161		34	

Psychopathological Matrix

Far from being a single factor, psychopathology may thus be regarded as a multifactorial matrix—interpersonal, intrapsychic and, on occasion, sociopathic—which intimately affects the asthmatic pattern in individual cases. Viewed against this backcloth, emotional precipitants like specific allergens may operate as triggers for individual attacks.

The Allergic Contribution

The analogue in terms of allergy is the immunological substrate underlying every case of asthma. In practice, however, it has always proved difficult to evaluate the importance of particular allergens in activating this substrate. Skin testing by itself is notoriously unreliable, so that results should always be interpreted in the light of a careful history. In this series, for example, of the 53 per cent who had had skin testing, about half showed positive reactions to common allergens; the rest had minor or negative results. These findings in isolation are inconclusive.

As a practical procedure, desensitization has proved to be more successful in Group II asthmatics than in Group III, although the lability index remains unchanged (R. S. Jones, personal communication). Conversely, children with allergen-precipitated attacks may achieve dramatic improvement without altering their allergic diathesis or reducing their allergic sensitivity by one iota—through psychotherapeutic intervention. The subject remains allergic but presumably the antigen–antibody reaction which forms the basis of the asthmatic attack is no longer 'detonated' because the contributory emotional tension has been successfully deflected and the sequence thereby 'defused'.

Steroid

The widespread use of steroid in intractable asthma is a cause for some concern. Of the present sample, the majority of cases so treated could be adequately stabilized both clinically and physiologically without steroid therapy, given successful correction of psychopathology or withdrawal of the child from its sphere of influence. In short, proper attention to emotional pathology in refractory asthma may obviate the need for steroid, thereby reserving this potentially hazardous therapy for its proper indication—the physiologically severe case. Incidentally, although this group is already prone to stunting of growth which steroid may well aggravate, there is no convincing evidence that substitution of ACTH is superior in avoiding this adverse side effect (Norman and Sanders, 1969). Strictly speaking, the term 'steroid dependency' should be confined to cases in which, despite comprehensive management, withdrawal of steroid cannot be achieved safely. Conversely, the more dramatic the response to steroid, in other than emergency situations, the more suspect the need to employ it at all.

Deaths

Attention has been drawn (Speizer *et al.*, 1968) to the recent alarming increase in death rate from asthma among children in the age range 10 to 14. Allowing for greater accuracy and refinement in diagnsotic procedure, this is still regarded as an absolute rather than a relative increase. In the present series, which is not a strictly representative sample, there were eleven fatal cases, average age at death 11·8 years. The majority were in Group III physiologically, most had had corticosteroid therapy and five were on steroid when they died. These factors are in keeping with previous reports (Williams and Leopold, 1959; Bruce Pearson, 1968).

Most of these children died at home in status asthmaticus, the treatment of which appeared inadequate. Only one child died suddenly. One lesson to be learned is that steroids should be administered much more generously to the Group III asthmatic, and particularly in status asthmaticus where massive intravenous therapy is indicated (D. A. Williams and S. Davies, personal communication).

Despite the incrimination of sympathomimetic amines as a possible contributory factor in the recent increase in death rate

(Speizer *et al.*, 1968) only one death in this series was temporally related to the use of isoprenaline aerosol. It seems likely that abuse of this form of treatment is potentially most dangerous among patients already suffering myocardial impairment resulting from hypoxia during severe episodes, although habituation to bronchodilator aerosols is a separate and definite hazard in the asthmatic patient, irrespective of severity.

Significant psychopathology characterized all the fatal cases in this sample; mostly this was associated with 'a negative aura'. Of equal significance was the fact that in most cases there had been little, if any, attempt to deal with this relevant psychopathology.

CONCLUSIONS AND PRINCIPLES OF MANAGEMENT

From this study certain principles emerge which govern the rational management of childhood asthma.

It is incorrect and dangerously misleading to refer to 'allergic', 'infective' and 'psychogenic' types:

incorrect because all cases have an immunological basis irrespective of history or identification of particular allergens;

false because intercurrent infection may complicate any case when superimposed upon bronchoconstriction, especially in the presence of excessive mucoid secretion; this is particularly true of younger children more prone to infection in any event;

misleading because, while neither primary nor specific psychogenesis obtains, every case involves potential psychopathology in that its course may be affected by psychodynamic factors.

All three contributions therefore apply but their relationship is complementary, not mutually exclusive, and their impact summative not disparate.

Often enough the relevant dynamics are simply those of any normal family—with one vital difference—the presence of an inherently unstable bronchial tree, which all too readily reflects the normal stresses of intra-familial interaction.

Because of this genetically determined substrate, ventilatory function tests should always form the basis for evaluating true severity and potential for improvement. Cases most likely to develop serious and even fatal ventilatory failure, do not achieve normal readings without the help of steroid, whereas intractability is more a clinical rating not necessarily associated with serious ventilatory impairment. Nevertheless, no asthmatic should ever be dismissed as trivial since the abnormal propensity for bronchoconstriction means that he is more at risk than normal.

'At risk', moreover, may be as much a function of psychopathology as of pathophysiology, especially when non-accepting attitudes carry hostile or carping overtones. Thus, where residential placement is considered necessary to reorientate attitudes, great care must be taken not to aggravate existing psychopathology through successful competition with the atmosphere at home. To the extent that parentectomy achieves symptomatic improvement, the risk of challenging already hostile parents increases, with potentially disastrous repercussions should parents or child misinterpret this concrete demonstration.

In other words, separating child from parents should always be designed to repair relationships. If, instead, these are impaired, short-term progress will be achieved only at the cost of adverse outcome in the longer term.

The concrete demonstration can be of value, however, provided it is engineered with due cognizance of the psychodynamic investment prevailing (Pinkerton, 1965). For example, the dramatic improvement in the over-dependent anxiety-prone child once removed from his 'hot-house' home atmosphere can be made the focal point around which to promote parental insight and overcome iatrogenic misgivings, provided that the basic investment is warmly benign. Realignment of family dynamics often restores trouble score to a level in keeping with physiological status. This is clearly preferable to the exhibition of steroids.

Disodium cromoglycate undoubtedly represents a significant therapeutic advance, especially in Group II subjects, because of their enhanced lability (Jones and Blackhall, 1970). Specifically, the prevention by this drug of post-exercise fall in FEV_1 provides the most convincing indication for its use. The basis of this action is thought to be local interference with the antigen–antibody reaction which initiates bronchospasm, but even this may be influenced by environmental factors. For example, some of our children who showed dramatic improvement on this regime within the stable setting of hospital or residential school, reported a discouraging slump in response at home on equivalent dosage. Therefore, although this is the latest addition to our armamentarium, it is not the ultimate panacea, nor is any other single measure. Although unquestionably effective, its efficacy remains relative—like everything else about this complex and baffling disorder. Even steroid therapy is affected by situational variations, higher doses being required under less stable or more challenging circumstances to achieve equivalent response. Similar fluctuation in efficacy is reported frequently in respect of bronchodilator drugs.

Not only is progress governed by environmental circumstances, but equally by the patient's motivation to improve. As doctors, we tend to assume that every patient wishes to be relieved or cured (Balint, 1957) whereas, in practice, every physician is familiar with the asthmatic's exasperating resistance at times to all our therapeutic overtures—and the more vigorous our approach, the more obstructive his defence.

As with the asthmatic child and his family, so with the doctor; the key to successful management lies in all-round acceptance of the problem—prescribing pharmaceutically as indicated, promoting psychodynamic reorientation where relevant, combating secondary infection where suspected, desensitizing where appropriate—but above all providing continuous comprehensive and consistent support on an out-patient basis if possible and without obtruding. This is especially important in cases with irremediable psychopathology and/or severe pathophysiological involvement.

Essentially, the need is for a service rather than a cure, the aim being to stabilize the labile bronchus. This is the crux of the problem.

REFERENCES

Aas, K. (1969). 'Allergic Asthma in Childhood.' *Archs Dis. Childh.*, **44,** 1.

Abramson, H. A. (1954). 'Evaluation of Maternal Rejection Theory in Allergy.' *Ann. Allerg.* **12,** 129.

— and Peshkin, M. M. (1960). 'Psychosomatic Group Therapy with Parents of Children with Intractable Asthma.' *Ann. Allerg.*, **18,** 87.

— — (1961). 'Group Psychotherapy of the Parents of Intractably Asthmatic Children.' *J. Child. Asthma Res. Inst. Hosp.*, **1,** 77.

Alcock, T. (1960). 'Some Personality Characteristics of Asthmatic Children.' *Br. J. med. Psychol.*, **33,** 133.

Alexander, F. (1950). *Psychosomatic Medicine: Its Principles and Applications.* New York: Norton.

Appel, J. and Rosen, S. R. (1951). 'Psychosomatic Disorders in Psychoses.' *Psychosom. Med.*, **13,** 314.

Balint, M. (1957). In *The Doctor, his Patient and the Illness.* London: Pitman.

Bernstein, I. L., Allen, J. E., Kriendler, L., Ghory, J. E. and Wohl, T. H. (1960). 'A Community Approach to Juvenile Intractable Asthma.' *Paediatrics*, **26,** 586.

Block, J., Jennings, P. H., Harvey, E. and Simpson, E. (1964). 'Interaction between Allergic Potential and Psychopathology in Childhood Asthma.' *Psychosom. Med.*, **26,** 307.

— — — — (1966). 'Clinicians' Conceptions of the Asthmatogenic Mother.' *Archs Gen. Psychiat.*, **15,** 610.

Bruce Pearson, R. S. (1968). 'Asthma—Allergy and Prognosis.' *Proc. R. Soc. Med.*, **61,** 467.

Burton, Lindy (1968). *Vulnerable Children.* London: Routledge & Kegan Paul.

Buston, M. H. (1966). 'Factors Affecting Ventilatory Function in the Child with Asthma.' *Archs Dis. Childh.*, **41,** 509.

Coolidge, J. C. (1956). 'Asthma in Mother and Child as a Special Type of Intercommunication.' *Am. J. Orthopsychiat.*, **26,** 165.

Dawson, B., Horobin, G., Illsley, R. and Mitchell, R. (1969). 'A Survey of Childhood Asthma in Aberdeen.' *Lancet*, **1,** 827.

Dees, S. S. and Lowenback, H. (1948). 'The E.E.G. of Allergic Children.' *Ann. Allerg.*, **6,** 99.

Dekker, E., Barendregt, J. T. and de Vries, K. (1960). 'Allergy and Neurosis in Asthma.' *Adv. Psychosom. Med.*, **1,** 235.

Dubo, S., McLean, J. A., Ching, A. Y., Wright, H. L., Kauffman, P. E. and Sheldon, J. M. (1961). 'A Study of Relationships between Family Situation, Bronchial Asthma and Personal Adjustment in Children.' *J. Pediat.*, **59,** 402.

Dunbar, H. F. (1938). 'Psychoanalytic Notes Relating to Syndromes of Asthma and Hay Fever,' *Psychoanal. Q.*, **7,** 25.

Falliers, C. J., McCann, W. P., Ellis, E. F. and Chai, H. (1966). 'Clinical Methods for the Longitudinal Study of Asthma.' *J. Allergy*, **38,** 1.

Feingold, B. F., Singer, M. T., Freeman, E. H. and Deskins, A. (1966). 'Psychological Variables in Allergic Disease: a Critical Appraisal of Methodology.' *J. Allergy*, **38,** 143.

Fenichel, O. (1945). *The Psychoanalytical Theory of Neurosis.* London: Kegan Paul.

Fitzelle, G. T. (1959). 'Personality Factors and Certain Attitudes toward Child Rearing among Parents of Asthmatic Children.' *Psychosom. Med.*, **21,** 208.

Freeman, E. H., Feingold, B. F., Schlesinger, K. and Gorman, F. J. (1964). 'Psychological Variables in Allergic Disorders.' *Psychosom. Med.*, **26,** 543.

French, T. M. (1939). 'Psychogenic Factors in Asthma.' *Am. J. Psychiat.*, **96,** 87.

— and Alexander, R. (1941). 'Psychogenic Factors in Bronchial Asthma.' *Psychosom. Med.*, Monograph IV, Nat. Res. Council, Washington.

Graham, P. J. and Rutter, M. L. (1968). 'The Reliability and Validity of the Psychiatric Assessment of the Child. II. Interview with the Parent.' *Br. J. Psychiat.*, **114,** 581.

— — Yule, W. and Bless, I. B. (1967). 'Childhood Asthma: A Psychosomatic Disorder? Some Epidemiological Considerations.' *Br. J. Prev. Soc. Med.*, **21,** 78.

Groen, J. J., Van der Valk, J. M., Bastiaans, J., Dekker, E., Ledeboer, R. C., Defares, J., Heemstra, H., Barendregt, J. T. and de Vries, K. (1965). *Psychosomatic Research*, p. 52. Oxford: Pergamon.

Herbert, M. (1965). 'Personality Factors and Bronchial Asthma: A Study of South African Indian Children.' *J. psychosom. Res.*, **8,** 353.

Howell, J. B. L. and Altounyan, R. E. C. (1967). 'A Double-Blind Trial of Disodium Cromoglycate in the Treatment of Allergic Bronchial Asthma.' *Lancet*, **2,** 539.

Ishizaka, K., Ishizaka, T. and Hornbrook, M. M. (1966). 'Physiochemical

Properties of Reaginic Antibody. V. Correlation of Reaginic Activity with E-globulin Antibody.' *J. Immunol.*, **97,** 840.

Johansson, S. G. O. (1967). 'Raised Levels of a New Immunoglobulin Class (IgND) in Asthma.' *Lancet*, 2, 951.

Jones, R. H. Trefor and Jones, R. S. (1966). 'Ventilatory Capacity in Young Adults with a History of Asthma in Childhood.' *Br. med. J.*, **2,** 976.

Jones, R. S. (1966). 'Assessment of Respiratory Function in the Asthmatic Child.' *Br. med. J.*, **2,** 972.

— and Blackhall, M. I. (1970). 'The Role of Disodium Cromoglycate (Intal) in the Treatment of Childhood Asthma.' *Archs Dis. Childh.*, **45,** 49.

— Wharton, M. J. and Buston, M. H. (1963). 'The Place of Physical Exercise and Bronchodilator Drugs in the Assessment of the Asthmatic Child.' *Archs Dis. Childh.*, **38,** 539.

Knapp, P. H. and Nemetz, S. J. (1957). 'Personality Variations in Bronchial Asthma.' *Psychosom. Med.*, **19,** 443.

Lask, Aaron (1966). *Asthma: Attitude and Milieu*, Ed. by M. Balint. Philadelphia and Montreal: Lippincott.

Leigh, D. and Doust, J. W. L. (1953). 'Asthma and Psychosis.' *J. ment Sci.*, **99,** 489.

— and Marley, E. (1967). *Bronchial Asthma*. Oxford: Pergamon.

— and Rawnsley, K. (1956). *Int. Archs Allergy appl. Immun.*, **9,** 305.

Lindt, H. and Goldman, A. S. (1961). 'A Study of "Special Pressures" and their Impact on the Relationship between Mothers and their Asthmatic Children.' *Texas Rep. Biol. Med.*, **19,** 300.

Long, R. T., Lamont, J. H., Whipple, B., Bandler, L., Blom, G., Burgin, L. and Jessner, L. (1958). 'A Psychosomatic Study of Allergic and Emotional Factors in Children with Asthma.' *Am. J. Psychiat.* **114,** 890.

McDermott, N. T. and Cobb, S. (1939). 'A Psychiatric Survey of Fifty Cases of Bronchial Asthma.' *Psychosom. Med.* **1,** 203.

Macdonald, P. J. and Weaver, C. M. (1970). 'Some Personality Characteristics of Asthmatic Children.' In Press.

Margolis, M. (1961). 'The Mother-Child Relationship in Bronchial Asthma.' *J. abnorm. soc. Psychol.*, **63,** 360.

Maurer, E. (1965). 'The Child with Asthma: An Assessment of the Relative Importance of Emotional Factors in Asthma.' *J. Asthma Res.*, **3,** 25.

Miller, H. and Baruch, D. W. (1957). 'The Emotional Problems of Childhood and their Relation to Asthma.' *Am. J. Dis. Child.*, **93,** 242.

Mitchell, J. H., Curran, C. A. and Myers, R. N. (1947). 'Some Psychosomatic Aspects of Allergic Diseases.' *Psychosom. Med.* **9,** 184.

Monsour, K. J. (1960). 'Asthma and the Fear of Death.' *Psychoanal. Q.*, **29,** 56.

Morris, R. P. (1961). 'Effect of the Mother on Goal-Setting Behaviour of the Asthmatic Child.' *Ann. Allergy*, **19,** 44.

Morrison Smith, J. and Devey, G. F. (1968). 'Clinical Trial of Disodium Cromoglycate in Treatment of Asthma in Children.' *Br. med. J.*, **2,** 340.

Munro Ford, R. (1968). 'Treatment of Intractable Childhood Asthma by Medium-Term Separation from Home Environment.' *Med. J. Aust.*, **1,** 653.

Neuhaus, E. C. (1958). 'A Personality Study of Asthmatic and Cardiac Children.' *Psychosom. Med.*, **20,** 181.

Norman, A. P. and Sanders, S. (1969). 'Effect of Corticotrophin on Skeletal Maturation and Linear Growth in Six Patients with Severe Asthma.' *Lancet*, **1,** 287.

Palmer, K. N. V. and Diament, M. L. (1967a). 'Spirometry and Blood-Gas Tensions in Bronchial Asthma and Chronic Bronchitis.' *Lancet*, **2,** 383.

—— (1967b). 'Effect of Aerosol Isoprenaline on Blood-Gas Tensions in Severe Bronchial Asthma.' *Lancet*, **2,** 1232.

—— (1968a). 'Hypoxaemia in Bronchial Asthma.' *Lancet*, **1,** 318.

—— (1968b). 'Relative Contributions of Obstructive and Restrictive Ventilatory Impairment in the Production of Hypoxaemia and Hypercapnia in Chronic Bronchitis.' *Lancet*, **1,** 1233.

—— (1969a). 'Dynamic and Static Lung Volumes and Blood-Gas Tensions in Bronchial Asthma.' *Lancet*, **1,** 591.

—— (1969b). 'Effect of Salbutamol on Spirometry and Blood-Gas Tensions in Bronchial Asthma.' *Br. med. J.*, **1,** 31.

Panzani, R., Boyer, R. and Turner, M. (1956). In *Atti del III Congresso Europea di Allergologia*, Il Pensiero Scientifica.

Peshkin, M. M. (1930). 'Asthma in Children Refractory to Treatment—a Plea for a "Home" as a Restorative Measure.' *Am. J. Dis. Child.*, **39,** 774.

— (1959). 'Intractable Asthma of Childhood. Rehabilitation at the Institutional Level with Follow-up of 150 Cases.' *Int. Archs Allergy appl. Immun.*, **15,** 91.

— (1960). 'Management of the Institutionalized Child with Intractable Asthma.' *Ann. Allergy*, **18,** 75.

— (1963). 'Diagnosis of Asthma in Children: Past and Present.' In *The Asthmatic Child*, p. 1, Ed. by H. K. Schneer. New York: Hoeber.

— (1964). 'The Role of Emotions in Children with Intractable Bronchial Asthma.' *J. Asthma Res.*, **2,** 143.

Pinkerton, P. (1965). In *Modern Perspectives in Child Psychiatry*, p. 313, Ed. by J. G. Howells. Edinburgh and London: Oliver & Boyd.

— (1967). 'Correlating Physiologic with Psychodynamic Data in the Study and Management of Childhood Asthma.' *J. Psychosom. Res.*, **11,** 11.

— (1969). 'Patho-Physiology and Psychopathology as Co-Determinants of Pharmaco-Therapeutic Response in Childhood Asthma.' In *Psychotropic Drugs in Internal Medicine*, Ed. by A. Pletscher and A. Marino. International Congress Series No. 182, June, 1969. Amsterdam: Excerpta Medica Foundation.

Purcell, K., Bernstein, L. and Bukantz, S. C. (1961). 'A Preliminary Comparison of Rapidly Remitting and Persistently "Steroid-Dependent" Asthmatic Children.' *Psychosom. Med.*, **23,** 305.

Rackeman, F. M. and Edwards, M. C. (1952). 'Asthma in Children. A Follow-up Study.' *New Engl. J. Med.*, **246,** 815.

Rees, H. A., Millar, J. S. and Donald, K. W. (1967). 'Adrenaline in Bronchial Asthma.' *Lancet*, **2,** 1164.

Rees, L. (1956a). 'Physical and Emotional Factors in Bronchial Asthma.' *J. Psychosom. Res.*, **1,** 98.

— (1956b). 'Psychosomatic Aspects of Asthma in Elderly Patients.' *J. Psychosom. Res.*, **1,** 212.

Rogerson, C. H. (1937). 'The Psychological Factors in Asthma-Prurigo.' *Q. Jl. Med.*, **30,** 367.

Rubin, S. and Moses, L. (1944). 'E.E.G. Studies in Asthma with some Personality Correlates.' *Psychosom. Med.*, **6,** 1.

Rutter, M. and Brown, G. W. (1966). 'The Reliability and Validity of Measures of Family Life and Relationships in Families Containing a Psychiatric Patient.' *Soc. Psychiat.*, **1,** 38.

— and Graham, P. (1968). 'The Reliability and Validity of the Psychiatric Assessment of the Child. I. Interview with the Child.' *Br. J. Psychiat.*, **114,** 563.

Saul, L. J. and Lyons, J. W. (1954). 'Motivation and Respiratory Disorders.' In *Recent Developments in Psychosomatic Medicine*, Ed. by E. D. Whitkower and R. A. Cleghorn. Philadelphia: Lippincott.

Scadding, J. C. (1963). 'Meaning of Diagnostic Terms in Broncho Pulmonary Disease.' *Br. med. J.* (1970). **2,** 1425.

Schubert, J. and Weaver, C. M. (1970). 'Parental Attitudes in Childhood Asthma.' In Press.

Schwartz, M. (1952). 'Heredity in Bronchial Asthma.' *Acta allerg.* (*Kbh.*), Suppl. 2.

Siegel, S. C. and Lovin, B. J. (1960). 'Pediatric Allergy—a Critical Review of Literature.' *Ann. Allergy*, **18,** 1244, 1359.

Speizer, F. E. and Doll, R. (1968). 'A Century of Asthma Deaths in Young People.' *Br. med. J.*, **2,** 245.

— — and Heaf, P. (1968). 'Observations on Recent Increase in Mortality from Asthma.' *Br. med. J.*, **1,** 335.

— — — and Strang, L. B. (1968). 'Investigation into Use of Drugs Preceding Death from Asthma.' *Br. med. J.*, **1,** 339.

Tai, E. and Read, J. (1967). 'Blood-Gas Tensions in Bronchial Asthma.' *Lancet*, **1,** 644.

Tuft, H. S. (1957). 'The Development and Management of Intractable Asthma in Childhood.' *Am. J. Dis. Child.*, **93,** 251.

Turnbull, J. (1962). 'Asthma Conceived as a Learned Response.' *J. Psychosom. Res.*, **6,** 5.

Walsh, S. D. and Grant, I. W. B. (1966). 'Corticosteroids in Treatment of Chronic Asthma.' *Br. med. J.*, **2,** 796.

Weaver, C. M. and Pinkerton, P. (1970). 'Implications of Parentectomy in Childhood Asthma Re-defined in Psycho-Socio-Pathophysiologic Terms.' *Proc. VIIth Int. Cong. Child Psychiat.*, Jerusalem.

Williams, D. A. and Leopold, J. (1959). 'Death from Bronchial Asthma.' *Acta allergologica*, **14,** 83.

CHAPTER 7

PSYCHOSOMATIC ASPECTS OF DIABETES MELLITUS

LESTER BAKER and AVNER BARCAI

INTRODUCTION

The literature concerning the psychosomatic aspects of diabetes mellitus is filled with conflict and confusion. This has been accompanied by a virtual standstill in papers devoted to this subject: of over 35,000 articles covered in the *Diabetes* indices for the years 1960 to 1968, less than 30 pertinent references were found under the key-words 'emotions', 'psychiatry', or 'psychosomatic'. Much of the confusion stems from arguments caused by authors who use the same words to convey entirely different meanings. As Starr (1955) bluntly put it, 'the term psychosomatic disorder has served as a convenient "wastebasket" diagnosis which has not allowed for a comprehensive grasp of the multiple syndromes which fall under such a category'.

This review will not attempt to be all inclusive, but will rather concentrate on a critical updating of the literature concerning diabetes and emotions. Emphasis will be placed on current work which has provided a new direction, and which may stimulate further endeavours. Since many of the classic physiological studies in the diabetic psychosomatic field were published before knowledge had accrued concerning the key role of free fatty acids in energy metabolism, a brief review of the relationships between emotions and free fatty acids would thus appear to be an appropriate starting-point.

EMOTIONS AND FREE FATTY ACIDS

Free fatty acids play a role in fat metabolism analogous to that of glucose in carbohydrate metabolism (Wertheimer, 1965). Free fatty acids are a prime source of energy in fasting man, and they may be indeed the preferred substrate of muscle at all times. Triglyceride in

The work described in this chapter was supported in part by U.S. Public Health Service Funds, Grant Nos. HD00444, AM13518, FR00240, and a Grant-in-Aid from the Wagman Foundation.

adipose tissue represents a storage form of free fatty acids similar to liver glycogen as a storage form of glucose. The factors responsible for triglyceride synthesis and lipid mobilization have been the focus of much recent attention (Steinberg and Vaughan, 1965).

The prominent role of the catecholamines in lipolysis led to early studies designed to see whether emotional 'stress' or 'arousal', presumably by acting through the autonomic nervous system, could also cause a rise in free fatty acid concentrations. Cardon and Gordon (1959) documented that a sham traumatic procedure intended to produce fear in normal volunteers was accompanied by a rapid and significant elevation of free fatty acids. Bogdonoff, Estes and Trout (1959) showed that an interview centering about areas of personal conflict, anxiety, anger and hostility produced striking elevations of free fatty acids in three of four volunteer students.

Expanding this work further, Bogdonoff *et al.* (1960), Bogdonoff and Estes (1961) and Bogdonoff and Nichols (1965) studied a series of senior medical students undergoing a 15-minute oral examination considered by the students to be difficult and challenging. In this life situation, marked increases of free fatty acids were found in all 20 subjects. This was accompanied by rises in blood glucose concentration, by an increase in heart rate, and by a rise in urinary epinephrine excretion. Post-examination interviews designed to quantify the intensity of affect arousal showed that anxiety predominated. Those subjects thought to have the highest affect arousal ratings also had the largest mean changes in plasma free fatty acid concentrations and in heart rate. It was also demonstrated (Bogdonoff *et al.*, 1964) that the characteristics of social interaction could modify the physiological responses which accompany a challenging task. That is, an individual who participated in a laboratory testing experience in the company of 'friends' consistently demonstrated less lipid mobilization and emotional 'arousal' than that seen for individuals working among 'strangers'.

A standardized challenging task has also been used by Levi and co-workers to study the changes of plasma free fatty acids. In a series of papers (Levi, 1961, 1967a and b; Carlson, Levi and Oro, 1968), a two hour 'stress' period preceded a similar two hour interval in which no 'stress' occurred. The 'stress' consisted of an industrial task of sorting small, shiny steel balls of four similar sizes in the presence of loud industrial noise, variations in light, rush due to lack of time, and standardized criticism. Plasma free fatty acid concentrations rose significantly during the 'stress' period. The authors raised the question as to whether this kind of 'stress', similar to that found in many aspects of our modern industrial society, could cause a chronic state of accelerated adipokinesis, which in turn might be a significant contributing factor to the major health problem of coronary artery disease.

While Bogdonoff had indicated that a variety of emotional stimuli could cause free fatty acid changes, Gottschalk *et al.* (1965) found only anxiety to have a positive correlation with plasma free fatty acids. On a scale designed to measure anxiety and three forms of hostility it was found that anxious subjects had higher free fatty acid levels and sharper rises in the concentration of free fatty acids than did non-anxious subjects in reaction to venipuncture and to five minutes of free association. These authors called attention to the fact that the three indices of hostility showed no correlation with free fatty acid levels or responses. It was suggested therefore that different emotions might be associated with different biological concomitants.

Pinter *et al.* (1967) also pointed out that different states of emotional arousal have different adipokinetic effects. A hypnotic state was induced in 17 patients. Two anxiety-provoking suggestions were made: the first was a 'stressful' situation with a possibility of escape by active effort; suggestion number two was a 'stressful' situation without hope of escape, forcing the subject to be passive. Suggestion number two was followed by a much greater increment of free fatty acid concentrations. Indeed, it was found that this situation had an adipokinetic potency equal to approximately 85 per cent of an intravenous epinephrine infusion (0·5 μg./kg. for 15 minutes). Using radioactively labelled free fatty acid tracers, it was clearly documented that the increase in free fatty acid concentrations was due to increased lipolysis.

This brief review of emotions and free fatty acids serves to highlight several points:

(1) Emotional stimuli can produce rapid and significant increases of plasma free fatty acid concentrations. There appear to be differences in the kind of emotional stimuli which can produce this effect, with anxiety apparently a major factor. There also seem to be different states of emotional 'arousal'. Further work in this area must seek to define more clearly such global terms as emotional 'stress' and emotional 'arousal'.

(2) The increase in plasma free fatty acids caused by psychogenic factors is clearly due to an increased rate of lipolysis. Although this has been shown most elegantly by tracer studies of Pinter *et al.* (1967), it is also implicit in the ability of ganglionic blockers (Bogdonoff and Estes, 1961), nicotinic acid (Carlson, Levi and Oro, 1968), and beta adrenergic blocking agents (Pinter *et al.*, 1967; Baker *et al.*, 1969a) to cause a reduction of the anticipated free fatty acid response. It is

still an unsettled question as to whether the stimulation of lipolysis is mediated through the norepinephrine released at the adipose tissue site by the autonomic nervous system, or by the adrenal release of epinephrine.

(3) The implication that chronic hyperadipokinesis caused by emotional 'stress' is related to coronary artery disease is an intriguing area in which much further work must be done.

(4) The identification of the adrenergic beta receptors as the pathway for the stimulatory effect of catecholamines on adipose tissue lipolysis has important therapeutic implications. This approach has already been used by Baker *et al.* (1969a) to treat a group of juvenile diabetics who were hospitalized frequently because of repeated bouts of severe diabetic ketoacidosis. The documentation and treatment of a hyperdynamic beta adrenergic circulatory state (Frohlich, Terazi and Dustan, 1969), and the recent work of several groups with beta adrenergic blockers in anxiety neuroses (Granville-Grossman and Turner, 1966; Pitts and McClure, 1967; Pitts, 1969) may also be relevant here.

DIABETES AND EMOTIONS

The studies concerning the relationships between emotional factors and diabetes may be grouped as follows (Kubany, Danowski and Moses, 1956; Treuting, 1962):

(1) The role of the emotional factors in the *aetiology* of diabetes.

(2) Characterization of *personality patterns* of diabetics which might distinguish them from normal subjects and from individuals with other chronic disease states.

(3) The role of emotional factors in the *course and control* of the diabetic state.

The Role of Emotional Factors in the Aetiology of Diabetes

Treuting (1962) has recently reviewed the pertinent literature in this area. Few new observations have been reported (Slawson, Flynn and Kollar, 1963; Quichaud, 1963; Félix *et al.*, 1965, 1966; Larcan, 1966; Félix, 1967). The current consensus would appear to be best summed up by Danowski's editorial comments (Danowski, 1963): 'It still appears therefore that at present the contention that emotional stress can by itself produce permanent diabetes mellitus in a totally non-diabetic individual cannot be confirmed by clinical data, whereas considerable indirect and direct evidence can be assembled in support of the view that stress intensifies known preexistent diabetes mellitus, brings to clinical recognition previously unrecognized actual diabetes, and may convert pre-diabetes to actual diabetes.'

It would be important in any future considerations of the aetiological role of emotions in diabetes to take into account the varying states of hyperadipokinesis which may be induced by emotional arousal (see previous section). It is theoretically possible that these elevated lipid levels could create a state of insulin antagonism which might eventually progress to overt diabetes.

Evaluation of Personality Patterns

Diabetes is unique among chronic diseases in its demands on the patient: the need for self-discipline with regard to urine testing and dietary habits; the need for daily insulin injections; the possibility of serious complications during intercurrent infections; hypoglycaemic reactions; and the long-term threat of the diabetic sequelae. The impact of these circumstances upon the individual and the family of the diabetic can readily be appreciated (Benedek, 1948; Fischer, 1948; Wagner, 1952; Kennedy, 1955; Palmer, 1958), yet the literature in this area still contains many conflicting and contradictory reports. On the one hand, several authors have presented a personality type felt to be characteristic of the diabetic (Menninger, 1935; Lindberg, 1936; Dunbar, 1954). Others have presented data to support the thesis that there is no behavioural pattern which is characteristic of the diabetic (Brown and Thompson, 1940; Lisansky, 1948; Bruch, 1949; Kubany, Danowski and Moses, 1956). Crowell (1953) found no personality criteria which could be used to distinguish diabetics from patients with rheumatic fever.

The attitudes and reactions produced by the disease (the 'somatopsychic' factors) are also generally included in this category. The problems found here have often been most exaggerated in the patients with juvenile diabetes mellitus, and have drawn attention from many authors (Fischer, 1948; Wagner, 1952; Sheppe and Sheppe, 1954; Hinkle *et al.*, 1959; Schiff, 1964; Isenberg and Barnett, 1965). Swift and Seidman (1964) and Swift, Seidman and Stein (1967) evaluated 50 juvenile diabetics and found this group to be different from a matched control group in dependence–independence balance, self-percept, manifest and latent anxiety, actual identification, constriction, and hostility expression. The diabetic children showed significantly poorer adjustment with parents, siblings, and peers.

In marked contrast to the above is the careful study of Sterky (1963) presenting the social and family structure of 145 diabetic children and 126 matched controls. An effort was made to obtain the social and psychological histories of the diabetic children antedating the onset of their disease. While the diabetic group had a significantly increased frequency of mothers with anxiety symptoms, the frequency of mental symptoms in the children was the same for both study groups. The most common problems of the diabetics were emotional lability and difficulty with companions. The author felt that this study essentially corroborated that of Danowski (1957): 'The diabetic child is not doomed to personality disturbances as an intrinsic manifestation of his metabolic disturbance.'

It would appear that a major reason for these contradictory conclusions is the tendency to group all diabetics together when making comparisons with either normal individuals or with subjects with other chronic diseases. There are children with diabetes who are reasonably well adjusted to their disease, give no problem to the physician, to their families, or to society; they constitute the largest group. On the other hand, several other categories of diabetic children exist with varying degrees of emotional disturbances. In some instances, the personality difficulties antedated the disease, while in others the impact of the disease caused adjustment difficulties. As will be expanded in the next section, further progress in this area would be aided by the use of a viable psychiatric classification of personality and emotional patterns in diabetic patients. Such a classification was previously suggested by Starr (1955), and has recently been revised by Barcai and Baker (1970).

Role of Emotional Factors in the Course and Control of the Diabetic State

The literature has been plagued by lack of precision as to the ways in which emotions do or do not affect the course of diabetes. Nabarro's comments (1965) exemplify the situation. In reviewing the predisposing causes of 72 cases of severe diabetic ketoacidosis, he found that almost 15 per cent of the patients developed ketosis following an emotional disturbance. He states, 'It was impossible to discover whether they had omitted insulin injections, or whether psychological factors had produced an intense resistance to insulin action.' Other authors have been less judicious, and have tended to present those cases to strengthen one or the other of these alternatives.

Hinkle, Evans and Wolf (1951a) presented three young patients in whom 'exacerbation of the diabetes, associated with ketosis and coma, very frequently appeared in association with acutely stressful life situations'. In the opinion of these authors, the emotional state of the patient triggered the episodes of ketoacidosis. On the other hand,

Rosen and Lidz (1949), in studying 12 patients who had repeated bouts of ketoacidosis, came to the opposite conclusion: that is, that emotions were at best secondary factors, leading to abandonment of the diabetic regimen, and thus resulting in diabetic ketoacidosis. Cohen *et al.* (1960) found that the most common precipitating factor in diabetic ketoacidosis was the omission of insulin; 50 per cent of the patients who neglected to take insulin were found to have specific emotional disturbances which directly related to the disregard of the insulin. Stearns (1959) presented several case reports of self-destructive behaviour in young patients, which included the omission of insulin to precipitate acidosis, or the purposeful neglect of a serious infection. Deliberate omission of insulin, however, did not seem to be the primary factor in many other patients described in the literature (Peck and Peck, 1956; Slawson, 1963; Schless and von Laveran-Stiebar, 1964; Baker *et al.*, 1969a). It would appear that attempts to continue to consider as one group all diabetic patients who demonstrate either 'excessive lability' or frequent bouts of ketoacidosis will only result in furthering the confusion. There are certain patients who 'use' the diabetic state either to get out of unpleasant life situations, or as a weapon against themselves, their families, or their environments. These individuals are clearly different from other diabetics in whom ketoacidosis supervenes despite conscientious administration of normal or supplemental insulin doses. Further knowledge in this area, from both the psychological and the metabolic points of view, can only be gained by consideration of these groups as separate and distinct entities (see proposed classification system, next section).

The experimental approach to the role of emotions in diabetes has similarly been beset by many problems. Although the studies of Hinkle and collaborators (Hinkle and Wolf, 1949, 1952a and b; Hinkle, Conger and Wolf, 1950; Hinkle, Evans and Wolf, 1951a and b) stand out as classics, it was never possible in their studies to correlate whether a particular 'stress' would cause the blood glucose to go up or down. The role of free fatty acids, especially with relationship to diabetic ketoacidosis, was not fully appreciated until the mid-1950s, several years after their major studies. It is also possible that Hinkle and co-workers over-interpreted their data in an attempt to support their hypothesis that emotional deprivation in certain diabetics resulted in a metabolic pattern of starvation which, superimposed on the diabetic state, caused ketoacidosis.

Very few recent papers have appeared in this area, but those by Vandenbergh, Sussman and Titus (1966) and Vandenbergh, Sussman and Vaughan (1967) illustrate current methodological difficulties. The authors documented a significant decrease in blood glucose, and a non-significant increase in free fatty acids, following both hypnotically induced 'stress' and physical–anticipatory 'stress'. The authors called attention to the problem intrinsic to this research of measuring accurately and regulating the amount of 'stress' which each individual patient perceives. Two other points are, however, equally important in judging their data: the experimental plan was such that insulin was given on the day of the experiment, and the data of the 'stress' day were compared to data obtained during a similar interval on a non-stress day. On the basis of what is known concerning the daily metabolic lability of patients with diabetes, it would not seem appropriate to compare data obtained in this manner. The grouping together of individuals with different types of diabetes (juvenile and maturity onset) also would tend to detract from the results.

This brief review of emotions and diabetes has served to highlight the following points:

(1) The grouping together of all patients in whom diabetes and emotional symptoms co-exist has not allowed meaningful insights into the exact relationships between psychiatric and metabolic events.

(2) The use of the words 'stress' and 'emotional arousal' by various authors to convey different meanings has tended to obscure those instances in which emotional factors do seem to play a causal role in the course of the diabetes.

(3) Further definition is needed of those factors responsible for creating a state of insulin resistance during emotional 'stress'. The blanket invocation of a pituitary–adrenal axis response to such emotional 'stress' is obviously not sufficient as a pathophysiological explanation.

NEW DIRECTIONS

The recent studies of Baker, Barcai and co-workers represent a response to the type of problems outlined in the preceding section. These authors have attempted to deal with the psychosomatic aspects of juvenile diabetes by trying to distinguish the different sub-groups within the larger one, and by calling attention once again to the difficulties created by global views of 'stress'. They have delineated a sub-group of juvenile diabetics, the 'super-labile' group, and have clearly demonstrated that the diabetic decompensation seen following emotional 'arousal' in these patients is mediated by endogenous catecholamines. This information has been used in an effective therapeutic manner.

Their attention was first drawn to this area during studies designed to elucidate the non-insulin factors involved in the metabolic homeostasis of patients with juvenile diabetes (Baker *et al.*, 1969b; Baker, Kaye and Haque, 1969). An increased ketone responsiveness to epinephrine stimulation in the diabetic child was documented. The opportunity to re-examine the possible relationship between catecholamines, emotions, and diabetic acidosis was afforded these investigators when two pre-adolescent girls were referred to their hospital because of a diabetic pattern characterized by frequent and severe bouts of ketoacidosis. These children were incapacitated by their disease: acute hospitalizations averaged approximately one admission every 3–4 weeks per child. Exhaustive study of these patients failed to uncover any organic cause (Molnar, 1967) for the frequent bouts of ketoacidosis. A variety of therapeutic approaches, including supportive psychotherapy, failed to prevent this pattern from continuing.

The authors used a series of psychiatric interviews in order to document the relationship between emotional arousal and diabetic ketoacidosis, and to study the humoral mechanisms which might be implicated (Baker *et al.*, 1969a). A 'specific stress' interview was defined as a deliberate attempt to reproduce a conflict to which the patient was felt to be specifically vulnerable. The actual psychiatric manoeuvre used was based on analysis of both the individual and family psychodynamics. Two 'specific stress' interviews were held; during one of these, acute beta adrenergic blockade was induced by intravenous infusion. A non-provocative interview, termed 'non-specific stress' because of its novelty to the patient, was used as a control. Evidence that the 'specific stress' interviews were indeed successful in producing major emotional arousal was seen both on the clinical and humoral levels. In addition to the appearance of the child, evidence of a pituitary–adrenal response to 'stress' was documented by significant increments in plasma growth hormone and corticoid concentrations, as well as an increase in the urinary excretion of epinephrine.

The metabolic consequences of these interviews can be seen graphically in *Figure 1*. While the 'non-specific stress' interview was associated with no change in free fatty acid concentrations, the 'specific stress' interview caused a 100 per cent rise. The repeat 'specific stress' interview preceded by beta adrenergic blockade was felt to result in an identical state of emotional 'arousal', but was not associated with any metabolic changes of consequence. These data were interpreted to show that endogenous catecholamines play a key role in the mediation of diabetic decompensation following emotional 'stress'. These acute studies were then followed by long-term therapeutic trials of oral beta adrenergic blockade in these children. A dramatic improvement in the clinical course was seen.

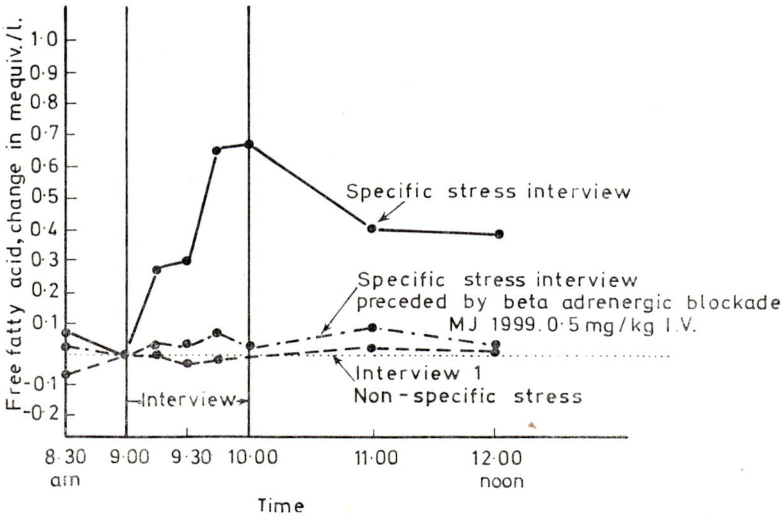

Figure 1. Metabolic consequences of specific stress interviews

The authors have studied and treated several similar patients since that initial report. These patients appear to be so similar in their diabetic course and emotional pattern that they have been placed in a separate sub-group, to which the name 'super-labile' juvenile diabetes has been applied. The families of these patients so resemble one another that a characteristic psychiatric profile may be drawn of them. These individual and family profiles are currently being prepared (Barcai and Baker, 1970). The use of beta adrenergic blockade, along with crisis-induced family psychotherapy (Minuchin and Barcai, 1969), has been an effective therapeutic modality. Corroboration of this approach has also come from two other groups (Schultz, 1969; Werner, 1969).

Barcai and Baker (1970) have presented a classification system of psychosomatic disorders in juvenile diabetes updating that of Starr (1955). It offers diagnostic, aetiologic, and therapeutic implications. A brief table showing this classification is presented here (Table 1), but the reader is referred to the original study for more comprehensive discussion. It is recognized, of course, that all patients will not fall neatly into only one category. The classification is offered as a working hypothesis, intended to stimulate further studies.

TABLE 1

Emotions and Diabetes: Proposed Classification

Syndrome	I: 'NORMAL' DIABETIC
Presenting Picture (*a*) Medical (*b*) Emotional	 Usual diabetic course Age appropriate responses
Formulation	Healthy adjustment
Therapeutic Approach (*a*) Medical (*b*) Psychiatric	No special measures necessary
Syndrome	II: 'PSEUDO-PSYCHOSOMATIC' REACTION (erroneously labelled as psychosomatic by virtue of a temporal association between the diabetic state and the emotional symptoms)
Presenting Picture (*a*) Medical (*b*) Emotional	 Usually no problems with respect to acute episodes of hypoglycaemia or acidosis. Occasional acetonuria without organic explanation. Patient may appear unco-operative with behavioural disturbances. Open expression of disagreement between the parents concerning aspects of the diabetic management.
Formulation	This is primarily a problem concerning the difficulty of the family members to negotiate issues. This overt conflict is transferred to the arena of the child's diabetic regimen.
Therapeutic Approach (*a*) Medical (*b*) Psychiatric	 No special manoeuvres necessary. Psychiatric referral often made with difficulty. Therapy aimed at conflicts between parents. Marriage counselling and supportive therapy may be necessary.
Syndrome	III: SOMATO-PSYCHIC REACTIONS (the somatic disease creates and triggers an emotional dysequilibrium with resultant psychiatric symptoms) A: TRAUMATIC REACTION
Presenting Picture (*a*) Medical (*b*) Emotional	 Reasonable normal diabetic course, with no major difficulties in medical management. Child may appear depressed and unhappy, or hostile and resentful towards parents, siblings, and peers.
Formulation	Unable to deal with the trauma of being a diabetic (fears of invalidism and death), the child may become depressed or hostile because of this personal 'injustice'. The manifestations tend to be purely psychiatric, with no overlap into difficulties concerning the diabetic regimen.

TABLE 1 *Continued*

Therapeutic Approach	
(*a*) Medical	Frank and thorough explanation of the diabetic state: appropriate emphasis on the realistic difficulties of being a diabetic, and its implications for the future. Deal with experiential anxiety of the patient secondary to the illness. Family interviews should allow them to work through this 'vulnerable child' syndrome by dealing with the impact of diabetes in an honest and open fashion.
(*b*) Psychiatric	Psychiatric referral often not necessary, since a good medical therapeutic approach (as outlined above) is usually sufficient.
	B: Iatrogenic Management Reaction
Presenting Picture	
(*a*) Medical	Usually referred to a teaching centre because of frequent insulin reactions or 'brittleness'. Diabetic regimen quite rigid with respect to diet, frequent blood glucose examinations, and insulin dosage manipulation to avoid glucosuria.
(*b*) Emotional	Child usually frightened, tense, and anxious. Child's home behaviour frequently characterized as irritable and highly strung. Often history of deterioration in school performance and self-esteem, with loss of friends.
Formulation	A fearful over-response in a highly conscientious family to the rigid approach of the physician who initially made the diagnosis. Part of the irritable behaviour may be due to inapparent hypoglycaemia secondary to over-manipulation of the insulin dosage with a 'Somogyi effect'.
Therapeutic Approach	
(*a*) Medical	Re-education concerning the legitimate goals of diabetic control. Hospitalization may be necessary: to test the Somogyi effect hypothesis, and to allow for more gradual liberalization of the diabetic regimen. Too rapid a shift of the diabetic programme may cause anxiety attacks, the symptoms of which can easily be confused with true hypoglycaemic reactions.
(*b*) Psychiatric	True psychiatric referral may not be necessary: these families do well with support during the process of re-education. Attention should be paid to undoing of fears engendered by the rigid and fearful approach.
	C: True Management Reaction
Presenting Picture	
(*a*) Medical	Often referred because of frequent hospitalizations for ketoacidosis. Difficulties are always found to be traceable to such problems as wilful omission of insulin, failure to report symptoms of insulin deficiency, falsification of urine test results, eating binges.
(*b*) Emotional	Negativistic patients who present behavioural disturbances: school attendance difficulties, flaunting of parental and teacher authority.

Formulation	The arena of diabetes is used as a testing ground for control in these families. Covert parental conflicts are often found, along with a chronic difficulty in the establishment of generational boundaries. Problems tend to be handled by denial or temporizing manoeuvres. Although currently manifested as diabetic problems, the issue of control is a generic one in these families.
Therapeutic Approach	
(*a*) Medical	Transfer responsibility to child for management of the disease, along with explanation of the rationale for the diabetic regimen. Hospitalization may be required, as parents often lack ability to confront child with this responsibility.
(*b*) Psychiatric	Psychiatric referral may be difficult because of the covert conflicts. Family intervention with open confrontation to divest the child of controlling influence in the family and in establishment of generational boundaries with authority delegated to parents.
Syndrome	IV: PRIMARY PSYCHOSOMATIC DISEASE (emotional difficulties appear to be causally related to metabolic problems) A: PSYCHOPHYSIOLOGIC REACTION, CHRONIC TYPE
Presenting Picture	
(*a*) Medical	Frequent acetonuria. Appears to be on verge of frequent acidotic episodes, although few hospitalizations necessary. Insulin requirements fluctuate widely, with usual dosage far greater than that expected for the size, weight, and duration of disease. Insulin resistance not due to immunological problems.
(*b*) Emotional	Child often appears to be anxious, unhappy, immature, or slightly withdrawn. Parental conflict over acceptance of disease.
Formulation	These families tend to repress all problems. The children lack ego strength, and many have identity difficulties. The children have a low coping capacity, and issues are transformed into a generalized chronic anxiety. This is associated with a state of insulin resistance, although the exact mechanism is not known.
Therapeutic Approach	
(*a*) Medical	Referral to psychiatrist. Close follow-up in order to reduce insulin dosage as emotional problems are resolved.
(*b*) Psychiatric	Assess underlying causes of anxiety state. Design therapeutic manoeuvres for individual and family accordingly.

TABLE 1 *Continued*

	B: Psychophysiologic Reaction, Acute Decompensating Type: The 'Super-Labile'
Presenting Picture	
(*a*) Medical	Multiple hospital admissions for severe bouts of ketoacidosis with no obvious organic cause. Remarkable response to small doses of insulin following hospitalization, in contrast to apparent marked insulin resistance to supplemental doses of insulin conscientiously given at home.
(*b*) Emotional	Child and family very pleasant, smiling, and co-operative. Usually regarded as model children by nurses. No apparent conflicts ever in these families.
Formulation	The family tends to be an enmeshed, over-protective group, where problems are dealt with by diffusion rather than by resolution. The children are non-coping and ineffective, and cannot deal effectively with new situations and challenges. Anxiety apparently provokes endogenous catecholamine activation which results in rapid diabetic decompensation despite supplemental insulin.
Therapeutic Approach	
(*a*) Medical	Careful evaluation to rule out any organic causes for this extreme 'brittleness'. Removal of possible sources of patient and physician error. Chronic oral beta adrenergic blockade therapy effective.
(*b*) Psychiatric	Referral to psychiatrist relatively easy, but therapeutic intervention difficult. Routine supportive therapy of family or child not effective. Vigorous family intervention by crisis induction method much more therapeutic.

Baker and Barcai (1970) have called attention to the problem created by the use of such global words as 'non-specific stress', 'specific stress', and 'emotional arousal'. In particular, they discuss a patient who was subjected to what was felt to be a 'specific stress' interview. Clinically, the patient was noted to be flushed, tense, and rigid for the first 30 minutes of the interview, but then appeared to be more relaxed and overtly aggressive in the latter phase of the interview. The hormonal studies during this interview documented an initial rise of plasma corticoids at the mid-point of the interview, followed by a decrease. A significant increment in the output of urinary epinephrine occurred during the interview time. Metabolically, a small rise in blood glucose was noted, but no change in the free fatty acid concentration occurred. Data such as this indicate that 'arousal' and 'stress' cannot be defined solely on clinical observations or pituitary–adrenal responses. One can speculate that a psychosomatic crisis depends upon at least two factors: (1) the triggering mechanism; and (2) the inability to 'turn it off'. The rise in corticoids and epinephrine may represent an 'arousal' or triggering phenomenon, but the ability of this particular patient to 'turn it off' at a critical time during the interview prevented those metabolic consequences which might have led to ketoacidosis. (Later questioning revealed that the patient's mother had told her to expect 'a difficult time' during the interview, and had implied to the patient that she need not take the interview seriously. Apparently, the patient recalled this advice during the course of the interview.) A major area for future investigation would thus appear to be an analysis of those psychiatric, hormonal, or metabolic factors which permit the return towards a homeostatic equilibrium. It was also pointed out by these authors that the selective use of different blocking agents, rather than the measurement of hormones in blood or urine, may yield more precise information as to which members of the pituitary–adrenal axis are playing significant roles in the diabetic state.

SUMMARY

A review of the literature concerning the relationships between emotions and free fatty acids has served as an introduction to a critical evaluation of the studies of emotions and diabetes. Emphasis has been placed on areas of controversy, many of which have occurred as a result of the grouping together of all diabetic individuals who manifest psychological symptoms. The lack of precision of such terms as emotional 'stress' has also contributed to the confusion in this area. The recent work which attempts to separate the different syndromes subsumed under the heading of 'Psychosomatic Disorders of Diabetes' appears to point in the proper direction, since it allows for more accurate delineation of the complex inter-relationships between psychiatric, hormonal and metabolic factors in the diabetic individual.

ACKNOWLEDGEMENTS

The authors wish to acknowledge the many contributions of Drs. Robert Kaye and Salvadore Minuchin to the development of this work. We also are indebted to Mrs. Liesel Baker for editorial assistance.

REFERENCES

Baker, L. and Barcai, A. (1970). 'Psychophysiologic Studies in Juvenile Diabetes Mellitus.' (In preparation.)

Baker, L., Kaye, R. and Haque, N. (1969). 'Metabolic Homeostasis in Juvenile Diabetes Mellitus. II. Increased Ketone Responsiveness to Epinephrine.' *Diabetes,* **18,** 421.

— Barcai, A., Kaye, R. and Haque, N. (1969a). 'Beta Adrenergic Blockade and Juvenile Diabetes: Acute Studies and Long Term Therapeutic Trial.' *J. Pediat.,* **75,** 19.

— Root, A. W., Haque, N. and Kaye, R. (1969b). 'Metabolic Homeostasis in Juvenile Diabetes Mellitus. I. Role of Growth Hormone.' *Metabolism,* **18,** 110.

Barcai, A. and Baker, L. (1970). 'A Proposed Classification for the Emotional Syndromes Seen in Juvenile Diabetes Mellitus.' (In preparation.)

Benedek, T. (1948). 'An Approach to the Study of the Diabetic.' *Psychosom. Med.,* **10,** 284.

Bogdonoff, M. D. and Estes, E. H., Jr. (1961). 'Energy Dynamics and Acute States of Arousal in Man.' *Psychosom. Med.,* **23,** 23.

— — and Trout, D. (1959). 'Acute Effect of Psychologic Stimuli Upon Plasma Non-Esterified Fatty Acid Level.' *Proc. Soc. exp. Biol. Med.,* **100,** 503.

— — Harlan, W. R., Trout, D. R. and Kirshner, N. (1960). 'Metabolic and Cardiovascular Changes During a State of Acute Central Nervous System Arousal.' *J. clin. Endocr. Metab.,* **20,** 1333.

— Klein, R. F., Back, K. W., Nichols, C. R., Troyer, W. G. and Hood, T. C. (1964). 'Effect of Group Relationship and of the Role of Leadership Upon Lipid Mobilization.' *Psychosom. Med.,* **26,** 710.

— and Nichols, C. R. (1965). 'Psychogenic Effects on Lipid Mobilization.' In *Handbook of Physiology,* Section 5: Adipose Tissue, Ed. by A. E. Renold and G. F. Cahill, Jr. Washington, D.C.: American Physiological Society.

Brown, G. D. and Thompson, W. H. (1940). 'The Diabetic Child: An Analytic Study of his Development.' *Am. J. dis. Child.,* **59,** 238.

Bruch, H. (1949). 'Physiologic and Psychologic Interrelationships in Diabetes in Children.' *Psychosom. Med.,* **11,** 200.

Cardon, P. V., Jr. and Gordon, R. A., Jr. (1959). 'Rapid Increase of Plasma Unesterified Fatty Acids in Man During Fear.' *J. Psychosom. Res.,* **4,** 5.

Carlson, L. A., Levi, L. and Oro, L. (1968). 'Plasma Lipids and Urinary Excretion of Catecholamines in Man During Experimentally Induced Emotional Stress, and Their Modification by Nicotinic Acid.' *J. clin. Invest.,* **47,** 1795.

Cohen, A. S., Vance, V. K., Runyan, J. W., Jr. and Hurwitz, D. (1960). 'Diabetic Acidosis: An Evaluation of the Cause, Course, and Therapy of 73 Cases.' *Ann. intern. Med.,* **52,** 55.

Crowell, D. H. (1953). 'Personality and Physical Disease: A Test of the Dunbar Hypothesis Applied to Diabetes Mellitus and Rheumatic Fever.' *Genet. Psychol. Monog.,* **48,** 117.

Danowski, T. S. (1957). *Diabetes Mellitus, with Emphasis on Children and Young Adults.* Baltimore: Williams and Wilkins.

Danowski, T. S. (1963). 'Emotional Stress as a Cause of Diabetes Mellitus.' *Diabetes*, **12,** 183.

Dunbar, F. (1954). *Emotions and Bodily Changes*. New York: Columbia University Press.

Félix, H. (1967). 'Étude critique du diabète sucré émotionnel.' *Diabète*, **15,** 41.

— Lacoste, J., Freyria, J., Lesbre, F. and Duprat, F. (1965). 'Étude critique du diabète sucré émotionnel de l'adulte jeune.' *J. med. Lyon*, **46,** 1281.

— — — — — (1966). 'Étude critique du diabète sucré émotionnel de l'adulte jeune.' *Lyon Med.*, **216,** 559.

Fischer, A. E. (1948). 'Factors Responsible for Emotional Disturbances in Diabetic Children.' *Nerv. Child.*, **7,** 78.

Frohlich, E. D., Terazi, R. C. and Dustan, H. P. (1969). 'Hyperdynamic Beta-Adrenergic Circulatory State.' *Archs intern. Med.*, **123,** 1.

Gottshalk, L. A., Cleghorn, J. M., Gleser, G. C. and Iacono, J. M. (1965). 'Studies of Relationships of Emotions to Plasma Lipids.' *Psychosom. Med.*, **27,** 102.

Granville-Grossman, K. and Turner, P. (1966). 'The Effect of Propranolol on Anxiety.' *Lancet*, **1,** 788.

Hinkle, L. E., Jr., Conger, G. B. and Wolf, S. (1950). 'Studies in Diabetes Mellitus: The Relation of Stressful Life Situations to the Concentration of Ketone Bodies in the Blood of Diabetic and Non-Diabetic Humans.' *J. clin. Invest.*, **29,** 754.

— Evans, F. and Wolf, S. (1951a). 'Studies in Diabetes Mellitus. III. Life History of Three Persons with Labile Diabetes in Relation of Significant Experiences in Their Lives to the Onset and Course of the Disease.' *Psychosom. Med.*, **13,** 160.

— — — (1951b). 'Studies in Diabetes Mellitus. IV. Life History of Three Persons with Relatively Mild, Stable Diabetes, and Relation of Significant Experiences in Their Lives to the Onset and Course of the Disease.' *Psychosom. Med.*, **13,** 184.

— Fischer, A., Knowles, H. C., Jr. and Stunkard, A. J. (1959). 'Role of Environment and Personality in Management of the Difficult Patient with Diabetes Mellitus—A Panel Discussion.' *Diabetes*, **8,** 371.

— and Wolf, S. (1949). 'Experimental Study of Life Situations, Emotions, and the Occurrence of Acidosis in a Juvenile Diabetic.' *Am. J. med. Sci.*, **217,** 130.

— — (1952a). 'A Summary of Experimental Evidence Relating Life Stress to Diabetes Mellitus.' *J. Mt Sinai Hosp.*, **19.** 537.

— — (1952b). 'The Effects of Stressful Life Situations on the Concentration of Blood Glucose in Diabetic and Non-diabetic Humans.' *Diabetes*, **1,** 383.

Isenberg, P. L. and Barnett, D. M. (1965). 'Psychological Problems in Diabetes Mellitus.' *Med. Clins N. Am.*, **49,** 1125.

Kennedy, W. B. (1955). 'Psychologic Problems of the Young Diabetic.' *Diabetes*, **4,** 207.

Kubany, A. J., Danowski, T. S. and Moses, C. (1956). 'The Personality and Intelligence of Diabetics.' *Diabetes*, **5**, 462.

Larcan, A. (1966). 'Stress et diabète.' *Aggressologie*, **7**, 447.

Levi, L. (1961). 'A New Stress Tolerance Test with Simultaneous Study of Physiological and Psychological Variables.' *Acta Endocr.*, **37**, 38.

— (1967a). *Emotional Stress: Physiological and Psychological Reactions—Medical, Industrial, and Military Implications*. New York: Elsevier.

— (1967b). 'Sympatho-adrenomedullary Responses to Emotional Stimuli: Methodologic, Physiologic and Pathologic Considerations.' In *An Introduction To Clinical Neuroendocrinology*, Ed. by E. Bajusz. Basel: Karger.

Lindberg, B. J. (1936). 'Diabetic Psychosis.' *Acta psychiat.* (*Kbh.*), **11**, 267.

Lisansky, B. S. (1948). 'Convulsive Disorder and Personality.' *J. abnorm. Soc. Psychol.*, **43**, 29.

Menninger, W. C. (1935). 'The Interrelationship of Mental Disorders and Diabetes Mellitus.' *J. ment. Sci*, **81**, 332.

Minuchin, S. and Barcai, A. (1969). 'Therapeutically Induced Family Crises.' In *Science and Psychoanalysis*, Ed. by J. Massermann, Vol. 14. New York: Grune and Stratton.

Molnar, G. D. (1967). '"Brittle" Diabetes.' In *Diabetes Mellitus: Diagnosis And Treatment*, Ed. by G. J. Hamwi and T. S. Danowski, Vol 2. New York: American Diabetes Association.

Nabarro, J. D. N. (1965). 'Diabetic Acidosis: Clinical Aspects.' In *On The Nature And Treatment Of Diabetes*, Ed. by B. S. Leibel and G. A. Wrenshall. The Netherlands: Excerpta Medica Foundation.

Palmer, R. W. (1958). 'The Diabetic Personality.' *J. Indiana med. Ass.*, **51**, 1399.

Peck, F. B., Sr. and Peck, F. B., Jr. (1956). 'Tautologous Diabetic Coma—A Behaviour Syndrome.' *Diabetes*, **5**, 44.

Pinter, E. J., Peterfy, G., Cleghorn, J. M. and Pattee, C. J. (1967). 'The Influence of Emotional Stress on Fat Mobilization: The Role of Endogenous Catecholamines and the Beta Adrenergic Receptors.' *Am. J. med. Sci.*, **254**, 634.

Pitts, F. N., Jr. (1969). 'The Biochemistry of Anxiety.' *Scientific Am.*, **220**, 69.

— and McClure, J. M., Jr. (1967). 'Lactate Metabolism in Anxiety Neuroses.' *New Engl. J. Med.*, **277**, 1329.

Quichaud, J. (1963). 'Diabète sucré post-traumatique. Rôle de l'émotion dans son déclenchement.' *Ann. Med. Leg.* (*Paris*), **43**, 171.

Rosen, H. and Lidz, T. (1949). 'Emotional Factors in the Precipitation of Recurrent Diabetic Acidosis.' *Psychosom. Med.*, **11**, 211.

Schiff, L. J. (1964). 'Emotional Problems of Diabetic Children and Their Parents.' *Psychosomatics*, **5**, 362.

Schless, G. L. and von Laveran-Stiebar, R. (1964). 'Recurrent Episodes of Diabetic Acidosis Precipitated by Emotional Stress.' *Diabetes*, **13**, 419.

Schultz, R. (1969). Personal communication.

Sheppe, W. M. and Sheppe, W. M., Jr. (1954). 'The Psychogenic Problems of the Young Diabetic Patient.' *West Va med. J.*, **50**, 65.

Slawson, P. F. (1963). 'Emotional Factors in Repetitive Diabetic Acidosis.' *Psychosomatics*, **4**, **344**.

— Flynn, W. R. and Kollar, E. J. (1963). 'Psychological Factors Associated with the Onset of Diabetes Mellitus.' *J. Am. med. Ass.*, **185**, 166.

Starr, P. H. (1955), 'Psychosomatic Considerations of Diabetes in Childhood.' *J. nerv. ment. Dis.*, **121**, 493.

Sterns, S. (1959). 'Self-Destructive Behavior in Young Patients with Diabetes Mellitus.' *Diabetes*, **8**, 379.

Steinberg, D. and Vaughan, M. (1965). 'Release of Free Fatty Acids from Adipose Tissue *in vitro* in Relation to Rates of Triglyceride Synthesis and Degradation.' In *Handbook of Physiology*, Section 5: Adipose Tissue, Ed. by A. E. Renold and G. F. Cahill, Jr. Washington, D.C.: American Physiological Society.

Sterky, G. (1963). 'Family Background and State of Mental Health in a Group of Diabetic School Children.' *Acta paediat.*, **25**, 1.

Swift, C. R. and Seidman, F. (1964). 'Adjustment Problems of Juvenile Diabetes.' *J. Am. Acad. Child Psychiat.*, **3**, 500.

—— and Stein, H. (1967). 'Adjustment Problems in Juvenile Diabetes.' *Psychosom. Med.*, **29**, 555.

Treuting, T. F. (1962). 'The Role of Emotional Factors in the Etiology and Course of Diabetes Mellitus: A Review of the Recent Literature.' *Am. J. med. Sci.*, **244**, 93.

Vandenbergh, R. L., Sussman, K. E., and Titus, C. C. (1966). 'Effects of Hypnotically Induced Acute Emotional Stress on Carbohydrate and Lipid Metabolism in Patients with Diabetes Mellitus.' *Psychosom. Med.*, **28**, 382.

—— and Vaughan, G. D. (1967). 'Effects of Combined Physical-Anticipatory Stress on Carbohydrate-Lipid Metabolism in Patients with Diabetes Mellitus.' *Psychosomatics*, **8**, 16.

Wagner, R. (1952). 'Problems in Juvenile Diabetes Mellitus.' *J. Mt. Sinai Hosp.*, **19**, 249.

Werner, S. (1969) Personal communication.

Wertheimer, H. E. (1965). 'Introduction—A Perspective.' In *Handbook of Physiology*, Section 5: Adipose Tissue, Ed. by A. E. Renold and G. F. Cahill, Jr. Washington, D.C.: American Physiological Society.

CHAPTER 8

PSYCHOLOGICAL ASPECTS OF SOME DISORDERS OF WEIGHT

A. H. CRISP

INTRODUCTION

Over the centuries clinicians, novelists and playwrights have tended to identify and characterize the fat person with certain personality traits. More recently medical investigators have systematically identified a 'fat' factor associated with the endomorphic body build and with cyclothymic personality characteristics and a propensity for manic depressive illness. Also during this century, developmental psychopathologists, especially of the Freudian and Kleinian schools, have drawn attention to the mother–infant feeding relationship and the implications of its outcome for similar subsequent psychological characteristics and morbidity and also for certain feeding disorders (Winnicot, 1958).

It is less clear, although possible, that such observations have a partial and useful bearing on the variety of conditions seen in everyday medical practice and subsumed under the terms 'obesity' and 'anorexia nervosa', where the individual, if he becomes a patient, presents with the disorder of weight and its complications rather than directly with some psychiatric disorder. This chapter concerns itself with these two syndromes. Following some initial reference to biochemical and metabolic aspects, the reader will be referred elsewhere for more detailed information and the metabolic parameters will only thereafter be mentioned insofar as clinical, epidemiological and psychopathological factors are thought to illuminate the controversy over their relationship to the development of the disorders.

OBESITY

Obesity is a common state involving an excessive accumulation of fat usually leading to the individual's being overweight and associated with a variety of syndromes and complications. It is probable that multiple factors influence its development, even when a specific identified propensity exists such as for late onset diabetes, the inherited presence of glycerokinase or the existence of a discrete hypothalamic lesion (Mayer, 1966). Such multiple factors may vary between obese individuals and in any one individual over the course of time. In the majority of obese individuals, more so in some than others, there exists other characteristic metabolic and physical abnormalities which can often be seen to influence current body metabolism in the direction of generating obesity, but where it is also likely that they themselves have been generated or modified by the past nutritional behaviour of the individual from the time of his birth or conception. Such behaviour is likely itself to have been subject to multiple genetic, constitutional and experiential factors. When all such factors as these, related to the chronicity of the obesity (Fellner and Levitt, 1964; Mayer, 1964; Pawan, 1964, 1963), patterns of activity and heat loss (Miller, 1967), periodicity of eating (Fabry *et al.*, 1964), number of body fat cells (Sinclair, 1967) and gastro-intestinal absorptive characteristics have been identified and taken into account, it becomes true that fatness will increase if calorie intake is in excess of calorie expenditure. It therefore becomes important from the psychosomatic standpoint to examine psychosocial and psychoneurotic factors associated with acute and chronic obesity and its familial aspects, levels of activity, periodicity of eating, excessive food intake and, finally, the implications of ongoing obesity in terms of the way in which it may variously and perhaps increasingly meet the psychopathological needs of the individual himself.

Cultural and Familial Aspects

Nearly a century ago the probable major impact of 'good' nutrition on body build and weight was suggested by the finding that second generation immigrants to the U.S.A. whatever their racial origins, were often more similar in terms of their size and weight to the population mean than to their parental racial group. It is now estimated that about 10 per cent of children in the U.S.A. are obese if neither of their parents is fat. If one or both parents are fat then the figures rise to 40 and 80 per cent respectively. In slightly less prosperous Europe the figures are less, but the familial association is still quite evident. Thus Quaade (1955), in his major epidemiological study of childhood obesity in Copenhagen, found that about 11 per cent of children of obese mothers and 8 per cent of children of obese fathers were themselves obese, compared with less than 4 per cent of children who were obese if the parents were thin. He defined obesity in a statistical sense as including all those children whose largeness as measured by a weight–height index was greater than two standard deviations above the mean (he found the index to be relatively normally distributed in his population).

Other workers have attempted to define independent categories of acute and chronic obesity. More often than not obesity has been present from childhood although it can present for the first time in adolescence or later. Acute episodes can occur and have been described by Shorvon and Richardson (1949) but in the majority of cases the disorder presents a history of chronicity, sometimes with phases of more acute weight gain at such times as puberty, marriage and marital stress, pregnancy, puerperium and the menopause.

It is evident that large babies at birth are more likely than average sized and small babies to become large children and to grow more rapidly and to be obese adolescents and adults (Quaade, 1955; Mossberg, 1949; Crisp, 1965; Crisp *et al.*, 1970). The importance of genetics together with intra-uterine factors in determining adult weight has been shown by Shields (1962), who reports that monozygotic twins reared apart are closer in body weight than dizygotic twins reared together. Crisp (1966a, 1970a and b), in a study of factors influencing birth weight, has shown that direct genetic factors are not the only determinant and that maternal feeding habits and their neurotic determinants during pregnancy are an influential factor. Sinclair (1967) has suggested that the fixed number of fat cells which an individual is destined to thereafter possess, is determined during intra-uterine life. Thus the 'obese' baby is born with a propensity for obesity, sometimes already reflecting maternal and perhaps marital and family neurotic or reality related problems and insecurities, sometimes specific to the baby and already having been construed and dealt with by the mother or the family in nurturent terms.

Such family behaviour may be perpetuated during the infant's childhood. Quaade found that cultural and family neurotic attitudes in the families of obese children often centred around the high value they placed on food. The mothers of these families characteristically denied that their obese children were obese and such families were also characterized by the family's capacity and need always to eat all the food provided and to leave a clean plate at the end of the meal. Crisp (1969) has drawn attention to feeding patterns in the first year of life and the possibility that an uninterrupted feeding pattern such as either prolonged breast feeding or else bottle feeding *ab initio* during this period may be another factor setting the child's 'appestat' at a critical time and thereby influencing subsequent nutritional needs and feeding behaviour. Such mother–infant feeding patterns will also sometimes reflect and generate neurotic interactions, serving to endorse any emerging constitutional propensity for over-nutrition.

The psychosomatic study of obesity has often been complicated by the problems of selectivity in the hospital populations under study, whether in medical or psychiatric departments. For instance, it is quite clear that the majority of obese individuals do not seek treatment on account of their obesity or of psychological disturbance, although they are very likely as they pass through middle age to suffer increasingly from the complications of obesity which may then precipitate their presentation to doctors (Kemp, 1967). The epidemiological approach has therefore been essential to complement the extensive clinic observations of workers such as Bruch (1957). Thus Quaade (1955), in his epidemiological study, considered that intra-family neurotic factors in terms of identifiable psychoneurotic disability were only present in about 15 per cent of his population of obese children. Psychoneurotic character structure or ongoing inter-personal crises not giving rise to psychoneurotic disability but instead being dealt with by nurturent means within the family might be more difficult to examine, and could of course have existed unidentified in Quaade's study. Recently Silverstone and Solomon (1966), in another study covering two general practices in North London, used the psychiatric sections of the Cornell Medical Index as a measure and found evidence of 'neuroticism' in about one-third of a group of obese women attending a general practitioner clinic. However, once again, this measure was aimed at psychoneurotic behaviour rather than other forms of psychopathology. These workers defined obesity as a state of being 30 per cent or more above the ideal weight for height and sex. In a further epidemiological study Silverstone (1968) found obesity to be significantly more common in women than in men in middle age, at which time it was a feature of nearly 40 per cent of the female population and somewhat less than 20 per cent of the male population. This distinction was sharpened even more when social class factors were taken into account, obesity being particularly characteristic of women in the lower social classes.

In summary then it is likely that multiple genetic, cultural and neurotic factors operate within families and mingle over time as influences in the development of childhood obesity, such influences varying quantitatively between individuals and in the same individual over time.

Activity

Activity is once more being recognized as a major factor influencing body weight and composition. For many years now Mayer

(1953) has expressed the view that inactivity may well be an important premorbid feature of children and adults who become obese. On the basis of his animal laboratory studies he attributed such inactivity mainly to genetic factors. More recently (Mayer, 1964, 1966) he has been less emphatic on this point and it appears likely that, once again, such premorbid states of inactivity have multiple origins—genetic, metabolic, psychosocial and psychoneurotic. For instance, inactivity may come to characterize the non-obese child as a defensive posture against shyness, social anxiety, undue sensitivity, inferiority feelings, etc. If his state thereby becomes that much more readily compounded by obesity because of secondary familial nurturent factors of one kind or another then his social difficulties may be enhanced and his emotional development further stifled. In adults Stunkard (1957, 1958) has drawn attention to the factor of premorbid depression and its concomitant of inactivity as a contributory factor to the development, perpetuation or worsening of obesity.

Meanwhile, there is considerable clinical evidence that inactivity is a striking feature of established obesity. Such inactivity may reflect the neurotic or sensitive obese person's increasing need to withdraw from society. The burden of additional weight that he has to carry around will present complex mechanical difficulties inclining him to avoid being active. Inactivity may also be an inherent aspect of the physiological state of adiposity and is often clearly an immediately postprandial feature in many people. So far as the latter matter is concerned, however, it is evident that many inactive obese people whose weight is stable eat very sparingly. Crisp (1967a) has contrasted the non-sexual hyperactivity of anorexia nervosa patients with the more generally reduced activity of the obese, especially the massively obese. He found this latter group currently to report significantly less sexual activity than a control group when comparing the two groups at the times before and after the onset of the massive obesity in the probands. He suggested that this might have a mixed biological and neurotic basis and be meeting marital and other inter-personal neurotic needs in some instances. Bruch (1964), more than anyone else, has drawn attention to the probably great significance of inactivity in obese children. She states 'such children consistently over-eat and this, together with their passive, inactive way of life, represents a protection against more severe mental illness. Obesity serves as an alibi for the avoidance of threatening and unacceptable social demands and food indulgence permits the experience of at least a semblance of satisfaction in an otherwise dismal existence.'

In conclusion inactivity appears as a frequent accompaniment of obesity and may often significantly precede it. It is likely to be one other factor, having itself multiple determinants, and contributing to both the genesis, perpetuation and reinforcement of obese states.

Periodicity of Eating

There is evidence that the same amount of food eaten at less frequent intervals leads to a greater increase in body weight both in man and animals (Cohn and Joseph, 1960; Okey, Scheier and Reed, 1960; Gwinup *et al.*, 1963; Fabry *et al.*, 1964; Pawan, 1967). This is plausible when viewed from a biological standpoint, the body metabolism ensuring maximal utilization and hence also storage as fat of a larger residue of food when subjected to and threatened by longer intervals of abstinence and hence relative starvation.

Obese patients display a wide variety and sometimes bizarre pattern of eating, ranging from constant nibbling to phases of prolonged abstinence, alternating with bulimic episodes, such patterns sometimes alternating in one individual over the course of time and often being as skilfully concealed as are the drug addict's ingestive habits. Others, especially obese adolescent girls, are prone to so-called 'compulsive' eating or more accurately the inability effectively to resist the impulse to over-eat. The occasions when this impulse becomes overwhelming tend to be those when they are feeling anxious or sad and when they are alone, especially at weekends and in the late evening—the night eating syndrome first described by Stunkard, Grace and Wolff (1955). Such behaviour also both precedes and emerges within the convalescent phase in roughly half the patients who have anorexia nervosa. In other women it is clear (Bruce and Russell, 1962) that weight gain as a feature of their premenstrual tension syndrome mainly has a similar basis. Crisp (1967a) has speculated on the metabolic basis for such 'compulsive' and 'addictive' behaviour in relation to carbohydrate.

Meanwhile, in terms of the metabolic substrate of such behaviours, it appears that the body's metabolism and metabolic responses are very sensitive to changes in dietary pattern, certainly in terms of carbohydrate and fat metabolism in relation to changes of carbohydrate intake (Hales and Randle, 1963b; Crisp, Ellis and Lowry, 1967; Crisp and Stonehill, 1967; Blendis and Crisp, 1968; Crisp, Blendis and Pawan, 1968; Crisp, 1970c; Mishkel, 1968).

Individual Psychopathology

Feeding behaviour is known to be governed by cerebral centres of organization in the hypothalamus and visceral brain. Discrete lesions in these or related sites (e.g. brain damage stemming from trauma, tumour, anoxia, leucotomy operations, etc.) can lead to disorders of feeding and weight, including obesity. For further information of this aspect the reader is referred to reviews by Anand (1961) and Russell (1968).

At the same time it is difficult to provide any comprehensive view of individual dynamic psychopathology. As previously stated obesity is commonplace in the general population and we know very little concerning the possible extent of its neurotic basis in this population. It will be recalled that Quaade found evidence, at interview, of neurotic factors present in a minority of his cases and families under epidemiological study. Moreover, such neuroticism may not always have led to the development of the obesity, nor is it evidently specific to obesity. In some instances it may have been intensified by the obesity; it may be a relatively independent factor but making it more likely that the patient will seek help from doctors and others, thus leading to the over-representation of neurotic factors associated with obesity in the medical clinic. However, others claim that the aetiological neurotic difficulties of the obese are of a characterological and inter-personal rather than individual neurotic behavioural kind, often including the patient's neurotic denial of emotional difficulties, and not being readily accessible to interview techniques and questionnaire methods. Such diversity of opinion is revealed once again, comparing Silverstone's findings, referred to earlier, together with Simon's (1963) findings in which he found reduced depressive illness amongst a 'healthy' and uncomplaining obese army population compared with a comparable non-obese population, with the findings of most other workers (Bruch, 1957; Stunkard, 1957; Fellner and Levitt, 1964; Werkman and Greenberg, 1965), who report an increased prevalence of psychiatric morbidity and emotional problems amongst obese people who, however, have often been medical clinic attenders. At the same time one is reminded of the known link between manic depressive psychosis and the endomorphic or pyknic body build (Mayer-Gross, Slater and Roth, 1960) which clearly overlaps with the state of obesity.

Despite such complexities, many investigators have attempted synthesizing and global theories aimed at accounting in dynamic psychopathological terms for the generation of obesity through the interaction of abnormal and neurotic feeding habits and other family neurotic mechanisms. In particular Bruch has drawn attention to the guilty provision of excessive food to the young child by its mother or mother-surrogate as a substitute for her love and affection, which is lacking or unavailable because of her strong though sometimes unrecognized feelings of hostility, rejection, or ambivalence towards the child. Such feelings may themselves clearly have many origins reflecting such factors as the mother's and father's individual psychopathologies, the state of their marriage and the factors leading to the conception of this particular child. Certainly one sees children often enough given food as a solace when they are angry or miserable and also as a reward when they have been helpful or compliant. It seems plausible then that some such children might grow up prizing food more than human relationships. At the same time many people set great store by food as a source of strength and well being; the opposite of weakness, wasting, disease and death. Doctors have often endorsed this attitude with their concern for 'good' feeding and weight gain in the children attending their post-natal clinics. Such attitudes probably also contribute to the popular though so often false (Werkman and Greenberg, 1965) cultural and literary image of the obese person as being confident, reliable, jolly and, so to speak, super-stable.

One ambitious attempt at classification of psychopathology in terms of family dynamics was that by Frazier *et al.* (1955). In a clinical and psychodynamically oriented study of obese and skinny children and their parents, these workers claimed to recognize five specific patterns of family interaction: (1) The non-neurotic but 'culturally' fat family. (2) The skinny neurotic mother who views her child ambivalently and defensively, over-feeds her and renders her obese. (3) The obese neurotic mother who views her child ambivalently and denies it food because of her own need for it and renders the child skinny. (4) Families where mutual ambivalence and guilt for eating is associated with peptic ulceration. (5) Where the neurotic, predominantly critical mother symbolically withholds food and precipitates anorexia nervosa in the child. In the clinical situation it is certainly sometimes evident where a patient has lost weight with anorexia nervosa that those in the family around her have gained a roughly corresponding amount of weight through her devotion to feeding them up whilst, conversely, when an obese patient, especially from a parental home, comes into hospital for prolonged treatment and loses weight, then not infrequently the mother left behind in the home gains a considerable and sometimes comparable amount of weight (Crisp and Stonehill, 1970). Meanwhile, Stunkard (1958) has drawn attention, as previously stated, to depression as a premorbid feature of some patients, possibly predetermining their obesity. In this connection it is noteworthy that whilst the majority of depressed patients lose weight, a minority gain weight excessively even sometimes to the extent of developing a syndrome of over-weight and hypersomnia which becomes difficult to distinguish from the so-called Kleine-Levin syndrome. Crisp (1967b) has emphasized the differences between childhood feeding disorders and adult disorders of weight, suggesting that, during adolescence, the factor of weight or abnormal weight takes on increasing significance for the individual, sometimes overriding the neurotic significance of food and eating. Thus, the adolescent girl in particular may find herself comforting herself by over-eating, precipitating herself into progressive obesity and thereby merely generating or worsening her sensitive feelings of insecurity and inferiority for which she increasingly blames her obese appearance. In the clinic at least, obese adolescents often show evidence of psycho-sexual immaturity and present major 'identity' problems. Additionally, massive obesity often comes eventually to be associated with sexual inactivity which may be rewarding for some as a neurotic solution to their other emotional difficulties. As the obese person ages, consequences of such unresolved problems are likely to become multiplied and increasingly entrenched.

Finally, there is the vexed question of whether or not an excessive amount of psychiatric morbidity is precipitated by attempts at weight loss by the obese population especially in the (enforced) treatment situation. As previously mentioned, Bruch (1957) has described a sub-group of obese subjects who develop severe depressive states when dieting and/or losing weight, whilst Stunkard (1957), working in a nutritional clinic in the U.S.A., found that 54 per cent of 72 obese subjects who attempted to lose weight by dieting reported untoward emotional reactions. In a co-study he found that 9 out of 25 obese subjects subjected to weight reduction programmes became severely depressed. He emphasized the difficulties of drawing conclusions concerning causality of obesity from such observations. Reference has also already been made to the report by Silverstone and Solomon (1966), in which they concluded that only one-third of 31 obese women, who were attending a general practitioner and agreed to treatment, aimed at reducing their weight, showed evidence of being 'neurotic'. These patients were treated with a restricted diet for one year. The authors claim that no untoward emotional reactions were detected during this time, in which the non-neurotic patients who continued to attend lost an average of 30 lb. in weight and the neurotic patients 10 lb. in weight. However, this follow-up was incomplete and referred to only about half of the original patient group. Meanwhile, Crisp (1967a) has emphasized that, while psychiatric morbidity in the form of illness may not emerge during weight reduction, when massively obese patients attempt to lose weight down to truly normal levels and approach these levels, then characterological and inter-personal problems arise or sometimes re-emerge and which are of such intensity that relapse is inevitable. For example, increased sexual activity sometimes occurs under such circumstances in a way which cannot be tolerated by the individual or those with whom he or she is involved. At other times the barrenness of the individual's life situation has become increasingly and intolerably self-evident to them.

Treatment

Within this brief survey there is little space to comment on the vast literature concerned with treatment of obesity. The relevant psychotherapeutic literature, including reports of studies where psychotherapy has been combined with dietetic treatment, has been reviewed recently by Chesser (1969) and also referred to by Crisp (1967a) and Crisp and Stonehill (1970). Overall, the evidence is that the condition is often resistant to the most intensive forms of treatment and even if considerable weight loss is achieved in the short term. The natural history of the condition includes a pattern of spontaneous remission in a small number of obese patients. Anecdotal reports of long-term recovery in relation to treatment must therefore be regarded with caution, especially since it may be such a sub-group of individuals who are motivated to seek out treatment. It may also be that this group of individuals demonstrate, by their capacity to recover, either a relative absence of or their increased capacity to cope with associated neurotic factors. Psychotherapeutic treatment alone rarely seems to become associated with weight loss but often appears to lead to the patient becoming better adjusted to their obesity and to an improvement in their existing personal relationships and life situation. Perhaps the most promising therapeutic regime is a combined one in which extensive restriction of dietary intake over a prolonged period of time, at least a year, and probably requiring hospitalization, is combined with psychotherapy aimed at helping the patient to make the new kind of adjustment made necessary by the physical change in herself. This is not a form of treatment which can be made available to everyone with obesity. In the writer's view it is likely that age will prove to be an important factor influencing response to treatment. The young, socially uncommitted person is likely to do best.

Conclusion

It seems likely that multiple cultural and psychoneurotic factors influence the course of obesity, varying in importance between individuals and in the same individual over the passage of time. The varieties of possible interplay between the individual's lifetime of experiences affecting his emotional development on the one hand and his feeding habits and metabolic status on the other, appear to be innumerable. It is probable, therefore, that no one factor other than perhaps the more basic cultural overtones and significance of food as a factor in human survival, can be safely and generically ascribed to the developmental psychopathology of obesity. For the latter one must also search in the individual patient for such factors as the other meanings of food, physical appearance, biological and inter-personal activities of various kinds and their coming together and compounding over the years. The identification of accessible and reversible neurotic factors within this pathology will often be the first task of treatment for the patient with established obesity. Other than this we must hope for increasing help from the public health and preventative medicine field; offering help to families who seek it, at the earliest possible stages in their committal to succouring children.

ANOREXIA NERVOSA

In contrast to obesity, anorexia nervosa is a rare condition, especially in the clinic. Nevertheless it has always excited wide clinical interest. This report is concerned with primary anorexia nervosa or weight phobia and not with the larger and more diffuse field of 'nervous malnutrition' (Bliss and Branch, 1960). Primary anorexia nervosa usually has the characteristics of this latter syndrome, namely features of reduced food intake, low weight, accompanying reduced metabolic activity and increased motor restlessness. It is further characterized by its occurring mainly in adolescent females who have initially restricted carbohydrate from their diet in a more universal wish to slim in a culturally fashionable and acceptable way. Subsequently, however, they have come to almost totally avoid such foods within the context of an increasing concern and need to lose weight down to abnormally low levels and an associated and increasing fear and sense of desperation whenever they do eat and thereby gain any small amount of weight. Menstrual bleeding always ceases. Such patients can no longer contemplate and accept the prospect of restoration of weight back to normal adolescent levels. The proposition frightens or disgusts them and the danger of it leads them to deceive those around them ingeniously. Thus others may not be aware of their concern about their weight and they may successfully conceal much of the above behaviour even from those with whom they are living. They rarely wish to change and seldom seek help.

At a metabolic level the patient's condition is characterized by the consequences of severe carbohydrate starvation and the bizarre periodicity and patterns of eating other foods. Sometimes, and usually later on, the condition can become further complicated by periodic eating of carbohydrate and inter-related patterns of total abstinence or excessive vomiting and purging behaviour. The evolution of these patterns of behaviour has been described in more detail elsewhere (Crisp, 1967b, 1970c).

Our present knowledge of the natural history of the condition merits some attention being paid to premorbid features. Thus there is no evidence that the disorder is related to psychotic illness but some evidence that psychoneurotic illness occurs more commonly than usual in the families of these patients. The disorder itself cannot usefully be construed in terms of conventional psychoneurotic classifications although, psychopathologically speaking, perhaps Crighton-Miller (1938) has come closest when describing it as a 'partial suicide', whilst Crisp (1967b) has attempted to define it in terms of a phobic avoidance response of normal adolescent weight inspired by the progressive psychobiological effects of the over-determined dieting behaviour. Bruch (1966) has recently termed it 'pursuit of thinness'. There is some agreement that a significant number of these patients reveal a history of some degree of obesity immediately premorbidly. It also seems that 'oral' behaviour of a variety of kinds characterizes the families—more than usual involvement in the nurturent professions, alcoholism, obesity, drug dependence, and primary anorexia nervosa itself. Nevertheless, evidence to date does not suggest that the actual development of anorexia nervosa has any simple genetic basis (Crisp, 1969a). Furthermore, many patients with anorexia nervosa do not provide family histories of the above kinds.

The final common clinically evident pathway to the disorder appears to be dieting behaviour, although this may later be vigorously denied by the patient. Perhaps it is on this account that the obese population are significantly highly represented in the families of anorexia nervosa patients and in the premorbid state of the patients themselves. Thus, the patients themselves tend to be similar to an obese population in terms of high birth weight and high growth rate although once again these characteristics are by no means necessary for the condition to develop. It is likely that they represent one of the possible complex psychosomatic predeterminants in primary anorexia nervosa.

Kay and Leigh (1954), who reported from their systematic study the high incidence of psychoneurotic illness in the families of anorexia nervosa patients, also reported a high incidence of reported childhood neurotic disorder, feeding and weight disorder, in their probands. However, other authors (Crisp, 1965b; Dally, 1969; Warren, 1968) have been equally struck by the reported absence of childhood neurotic behaviour in their patients who have instead been described as being 'compliant, good children', although often ultra-sensitive, shy, socially anxious and lacking in confidence. This trait cluster is similar to that described by Bruch (1964) in her reported study of obese children.

Crisp has also attempted to identify the psychopathological determinants of anorexia nervosa in terms of the family psychodynamics. He has found a variety of disturbed family relationships (*see* p. 141) not specific to the condition but commonly found in the whole range of adolescent disorders and ill health. The family psychopathology then may usefully be examined in terms of its relationship to the patient as an adolescent. The origins of the specific disorder (in this case anorexia nervosa) in those adolescents who prove vulnerable appears to depend upon 'organ vulnerability' or specific 'behaviour patterns', perhaps laid down in earlier life and which may or may not have a developmental interaction with the family psychodynamics. This takes one into the arena of complex interacting genetico-experiential factors and their multifactorial relationships and contribution to specific 'choice' of disease in later life. The writer (Crisp 1966a) has attempted to present his views on this relationship in many patients who present with primary anorexia nervosa, in greater detail elsewhere.

Our views on the natural history of the disorder (*Figure 1*) are probably coloured by the marked tendency for only the most ill patients to be referred to the clinic. Whilst this may be a universal tendency with disease it is particularly marked in this condition. Many patients recover spontaneously without being brought to the clinic and sometimes without their parents or other family knowing that they have been ill. In such cases it may be a schoolteacher who has observed the condition in passing or else it is revealed later in life as part of the patient's history when she presents on some other account. Even amongst these patients who are referred for treatment the majority will completely recover from their anorexia nervosa in later life (Crisp, 1968a; Seidensticker and Tzagournis, 1968). However, some of these will have other illnesses possibly related to their ongoing, unaltered psychopathology. Others will not recover, and most investigators (Crisp 1965a; Dally, 1967; Farquherson and Hyland, 1966; Kay and Leigh, 1954; Seidensticker and Tzagournis, 1968) report a 5–15 per cent mortality in their follow-up studies.

Such patients are usually those who have been ill for five years or more, often much longer. Death is usually from direct suicide or inanition with or without severe metabolic derangement. These patients tend to be those who have failed to respond to repeated attempts at medical treatment and who may have defied diagnosis. At this stage, therefore, it is appropriate to consider the differential diagnosis and the complexities brought to it by the severe secondary metabolic derangements (referred to in detail elsewhere—Crisp, 1969d), especially when the patient is denying and concealing the origins of these. First, the distinction between the condition and Simmond's disease is simple enough on physical examination alone.

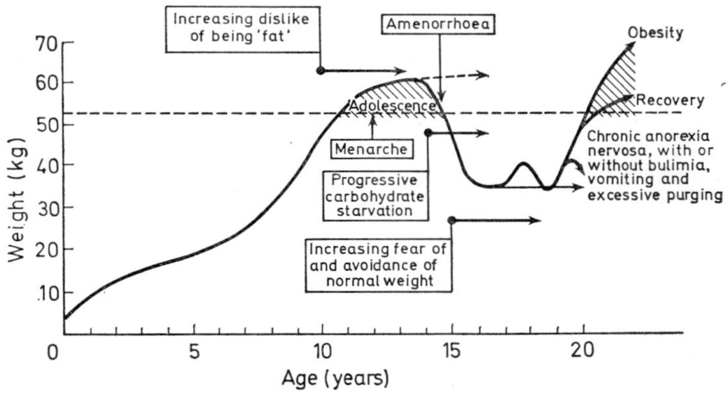

MTPM (8·1)

Figure 1. Some typical developments found in a series of 82 patients with primary anorexia nervosa or weight phobia

Reproduced by courtesy of the Editor of *Hospital Medicine*

Patients with anorexia nervosa are usually emaciated, hirsute, restless and show marked poor peripheral circulation as well as general hypometabolism. The condition is much more difficult to recognize when it masquerades under one of its prominent or revealed symptoms in the general medical clinic, usually as unexplained diarrhoea (secret purgation), abdominal pain, vomiting, amenorrhoea, hirsutes, chilblains, or periodic oedema. Patients with anorexia nervosa have undergone appendicectomy significantly more often than other comparable subjects. A low basal metabolic rate and bradycardia, combined with a high serum cholesterol level have sometimes wrongly focused attention on thyroid activity as a possible primary aetiological factor. When the patient has been secretly overeating and presents with breathlessness, sweating, tachycardia, a racing pulse, a bitter complaint of feeling overwhelmingly hungry and shows an inflated BMR then the condition may be initially difficult to distinguish from thyrotoxicosis. Such patients may have gained 10 kg. or more in weight within a few days. Disorders of fluid balance may become profound as the condition progresses and become complicated by the effects of general starvation, punctuated by periodic and sometimes secret carbohydrate binges, vomiting, excessive purging and, occasionally, secret polydipsia deriving from the patient's frantic efforts to assuage her desire to eat. At the height of the disorder symptomatic high normal levels of plasma cortisol and androgens accompanied by a low urinary output of steroid degradation substances, and, in conjunction with amenorrhoea, hirsutes and denial of other symptoms and behavioural disturbances, may focus the doctor's attention predominantly on the adrenal function. In the presence of excessive vomiting and purgation hypokalaemia may specifically claim the doctor's attention. Such patients sometimes appear to be able to tolerate remarkably low levels of serum potassium, in the range 1–2 mEquiv./100 ml., perhaps through the processes of adaptation over the years.

The illness may also be difficult to recognize in the psychiatric clinic where it can present as a periodic disturbance in which the patient becomes intensely distressed, ashamed of herself, convinced that she is pregnant, and is sometimes suicidal, in association with bouts of fluid retention. Such cases may be difficult to distinguish from and perhaps blend into those periodic psychoses described as having similar manifestations but without an evident underlying disorder of weight at the psychopathological level. The disorder may present to the psychiatrist with its affective or obsessional features together with hyperactivity to the fore, and diagnostic attention, especially when denial and secretive behaviour are a feature of the patient's state, is diverted towards these aspects. Those chronic patients who have progressed to a state of over-eating and vomiting not infrequently appear to become dominated by 'oral' behaviour and may sometimes present with alcoholism. It is this group too who contribute mainly to the 10 per cent incidence of clinical epilepsy in this condition. Such epilepsy appears to be related to features of chronicity and severe electrolyte depletion; also possibly to the withdrawal effects of barbiturates prescribed symptomatically for the condition and frequently vomited up. Although such epilepsy appears to be secondary to the metabolic upheaval, a small part of the EEG abnormalities and propensity for clinical epilepsy which these patients display appears to be a more prevailing characteristic. For instance EEG spike and wave phenomena characterized an identical twin pair discordant for anorexia nervosa (Crisp, Fenton and Scotton, 1968).

Occasionally the disorder presents with its social accompaniments and complications to the fore. The younger patient brought up to the clinic by her parents or the chronically ill patient now bereft of her parents, presents with problems of social isolation and incapacity any longer to work or fend for herself. A common feature of such patients is the absence of sexual interest or activity but a few, usually those who over-eat and vomit and whose weight fluctuates, are sporadically sexually active and sometimes promiscuous. Once again, if the patient's concealment of her abnormal feeding behaviour is successful, the underlying disorder may escape recognition.

TREATMENT

Patients precipitated into hospital by an acute medical crisis require immediate medical attention. For instance, if the patient arrives weak and semi-comatose weighing say, 30 kg., in a state of extreme hypometabolism, with a body temperature several degrees below normal, she has often been totally without carbohydrate intake for several weeks. It may then be primarily important to provide her with intravenous carbohydrate, cautiously administered by drip. At the same time the electrolytic state and fluid balance may require expert medical attention. Epilepsy may need to be brought symptomatically under control at the same time by anti-convulsant treatment provided the sedative effect is not overwhelming. As soon as possible, tube feeding should be established. However, it should be remembered that these patients show abnormality of gastric function; often reduced function and occasionally acute gastric dilatation (Crisp, 1968b; Russell, 1966). Pyrexia, lymphocytosis and diarrhoea are amongst the transitory physiological response to restoration of feeding.

There is no one agreed form of longer term treatment. In the author's view psychotherapy in isolation is probably not helpful and can be dangerous, leading to unnecessary perpetuation of the phobic disorder and sometimes worsening of the condition. Equally, isolated restoration of weight, either partially or completely is rarely helpful unless the patient is on the brink of spontaneous recovery. Indeed, precipitation back into a state of normal weight is likely to reinforce the patient's need to be under-weight and she is anyway unlikely to allow such a thing to happen, discharging herself from hospital well beforehand. The author has developed a treatment regime whereby the patient is brought into hospital and subjected to strict control, e.g. complete bed rest; firmness over eating a normal diet (i.e. about

2,500–3,000 calories and containing adequate carbohydrate). She is not allowed to eat more than the prescribed diet—a control she sometimes welcomes since it is often her fear that, like the alcoholic, if she once starts eating she will not be able to stop. She is likely to have to stay totally in bed for the first eight to ten weeks, this being followed by a period of progressive mobilization whilst she learns that she can be normally active, eat sensibly and maintain a steady weight. During this first period she will gain weight at the rate of about 2 kg. a week. She will have been told firmly before admission that the initial aim is to restore her weight to a specific level—the population mean for her height and sex at the age at which she fell ill, not her present age. Furthermore that, as she is gradually re-exposed to this weight and its implications (they will include the 'pubertal' processes of re-emergence of gonadotropic activity—Russell *et al.* (1965)—and the associated re-kindling of her adolescent biological self and its psycho-social implications for her), the doctor's psychotherapeutic concern will be to help her to begin to cope with her emerging difficulties and to deal with them differently this time. Such psychotherapy has as its theoretical basis the need that the patient has to be helped literally to 'grow up'. Clearly since the patient has failed to achieve this previously and has needed instead to regress back into psychobiological childhood, the task may be a major if not an insuperable one in the more severely ill patients. If the therapist allows himself to become concerned with only his patient's psychopathology then he may find himself involved in a major 'transference' orientated psychotherapy and possibly an evidently hopeless task. It is therefore important to explore the possibilities, when the patient is still adolescent in chronological age and living at home or with strong parental home links, of helping the patient's parents and thereby helping them to help the patient. In this connection it has not infrequently appeared to be the case that the overwhelming threat to the patient precipitating her illness was the prospect that her parents were waiting for her to show evidence of maturity and independence in her adolescence so that they could separate. Often such parents had dutifully and painfully waited for this occasion for years. Sometimes the patient's very conception and existence reflected a desperate and at the time successful attempt by one of the parents to secure the marriage which would otherwise have probably broken up. Under such circumstances the overt hostility and rejection from the other parent was sometimes formidable. In other instances adoptive parents were finding themselves unable to cope with their (illegitimate) adopted daughters once they had reached adolescence. Such adoptive parents were usually in unconsummated marriages, having failed to make any sort of adolescent sexual adjustment themselves. In other family situations the patient has been unable to cope with her emergent adolescent needs, increasingly conflicting with strict moralistic parental attitudes. Sometimes this situation was complicated by major oedipal conflicts in the patient which had been resolved for her once her illness had developed, at least in their genital form, but which on restoration of weight could once again be seen to be influencing her adolescent sexual needs and forays.

Sometimes such family situations lent themselves to psychotherapeutic help. The parents could be assisted occasionally merely by clarification of the problem and sympathetic help, to support their daughter for a little longer whilst she attempted to find her feet. At other times subconscious or conscious hostility, resentment and bitterness towards the patient from one or other or both parents or a combination of excessive and seductive over-protection by one and jealousy and rejection by the other was too overwhelmingly fixed and established for it to be possible to usefully intervene at that level. In some patients the introjected family psychopathology was clearly evident, with the patient feeling intense fear, guilt and shame about her adolescent temptations and behaviour. Certainly with greater chronicity of the condition patients increasingly focused their attention upon such areas, especially in relationship to pregnancy and their dislike and disgust of their own bodies. Other patients who had always been exceptionally diffident, socially anxious and reluctant to explore during childhood, had merely found that the extra demands of adolescence had been the overwhelming factor and appeared doomed to lead a restricted life. More often than not, however, it was the patient's conflicting and ambivalent attitude to adolescent activity rather than her capacity contentedly to avoid it and be a non-participant, which was the striking feature. Other older and more chronically ill patients present special difficulties for treatment. Those who have been ill for as much as 10 years or more often find it very difficult to tolerate the treatment regime just described. Usually a more modest goal of trying to help them survive, albeit at an abnormally low weight, is all that should be aimed at. Too much enforced weight gain can precipitate severe depression or suicide in this group. Particularly difficult to help are those patients who have married subsequent to developing their anorexia nervosa, thereby achieving a limited social and inter-personal adjustment often demanding that they remain unchanged. The risks of leucotomy as a treatment measure have been referred to elsewhere (Crisp, 1967b).

In this range of descriptive psychopathology, so far no reference has been made to the 10 per cent of patients who are male. In the writer's experience the factors leading to the disorder in males are not strikingly different from those in females except that in about 50 per cent of the male patients he has seen the immediate adolescent sexual conflict preceding the disorder was in the realm of homosexual activity. Whereas the female adolescent is vulnerable to having her future blighted by the risks of heterosexual activity, perhaps homosexual activity in the male in adolescence is the closest that he comes to risking similar social sanctions. Other than this factor it has been suggested that factors accounting for the relative rarity of the condition in males might include the relative absence of dieting behaviour in adolescent males and also the slower rates of growth to which they are subjected and the consequent relative absence of adolescent obesity and puppy fat.

CONCLUSION

Primary anorexia nervosa is a rare and often clearly definable condition which has attracted wide clinical interest. It remains a major clinical challenge. It is evidently an important potential source of metabolic research work, especially in the field of carbohydrate and lipid metabolism.

Recently several reports have appeared of studies of large series of patients with primary anorexia nervosa. Some agreement has been reached that the disorder cannot usefully be construed in conventional psychiatric terms. At a clinical descriptive behavioural level it appears unrelated to the psychoses. It is perhaps most usefully viewed as a 'functional' psychosomatic disorder deriving from these individuals' capacity to mobilize excessive carbohydrate starvation and its consequences as a necessary means of coming to avoid emerging adolescent emotional difficulties of a non-specific kind. The early characteristic feature and common denominator of the condition—namely dieting behaviour—may partly explain why the anorexia nervosa population as a whole reveals some constitutional and clinical overlap with the childhood and adolescent obese population.

It is a disorder which sometimes, perhaps often, remits spontaneously. However, not uncommonly it becomes chronic and can progress to early death. It is difficult to evaluate the effects of treatment against such a variable clinical background but, in the present writer's view, intensive treatment of the kind described can have a highly significant effect on the outcome. This is especially so when the patient has not been ill for so long a period, her illness become so complicated socially and metabolically or her basic personality resources always been so limited, that the task before her with the physician's help, of re-establishing herself in life as a viable prospecting adolescent, has become too great.

REFERENCES

Anand, B. K. (1961). 'Nervous Regulation of Food Intake.' *Physiol. Rev.*, **41,** 677.

Blendis, L. M. and Crisp, A. H. (1968). 'Serum Cholesterol Levels in Anorexia Nervosa.' *Postgrad. med. J.*, **44,** 327.

Bliss, E. L. and Branch, C. H. H. (1960). *Anorexia Nervosa.* New York: Hoeber.

Bruce, Joan, and Russell, G. F. M. (1962). 'Premenstrual Tension.' *Lancet*, **2,** 267.

Bruch, H. (1964). 'Psychological Aspects of Overeating and Obesity.' *Psychosomatics*, **5,** 269.

— (1966). 'Anorexia Nervosa and its Differential Diagnosis.' *J. nerv. ment. Dis.* **141,** 555.

— (1967). *The Importance of Overweight.* New York: Norton.

Chesser, E. (1969). 'Group Treatment of Obesity.' Paper Read at Ordinary Meetings of Society for Psychosomatic Research. To be published.

Cohn, C. and Joseph, D. (1960). 'Role of Rate of Ingestion of Diet on Regulation of Intermediary Metabolism (Meal Eating vs. Nibbling).' *Metabolism*, **9,** 492.

Crighton-Miller, H. (1938). 'Pre-psychotic Anorexia' (Discussion). *Lancet*, **2,** 1174.

Crisp, A. H. (1965a). 'Some Aspects of the Evolution, Presentation and Follow-up of Anorexia Nervosa.' *Proc. R. Soc. Med.*, **68,** 814.

— (1965b). 'Clinical and Therapeutic Aspects of Anorexia Nervosa—A Study of 30 Cases.' *J. psychosom. Res.*, **9,** 67.

— (1966a). 'A Psychosomatic Study of Anorexia Nervosa: a Controlled Study of Some Aspects of the Constitution and Premorbid Feeding Behaviour of Patients.' *M.D. Thesis*, University of London.

— (1966b). 'Anorexia Nervosa in an Identical Twin.' *Postgrad. med. J.*, **42,** 86.

— (1967a). 'The Possible Significance of Some Behavioural Correlates of Weight and Carbohydrate Intake.' *J. psychosom. Res.*, **11,** 117.

— (1967b). 'Anorexia Nervosa.' *Hosp. Med.*, **1,** 713.

— (1968a). 'Primary Anorexia Nervosa.' *Gut*, **9,** 370.

— (1968b). 'Some Aspects of Gastric Function in Anorexia Nervosa.' Proceedings 1st Congress of Italian Society for Psychosomatic Research, September, 1967, Ed. by F. Antonelli, O.P.I. S.p.A. Rome.

— (1969). 'Psychological Aspects of Breast Feeding with Particular Reference to Anorexia Nervosa.' *Br. J. med. Psychol.*, **42,** 119.

— (1970a). 'Some Premorbid Factors in Adult Disorders of Weights, with Particular Reference to Primary Anorexia Nervosa (Weight Phobia). A Literature Review.' *J. psychosom. Res.*, **14,** 1.

— (1970b). 'A Study of Reported Birth Weights and Growth Rates in a Group of Patients with Primary Anorexia Nervosa (Weight Phobia).' *J. psychosom. Res.*, **14,** 23.

— (1970c). 'Anorexia Nervosa, "Feeding Disorder", "Nervous Malnutrition" or "Weight Phobia".' In *World Review of Nutrition and Dietetics,* Vol. 12, p. 452. Basle: Karger.

— Blendis, L. M. and Pawan, G. L. S. (1968). 'Aspects of Fat Metabolism in Anorexia Nervosa.' *Metabolism,* **17,** 1109.

— Douglas, J. W. B., Ross, J. M. and Stonehill, E. (1970). 'The Natural Development of Abnormalities of Weight. An Epidemiological Study.' (Proceedings of 13th Annual Conference of Society for Psychosomatic Research, London). *J. psychosom. Res.* (in press).

— Ellis, Julia and Lowy, Clara (1967). 'Insulin Response to a Rapid Intravenous Injection of Dextrose in Patients with Anorexia Nervosa and Obesity.' *Postgrad. med. J.*, **43,** 97.

— Fenton, G. W. and Scotton, Leila (1968). 'A Controlled Study of the E.E.G. in Anorexia Nervosa.' *Br. J. Psychiat.*, **114,** 1149.

— and Stonehill, E. S. (1967). 'Hypercarotenaemia as a Symptom of Weight Phobia.' *Postgrad. med. J.*, **43,** 721.

— — (1970). 'Obesity. Treatment Aspects.' (Proceedings of 13th Annual Conference of Society for Psychosomatic Research, London). *J. psychosom. Res.* (in press).

Dally, P. J. (1967). 'Anorexia Nervosa—Long Term Follow-up and Effects of Treatment.' *J. psychosom. Res.*, **11,** 151.

— (1969). *Anorexia Nervosa.* London: Heinemann.

Fabry, P., Fodor, J., Hejl, Z., Braun, T. and Zvolánková, K. (1964). 'The Frequency of Meals; Its Relation to Overweight, Hypercholesterolaemia and Decreased Glucose Tolerance.' *Lancet,* **2,** 614.

Farquherson, R. F. and Hyland, H. H. (1966). 'Anorexia Nervosa; the Course of 15 patients Treated from 20–30 Years Previously.' *Can. med. Ass. J.*, **94,** 411.

Fellner, C. H. and Levitt, H. (1964). 'A New Approach to Overweight.' *Am. J. clin. Nutr.* **15,** 50.

Frazier, S., Faubion, M., Griffin, M. and Johnson, A. (1955). 'A Specific Factor in Symptom Choice.' *Proc. Staff Meet. Mayo Clin.*, **30,** 227.

Gwinup, G., Byron, R. C., Roush, W. H., Kruger, F. A. and Hanwi, G. J. (1963). 'Effect of "Nibbling" vs. "Gorging" on Serum Lipids in Man.' *Am. J. clin. Nutr.*, **13,** 209.

Hales, C. N. and Randle, P. J. (1963). 'Effects of Low Carbohydrate Diet and Diabetes Mellitus on Plasma Concentration of Glucose, Nonesterified Fatty Acids and Insulin during Oral Glucose Tolerance Tests.' *Lancet,* **1,** 790.

Kay, D. W. K. and Leigh, D. (1954). 'The Natural History, Treatment and Prognosis of Anorexia Nervosa Based on a Study of 38 Patients.' *J. ment. Sci.*, **100,** 411.

Kemp, R. (1967), 'Obesity, the Clinical Background.' *Med. News Mag.*, January, 3.
Mayer, J. (1953). 'Genetic, Traumatic and Environmental Factors in the Aetiology of Obesity.' *Physiol. Rev.*, **33,** 472.
— (1964). 'Appetite and the Many Obesities.' *Aust. Ann. Med.*, **13,** 282.
— (1966). *Therapeutic Notes*, No. 3, 71.
Mayer-Gross, W., Slater, E. and Roth, M. (1960). *Clinical Psychiatry*, p. 201. London: Cassell.
Miller, D. S., Mumford, Pamela, and Stock, M. J. (1967). 'Gluttony: 2. Thermogenesis in Overeating Man.' *Am. J. clin. Nutr.*, **20,** 1223.
Mishket, K. A. (1968). 'Xanthomatosis.' *Br. J. hosp. Med.*, **1,** 223.
Mossberg, H. D. (1948). 'Obesity in Children.' *Acta paediat.*, **35,** Suppl. **2.**
Okey, R., Scheier, G. and Reed, R. (1960). 'Food Restriction and Cholesterol Metabolism.' *J. Am. diet. Ass.*, **36,** 441.
Pawan, G. (1963). 'Metabolic Aspects of Human Obesity.' *Acta neuroveg.*, 525.
— (1964). 'Dietary Treatment of Obesity. Experimental Observations and Metabolic Studies.' In a Symposium Ed. by G. Blix, p. 128. Uppsala: Almqvist & Witsells.
— (1967). 'Metabolic Consequences of Altering the Feeding Pattern of Mice on a Constant Diet. Carbon and Energy Balance. Respiration and Carcass Composition Studies. In Proc. Seventh International Congress of Nutrition, Hamburg. Vol. 2: Regulation of Hunger and Appetite. London: Pergamon Press.
Quaade, F. (1955). *Obese Children: Anthropology and Environment.* Copenhagen: Danish Service Press.
Russell, G. F. M. (1966). 'Acute Dilatation of the Stomach in a Patient with Anorexia Nervosa.' *Br. J. Psychiat.*, **112,** 203.
— (1968). 'The Neuroendocrinology of Human Undernutrition with Special Reference to Anorexia Nervosa.' In *Physiopathology of Adipose Tissue.* Excerpta Medica Monographs, No. 404.
— Lorraine, J. A., Bell, E. T. and Harkness, R. A. (1965). 'Gonadotrophin and Oestrogen Excretion in Patients with Anorexia Nervosa.' *J. psychosom. Res.*, **9,** 79.
Seidensticker, J. F. and Tzagournis, M. (1968). 'Anorexia Nervosa—Clinical Features and Long Term Follow-up.' *J. chron. Dis.*, **21,** 361.
Shields, J. (1962). *Monozygotic Twins Brought Up Apart and Brought Up Together.* Oxford University Press.
Shorvon, H. S. and Richardson, S. S. (1949). 'Sudden Obesity and Psychological Trauma.' *Br. med. J.* **2,** 951.
Silverstone, J. T. (1968). 'Psychosocial Aspects of Obesity.' *Proc. R. Soc. Med.*, **61,** 371.
— and Solomon, T. (1966). 'Psychiatric and Somatic Factors in the Treatment of Obesity.' *J. psychosom. Res.*, **9,** 249.
Simon, R. I. (1963). 'Obesity as a Depressive Equivalent.' *J. Am. med. Ass.*, **183,** 208.

Sinclair, H. M. (1967), 'Accurate Mechanism for Controlling Eating.' *Med. News. Mag.*, January, 13.

Stunkard, A. J. (1957). 'The Dieting Depression.' *Am. J. Med.*, **23,** 77.

Stunkard, A. J. (1958). 'Physical Activity, Emotions, and Human Obesity.' *Psychosom. Med.*, **20,** 366.

— Grace, W. J. and Wolff, H. G. (1955). 'Night-eating Syndrome; Patterns of Food Intake Among Certain Obese Patients.' *Am. J. Med.*, **19,** 78.

Warren, W. (1968). 'A Study of Anorexia Nervosa in Young Girls.' *J. Child. Psychol. Psychiat.*, **9,** 27.

Werkman, S. L. and Greenberg, E. S. (1965), 'Abnormal Personality and Interest Patterns in Obese Adolescent Girls.' (Abstr.). *Psychosom. Med.*, **27,** 482.

Winnicot, D. W. (1958). *Collected Papers*, p. 33. London: Tavistock Publications.

CHAPTER 9

FUNCTIONAL VOMITING, ABDOMINAL PAIN AND DIARRHOEA

OSCAR W. HILL

INTRODUCTION

About one half of the patients seen in a medical clinic have no organic lesion to account for their symptoms (McClay, 1965). This is especially the case with symptoms referred to the gastro-intestinal tract. Edwards and Coghill (1968), in a large series of patients complaining of dyspepsia, found that 40 per cent had no organic lesion that could account for their symptoms. Kirsner and Palmer (1958) estimated that, of their patients with digestive symptoms, 50–70 per cent were due to the irritable colon syndrome. Purtell, Robins and Cohen (1951) found that anorexia, nausea, vomiting and abdominal pain were very common complaints in a group of patients whose symptoms were thought to be of hysterical origin. Although further study after a period of time may reveal a lesion that was initially occult this becomes less likely when the complaint has persisted over a lengthy period. However, it is unwarranted without further psychological study to assume that functional disorders are necessarily psychogenic as further progress in knowledge may reveal a hitherto unknown aetiology. (In this chapter the word 'functional' is used to describe a symptom that is not related to a demonstrable, structural or biochemical abnormality.) Caution is engendered by the recent work on lactase deficiency as a possible further organic cause of diarrhoea (McMichael, Webb and Dawson, 1965). Nonetheless, in many 'functional' disorders it is possible to define psychological and psychophysiological mechanisms which, together with adverse circumstances operating upon a vulnerable personality, can be seen as a causal sequence leading to the functional symptom. Assessment of these patients becomes much less controversial if it is accepted that psychological factors operate upon physical predispositions across the whole range of disorder from the 'functional' to the 'organic'.

In this chapter three functional gastro-intestinal complaints will be described. In some ways it would be more logical to start with the individual disturbed in his general function and relationships and then to describe some of his physical symptoms, as on further investigation they frequently prove to be peripheral to other more important problems. In practice the patient presents with his symptom and nearly always to a non-psychiatrist. Hence the symptom has been taken as the starting-point even though, from the psychiatric point of view, this approach results in heterogeneous groups especially in the patients with 'abdominal pain and discomfort' in whom a variety of distinct psychological mechanisms are found.

VOMITING

Vomiting, when it is not an involuntary response to an organic lesion, may be either self-induced or functional. It has commonly been said of these patients that 'they complain bitterly but look well' (Cecil and Loeb, 1959), but more recently it has become increasingly appreciated that such vomiting may lead to serious metabolic problems (Hill, 1967; Wallace *et al.*, 1968; Wolff *et al.*, 1968).

Self-induced Vomiting

Eight per cent of patients with a peptic ulcer will admit to self-induced vomiting (Edwards and Coghill, 1968) which is used as a means of relieving pain and discomfort. With some patients the vomiting seems excessive beyond the needs of pain relief and resistant to medical intervention. In these patients some gratification beyond that of pain relief is probably present. This element may lead some of these patients to conceal their vomiting, as in an extreme case reported by Wallace *et al.* (1968).

Self-induced vomiting is a common feature of anorexia nervosa. The vomiting is nearly always concealed and serves the purpose of demonstrating compliance to authority without the danger of putting on weight or it may come as the climax of an orgy of over-eating to which these patients are prone. The behaviour may also be sexualized (*see* Chapter 8).

Functional Vomiting

It is commonly recognized that vomiting may be induced psychologically as a reaction to some disgusting sight, smell or suggestion or by a conditioned reflex as in the poor sailor who sometimes vomits as he walks up the gang-plank to board a stationary vessel.

Trethowan and Conlon (1965) have observed a significantly high incidence of nausea or sickness as part of the Convade syndrome in the husbands of pregnant women.

Wilbur and Washburn (1938) described a group of patients, predominantly female, with functional or nervous vomiting but limited their study to the physical aspects. More recently Cleghorn and Brown (1964) have reviewed accounts of the individual psychopathology in patients suffering from psychogenic vomiting. Broadly speaking they concluded that they were immature persons and that the vomiting was often related to sexual fears.

Hill (1968) has described a group of functional vomiters. The most prominent features in these patients were the extent to which they had been orphaned in childhood, the incidence of vomiting in childhood and of a family history of vomiting, and finally the way in which so many of the patients felt trapped in a current major relationship.

Almost half of these patients had been orphaned in childhood, a proportion greatly in excess of the 18 per cent found in a large psychiatric population (Hill and Price, 1967), despite the likelihood that orphans would be excessively represented in this control population. There were in addition some major separation experiences in some of the vomiters who had not been orphaned.

Half of the vomiters gave a history of recurrent vomiting in childhood and a number of them could remember that their vomiting had begun in association with a significant death or other separation. Keeler (1954) has recorded vomiting as one of the components in a child's grief reaction and Maddison and Viola (1968) record it as one of the physical accompaniments of grief in the adult.

Taken by itself it is not easy to see what connection orphanhood may have with psychogenic vomiting in adult life. If vomiting had been associated with grief at that time it could be that the vomiting might tend to recur as a conditioned accompaniment of despair in later life. The observation may become more meaningful if it is considered in conjunction with another finding that emerged in this group of patients. When compared with a control population of patients with functional abdominal pain who had been very similarly investigated, the vomiters were found to a significant degree to be living with a person, usually a spouse, to whom they felt very hostile but from whom they could not separate. An interesting sub-group consisted of four of the female patients who had a very trying aged parent living with or near them. A word that was frequently used by many of the vomiters was 'duty' and their conception of duty impelled them into many situations that they found distasteful. As a typical example, one patient had loathed her husband for many years, had barely spoken to him but still felt that she must prepare his meals. It may well be that the significance of the orphanhood in this group is that the subsequent insecurity, together with their sensitization to loss, may make them unwilling to suffer a further separation even when by commonly accepted standards they might be better off if they withdrew and tried to form a more satisfactory relationship with someone else.

Jacobson and Ryder (1969) have investigated marriages in which one of the partners had lost a parent by death in childhood. They rated the couple for 'marriage closeness', which was largely a measure of free communication and mature relationship. They found a significantly lower score in pairs where the loss had occurred at the age of 12 or younger, compared with pairs who had lost a parent at any other time previous to the marriage.

Hill (1969) has noted that in a population of depressed women, those who were orphaned in childhood were far more likely to attempt suicide. This may underline the greater despair that overwhelms these individuals when they suffer a further loss—a despair that the vomiters may be unable to face. It is worthy of note that only one of the vomiters appeared depressed despite the generally high incidence of adverse life situations. It is also of interest that our use of language gives some recognition to the way in which a hostile relationship may provoke nausea and vomiting. Phrases such as 'you make me sick' or 'it's enough to make you vomit' are commonly used in antagonistic situations. Another feature of these relationships is that the hostile pair in the great majority of cases live under the same roof. Of the various joint activities that are abandoned in the course of a deteriorating relationship, the eating of meals together is one of the last to go. It needs little imagination to conjure up the scenes of recrimination or hostile silence that must be the accompaniment of such meals and the effect that the associated emotions may have on gastric function.

The family history of vomiting in these patients was striking and often extended to three generations. Taken in conjunction with the frequent history of childhood vomiting it may be that these patients inherited a physiological apparatus with a lower threshold for vomiting. Alternatively it may be that the child's experience of parental vomiting may be the determining factor. Certainly, the disgust and sympathetic response aroused in one subject by another's vomiting is a potent stimulus to vomiting and if that vomiting is rewarded by sympathetic attention it may become conditioned to appear when the subject feels the need for such attention. We know that vomiting can be conditioned (as in the sea-sick sailor), as indeed can other autonomic responses (*see* Chapter 3). Apley and MacKeith (1962) observed that children who suffer from nervous vomiting often have parents who also vomit. Hoyt and Stickler (1960) carried out a follow-up study of childhood vomiting and found that in about a quarter the vomiting persisted. Unfortunately the follow-up period in most patients was less than five years.

Thus we may conclude tentatively that in patients with psychogenic vomiting there is evidence already in childhood of a predisposition to react to stress with vomiting. This tendency may be inherited or learnt from parents or possibly both. This tendency may have been heightened by the increased stresses of an orphaned childhood or even by some more specific evocation of vomiting by death and separation. A disturbed and insecure childhood may predicate disturbed relationships in adult life and the earlier experience of loss may make the patient more reluctant to suffer a further loss. She is more likely to persist in an unsatisfactory relationship and vomit as a reaction to the general stress, and more specifically, as a reaction of disgust and rejection.

Although the vomiting reaction is deeply ingrained and the current conflictual situation usually unresolvable, these patients can often be helped symptomatically with phenothiazines and the opportunity to 'bring up' their problems and obtain verbal catharsis. When one patient came to the subject of her husband she began to vomit and in this way strikingly demonstrated where her difficulties lay. She felt much better afterwards.

ABDOMINAL PAIN

As has been stated above, 40 per cent of patients with dyspepsia have no organic lesion to account for their complaint. Merskey (1965) found in a series of patients complaining of pain in the setting of recognized psychological illness that after the head, the abdomen was the commonest site of such pain; 17 per cent of patients gave the abdomen as their primary location of pain and a further 12 per cent had abdominal pain in addition to some other pain.

Edwards and Coghill (1968) have contrasted the clinical pictures of non-ulcer dyspepsia to dyspepsia in the presence of a peptic ulcer. They rank twelve main features of the history of the symptoms that tend to distinguish the two conditions. They make the special point that severe pain is a feature of ulcer and that the non-ulcer patients present their symptom more in terms of discomfort.

Hill and Blendis (1967) investigated a consecutive series of patients who presented at a gastro-enterological clinic with a complaint of abdominal pain or discomfort for which no organic cause could be found. When contrasted with a series of patients suffering from peptic ulcer the distinguishing features were similar to those found by Edwards and Coghill—chiefly the exacerbation and failure of relief by food, family history of dyspepsia and the description of the symptom in discomfort rather than pain terms. Nausea, distension and belching featured more prominently in the Hill and Blendis series. The psycho-social status of these patients was investigated and comparisons were made with a control population. The occurrence of abdominal pain in the parents of these patients was a most prominent feature, present in just over half of the patients—greatly in excess of expectation in the normal population. It was not easy to ascertain the cause of the parental pain but in roughly half the cases there appeared to have been an organic cause and the remainder were probably functional. About a quarter of the patients had a parent whose death had been associated with a painful abdominal condition.

A third of the patients first developed their pain in close association with the death of a parent. The majority of this group of parents had suffered abdominal pain during their lifetime, many dying to the accompaniment of abdominal pain. The relevance of family history may lie in a number of possible mechanisms. There may be an inherited excessive reactivity of the abdominal viscera and autonomic nervous system in situations of stress. On the other hand, parental suffering may have impressed on the infant mind the vulnerability of abdominal function with a consequent increase in awareness of and anxiety about an area whose normal function is otherwise taken for granted in the remainder of the population. Another possibility is that a family culture is established in which the most acceptable way of conveying distress and eliciting attention would be to complain of abdominal pain.

Of possible relevance to this last point is the observation that the size of the sibship to which these patients belonged was significantly greater than the average. We can speculate that the association may be partly due to the relative lack of parental attention in larger families and the way in which a complaint of pain would of nece sity elicit attention that would be otherwise lacking. Both Gonda (1962) and Merskey (1965) have observed that patients with psychogenic pain come from large sibships, although Merskey also found that the report of pain was correlated with lower social class and lower educational attainment. He was inclined to consider that the correlation with size of sibship was an artifact related to these two factors. However, in the Hill and Blendis study, the control group was matched for social class, so that the finding of a larger sibship cannot be invalidated on those grounds. Merskey has also ascertained in his group of patients that there is a more frequent family history of painful suffering than in a control population. Apley (1959) found in a group of children with functional abdominal pain that a history of such pain in the mother was very common. In some of these children who were followed into adult life the complaint of abdominal pain persisted.

The development of abdominal pain in close association with the death of a parent suggests some other mechanisms additional to those already mentioned for the production of psychogenic pain in this group of patients. In the great majority of this sub-group the parent had either died with a painful abdominal condition or had during their lifetime suffered considerably from abdominal pain. It is a well-known phenomenon that the dead tend to be idealized by the bereft who often proceed to the extent of adopting the mannerisms, dress, goals, etc. of the departed. Much of the behaviour of the bereaved can be usefully understood in terms of coping with their guilty ambivalence towards the dead and a fear that retribution may be brought about by the dead person. The common response to these threats is a simultaneous denial of malice and placation of the dead through their idealization. Another possible defence is through the invocation of the law of talion in which the bereaved, by suffering in a similar fashion to the dead person, 'chooses' an exact manner of expiating his guilt (Krupp, 1965). It is important to make it clear to the non-psychiatrist that these reactions are involuntary responses. Just as the body has protective responses to physical pain, so there are psychological mechanisms that protect the individual from excessive mental pain.

The association between bereavement and pain may also be brought about through the depression that the loss may initiate. In this series of patients with abdominal pain, one fifth was clinically depressed and both their mood and pain appeared to respond well when treatment was directed at their depression. The relationship between pain and depression has been discussed by Joffe and Sandler (1965, 1967) and by Engel (1959) who also gives a general description of the developmental factors that may make an individual prone to psychogenic pain and the various precipitating circumstances that may operate on this vulnerability to produce an episode of pain. The complaint of bodily suffering is a prominent feature in depressive illness. Lewis (1934), in his study of 61 depressed patients, found that 25 had some hypochondriacal preoccupation or physical symptomatology. Bradley (1963) has described some striking cases of pain associated with depression. Kreitman *et al.* (1965), in a series of patients with prolonged 'hypochondriasis', found that most were suffering from a depressive illness, which had often been obscured by the somatic overlay. It is of interest that these authors also observed a significant similarity of physical symptoms in the patient and his mother. In psychological terms this may be seen either as a defensive mechanism whereby guilt and mental pain generally may be mitigated by the exaction of physical suffering or perhaps that in our current cultural climate, suffering is conceptualized largely in physical terms and requires physical explanations, just as some centuries ago all suffering, even that due to physical disease, was likely to be thought of in terms of a disorder of the spirit.

Viewed from the somatic side of the mind–body dichotomy, some understanding of the association of pain and depression may arise from a more extensive knowledge of the physiological accompaniments of depression by analogy with the better understood relationship in anxiety. We know that in patients who are depressed there may be changes in electrolytes (Coppen and Shaw, 1963), steroid levels (Hullin *et al.*, 1967), hypothalamic–pituitary reactivity (Caroll, 1969), gut motility (Grace, Wolf and Wolff, 1951), salivation (Palmai *et al.*, 1967), etc., and some of these changes together with those in parameters as yet undefined, may have something to do with the disturbed bodily sensations in depressive illness.

In helping patients with a possible psychogenic pain it is of great practical importance to entertain the possibility of its being a symptom of a depressive illness. The trained psychiatrist needs little reminder of this necessity but the majority of these patients will present themselves to non-psychiatric doctors. The patient may mention that in addition to his physical symptoms he feels depressed but will usually attribute his depression to the discomfort of his physical condition and his anxieties about his health. If the physician has been trained with the same cultural bias to the physical he may well adopt the patient's erroneous view of his symptoms.

The therapeutic approach, of necessity, will be dictated by the formulation of the individual problem. Where a depressive illness is found, an appropriate regimen should be instituted with either physical treatments, psychotherapy or adjustment of milieu or any combination of these as indicated. Whether, despite the absence of a depressive mood, it may be useful to view some of these patients as suffering from a depressive illness and to treat them accordingly even with physical treatments, must remain an open question. Atypical facial neuralgia is a largely psychogenic condition (Engel, 1951). Lascelles (1966) investigated a group of these patients and found that the majority had depressive features to their illness. With treatment for their depression many improved and lost their pain—the remainder took part in a controlled trial of phenelzine in which the drug proved valuable. Lance and Curran (1964) and Dalessio (1967) have claimed that pain in a variety of conditions has been relieved by the use of the tricyclic anti-depressant drugs. It remains a possibility that these drugs may affect pain through ways other than by the relief of depression. About half of the patients in the series discussed here had been complaining of pain for six years or more. As with so many patients who present with a psychogenic physical symptom, they often lack psychological awareness of what is going on in their lives but sometimes it is possible to give some relief by helping the patient to ventilate his problems. A patient may complain bitterly of a psychogenic symptom, but at an unconscious level the symptom may serve a purpose in warding off a more threatening disturbance. This is one reason why such symptoms may prove so intractable. In recent years, led by Engel (*see* Chapter 1), it has become increasingly accepted that many of these pains may best be viewed as hysterical phenomena sharing with classical hysteria all the factors that make for chronicity. Ljungberg (1957) showed in his prognostic study of hysterical conversion symptoms that if the symptom persisted for five years it was most unusual for improvement to take place thereafter.

There are other patients in whom the dominant mechanism may be a psychophysiological reaction through the mediation of air swallowing, heightened autonomic reactivity, increased tension in the muscles of the abdominal wall or an exaggerated awareness of a bodily part through excessive attention. In such cases the tranquillizers and drugs that dampen autonomic responses, e.g. propantheline, may be of value.

Appendicitis

One common presentation of functional abdominal pain is as 'appendicitis'. A considerable proportion of the appendices removed for suspected appendicitis are histologically normal. Harding (1962), in a series of 1,300 appendices removed for 'appendicitis', found that amongst male patients 29 per cent of appendices appeared normal with a peak of 36·5 per cent in the 21–30 age group and amongst females 47·7 per cent were normal with a peak of 62 per cent at age 11–20. The significance of this observation is hotly debated. It is difficult to find agreement on the criteria of normality in an appendix. Some pathologists feel that even a few inflammatory cells may be abnormal—on the other hand, Thackray (1959) compared the histology of a series of appendices removed for 'chronic appendicitis' with appendices removed routinely at gynaecological operations and found that the incidence and degree of pathology was similar in the two series. Some surgeons believe that some apparently normal appendices may give rise to symptoms by colicky contraction.

The absence of convincing organic pathology does not mean that these patients are necessarily suffering from an emotional disturbance that is causing their symptoms but the possibility of this sequence must be greater for the group as a whole.

Ingram *et al.* (1965) investigated 134 female patients aged 15–35 whose appendices were removed for suspected appendicitis. The authors found that 89 per cent of the elective appendicectomies were normal but only 49 per cent of the emergency appendicectomies were found to be normal. A social worker assessed the extent to which emotional problems were present (in ignorance of the findings at appendicectomy). She observed a highly significant excess of these problems in those patients whose appendices proved to be normal. In a follow-up study it was established that patients for whom a diseased appendix had been removed were more likely to have been relieved of their symptoms—again the difference was highly significant.

Barraclough (1968) examined a group of 89 female patients whose appendices had been removed for suspected appendicitis—49 per cent had normal appendices. A brief psychiatric assessment was made and the patients also completed a questionnaire on anxiety. No significant difference was found in these measures between patients with normal and abnormal histology. When a division was made on the basis of symptomatology (single attack, recurrent attacks of pain or continuous pain), an independent rating of the psychosocial position assessed a significantly greater number of patients with chronic pain as being in need of psychiatric help for problems other than their pain. The 'chronic pain' patients also showed a greater general anxiety about matters unrelated to their appendix.

In a similar series of 61 men Barraclough (1967) found 13 patients with a normal appendix and on the basis of questionnaire data and interview they were significantly more disturbed than the patients with an abnormal appendix.

From the practical point of view it is better to remove some normal appendices rather than run the risk of leaving an inflamed appendix inside the abdomen but it is apparent that the group here defined contains a considerable number of psychologically disturbed patients who require some psychiatric attention.

DIARRHOEA

Self-induced

Schwartz and Relman (1953) were the first to draw attention to the syndrome of addiction to purgatives and the serious metabolic disturbances that ensued. More recently Perrier (1960) and Rawson (1966) have contributed excellent reviews of the subject.

The great majority of the patients are women with a horror (at a superficial level) of the evil consequences of inadequate evacuation of the colon and will go to great lengths to obtain purgatives and to conceal their habit from any threat of interference. They often complain of a feeling of tightness in the abdomen that can be relieved only by the taking of purgatives. These patients often became oedematous and feel bloated as a result of their electrolyte disturbance and this feeling may reinforce their desire for purging with consequent increase in bloating. These patients usually develop hypokalaemia and on barium enema there are features characteristic of the 'cathartic colon' (Rawson, 1966). This addiction is notoriously resistant to treatment.

Purgative addiction is a common feature in anorexia nervosa. From the psychopathological point of view it may be seen as one way of keeping weight down and more specifically of rendering the abdomen flat and empty. Patients with anorexia nervosa are particularly fearful of increasing their girth, usually in relationship to fears and fantasies of pregnancy.

Direct Observations of the Effect of Emotion upon the Colon

Grace, Wolf and Wolff (1951) made extended observations in four fistulous subjects of the relationship between emotion and colonic activity. They characterized two types of response: hyperdynamic with diarrhoea and hypodynamic with constipation.

The hyperdynamic response was characterized by hyperaemia, a contraction of longitudinal muscles, together with shortening of the colon, and increase in rhythmic contractile activity of circular muscles in all parts of the colon except the descending and sigmoid, in which longitudinal muscle activity predominated producing a rigid tubular shape with a pallor of the mucosa in that region. This reaction was provoked by any assault upon the mucosa and also by symbolic assaults such as with words, when they elicit anger, resentment, anxiety and conflict. By contrast, the hypodynamic reaction was encountered when the patient reacted to a symbolic threat with dejection and a sense of defeat. In this reaction there was a general decrease of motor activity apart from the sphincter which became contracted. The mucosa was pale and mucous secretion reduced.

Extensive studies have been made of pressure changes in the lumen of the bowel. The findings are not always easy to interpret, especially in terms of flow which is a function of pressure and resistance. There is the paradox that the 'painless diarrhoea' sub-syndrome of irritable colon is associated with subnormal motor activity (Chaudhary and Truelove, 1961), although Ritchie and Tuckey (1969) dissent from this finding. Chaudhary and Truelove have found that where the irritable colon is accompanied by pain there is a hyperactive pattern of motor activity which disappears when the patient is in remission, but there is an excessive response to prostigmine which persists even in remission. If pressures are recorded during interview, when emotional material is brought up, this will produce heightened colonic activity in about a quarter of all subjects without distinction as to whether they suffer from irritable colon, ulcerative colitis or are normal. Pressures exceeding 60 mm.Hg were recorded which would last for as long as 30 seconds. Wangel and Deller (1965) confirm this observation and extend it by their observation that all conditions producing diarrhoea, organic as well as functional, show a symptomatic exacerbation under emotional stress. Holdstock, Misiewicz and Waller (1969) demonstrated that in seven out of nine patients with 'functional' abdominal pain, there was a correlation between gut contraction and the experience of pain. The pain responded very well to intravenous propantheline. Five of the patients had the irritable colon syndrome. Nonetheless, two of the patients had no pain induced despite intraluminal pressures of over 100 mm. Hg, so that some other factors must be needed if pain is to be produced. Wright and Das (1969) have found that a metabolite of adrenaline is increased in the urine of patients with nervous diarrhoea and speculate that this may be attributable either to heightened anxiety or an excessive production in the gut itself.

Irritable Colon

'Irritable colon' is a common condition and some gastro-enterologists claim that it is responsible for the symptoms of more than half the patients in their clinics (Kirsner and Palmer, 1958).

Although the contribution made by psychological factors to this syndrome had been long recognized, White, Cobb and Jones (1939) gave the first systematic description in which considerable weight was given to the character structure and stressful experience of these patients. As with other large series there was a predominance of women in this group. Patients had shown evidence of the condition for an average of ten years, the most usual age at which the symptoms had begun was in the early twenties. The sequence that they depict is of anxiety, guilt and resentment, leading to a state of tension which precipitates the physical symptoms. They quote many case histories that convincingly demonstrate the relationship of the physical symptoms to stressful circumstances.

The findings of Chaudhary and Truelove (1962) on a large series also underline the importance of psychological factors. They identified many different kinds of adverse situations in their patients. The most frequent comment on the female patients was that they were 'obsessional over trivial problems'. These authors divided the patients into the two clinical groupings of 'spastic colon' and 'painless diarrhoea'. The former was by far the most common and consisted of abdominal pain usually over the colon, usually but not always associated with diarrhoea or sometimes with constipation. A third of their patients had been submitted to appendicectomy or a gynaecological operation for what in some could be seen retrospectively as symptoms due to their irritable colon.

Jeffcoate (1969) considers that in many women with chronic pelvic pain, especially those with unilateral 'dysmenorrhoea', the symptoms are not produced by the genitalia but by an irritable colon. In this context it is interesting to note that the individuals are usually constipated in the premenstruum and then have some diarrhoea with the commencement of the period. They are sometimes led by primitive logic to purge themselves during the premenstruum in an attempt to remove the symptoms of premenstrual tension. The experience of these patients may be relevant to the psychopathology of the more serious purgative addicts.

A series of 31 patients with functional diarrhoea seen by Hill (1970) conformed very much to the above descriptions: 10 had previously lost their appendix; 5 gave a history of irritable colon in a first degree relative. Most of the patients were involved in considerable life difficulties and they often noted that attacks of diarrhoea came in relation to these difficulties. Many were also aware of anxiety symptoms such as sighing respiration and palpitations. One patient had been invalided out of the army with da Costa's syndrome ('circulatory neurasthenia') and then later developed an irritable colon. A most interesting feature of the personality structure of these patients was the extent to which they suffered phobias or compulsive symptoms. This feature was more prominent among the women, of whom 12 out of 17 had these symptoms. Phobias of water and spiders were the most common. In a control series made up of women with other physical symptoms who had been seen by the same psychiatrist, the frequency of phobias and compulsions was 4 out of 21. The difference is statistically significant ($X_1 = 10{\cdot}4$, $p = < 0{\cdot}01$).

The association may be due to the greater anxiety in these patients either directly evoked by their specific fear or arising at a deeper level from unconscious conflict, of which the phobia may be an external sign. The formation of phobias may also be seen as an index of the difficulty that these patients have in coping with their problems in a more direct fashion.

Cohen and Reed (1967) describe a small series of patients with 'nervous diarrhoea' and other autonomic disturbances, provoked directly by specific phobias. These patients were helped by desensitization to the phobic situation (*see* Chapter 16).

Therapy

A psychiatric assessment may reveal avenues whereby the patient may be helped with specific problems, using the entire range of psychiatric aid.

Failing such scope, symptomatic treatment with tranquillizers, propantheline and I-so-gel may be helpful. As a group these patients respond very well to a physician who is willing to allow them a supportive relationship. In a prognostic study, Waller and Misiewicz (1969) emphasize the chronicity of the condition and its tendency to recurrent remission and relapse. The location of any pain tends to remain constant in any individual.

It is of interest to note that there is considerable evidence that irritable colon may be a precursor of diverticulosis (Manousos, Truelove and Lumsden, 1967).

CONCLUSION

In many ways the conditions discussed in this chapter can be seen as a paradigm of psychosomatic mechanisms.

First, we see a predisposition to a particular physical reaction derived part from inheritance, part from the learning experiences in childhood. In most of the patients we can see a current situation operating upon a vulnerable personality to produce the specific reaction.

This sequence is not confined to the purely 'functional' disorders but extends, for example, to diarrhoea associated with anatomical lesions and indeed to much, if not the whole, of disease.

REFERENCES

Apley, J. (1959). *The Child with Abdominal Pains*. Oxford: Blackwell.

— and MacKeith, R. (1962). *The Child and His Symptoms: A Psychosomatic Approach*. Oxford: Blackwell.

Barraclough, B. M. (1967). 'Appendicectomy in Men.' *J. psychosom. Res.*, **11,** 203.

— (1968). 'Appendicectomy in Women.' *J. psychosom. Res.*, **12,** 231.

Bradley, J. J. (1963). 'Severe Localized Pain Associated with the Depressive Syndrome.' *Br. J. Psychiat.*, **109,** 741.

Carroll, B. J. (1969). 'Hypothalamic—Pituitary Function in Depressive Illness.' *Br. med. J.*, **3,** 27.

Cecil, R. L. and Loeb, R. F. (1959). *Textbook of Medicine*, 10th ed., p. 798. Philadelphia: Saunders.

Chaudhary, N. A. and Truelove, S. C. (1961). 'Human Colonic Motility.' *Gastroenterology*, **40,** 1, 18, 27.

— — (1962). 'The Irritable Colon Syndrome.' *Q. Jl Med.*, **31,** 307.

Cleghorn, R. A. and Brown, W. T. (1964). 'Psychogenesis of Emesis.' *Can. psychiat. Ass. J.*, **9,** 299.

Cohen, S. I. and Reed, J. L. (1968). 'The Treatment of "Nervous Diarrhoea" and Other Conditioned Autonomic Disorders by Desensitization.' *Br. J. Psychiat.*, **114,** 1275.

Coppen, A. and Shaw, D. M. (1963). 'Mineral Metabolism in Melancholia.' *Br. Med. J.*, **2,** 1439.

Dalessio, D. J. (1967). 'Chronic Pain Syndromes and Disordered Cortical Inhibition: Effects of Tricyclic Compounds.' *Dis. nerv. Syst.*, **5,** 325.

Edwards, F. C. and Coghill, N. F. (1968). 'Clinical Manifestations in Patients with Chronic Astrophic Gastritis, Gastric Ulcer and Duodenal Ulcer.' *Q. Jl Med.*, **37,** 337.

Engel, G. L. (1951). 'Primary Atypical Facial Neuralgia. An Hysterical Conversion Symptom.' *Psychosom. Med.*, **13,** 375.

— (1959). '"Psychogenic" Pain and the Pain Prone Patient.' *Am. J. Med.*, **26,** 899.

Gonda, T. A. (1962). 'The Relation Between Complaints of Persistent Pain and Family Size.' *J. Neurol. Neurosurg. Psychiat.*, **25,** 277.

Grace, W. J., Wolf, S. and Wolff, H. G. (1951). *The Human Colon*. London: Heinemann.

Harding, H. E. (1962). 'A Notable Source of Error in the Diagnosis of Appendicitis.' *Br. med. J.*, **2,** 1028.

Hill, O. W. (1967). 'Psychogenic Vomiting and Hypokalaemia.' *Gut*, **8,** 98.

— (1968). 'Psychogenic Vomiting.' *Gut*, **9,** 348.

— (1969). 'The Association of Childhood Bereavement with Suicidal Attempt in Depressive Illness.' *Br. J. Psychiat.*, **115,** 301.

— (1970). 'Functional Diarrhoea.' In preparation.

— and Blendis, L. (1967). 'Physical and Psychological Evaluation of "Non-organic" Abdominal Pain.' *Gut*, **8,** 221.

Hill, O. W. and Price, J. S. (1967). 'Childhood Bereavement and Adult Depression.' *Br. J. Psychiat.*, **113,** 743.

Holdstock, D. J., Misiewicz, J. J. and Waller, S. L. (1969). 'Observations on the Mechanism of Abdominal Pain.' *Gut*, **10,** 19.

Hoyt, C. S. and Stickler, G. B. (1960). 'A Study of 44 Children with the Syndrome of Recurrent (Cyclic) Vomiting.' *Pediatrics*, **25,** 775.

Hullin, R. P., Bailey, A. D., McDonald, R., Dransfield, G. A. and Milne, H. B. (1967). 'Variation in 11-Hydroxycorticosteroids in Depression and Manic-depressive Psychosis.' *Br. J. Psychiat.*, **113,** 593.

Ingram, P. W., Evans, G. and Oppenheim, A. N. (1965). 'Right Iliac Fossa Pain in Young Women.' *Br. med. J.*, **2,** 149.

Jacobson, G. and Ryder, R. G. (1969). 'Parental Loss and Some Characteristics of the Early Marriage Relationship.' *Am. J. Orthopsychiat.*, **39,** 779.

Jeffcoate, J. N. A. (1969). 'Pelvic Pain.' *Br. med. J.*, **3,** 431.

Joffe, W. G. and Sandler, J. S. (1965). 'Notes on Pain, Depression and Individuation.' *Psychoanal. Study Child.*, **20,** 394.

—— (1967). 'On the Concept of Pain with Special Reference to Depression and Psychogenic Pain.' *J. Psychosom. Res.*, **11,** 69.

Keeler, R. (1954). 'Children's Reaction to the Death of a Parent.' In *Depression*, Ed. by P. H. Hock and J. Zubin. New York: Grune and Stratton.

Kirsner, J. B. and Palmer, W. L. (1958). 'The Irritable Colon.' *Gastroenterology*, **34,** 490.

Kreitman, N., Sainsbury, P., Pearce, K. and Costain, W. R. (1965). 'Hypochondriasis and Depression in Out-patients at a General Hospital.' *Br. J. Psychiat.*, **111,** 607.

Krupp, G. R. (1965). 'Identification as a Defence against Anxiety in Coping with Loss.' *Int. J. Psycho-Anal.*, **46,** 303.

Lance, J. W. and Curran, D. A. (1964). 'Treatment of Chronic Tension Headache.' *Lancet*, **1,** 1236.

Lascelles, R. G. (1966). 'Atypical Facial Pain and Depression.' *Br. J. Psychiat.*, **112,** 651.

Lewis, A. J. (1934). 'Melancholia: A Clinical Survey of Depressive States.' *J. ment. Sci.*, **80,** 1.

Ljungberg, L. (1957). 'Hysteria: A Clinical Prognostic and Genetic Study.' *Acta. psychiat. scand.*, **32,** Suppl. 112.

Maclay, I. (1965). 'The "Functional" Medical Out-patient.' *Br. J. Psychiat.*, **111,** 34.

McMichael, H. B., Webb, J. and Dawson, A. M. (1965). 'Lactase Deficiency in Adults. A Cause of "Functional" Diarrhoea.' *Lancet*, **1,** 717.

Maddison, D. and Viola, A. (1968). 'The Health of Widows in the Year Following Bereavement.' *J. psychosom. Res.*, **12,** 297.

Manousos, O. N., Truelove, S. C. and Lumsden, K. (1967). 'Transit Times of Food in Patients with Diverticulosis or Irritable Colon Syndrome and Normal Subjects.' *Br. med. J.*, **3,** 760.

Merskey, H. (1965). 'Psychiatric Patients with Persistent Pain.' *J. psychosom. Res.*, **8,** 299.

Palmai, G., Blackwell, B., Maxwell, A. E. and Morgenstern, F. (1967). 'Patterns of Salivary Flow in Depressive Illness and During Treatment.' *Br. J. Psychiat.*, **113,** 1297.

Perrier, C. (1960). 'Une forme spéciale d'hypokaliémie: La dénutrition psychogène par abus de laxatifs.' *Rev. Franç. Études Clin. Biol.* **5,** 792.

Purtell, J. J., Robins, E., Cohen, M. E. (1951). 'Observations of Clinical Aspects of Hysteria.' *J. Am. med. Ass.*, **146,** 902.

Rawson, M. D. (1966). 'Cathartic Colon.' *Lancet*, **1,** 1121.

Ritchie, J. A. and Tuckey, M. S. (1969). 'Intraluminal Pressure Studies at Different Distances from the Anus in Normal Subjects and in Patients with the Irritable Colon Syndrome.' *Clin. J. digest. Dis.*, **14,** 96.

Schwartz, W. B. and Relman, A. S. (1953). 'Metabolic and Renal Studies in Chronic Potassium Depletion Resulting from Overuse of Laxatives.' *J. clin. Invest.*, **32,** 258.

Thackray, A. C. (1959). ' "Chronic Appendicitis": Some Pathological Observations.' *Br. J. Radiol.*, **32,** 180.

Trethowan, W. H. and Conlon, M. F. (1965). 'The Couvade Syndrome.' *Br. J. Psychiat.*, **111,** 57.

Wallace, M., Richards, P., Chesser, E., and Wrong, O. (1968). 'Persistent Alkalosis and Hypokalaemia Caused by Surreptitious Vomiting.' *Q. Jl. Med.*, **37,** 577.

Waller, S. and Misiewicz, J. J. (1969). 'Prognosis in the Irritable-bowel Syndrome.' *Lancet*, **2,** 753.

Wangel, A. G. and Deller, D. J. (1965). 'Intestinal Motility in Man: Mechanisms of Constipation and Diarrhoea with Particular Reference to the Irritable Colon Syndrome.' *Gastroenterology*, **48,** 69.

White, B. V., Cobb, S. and Jones, C. M. (1939). 'Mucous Colitis: a Psychological Medical Study of 60 Cases.' *Psychosomatic Medicine Monograph*, No. 1. National Research Council, Washington.

Wilbur, D. L. and Washburn, R. N. (1938). 'Clinical Features and Treatment of Functional or Nervous Vomiting.' *J. Am. med. Ass.*, **110,** 478.

Wolff, H. P., Vescei, P., Krück, F., Roscher, S., Brown, J. J., Düsterdieck, G.O., Lever, A. F. and Robertson, J. I. S. (1968). 'Psychiatric Disturbance Leading to Potassium Depletion, Sodium Depletion, Raised Plasmarenin Concentration and Secondary Hyperaldosteronism.' *Lancet*, **1,** 257.

Wright, J. T. and Das, A. K. (1969). 'Excretion of 4-Hydroxy–3-Methoxy Mandelic Acid in Cases of Ulcerative Colitis and Diarrhoea of Nervous Origin.' *Gut*, **10,** 628.

CHAPTER 10

THE DECLINE OF DUODENAL ULCER

THOMAS ARIE

Duodenal ulcer is on the decline in this country. Until recently it has not been possible to say whether the decline has been merely in the severity of the disease, or whether the rate at which people are contracting the disease has really fallen. This is because information has come from mortality data on the one hand, which in a disease with a very low case fatality is a poor indicator of prevalence, and on the other hand from data on 'crises' in the disease such as referral to hospital, bleeding, perforation and elective surgery. A decline in the rate of any of these 'crises' could be evidence merely of a decline in the severity of the disease, which could result from advances in treatment, or from factors known to influence the course of the disease, such as decline in cigarette smoking (Doll and Hill, 1964). But has there been a real fall in the rate at which people are contracting the disease—the 'incidence'?

Incidence studies of the sort needed to settle this question are difficult, in that few populations are available in which the diagnosis and the recording of new cases are accurate and uniform over the years. The present note describes such an incidence study, the results of which seem, at least for the population investigated, to point to a real decline in the incidence of duodenal ulcer. The work has been reported elsewhere (Meade *et al.*, 1968) as part of a more general epidemiological study, and we describe it again here since the findings have a special importance for workers in the field of psychosomatic medicine. Why a disease which has traditionally been so firmly set among the psychosomatic disorders should now be in decline is not a question to which we can offer any good answers.

The epidemiology of peptic ulcer has been reviewed in detail by Doll (1952) and more recently, with special emphasis on causation, by Susser (1967). Kessel and Munro (1964) and Cooper (1964) have discussed the results and limitations of the application of epidemiological methods to psychosomatic disease. For the purposes of the

My thanks are due to the workers with whom the original study was done: Professor J. N. Morris, Dr. T. W. Meade, Dr. M. Brewis of the M.R.C. Social Medicine Unit and Mr. D. J. Bond of the Medical Sickness Annuity and Life Insurance Society.

present account a short summary of the changing picture of the disease during this century will suffice.

It has only relatively recently been the rule to attempt firm distinction between duodenal and gastric ulcer, and diagnostic fashions are anyway changeable. These considerations, together with the lack of adequate morbidity statistics, have hampered the reliable definition of secular trends in the disease. Nonetheless some aspects of these trends have been so gross as to be obviously real; for example, up to the turn of the century perforations were most common in young women and occurred mostly in the cardiac region of the stomach (Jennings, 1940).

Since World War I nine-tenths of perforations have occurred in men. Duodenal ulcer began to make its appearance in the early part of the century and by the 1930s and 40s was an epidemic disease of men. Unlike gastric ulcer which is most common in men of low social class, duodenal ulcer in middle-aged men shows no clear relationship to social class, although a survey by Doll, Avery Jones and Buckatzsch (1951), which was conducted shortly after World War II showed occupational variations in prevalence, some at least of which (for example the high rates in managers and foremen and the low rates in agricultural labourers) were thought to be real. Gastric ulcer mortality began to decline in the 1930s, at first in young men and in subsequent decades this decline has affected all age groups.

Data on the experience of peptic ulceration in middle-aged men were collected by Morris (1964) and the decline which he noted in mortality, in-patient treatment and sickness absence has in general persisted (Tables 1, 2 and 3). The evidence of decline which these sources indicate is subject to the limitations already mentioned, namely, that it does not tell us anything about the rate at which new cases are developing; however, the trend which the data show is the more impressive for the way in which the various sources corroborate each other. It was this evidence that led us to undertake an incidence study.

TABLE 1

Mortality due to Peptic Ulcer in Men aged 45–64
(rates per 100,000 per year)

	G.U.	P.U.
1936–8	28·8	16·5
1950	18·0	17·6
1955	11·6	14·9
1960	7·7	9·7
1965	6·2	6·0
1967	5·3	5·7

Registrar General, E. & W.

TABLE 2

Diagnoses of Hospital In-patients: Men aged 45–64
(rates per 100,000 per year)

	Total peptic ulcer	*Perforations*		*'Cold' surgery**		*'Hot' medicine†*	
		GU	DU	GU	DU	GU	DU
1953–5	584	23	52	97	156		
1956	478	16	55	84	126		
1959	412	16	40	70	98	58	66
1962	428	13	32	64	105	54	70
1964	395	9	35	47	101	45	69
1966	362	9	32	44	100	37	54

* i.e. elective operations.
† i.e. bleeding ulcers medically treated.
Hospital In-patient Enquiry; and J. S. A. Ashley, personal communications.

TABLE 3

Incapacity to Work: Men aged 45–64 (rates per 100,000 per year)

	Spells		*Gastritis, etc.*	*Days*		*Gastritis, etc.*
	GU	DU		GU	DU	
1951	570	490	1310			
1954–5	600	450	1310	38,000	30,000	29,000
1959–60	490	340	1240	26,000	20,000	23,000
1962–3	470	310	1240	26,000	19,000	24,000
1964–5	440	320	1220	22,000	18,000	24,000
1966–7	430	340	1210	23,000	19,000	23,000

Department of Health and Social Security.

THE INCIDENCE STUDY

To tackle the question whether there has been a change in incidence we made use of an unusual opportunity to study a population of which the M.R.C.'s Social Medicine Unit had made previous studies (Morris, Heady and Barley, 1952).

This population comprised all those male doctors aged 35 to 64 who held policies for immediate sickness benefit with the Medical Sickness Annuity and Life Assurance Society Limited. These doctors, something over 6,000 of them at the beginning of the period which we studied and something over 7,000 at the end, were insured against sickness causing them to be absent from their work and the population thus had some unusual advantages: first, our subjects were motivated by the very fact that they were insured to report episodes of sickness as fully as possible—in other words it is reasonable to assume that reporting was virtually complete; secondly, the accuracy of routine diagnosis was likely to be as high in this population, by virtue of their being doctors, as in any population that one might study.

It is difficult to define the onset of a chronic disease and in any such condition the definition of incidence must be operational. We defined it as a first episode of sickness lasting one week or more (although sickness payments dated immediately from the beginning of the absence, absences were not notifiable until a week after their onset, since benefit was not payable for absences of less than a week or for death). We examined the records of the Society for three periods, 1947–1950, 1957–1960 and 1961–1965, and we extracted from the records the case files of all those male doctors in our age groups with immediate sickness benefit certified as having any type of intra-abdominal pathology. We then scrutinized the files, selecting those who appeared to have either definite or possible duodenal ulcer and rejecting those who had any previous history of dyspepsia or peptic disorder; this latter category of course included those who mentioned relevant symptoms in their original proposal form. We then recorded all episodes of sickness occurring during the periods of our study. The resulting positive cases we classified into two categories: on the one hand, 'definite' duodenal ulcers; these were the instances in which the medical certificate mentioned duodenal ulcer specifically or where there was reference to definite radiological evidence of duodenal ulcer. The second category was that of 'possible' duodenal ulcer, which included: (1) cases of haematemesis and/or melaena where the direct cause was not specifically given; (2) a further small number of cases in which uncertain terminology nevertheless indicated likely duodenal ulcer—for example 'duodenitis'; and (3) cases where the diagnosis was given simply as 'peptic ulcer' with no further information. Finally, all cases certified as 'gastric ulcer' were classified separately; there were too few in any of the periods to calculate rates.

The results are set out in Table 4 and show a substantial fall in the incidence both of 'definite' duodenal ulcer and of 'definite plus possible' duodenal ulcer. It is perhaps even more remarkable that this fall is not only a consistent trend over all the age groups but is in fact present at each age group for each period compared (with the exception of the 45–54 age group between 1957 to 1960 and 1961 to 1965, when the rate is constant). This consistency gives added strength to the findings.

TABLE 4

Incidence of Duodenal Ulcer in Medical Practitioners, 1947–50, 1957–60, and 1961–5: Men aged 35–64, inclusive, Holding Policies for Immediate Sickness Benefit (average annual rates per thousand)

Age	1947–50	1957–60	1961–5
	Incidence of Definite Duodenal Ulcer		
35–44	1·9	1·3	0·7
45–54	2·5	1·0	1·0
55–64	2·0	1·7	1·3
Average population	6,180	7,114	7,026
Total new incidents	54	37	34
Standardized* incidence rates per 1,000 (ages 35–64)	2·1	1·3	1·0
	Incidence of Definite and Possible Duodenal Ulcer		
35–39	2·8	1·4	1·3
40–44	2·9	2·6	1·7
45–49	3·1	1·9	1·3
50–54	4·2	3·0	2·0
55–59	3·6	1·7	1·5
60–64	—	4·0	2·6
Total new incidents	78	66	60
Standardized* incidence rate per 1,000 (ages 35–64)	3·1	2·4	1·7

Rates not calculated where there are fewer than five new episodes.
*Standardized on the 1966 male home population of England and Wales.

DISCUSSION

Some technical points have to be borne in mind in interpreting the results. Underwriting policy towards proposals from doctors with previous or present histories of duodenal ulcer, its complications, or severe recurring dyspepsia, have remained unchanged throughout the period of the study; in these cases the policy has excluded benefit from sickness 'due to or arising from' these conditions. The characteristics of the exposed populations may have altered between the late 1940s and the early 1960s. For instance in 1947–50, 35 per cent of the population were aged 50–64 whereas in 1961–5 the corresponding figure was 48 per cent as the numbers of men applying for immediate sickness benefit policies declined slightly between the last two periods of the study. We have, of course, calculated age specific rates throughout, but we have no practicable way of telling whether there may have been other important changes in the population over the period, which is unlikely. In particular, the proportion of general practitioners has been remarkably constant.

As regards the cases ascertained, there are various possibilities to be considered. One is that diagnostic fashions may have altered and that doctors were less likely to label a particular clinical picture as 'duodenal ulcer' in 1961–5 than in 1947–50 or in 1955–60. With easy access to radiology throughout the period this seems unlikely. A related possibility is that there may have been changes in terminology so that, for example, what was called 'duodenal ulcer' in 1947–50 was called something else in 1961–5; this would have had the effect of artificially lowering incidence rates. It is impossible to settle this point conclusively but in our initial scan of the records taking out all mentions of any kind of intra-abdominal pathology, we found no evidence at all of changes in terminology of sufficiently significant kind.

There is another important possibility that we had to consider and this is that sickness absence from duodenal ulcer may be becoming shorter. If there were any increase in instances where a doctor with a duodenal ulcer either had an absence of less than a week or in which he was not away from work at all—perhaps because the condition is becoming milder—a misleading fall in rates might occur. Among the doctors, as for the general population (Morris, 1964), absences for duodenal ulcer tend to be long, presumably mainly because of complications. In 1947–50 and 1957–60 the average length of absence for definite duodenal ulcer was 52 days; in 1961–5 it was 43 days. It is most unlikely that this fall in length of absence could account for the fall in incidence rates. Moreover, we have shown a *trend* in the fall in the incidence rates between each of our periods and there is no corresponding trend in length of absence, the figure for the middle period being identical with that for the first. Further, in 1947–50, 8 per cent of first absences for duodenal ulcer in the doctors were for less than two weeks and the corresponding figures in the second two periods were 5 per cent and 6 per cent. There is thus no evidence of a material change in the frequency of short absences.

CONCLUSION

The evidence from national statistics and from our own study firmly points to a decline in duodenal ulcer, and other recent studies in this country have shown a similar trend; in York, Pulvertaft (1968) observed a decline in the rate at which men presented with duodenal ulcer at hospitals and in private practice between the early 1950s to the early 1960s, whilst Mackay (1966) reported a decline in the frequency of perforated peptic ulcer in men in the West of Scotland over a similar period. Regional differences persist and remain largely unexplained: thus, high rates of peptic ulceration in Aberdeen (Weir and Backett, 1968) contrast with low rates of perforation in Oxford (Saunders, 1967). The rates for men have fallen more steeply than for women, though women too have shared in the fall in mortality (Registrar General, 1969) and in hospitalization (Report of Hospital In-Patient Enquiry for 1966).

Why the decline has occurred is not at all clear. The fall in incidence, as well as apparently in complications, means that advances in treatment cannot alone be responsible. Susser and Stein (1962), analysing mortality trends by age argue for a 'generation effect': cohorts of men born in the late nineteenth century experienced, they suggest, environmental influences (the nature of which is unknown) which enhanced their chances of developing peptic ulcer, whilst for subsequent cohorts these influences have waned. However, as we have already noted in a disease with such low case fatality, mortality is a poor indicator of secular trend.

Predominantly psychological explanations of the causation of duodenal ulcer, in terms either of specific personality types or of 'stress' are hard to reconcile with the current decline, and their review forced Kessel and Munro (1964) to conclude that 'the epidemiological evidence for any form of direct relationship between personality factors or emotional status and the development of peptic ulcer is obscure'. This is not to say that such factors may not play a part in a complex multifactorial causation, such as we have learnt to expect in the common chronic non-communicable diseases; indeed there is probably now sufficient evidence that psychological factors play *some* part in duodenal ulceration, if not necessarily a predominant part. At the same time the steady increase in the amount of sedative and tranquillizing medication prescribed under the National Health Service (Department of Health and Social Security, Annual Reports) must surely be evidence that stress, or perception of stress, has not declined.

Are there then increases in the incidence of other 'psychosomatic' diseases, 'compensating' for the decline of duodenal ulceration? Where definition and diagnosis are the subject of so much disagreement,* data on which to base reliable estimates of changes in incidence are scanty or non-existent. Or are psychological difficul-

* Kessel and Munro wryly conclude that 'the more difficult it is to define an illness and to be sure of its presence the more likely it is to be regarded as psychosomatic'.

ties increasingly expressing themselves in overt psychiatric illness, or in other disturbed behaviour, rather than as 'psychosomatic' disease? Ought we to turn more in directions other than psychological for explanations of duodenal ulcer? Could it even be that the greatly increased use of sedative drugs is itself helping to prevent duodenal ulceration? The questions pose themselves readily enough but at present there are no convincing answers.

REFERENCES

Cooper, B. (1964), 'The Epidemiological Approach to Psychosomatic Medicine.' *J. chron. Dis.*, **8,** 9.

Department of Health and Social Security, Annual Reports. London.

Doll, R. (1952). 'Peptic Ulcer: Endemiology.' In *Modern Trends in Gastroenterology*, Ed. by F. Avery Jones. London: Butterworths.

— Avery Jones, F. and Buckatzsch, M. M. (1957). 'Occupational Factors in the Aetiology of Gastric and Duodenal Ulcers.' Special Report Series Medical Research Council, No. 276. London.

— and Hill, A. B. (1964). 'Mortality in Relation to Smoking: Ten Years' Observations of British Doctors.' *Br. med. J.*, **1,** 1399, 1460.

Jennings, D. (1940). 'Perforated Peptic Ulcer: Changes in Age, Incidence and Sex-distribution in the Last 150 Years.' *Lancet*, **1,** 395, 444.

Kessel, N. and Munro, A. (1964). 'Epidemiological Studies in Psychosomatic Disease.' *J. chron. Dis.*, **8,** 67.

Mackay, C. (1966). 'Perforated Peptic Ulcer in the West of Scotland: A Survey of 5343 Cases during 1954–63.' *Br. med. J.*, **1,** 701.

Meade, T. W., Arie, T. H. D., Brewis, M., Bond, D. J. and Morris, J. N. (1968). 'Recent History of Ischaemic Heart Disease and Duodenal Ulcer in Doctors.' *Br. med. J.*, **2,** 701.

Morris, J. N. (1964). *Uses of Epidemiology*, 2nd ed. Edinburgh: Livingstone.

— Heady, J. A. and Barley, R. G. (1952). 'Coronary Heart Disease in Medical Practitioners.' *Br. med. J.*, **1,** 503.

Pulvertaft, C. N. (1968). 'Comments on the Incidence and Natural History of Gastric and Duodenal Ulcer.' *Postgrad. med. J.*, **44,** 597.

Registrar General for England & Wales (1968). Annual Review of Statistics: Part 1. Medical 1967. London.

Report of the Hospital In-Patient Enquiry for 1966 (1969). London.

Sanders, R. (1967). 'Incidence of Perforated Duodenal and Gastric Ulcer in Oxford.' *Gut*, **8,** 58.

Susser, M. (1967). 'Causes of Peptic Ulcer: A Selective Epidemiological Review.' *J. chron. Dis.*, **20,** 435.

— and Stein, Z. (1962). 'Civilisation and Peptic Ulcer.' *Lancet*, **1,** 115.

Weir, R. D. and Backett, E. M. (1968). 'Studies of the Epidemiology of Peptic Ulcer in a Rural Community: Prevalence and Natural History of Dyspepsia and Peptic Ulcer.' *Gut*, **9,** 75.

CHAPTER 11

A COMPREHENSIVE APPROACH TO THE TREATMENT OF ULCERATIVE COLITIS

JOHN F. O'CONNOR

INTRODUCTION

The psychiatrist working in a general hospital is in the enviable position of being able to correlate environment, past and present, with the end product—a psychophysiological disorder. During the early 1930s, psycho-analytically trained physicians working within a hospital setting established the basis of many of our present-day psychosomatic concepts. Much of this original work was contributed by Murray (1930) and Daniels (1940) at the Columbia-Presbyterian Medical Center and by Sullivan and Chandler (1932) at Yale, in their studies of chronic, non-specific ulcerative colitis.

The management of the more seriously ill patient generally requires a co-operative effort on the part of the internist, psychiatrist and surgeon. Unfortunately, in many situations a disagreement arises which eventually results in suffering on the part of patients. A well co-ordinated approach leads to better management and earlier intervention by the specialist who is needed at a particular time, be it psychiatrist or surgeon, and eventually a better prognosis for the patient. The multiple complications associated with ulcerative colitis require a more comprehensive approach than those in other psychophysiological disorders.

DIAGNOSIS

This disease is characterized by inflammation and ulceration of the colon; its course is marked by remission and exacerbation and frequently is accompanied by arthritis, erythema nodosum or other systemic manifestations. Causation has been variously attributed to allergic, genetic, vascular, infectious and psychologic aetiology.

Diagnosis is easily established by history, stool examination, x-ray

Credit for contributions to this chapter has to be given to Drs. George Daniels, Richard Druss, Aaron Karush and Mrs. Lenore Stern.

and proctoscopy. Onset may be at any time of life, but occurs most frequently between 20 and 40 years of age in both sexes. It can be an acute, fulminating process, but more often than not, is insidious and slow in developing. After the fourth decade, the disease generally tends to be moderate, but when it originates in childhood, the prognosis is poor and the course of illness likely to be severe (Michener *et al.*, 1961; Kirsner, Raskin and Palmer, 1955; Bargen and Kennedy, 1955).

Symptoms range from mild abdominal cramps with blood in the stool to anorexia, nausea, vomiting, severe cramps and stools consisting almost entirely of blood and mucus. Should the disease be confined to the rectum and sigmoid colon, stools will usually be formed, but when it extends further up into the colon, the tendency is towards diarrhoea. Physical signs are generally limited to those of infection with associated abdominal tenderness.

REVIEW OF THE LITERATURE

Various therapeutic approaches have been utilized to alleviate the psychological stresses associated with ulcerative colitis. Psychopharmacological agents have had widespread use in the management of emotional conflicts associated with this disease. Narcosis has been reported to be helpful in controlling acute exacerbations in seven patients (Harper, 1962). Levy *et al.* (1956) describe five cases treated by prefrontal lobotomy: three were doing well one year after (one died of obstruction and perforation a week after lobotomy, and one died six months after colectomy).

Recently the effects of psychotherapy have received more attention. Grace, Pinsley and Wolff (1954) published the results of a study of 34 ulcerative colitis patients whose treatment was directed mainly towards the alleviation of life stresses with 'a minimum of psychological intervention'. The initial response to this form of treatment was considered favourable. Weinstock (1961) originally reported poor results of short-term hospital psychotherapy in a group of patients who appeared to be severely ill. In a later study Weinstock (1962) described positive effects of long-term psychotherapy and psychoanalysis on the course of disease in 28 patients.

METHODOLOGY

By and large, literature describing the effects of psychotherapy and psycho-analysis refer to individual patients or a rather limited number of cases, with no control group being used to compare findings (Cushing, 1953; Karush and Daniels, 1953; Sperling, 1957). While these reports are valuable for establishing hypotheses, it was felt by Daniels that in order to more adequately assess the results of psychiatric treatment, larger series would be necessary. Accordingly, he initiated an intensive study of all ulcerative colitis patients treated at the Medical Center (O'Connor *et al.*, 1964).

Of the 900 cases reviewed, 104 had been seen by a psychiatrist. However, only 57 patients had an adequate follow-up period (a minimum of five years) or sufficient therapy to provide for an effective evaluation. The term 'psychotherapy' refers here to various methods of treatment ranging from short-term directive, environmentally oriented therapy to classical psycho-analysis. The majority of patients (38) were seen in psycho-analytically oriented psychotherapy: 13 received brief therapy (less than 20 sessions) and 6 had over 400 hours of psycho-analysis.

This 'study group' of 57 patients was matched to a control group that had not received psychiatric treatment on the basis of four variables: (1) severity of disease; (2) sex; (3) age at onset; and (4) use of steroids. Patients in the psychiatrically treated group were also rated on the basis of psychological changes—either favourable or unfavourable in their sexual and marital life, self-esteem, and vocational and social behaviour (*Figure 1*).

The most important prognostic factor was found to be the severity of disease. Accordingly, the treated and untreated groups were matched on the following bases: (1) symptomatic and proctoscopic ratings in the first recorded year of disease; and (2) the extent of colitis at the time—whether it was universal, segmental or partial. Essentially, the patient with proctitis has a good prognosis with or without psychotherapy; while the patient with severe colitis involving the total bowel has a poor prognosis.

Proctoscopic and symptomatic ratings were recorded only at the time of observation, thus eliminating the possibility of a retrospective distortion. For example, during the course of the study, two psychiatrists were questioned as to their patient's response to treatment. One, who had analysed his patient over a $2\frac{1}{2}$-year span, felt she had improved markedly, not only in her life adjustment, but also in terms of the colitis. In a separate interview, the patient concurred. However, the recorded data indicated there had been absolutely no change in the severity of the disease process from a point dating back three years before her analysis to ten years after its termination—a 13-year period. We could only ascribe the hypothetical change to the fact that the patient was dealing with the colitis more realistically and not using her symptoms for secondary gain.

The second psychiatrist had treated a patient psychotherapeutically for approximately 1½ years. His comment was 'Yes, there has been some physical improvement, but she was never very sick to start with'. On reviewing this patient's history, we found that the

Data card

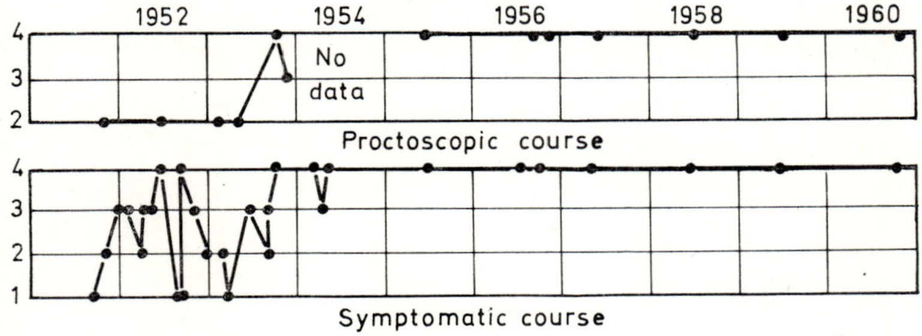

Hospitalization

11/51 7/52 3/53

Psychotherapy

3/53 1/54 134 Sessions

Significant environmental changes

• Entered own business

Emotional response to psychotherapy

Ratings	Before	After
Career	2	5
Sexual and marital	2	4
Family	2	3
Self esteem	2	5
Observer		4

Steroids: None

Psychiatric diagnosis: Personality disorder
Paranoid personality

Figure 1

early medical records revealed that her illness had indeed been severe and a three-year follow-up showed marked improvement. Due to the patient's personality structure in the course of the treatment she concentrated less on the colitis, and more on her emotional problems —marital difficulties, etc.

Observations such as these indicate how misleading the subjective reports of patients, or even physicians can be, and emphasize the need for currently recorded data in order to ensure an accurate evaluation. Clinical psychiatric research should be based on a demonstrable, not an undemonstrable or 'feeling proposition', which more often than not tends to be related to the observer and not the observed.

FINDINGS

Figure 2 illustrates the proctoscopic and symptomatic course of the

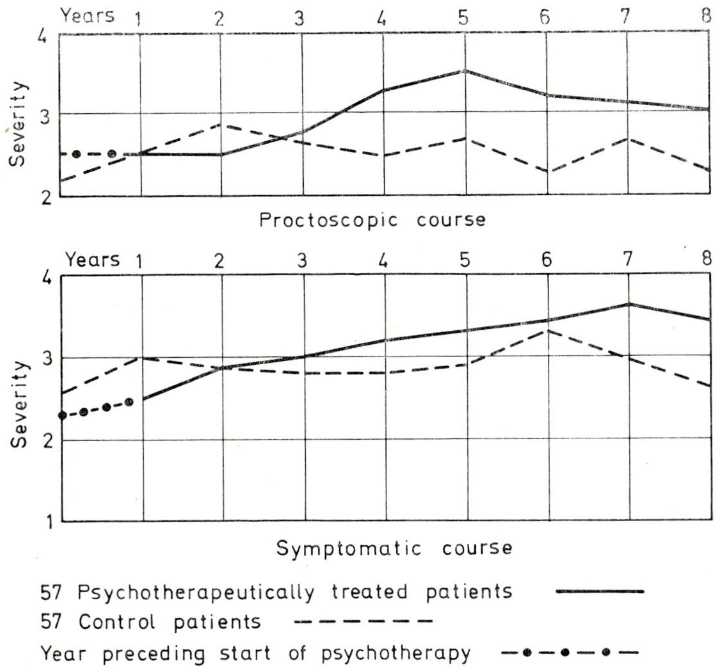

Figure 2. Proctoscopic and symptomatic ratings of psychotherapeutically treated patients and control patients

illness over an eight-year period. The patients averaged three proctoscopic examinations per year. The first year noted precedes the start of psychotherapy, the remaining seven years are those following its inception.

Findings in a single year might indicate that psychotherapy: (1) has no effect on the disease (third year); (2) is beneficial (fourth to eighth years); or (3) is detrimental (second year). However, when the overall course is observed, a definite pattern emerges. While in the first year of psychotherapy the treated patients rate consistently lower than the control group, by the third year a sustained improvement becomes apparent and at the time of final observation, the treated group shows considerable improvement, both symptomatically and proctoscopically. The control group, on the other hand, shows no improvement from its initial symptomatic rating, and a minimal gain proctoscopically.

As the study progressed, it became evident that those patients who were schizophrenic had a markedly unfavourable prognosis. Accordingly, this group was evaluated separately and their course of illness compared with that of the remaining treated and control patients (*Figure 3*). Proctoscopically, the schizophrenics who started

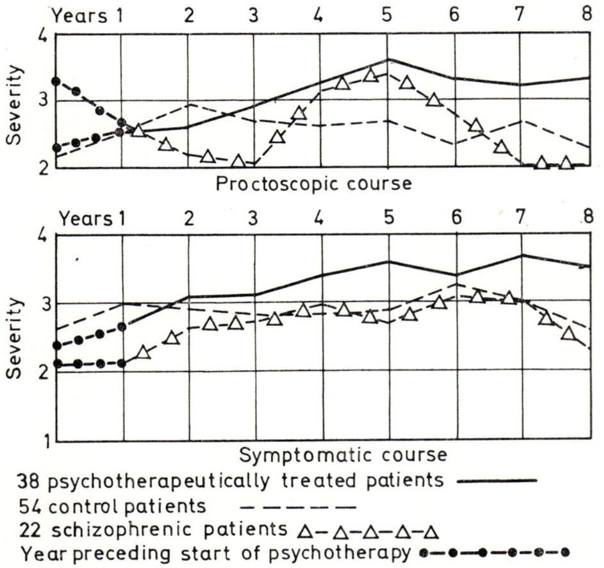

Figure 3. Proctoscopic and symptomatic ratings of psychotherapeutically treated patients and control patients with schizophrenic patients removed and charted as a separate group

off the eight-year period with the least evidence of disease (minimal inflammation), deteriorated steadily, dropping from their original high rating to the lowest possible one. The treated group except for the schizophrenics showed definite improvement while the controls remained essentially unchanged.

Symptomwise, those treated patients diagnosed as schizophrenic showed a slight gain after eight years, while the non-schizophrenic portion of the treated group improved markedly and ended the recorded period with a rating which denotes almost complete absence of symptoms. The controls remained much the same at the last year of measurement.

It should be noted that 19 (33 per cent) of the psychiatrically treated patients were diagnosed schizophrenic as compared to only 3 (6 per cent) of the controls. Yet the treated group fared significantly better than the control group, despite the high incidence of schizophrenia and its associated poor prognostic implications. These findings not only re-emphasize the value of psychotherapy in the treatment of ulcerative colitis, but also demonstrate the fallibility of using an individual patient to assess either the positive or negative effects of such treatment.

In a continuing investigation (O'Connor *et al.*, 1966), 40 schizophrenic patients were compared to a non-schizophrenic control group. Matching was on the basis of the previously established variables, with psychotherapy introduced as an additional criterion. The findings confirmed the poor prognosis for co-existing ulcerative colitis and schizophrenia. Both proctoscopically and symptomatically, the course of illness among the schizophrenics was one of decidedly greater severity (*Figure 4*). Even more striking was the discrepancy in mortality and surgical rates: the incidence of death and operative intervention for the schizophrenic group more than *doubled* that of the control group.

INTER-RELATIONSHIP OF PHYSICAL AND PSYCHOLOGICAL SYMPTOMS

The combined presence of ulcerative colitis and schizophrenia led to a further examination of the inter-relationship of physical and psychological symptoms. Accordingly, the schizophrenic series was reviewed in order to determine when, during the course of a somatic illness, overt signs of emotional disorder appeared most frequently—whether during an exacerbation or remission of disease (O'Connor and Stern, 1967). In most cases there was a simultaneous increase in psychological and somatic manifestations—a *concomitance*, rather than an *alternation* of symptoms (*Figure 5*). For 36 of the 40 schizophrenic patients (90 per cent), the earliest indication of obvious emotional disorder was at the onset of, or during an exacerbation of, colitis. Following the initial schizophrenic episode, 10 of these patients maintained a more or less constant degree of psychotic symptoms over a 10–20 year period and showed little, if any, change in emotional status with fluctuations of the colitis. It is interesting to

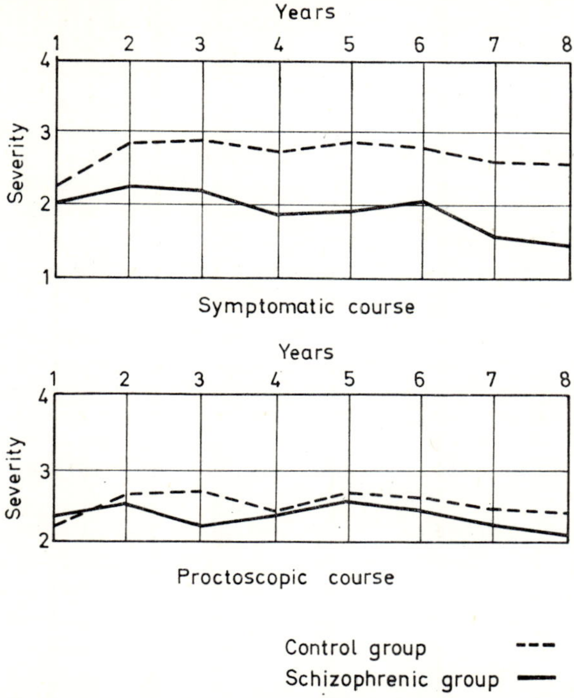

Figure 4. Symptomatic and proctoscopic ratings of 40 schizophrenic and 40 control patients over an eight-year period

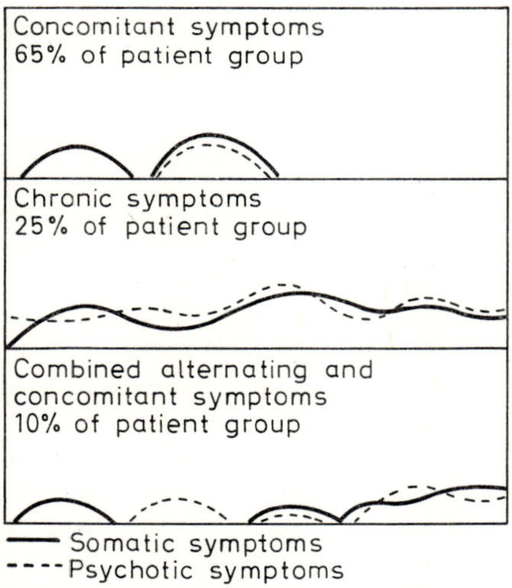

Figure 5. Representational graph: chronological relationship between somatic and psychotic symptoms in 40 patients with schizophrenia and ulcerative colitis

note that the somatic course of these 10 patients was also characterized more by chronicity than by periodic exacerbation and remission.

In 26 (65 per cent) of the schizophrenic patients, acute disturbances of a psychotic nature coincided timewise with physiological flare-ups. Four patients (10 per cent) exhibited both an alternation and concomitance of symptoms over the years, but the exacerbations of schizophrenia and colitis were too disparate chronologically to be related to each other:

> Between 1943 and 1945 one patient was hospitalized on six occasions for colitis. He recovered, but from 1946 to 1947 was institutionalized because of a schizophrenic reaction. In 1954, there was a moderate attack of colitis and another schizophrenic episode. He became symptom-free from 1958 to 62, but then required hospitalization for a severe exacerbation of colitis and an acute schizophrenic reaction. Neither disease process improved and he died in 1963.

The co-existence of somatic and psychological crises was most strikingly apparent in those patients undergoing surgery. In general, the possibility of psychosis in routine operative procedures is not a serious concern, even in patients with a history of emotional disturbance. A review of the literature indicates that the rates vary from 0·6 to 2 per cent (Knox, 1961; Lewis, 1955; Kelley, 1960). Recently, however, in open heart surgery, a most stressful surgical procedure, incidences ranging from 38 to 57 per cent have been reported (Blachley, 1964; Egerton and Kay, 1964; Kornfeld, Zimberg and Malm, 1965). In our group of schizophrenic patients, 52 per cent became grossly psychotic at time of colectomy, either just before operation, or immediately after. (In six patients, this was the first sign of overt emotional disorder.) Since an operative psychosis can be a major problem in terms of medical management, psychiatric consultation and follow-up should always be considered when surgery is contemplated for any ulcerative colitis patient, and is essential for the patient with overt psychological problems.

One would expect to see a higher incidence of emotional symptoms once surgery has been performed and the target organ removed if the concept of symptom alternation were valid. None of our patient group became psychotic, nor did any establish a new psychosomatic 'target organ' after colectomy. In 16 cases that were followed for several years after surgery, only one showed evidence of increased emotional disturbance, and this patient also had a steady downhill course somatically, terminating in death eight years later. Eight of the remaining post-operative cases, were markedly improved psychologically and seven slightly so, or essentially unchanged.

In assessing the inter-relationship of psychological and physical symptoms, it was observed that the same pattern of concomitant illness occurred among the non-psychotic patients in our series. Neurotic traits—i.e. severe anxiety, depression or obsessional manifestations—developed primarily at the time of an exacerbation of colitis. In many cases the combined psychological and somatic flare-ups appeared to be a direct response to some external stress.

Stress in psychophysiological disorders has to be well defined. While most patients react to 'normal' anxiety-provoking situations —death, loss of job, divorce, etc.—it is not infrequent to see a patient with a 'paradoxical' stress reaction, wherein an apparently pleasurable situation produces an increase in symptoms. One such case was an unmarried young female who for three summers, during vacation time, had experienced an exacerbation of her colitis. The vacation produced two very conflictual situations: (1) close contact with an authoritative mother, making unavailable the normal escape routes of visiting friends, etc.; and (2) dealing more directly with her sexual feelings towards the males at the resort.

One does encounter an occasional patient who demonstrates an alternation of symptoms. These cases are very dramatic and attract the attention of all involved; however, they are the exception, not the rule, and the physician cannot prognosticate on the basis of an hypothesis. Treatment has to be related to the individual patient and the existing medical, psychiatric or surgical problem, not to a premise that one syndrome, if alleviated, is likely to be replaced by another.

There has been recurrent conjecture as to whether or not steroids tend to precipitate psychosis. The frequency has probably been over-estimated (O'Connor, 1959; O'Connor and Musher, 1966). Early reports implicated steroids as aetiological in psychoses that were probably due to other factors. Of our 114 patients, only one had what could be considered a 'steroid-induced psychosis'.

When a patient being treated with steroids becomes psychotic, all other aetiological avenues should be investigated before medication is cancelled. Even if the patient does experience such a crisis, one might well decide to continue steroids as medically indicated, realizing that the psychosis will abate as the disease goes into remission, at which time the steroids can be safely reduced or withdrawn.

INDICATIONS FOR, AND METHODS OF, PSYCHIATRIC TREATMENT

Engel (1955) described patients with ulcerative colitis as being compulsive in nature, neat, orderly, punctual, conscientious and indecisive. Daniels (1940) has emphasized the presence of depression—others have added that these individuals are over-sensitive and susceptible to any hint of rejection or hostility. While it is true that, in a large series, the majority may have these character traits, the fact remains that many people who do not have ulcerative colitis show very much the same personality structure with similar patterns of depression and anxiety. When considering psychiatric treatment, equivalent factors of selection should apply whether or not the individual has ulcerative colitis. Even in the absence of physical illness, many of these patients would require psychotherapy. There does appear to be a higher level of emotional, familial and environmental difficulties than usually accompany the other psychophysiological disorders.

Psychiatric intervention is definitely indicated when the following conditions are present:

(1) An overt depression or anxiety.

(2) A history or evidence of psychosis.

(3) A poor environmental situation that the patient is unable to deal with.

In varying degrees, severe depression or anxiety are associated with ulcerative colitis and, within limits, are appropriate to the debilitating, threatening aspects of the disease, particularly during exacerbations. Understanding on the part of the physician and nursing staff, rest, tranquillizers or anti-depressants, and well-regulated visiting hours, can do much to allay such reactions. However, should the depression or anxiety become severe, psychiatric consultation and evaluation are definitely indicated.

Since schizophrenics were found to have a poor prognosis, psychiatric consultation should be routine for such patients. While insight therapy may not be possible, much can be done to relieve the currently existing emotional stress with an active programme of direction or support, and, at times, manipulation of the environment.

A poor environmental situation is always an indication for psychiatric consultation. If the patient is experiencing major stress at work, within the family, socially, sexually, etc., early therapeutic intervention can help to eliminate areas of conflict that in the future may become sources of chronic stress.

A young female at menarche experienced an acute, fulminating onset of colitis. Psychiatric consultation revealed that the mother, more than the daughter, was disturbed; also that the relationship between the two had markedly deteriorated when the daughter began to menstruate. At that time the mother began to check on her daughter continuously in all areas of life—even to the extent of accompanying her to the bathroom.

The girl resented this invasion of privacy, but was unable to express her anger, which might have effected a necessary change. She subsequently developed a severe attack of ulcerative colitis requiring long-term hospitalization. A treatment programme was established that centred chiefly on the mother's problems. Within a month of its initiation, the mother was able to accept the psychiatrist's suggestions to allow the girl more freedom and independence. The colitis subsided shortly thereafter.

This short-term psychiatric intervention was felt to be crucial in that it not only relieved the existing emotional stress, but also set a healthier pattern for the future relationship between mother and daughter. On an eight-year follow-up, the patient had been married, had a child of her own and had had no recurrence of the colitis.

At times it may be necessary to remove a patient from the situational conflict:

An 18-year-old male with moderately severe colitis lived in a household where his parents fought incessantly. The boy was constantly the target of his father's anger. Upon graduation from high school, the psychiatrist strongly recommended that he choose a college well removed from home. This advice was accepted and the young man has remained symptom-free for 15 years.

Under similar circumstances, another young man with colitis enrolled at a school some distance from his home town. Following graduation, he returned to live with his parents. A severe exacerbation occurred shortly thereafter and within a year he required colectomy.

Direct or supportive treatment does not necessarily require a psychiatrist; active participation by a physician, sensitive to the needs of his patient, is often sufficient to resolve the current crisis. A social worker, using support, suggestion, and environmental manipulation can be most helpful in favourably modifying an undesirable family or social situation.

It is important to understand that many patients will refuse to see a psychiatrist, or may be untreatable by psycho-analysis or psychoanalytically oriented therapy. Often, the most one should strive for is a good relationship based on a knowledge of the dependency needs of the patient which will enable him to function more effectively. This type of patient, when 'forced' to accept insights, may well develop an exacerbation of his colitis.

The psychiatrist must be flexible, moving slowly and guarding against too early and too active intervention. This is particularly necessary during a severe exacerbation. While interpretation of a problem provides a patient with valuable insight, it can also bring him face to face with a currently insoluble situation, which in and of itself, can increase anxiety or depression. The anxiety or depression, in turn, can aggravate the somatic symptoms.

It is useful when first seeing a seriously ill patient to take a detailed history and temporarily limit activity to a supportive type of treatment. Later, when the disease is in remission and a better understanding of the patient has been obtained, there is time to probe more deeply into the psychological difficulties. If one accepts the tenet that emotional factors contribute to the illness, then it is certainly important not to impose additional emotional stress.

In short, there are many factors that one must consider in evaluating the 'treatability' of a patient with ulcerative colitis. As of now, it appears that some can definitely benefit from psychotherapy or psycho-analysis—but a specific type of treatment must be carefully selected and be appropriately oriented towards the individual patient. Much work will have to be done before there is a fuller understanding of how psychiatric intervention favourably influences the course of ulcerative colitis. Intensive research with larger series of patients using physical criteria are required if the effects of psychological treatment on a physiological disease are to be understood.

PSYCHOTHERAPY

Currently under investigation are certain pre-existing psychogenic factors that can contribute to prognosis—favourable or unfavourable—in ulcerative colitis. There appears to be a concordance between the previous emotional state, the patient's handling of the disease and the eventual outcome. Data so far collected indicate there are many pre-morbid factors that can be related to the eventual course of the disease. Factors also arise from patient–therapist interaction that can influence the course of psychiatric treatment, and, as a result, the course of the colitis (Karush *et al.*, 1968, 1969).

It is important to deal with the patient's need to use the physical symptoms as a defence against psychological insights. This can be done by an apparent inattention to the constant recounting of somatic complaints, and a concentration on current and past psychological conflicts. The physical symptom can be interpreted early on as a mechanism of defence or, if the material is available, an expression of affect. This enables the physician to get through quickly to the defensive techniques or the affectual avoidance. At times the patient may use the 'diarrhoea and bleeding' as a means of manipulating the treatment to gain extra care and attention or to threaten the psychiatrist. This should be directly interpreted. In contrast to such a patient, another may, at times of extreme stress in treatment, experience a sharp increase in symptoms. With this type of patient it is wise to switch the focus of treatment temporarily until the patient is better able to handle the current conflict. In the course of treatment one should not under-estimate the need of a dependent relationship and the fear of death that is present in the ulcerative colitis patient. The transference, and the therapist's willingness to accept such a transference, is crucial. It allows a dependency which, if handled carefully and with understanding, can be utilized to eventually develop increasing independence, thereby reinforcing the ego assets of the patient.

It is important at the termination of treatment that the 'door be left open'. If an exacerbation occurs, return to a familiar therapeutic situation can be crucial for recovery. In our study group one patient felt 'ashamed' when the colitis recurred. She went to another medical facility where a questionable colon resection was performed. Later, she had an intestinal perforation and died. Another patient, who was seen over a 20-year period returned to her psychiatrist whenever an exacerbation occurred. She responded well to short-term intervention with a marked decrease in her colitis symptoms.

It appears that patients who use the colitis for 'secondary gain' are likely to have a poorer prognosis than those who tend to resent and ignore the disease. A sense of hopefulness on both the part of the psychiatrist and the patient seemed to lead to a better prognosis. The therapist must be sensitive to the personality structure and defensive techniques of the patient and adjust treatment accordingly. In this disease the psychological treatment has to be flexible, related to the psychopathology, the severity of colitis, the patient's current environment and other factors, not to a previously established formulation which may or may not be related to the individual.

RESULTS OF SURGICAL INTERVENTION

Following colectomy, many patients require virtually a year or more to adjust physically to the stoma. The colectomy often entails two or three additional hospitalizations for corrective surgery such as stoma revision, relief of obstruction, or prolapse. This possibility should be explained early to the patient, not as a complication or setback, but rather as a potential part of adjustment to the procedure. In our follow-up study of colectomy patients (Druss *et al.*, 1968), most felt that their general health was good to excellent, and that having an ileostomy was preferable to living with the debilitating effects of severe chronic ulcerative colitis.

However, good results in the performance areas of school, work and social activities did not always carry through to a sense of personal well-being. Many patients described subjective problems related to their ileostomy, i.e. sexual problems, fears of 'accidents', odour, 'straining themselves', and embarrassment. Most indicated that acceptance of the ileostomy by key figures in their life (family, employer), etc. was essential for a successful adjustment on their own part. Visits by the local ileostomy club members were considered most helpful, both in training and in providing successful models for identification.

The central role of the surgeon in this situation cannot be minimized. It is to him that the patient will turn for all aspects of his care after colectomy. The intense personal relationship between the patient and internist prior to operation may now shift to the surgeon, who must be aware of the many emotional difficulties that the patient is experiencing. The patient may be hesitant to verbalize these feelings. A 'contract of silence' in the doctor–patient relationship allows unrealistic fantasies and anxieties to develop in the mind of the patient.

One should not under-estimate the degree of depression and the extreme state of dependency that the post-colectomy patient is in (Druss, O'Connor and Stern, 1969). Consideration and support, and at times firmness, are necessary to pull him through this stage. A slight negative expression or remark on the part of the ward personnel can cause considerable psychological damage. Since, as a rule, the internist and psychiatrist play a small role in this stage of the patient's care the responsibility falls primarily on to the surgeon.

SUMMARY

To conclude, ulcerative colitis probably has both genetic and constitutional predeterminants. While gastro-intestinal symptoms are the most obvious manifestations, other organ systems are also involved—e.g. skin, joints, etc. Psychological factors have a significant effect in the onset of the individual exacerbation and in determining the patient's response to and handling of this illness.

The effects of psychotherapy or psycho-analysis on the course of ulcerative colitis are not yet fully understood. Individual case reports are optimistic and recent sizeable series, although less optimistic, have shown that it can favourably modify the course of the disease. Advantageous environmental changes have contributed significantly to somatic improvement in many cases. It appears that when psychotherapy does not improve the physical picture, it can still help the individual adapt more readily to the handicaps of chronic illness, thus providing a better life adjustment.

The treating physician has to be sensitive to the emotional stresses and conflicts of the individual and thoroughly aware of the status of the physical illness. Effective management of an ulcerative colitis patient requires conjoint participation of medicine, psychiatry and surgery; close contact and understanding between the various disciplines are essential if the goals of treatment are to be realized as fully as possible.

In this disease more than others, conflicts between various specialties tend to lead to inadequate treatment. Such conflicts should be kept to research or the literature—and not involve the patient.

REFERENCES

Bargen, J. A. and Kennedy, R. L. J. (1965). 'Chronic Ulcerative Colitis in Children.' *Postgrad. Med.* **17,** 127.

Blachley, P. H. (1964). 'Post-cardiotomy Delirium.' *Am. J. Psychiat.*, **121,** 371.

Cushing, M. W. (1953). 'The Psychoanalytic Treatment of a Man Suffering with Ulcerative Colitis.' *J. Am. Psychoanalyt. Ass.*, **1,** 510.

Daniels, G. E. (1940). 'Treatment of a Case of Ulcerative Colitis Associated with Hysterical Depression.' *Psychosom. Med.*, **2,** 276.

Druss, R. G., O'Connor, J. F., Prudden, J. and Stern, L. O. (1968). 'Psychologic Response to Colectomy.' *Archs gen. Psychiat.*, **18,** 53.

— — and Stern, L. O. (1969). 'Psychologic Response to Colectomy. II. Adjustment to a Permanent Colostomy.' *Archs gen. Psychiat.*, **20,** 419.

Egerton, N. and Kay, J. H. (1964). 'Psychological Disturbances Associated with Open Heart Surgery.' *Br. J. Psychiat.*, **110,** 433.

Engel, G. L. (1955). 'Studies of Ulcerative Colitis. III. The Nature of the Psychologic Processes.' *Am. J. Med.*, **19,** 231.

Grace, W. J., Pinsley, R. H. and Wolff, H. G. (1954). 'The Treatment of Ulcerative Colitis.' *Gastroenterology*, **26,** 462.

Harper, E. O. (1962). 'Prolonged Narcosis in the Treatment of Severe Ulcerative Colitis.' *Gastroenterology*, **42,** 758.

Karush, A. and Daniels, G. (1953). 'Ulcerative Colitis, Psychoanalyses of 2 Cases.' *Psychosom. Med.*, **15,** 140.

— — O'Connor, J. F. and Stern, L. O. (1968). 'The Response to Psychotherapy in Chronic Ulcerative Colitis. I. Pretreatment Factors.' *Psychosom. Med.*, **30,** 255.

— — — — (1969). 'The Response to Psychotherapy in Chronic Ulcerative Colitis. II. Factors Arising from the Therapeutic Situation.' *Psychosom. Med.*, **31,** 201.

Kelley, H. A. (1960). *Am. J. Obstet. Gynec.*, **79,** 498.

Kirsner, J. B., Raskin, H. F. and Palmer, W. L. (1955). 'Ulcerative Colitis in Children.' *Am. J. dis. Child.*, **90,** 141.

Knox, S. J. (1961). 'Severe Psychiatric Disturbances in the Post-operative Period.' *J. ment. Sci.*, **107,** 1078.

Kornfeld, D. S., Zimberg, S. and Malm, J. R. (1965). 'Psychiatric Complications of Open Heart Surgery.' *New Engl. J. Med.*, **273,** 287.

Levy, R., Wilkens, H., Herrmann, J., Lisle, A., Jr. and Rix, A. (1956). 'Experiences with Prefrontal Lobotomy for Intractable Ulcerative Colitis.' *J. Am. med. Ass.*, **160,** 1277.

Lewis, A. (1955). 'The Relationship Between Operative Risk and the Patient's General Condition.' In Report XVI, Congress International de Chirurgie, Copenhagen, 1955.

Michener, W. M., Gage, R. P., Sauer, W. G. and Strickler, G. B. (1961). 'The Prognosis of Chronic Ulcerative Colitis in Children.' *New Engl. J. Med.*, **265,** 1075.

Murray, C. D. (1930). 'Psychogenic Factors in the Etiology of Ulcerative Colitis and Bloody Diarrhea.' *Am. J. med. Sci.*, **180,** 239.

O'Connor, J. F. (1959). 'Psychoses Associated with Systemic Lupus Erythematosus.' *Ann. int. Med.*, **51,** 526.

— and Musher, D. (1966). 'Central Nervous System Involvement in Systemic Lupus Erythematosus.' *Archs Neurol.*, **14,** 157.

— and Stern, L. O. (1967). 'Symptom Alternation: An Evaluation of the Theory.' *Archs gen. Psychiat.*, **16,** 432.

— Daniels, G. E., Flood, C., Karush, A. Moses, L. and Stern, L. O. (1964). 'An Evaluation of the Effectiveness of Psychotherapy in the Treatment of Ulcerative Colitis.' *Ann. int. Med.*, **60,** 587.

— — Karush, A., Flood, C. and Stern, L. O. (1966). 'Prognostic Implications of the Psychiatric Diagnosis in Ulcerative Colitis.' *Psychosom. Med.*, **28,** 375.

Sperling, M. (1957). 'The Psychoanalytic Treatment of Ulcerative Colitis.' *Int. J. Psychoanal.*, **38,** 341.

Sullivan, A. J. and Chandler, C. A. (1932). 'Ulcerative Colitis of Psychogenic Origin: Report of 6 Cases.' *Yale J. Biol. Med.*, **4,** 779.

Weinstock, H. (1961). 'Hospital Psychotherapy in Severe Ulcerative Colitis.' *Archs gen. Psychiat.*, **4,** 509.

— (1962). 'Successful Treatment of Ulcerative Colitis by Psychoanalysts: a Survey of 28 Cases with Follow-up.' *J. psychosom. Res.*, **6,** 243.

CHAPTER 12

PSYCHOPHYSIOLOGICAL ASPECTS OF RHEUMATOID ARTHRITIS AND AUTO-IMMUNE DISEASE

GEORGE F. SOLOMON

INTRODUCTION

Psychosomatic research has richly documented correlations among personality variables, stress events and various disease states. Controversy persists, of course, about specificity of emotional factors for particular diseases and about the role of disease itself in inducing the observed personality traits. The time seems at hand for predictive studies and for greater efforts at elucidating physiological mechanisms, particularly nervous and hormonal, via which environmental factors and mental events play a role in pathogenesis of disease, the multifactorial causes of which may concern genetic, behavioural–nervous and immune inter-relationships (Salk, 1962). Host resistance and immunity and their relationship to stress and integrity of psychological defences may provide an underlying and unifying principle relating emotional factors to the onset and course, not only of infectious diseases and cancer, the resistance to which increasing evidence finds to be immunological in nature (Habel, 1963; Prehn, 1963), but also of auto-immune disease (Solomon, 1964). As will be discussed further, auto-immune diseases, conditions associated with immune reactivity against some component of an individual's own body, seem to be associated with states of relative immunological deficiency (Fudenberg, 1968), which in turn may be stress related (Solomon, 1969).

Auto-immune diseases are generally agreed to include rheumatoid arthritis, thyroiditis, acquired haemolytic anaemia, systemic lupus erythematosus (SLE), myasthenia gravis, polyarteritis nodosa, and polymyositis. Auto-immunity has been implicated in demyelinating disease, including multiple sclerosis, Graves' disease, idiopathic thrombocytopenic purpura, ulcerative colitis, and may play a role in some cases of pernicious anaemia, diabetes, and Addison's disease (Samter and Alexander, 1965). The role of auto-antibodies themselves in producing the lesions in auto-immune diseases remains uncertain, and they may even have a 'protective' effect (Paterson,

Jacobs and Coia, 1965). Cellular hypersensitivity may be the culprit, and serum auto-antibodies tend to be regarded as 'markers' or signals (Vaughn, 1965). Clinically and serologically there are many overlapping features and unclear boundaries among these diseases. For example, malignant rheumatoid arthritis with vasculitis blends with SLE, and a significant percentage of patients with ulcerative colitis have an arthritis indistinguishable from rheumatoid. Likewise, as we shall see, reports on psychological and personality factors in several of these diseases reveal similar features. Controlled psychological studies are not available for many of these conditions because of their relative rarity, and psychosomatic observations concerning others, such as diabetes, may not be relevant to this chapter in view of the lack of clarity of the role of immunological abnormalities in aetiology. For these reasons, because of the relative richness of available data, and because of the nature of my own clinical research, I shall emphasize findings in regard to social and personal factors in rheumatoid arthritis. (The correlation of psychological variables with the clinical course of rheumatoid arthritis is dealt with in Chapter 13.) I shall then go on to discuss possible pathogenetic mechanisms and the relationship of emotions and stress to immunity.

REVIEW OF THE LITERATURE ON PSYCHOSOMATIC ASPECTS OF RHEUMATOID ARTHRITIS

Moos (1963) reviewed reports on personality data on over 5,000 patients appearing in the literature. Many early investigators who did not utilize control groups agreed that emotional factors played a role in rheumatoid arthritis but differed in which factors were cited. Worry, pressure of work, marital disharmony and real or threatened loss of relatives could be documented immediately prior to onset of disease in nearly half the cases of one series (Ellman and Mitchell, 1936). Twenty rheumatoid arthritics were described as decent-looking, quiet, cheerful, reliable, conscientious, tending to hold the same job, self-limited and restricted in their expression of feelings and frigid (Halliday, 1942). Halliday's patients described their parents as strict and described themselves as shy and retiring in school, self-sacrificing, as having few friends but being loyal to them, and as being orderly, punctual, tidy and clean. An interview study of 43 arthritics concluded that they are immature, dependent, perfectionistic people who try to please and that the onset of their disease was often preceded by separation or loss of support (Robinson, 1957).

A psycho-analytic study of eight cases found a constant personality present before the onset of disease (Ludwig, 1955). Rheumatoid arthritics were extremely dependent, felt inadequate, had difficulty coping with their environment and with other people, and were severely blocked in emotional expression. They frequently denied their dependency by overcompensating with an outward façade of independence, self-assurance and self-control. Their attitude towards work and responsibility varied from an attempt to negate their dependence, both by accepting far more responsibility than they could handle and by over-work, to a manifestation of their dependency and inadequacy by avoidance of all responsibility and reliance upon others for guidance. They avoided closeness, were aware of strong unexpressible angry feelings, reacted over-sensitively to the slightest criticism or rejection, and tended to court others' favour, allowing themselves to be imposed upon. The patients also appeared to deal with their tensions defensively by varying degrees of over-activity. Ludwig agreed with others in stating that the single most important precipitating factor was the loss of, or separation from, important key figures upon whom these patients depended for support.

A clinical study of 33 patients concluded that patients learned to discharge aggression through muscle activity in ego syntonic channels, e.g. hard work, sports, gardening, and to relieve their guilt over this by serving others (Johnson, Shapiro and Alexander, 1947). Arthritic females tended to reject the feminine role, a rejection which was manifested by their being head of the house, by making decisions and by a predilection for the masculine posture in sexual relationships. The competitive relation with men served as a discharge for hostile feelings, while the excessive masochism served both as a discharge of hostility, allowing the arthritic woman to express her anger in an acceptable fashion, and as a denial of dependent demands.

A number of investigations prior to those of Moos and Solomon utilized control groups. Rorschach test and interview data on 73 arthritic patients and matched hypertensions were compared (Booth and Klopfer, 1936; Booth, 1937). Arthritics were predominantly introverted, righteous, obstinate, strict and rigid in moral matters, eager to conform to accepted social standards, and unrelenting and unforgiving. They showed poor sexual adjustment, were hypersensitive, and had an inordinate need to be dominant and controlling. Booth also observed that arthritics were restless and showed aimless muscular activities. He concluded that, 'the more closely one studies these patients, the more conviction grows upon one that the arthritic process is not merely frequently, but always, the expression of a personality conflict'.

The Minnesota Multiphasic Personality Inventory (MMPI) was utilized in two comparable studies of a total of 125 male arthritics and 175 controls (Cohen, 1949; Wiener, 1952). Findings indicated that arthritics over-reacted to their disease and showed symptoms of emotional disturbances. The arthritics obtained higher scores than non-disabled controls on the 'neurotic' scales of the MMPI; they had an unusual number of elevated scores; however, they generally obtained more normal scores than did a second group of neurotic patients.

A study of 29 male rheumatoid arthritic patients and 29 matched neurotic controls indicated that arthritics tended to turn hostility inward, that they were not as concerned as controls with obstacles that might provoke aggression, that they were more inclined to seek solutions to frustrating problems and not as inclined to be defensive, and that they attempted to conform to conventional modes of behaviour (Mueller and Lefkovits, 1956). The Rorschach data indicated that the arthritics had unresolved conflicts in the area of parental authority, that they operated on a level of defective personality integration, that they showed defective emotional responsiveness, and that they lacked emotional maturity and were constricted. The authors concluded that the arthritics were not significantly different from the neurotic controls. A further investigation by the same group had similar findings and concluded that arthritics tend to repress or suppress negative feelings more than controls (Mueller *et al.*, 1961).

Two well-controlled studies agreed on several findings (Cleveland and Fisher, 1954, 1960). In both, arthritics reported an intensive interest and participation in sports, athletics, and hunting and fishing and, contrastingly, an interest in household activities, especially cooking. They also emphasized the inconsistent nature of things and tended to show an excess of exhibitionistic and voyeuristic fantasies. Value was placed on the act of looking and being seen, and in most cases this impulse was denied and inhibited. Overtly, the arthritic appeared to be calm, composed and optimistic, rarely if ever expressing or even consciously feeling anger. He boasted of never fighting or getting angry, although he admitted that a 'smart alec or braggart' or 'a loud mouth guy' could get him angry. The arthritics complained of social shyness and inadequacy, tended to shun the limelight, and desired to be 'just average and not stand out at all'. They also complained of inability to say the right things at the right time, and were concerned about their looks, their clothes, and the impressions they made on others. The arthritics tended to describe the parents similarly. Mother was seen as a hardworking, efficient, self-sacrificing 'Christian' woman, who would give anyone anything and go without herself. She was also a compulsively clean and efficient housekeeper. However, she was the source of considerable frustration, since she tended to be a very strict disciplinarian. Father was perceived as being hardworking, honest, friendly, easy going and good-natured, but inconsistent. 'He was quiet, but watch out!' Father was either physically absent from home, beginning early in the patient's life, or he was psychologically weak. Cleveland and Fisher concluded that rheumatoid arthritics were psychiatrically sick and suggested that rheumatoid arthritis may be a defence against regression and personality disintegration.

Using the siblings of patients as controls, 18 sib–patient pairs were studied (Cormier *et al.*, 1957). Activity and impulsiveness, interest in games and sports, and competitive and aggressive fantasies had been dominant in rheumatoid arthritics. The sibs were quiet, shy, reserved and conforming, recalling that they had been jealous of their more active, now arthritic, sibs, and that they had shown less energy in athletics. Both groups described their parents as strict. The arthritics, however, were apt to regard parental demands as excessive and to react to them with impulsive defiance; whereas their sibs either uncomplainingly accepted similar demands or by-passed them unprovocatively. The sibs became disinhibited in adulthood and developed poise and self-confidence. Outbursts of rage tended to be more common and more violent in the arthritics than in the controls. However, the controls could 'forget it', while the arthritics were harassed by guilt and remorse, a need for self-punishment, and a fear that they had inflicted great harm on the object of aggression. The arthritics tried to be punctual, tidy and perfectionistic. They emphasized financial security and showed self-sacrificing and forgiving attitudes.

The most recent extensive and careful psychosomatic study of patients with rheumatoid arthritis primarily utilizing interviews was conducted in Finland on 102 consecutive female outpatients (Rimón, 1969). Aggression tests were controlled by comparison with other medical patients. Rimón had only 2 patients with a history of psychotic symptoms, these not occurring in parallel with rheumatoid symptoms, thus agreeing with previous observations of the rarity of coincidence of schizophrenia and rheumatoid disease (Nissen and Spencer, 1936; Gregg, 1939; Trevathan and Tatum, 1954; Pilkington, 1956; Rothermilch and Philips, 1963). Overt neurotic symptoms, excluding depressive ones, were manifested relatively infrequently. Other psychosomatic conditions, particularly hyperthyroidism (which may be associated with immunological disturbance), were relatively common. In evaluating the role of life stress in the onset of the rheumatic process, interestingly, Rimón's research provided evidence for two types of rheumatoid arthritis (analogous to the process and reactive forms of schizophrenia). 'In the first one, the disease begins suddenly and the symptoms appear distinct and even fierce. The onset of the disease is most often associated with a significant psychodynamic conflict situation, and a hereditary predisposition for rheumatoid arthritis is obviously lacking. In the other type, the onset of the disease is slow and the progression of the symptoms retarded. A correlation to an actual psychodynamic conflict situation is absent; whereas, a hereditary predisposition for rheumatoid arthritis does exist, judging by the relatively great number of other affected members of the family.' Rimón's 'non-conflict group' did not differ from a series of ordinary medical patients in direct expression of aggression. Those patients with an insidious onset of disease had no obvious inability to discharge aggressive impulses and to become conscious of aggressive tendencies.

STUDIES OF RHEUMATOID ARTHRITIC PATIENTS BY MOOS AND SOLOMON

Moos and I attempted to overcome some of the severe methodological problems limiting the generalizability of results of prior studies in a series of investigations by means of: (1) utilizing carefully matched control groups; (2) testing the assumption that similar underlying personality characteristics may manifest themselves in different and/or opposite ways; (3) utilizing different assessment methods and comparing their results; and (4) combining observations of investigators of different theoretical orientations to attempt to 'balance bias' (Moos and Solomon, 1965a and b). Sixteen female patients with rheumatoid arthritis classified as definite or classical by American Rheumatism Association criteria were compared with their closest aged, healthy sisters providing an automatic control for age, sex, parents' occupational status and many other background factors. We gleaned 140 statements from the literature, each suggested by at least one author to be descriptive of patients with rheumatoid arthritis. Three raters then independently rated these statements into personality trait dimensions to eliminate overlap and redundancy. Fifteen bipolar scales (e.g. dependency vs. denial of dependence, hyperindependence) emerged. If arthritics have underlying characteristics which may be manifested in opposite ways (as, for example, through the defence mechanism of reaction formation), they should show higher inter- or intra-individual variability than a control; so that differences might be reflected either in mean differences or *variability* differences on any of the scales. These personality trait dimensions were measured in three different independent ways: (1) by regular and rationally constructed scales for the MMPI; (2) by ratings made independently by two raters for a recorded 45-minute semi-structured interview; and (3) by a specially constructed personality test. Two raters categorized all 556 MMPI items as relevant to one of the dimensions. Raters scored interviews on a five-point scale on the dimensions and achieved very high inter-rater reliability. Since some personality characteristics of arthritics might manifest themselves in a situation-specific manner, i.e. arthritics may be overly dependent in some situations or with some people but overly independent in other situations or with other people, our Affective Reaction Inventory (ARI) comprised a number of situations, e.g. 'when I have a lot of things to do'. 'when I meet a group of new people', 'when I buy a big item', and several items under each situation relevant to one of the personality trait dimensions.

Our results on the MMPI scales showed patients were significantly higher on scales measuring perfectionism, compliance and subservience, nervousness and restlessness, reserve and introversion, depression, and sensitivity (to anger). Interview rating results were largely in agreement with MMPI data. The CSI significantly differentiated patients in only two personality trait dimensions, the masochism and self-sacrifice and the bound and repressed affect dimensions. However, a comparison between patients and siblings revealed 26 cases in which a personality characteristic manifested itself significantly in one specific situation. For example, patients scored significantly lower than siblings on the response 'I feel at ease' in the situation 'when I am with someone I like'. On the other hand siblings scored high on the response 'I tend to think of radical solutions' to the situation 'when things go wrong'. In regard to inter-individual variability, patients showed a greater number of extreme scores on 15 of the reaction dimensions on the ratings.

All the interviews covered the following areas: descriptions of self, sibling, mother, father, current and/or former husband; expression of anger; ability to manifest dependent behaviour; extent of present and previous physical activity; and events at the time of onset of symptoms. In addition, a short psychodrama was conducted. Each subject was told she had purchased a steam iron and found it defective. The interviewer played an unreasonable, hostile store complaint manager and tried to elicit anger, defiance and assertiveness in the subject by refusing to accept the iron, blaming her for damage, requesting money for repairs, etc. Each of the ten different content areas were transferred on to separate tapes, e.g. all patients' self-descriptions recorded on one tape. Recordings were analysed by an independent judge utilizing word counts of frequency of relevant material.

Vast differences in self-descriptive adjectives utilized by the two groups were clear. The patients generally described themselves as nervous, tense, worried, struggling, depressed, moody, highly strung, and easily upset; their siblings generally described themselves as liking people; as active and constantly busy; as easy to get acquainted with; as good, hard, productive workers; and as enjoying life in a generally unruffled manner. Thus, the patients saw themselves as far more 'pathologic' than the siblings saw themselves. Actual counts of adjectives and descriptive phrases used by the two groups indicated, further, that the patients put more emphasis on their emotional sensitivity, i.e. on being shy, inhibited, and hard to get to know; whereas, the siblings put more emphasis on being optimistic and easy going. Both groups seemed to have strong needs to see themselves as hardworking, productive, energetic, constantly busy individuals who successfully completed a large variety of tasks and continually saw progress in their lives. The siblings could in fact accomplish many of these goals, while the patients, in general, could not. These descriptions were in agreement with test results, which showed the patients to be higher on a variety of test scales measuring clinical symptomatology.

There are two other important findings relative to the patients' and siblings' descriptions of each other. First, the siblings showed greater freedom to express criticism. Second, the siblings tended to utilize negatively toned descriptive phrases in describing what the patients were like as children, i.e. before the onset of arthritis. For example, phrases such as 'poor little girl', 'always felt inferior', 'was told she was homely', was 'sickly and inactive', 'was shy, worried, and lazy', etc., were generally used by the sibling in describing the patient as a child. They were hardly ever used in the patients' descriptions of what their siblings were like as children.

The patients and siblings tended to agree on their descriptions of their mothers. The mothers were described in very positive terms, such as 'she worked very hard', 'she was never cross', 'she was very easy going', 'nothing ever bothered her', 'she took everything in her stride', 'she was sweet', 'she'd do anything for anyone to help them'.

This picture of the mothers was in close agreement with that given by Cleveland and Fisher's (1954) male arthritic patients. Interestingly, some patients did call their mothers intolerant, cold, unexpressive, overly submissive, impatient, and strict, while the siblings of these patients made essentially no critical comments about these same mothers. These differences suggest that the patients may have been more aware of and possibly more exposed to and/or bothered by their mothers' 'negative' traits and perhaps by what they perceived to be their mothers' inconsistency and rejection of them.

In general, fathers were described as representing one of two extremes. Some were seen as completely irresponsible, unreliable, unambitious, unreasonable, high-tempered, strict, overly dominating, etc. For example, one father was described as habitually drunk, as continually beating his wife, as burning the bed when his wife would not sleep with him, and as trying to 'get fresh with me, his own daughter'. Other fathers were described as easy going, gentle, determined, smart, hardworking, affectionate, lenient, wonderful, kind, good-natured, tolerant, yielding, etc. These rather stereotypic descriptions would suggest that neither the patients nor the siblings viewed their fathers very realistically.

Both patients and siblings tended to perceive both parents as being rather strict in discipline. The patients, however, viewed their fathers as stricter than the siblings viewed them. There was no evidence that the patients reacted to this discipline any more defiantly than their siblings. In those homes in which the parents were described as more lenient, the patients stated that they felt they knew what the boundaries were and never dared cross them. For example, one patient stated that her father 'was not strict and never hit us, he didn't have to'. The patients were, then, bothered more by the rejection they perceived from their mothers and the strictness they perceived from their fathers.

The patients' and siblings' descriptions of their spouses and their marriages showed striking differences. Almost all siblings tended to describe their marriages as reasonably happy and generally satisfactory, although with some problems. The patients, on the other hand, tended to describe their marriages in one of two extreme ways. Patients stated that their husbands were 'so good to me, it's pathetic'; 'marvellous, very easy going, calm, and relaxed'; or, in contrast, 'irresponsible, alcoholic, completely un-understanding'; 'mean, used to torture me'.

An even more noteworthy difference between the two groups was in their descriptions of the handling of disagreements between themselves and their husbands. There were no siblings who stated that they did not have any fights with their husbands, while 13 of the 16 patients so stated. Even those patients who had described very poor marriages still stated that they never argued with their husbands. These patients were martyr-like and masochistic in the extreme in relation to their husbands. For example, one patient described grotesque beatings she received from her husband. He stretched her mouth, would choke her and hold the bed covers over her head, would make her sit and watch him bowl for hours on end. She stated that she kept all her feelings inside and never complained. 'You can't blame him; he had a mean father.'

The siblings, as stated, mentioned that they did have arguments and disagreements with their husbands. In addition, they tended to react to situations more quickly and defiantly. For example, one sibling, who had had an alcoholic husband, told with some glee how she managed to get him to endorse a $900 cheque, had given him $30 in cash, and had then left, never to see him again.

The patients and siblings, as might be expected, also showed differences in their answers to the question, 'tell me the last time you got angry'. Almost all siblings either stated that they expressed their anger or provided at least one recent example of when they had expressed anger. Only two patients directly stated that they expressed angry feelings. There were no patient–sibling pairs in which the patient stated that she expressed anger more freely than the sibling. The siblings were apt to get angry at their husbands and children if provoked; the patients tended almost never to admit anger towards people who played significant roles in their lives. When patients did give examples of getting angry, these were far more remote in time than the examples given by the siblings. In addition, almost all patients made statements about feeling hurt, getting upset, or feeling bad when they were in situations which might, according to outside observers, be termed anger-provoking. The siblings did not mention these feelings nearly as often.

Examples convey the flavour of the patients' anger. One patient stated that the last time she had got slightly annoyed (not angry) was when she had a disagreement with a lady friend about what baseball team was playing in town. She found that she was wrong and stated that she felt very bad in that she had probably annoyed her friend and hurt her feelings. Another patient mentioned a 'serious' disagreement with her husband. When pressed for details, she stated that one night he had said that she was henpicking him. This caused her to leave the house immediately, drive away, park the car and think. This incident had occurred two years previously, and, since the patient remembered even the exact words her husband had spoken, it can be safely surmised that she was particularly sensitive to his anger.

During the psychodrama the interviewer attempted, by various techniques such as raising objections and questioning the honesty, trustworthiness, or sense of fair play of the subject, to induce some anger and assertiveness in each subject. The psychodrama was used in order to give a 'real-life' estimate of possible differences between the two groups in their tendency to express anger. Analysis of these data strongly supported earlier results. There were no patients who expressed more anger in this situation than did their siblings, and there were only two patients who were more assertive than their siblings. For example, many of the siblings stated that they would complain to the store manager, to the Better Business Bureau, to the company which had made the iron, or to a small claims court. This ability to threaten the mediation of a 'higher authority' was part of what was labelled an assertive handling of the problem. This was much more prevalent in the siblings than in the patients.

There was no evidence of a difference in dependency between the patients and their siblings. Almost every subject in the two groups described herself as being highly independent. The subjects made statements like 'I co-operate with others but never rely on them'; 'I don't think I ever relied on anyone'; 'I have never in the past asked anyone for favours'. In addition, the patients were only able to accept help if others strongly wished to give it and directly offered it. Patients felt pride in not asking others for favours and accepted favours only with an expressed fear of being obligated. On the other hand, patients frequently commented on how they derived pleasure from helping others.

Both groups were asked about the extent of their physical activity in childhood and at present. There were no differences in the amount of physical activity mentioned by the two groups; hence, the often-made hypothesis that rheumatoid arthritic patients involved themselves in more activity before their illness was not confirmed by these data. This negative finding seems related to the control group since both patients and sisters had shown considerable interest in sports. The patients had a certain keenness, delight and pleasure in discussing their past and present activity; whereas, the siblings seemed to be much more matter-of-fact in their descriptions.

Previous data on traumatic events in relation to onset of arthritis indicated that when large groups of matched patients and controls were questioned there were no differences in the number of such events mentioned by the two groups (Empire Rheumatism Council, 1950). Though uncontrolled for similar events in the lives of controls, almost every patient of ours did link the development of her arthritis with some acute or chronic stress situation. One patient talked of having to move from one town to another against her strong wishes; another talked of a traumatic experience associated with surgery; a third developed arthritis during a year in which her father had a stroke, her brother-in-law passed away, her mother-in-law, whom she did not care for, came to live with her, and her house caught fire; still another spoke about taking care of her mentally ill husband for three years.

A large-scale MMPI study compared 49 female rheumatoid arthritic patients and 53 of their healthy female family members utilizing our rationally derived scales, the regular three validation and nine clinical scales, and 113 published special scales (Moos and Solomon, 1964a). Statistical significance was evaluated by determining the percentage of MMPI scales that would show 'significant' differences between the groups on the basis of chance alone. Far more scales than would occur by chance showed significant differences between arthritics and family members and comprised scales reflecting: (1) physical symptoms; (2) depression, apathy and lack of motivation; (3) other general 'neurotic' symptoms such as anxiety, masochism, self-alienation and over-compliance; (4) psychological rigidity; and (5) similarity to the other psychosomatic conditions.

To summarize, our studies differed from previous ones in that there were no significant differences between patients and controls in dependency; both patients and siblings described themselves as being very independent though patients had somewhat more difficulty in accepting help from others. Both patients and siblings, likewise, had shown interest and earlier participation in sports, but patients spoke of their interest with great keenness and delight in physical activity, possibly as the result of the restriction of their disease. Evidence for at least some patients does suggest, however, that decreases in the amount of physical activity to which a patient had been accustomed may have *preceded* the development of arthritis, e.g. abandonment of participation in competitive sport because of the responsibility of family or advancing age. Observers but not patients themselves considered the patients more duty-oriented and conscientious. The clearest and most consistent finding related to the masochism, self-sacrifice and denial of hostility shown by arthritic patients. Although patients and siblings agreed reasonably closely in the descriptions of their parents, the patients were bothered more by the rejection they perceived from their mothers and the strictness they perceived from their fathers. The patients tended to describe their marriages either as extremely good or extremely bad; whereas, the siblings tended to describe their marriages as average and reasonably happy. The patients' unhappy marriages lasted for a considerable length of time, partially because the patients were almost completely unassertive and very strongly masochistic and self-sacrificing in relation to their husbands. The findings, in agreement with those of Cobb, Miller and Wieland (1959), suggest that patients will endure uncomfortable stressful situations longer than their siblings. It is possible, then, that chronic long-term stress, rather than simple discreet stress situations, may relate closely to later development of rheumatoid arthritis in at least some cases. As mentioned, practically every patient did link the development of her arthritis with environmental stress, and it seemed that more acute short-term stresses were prevalently mentioned in those cases where long-term stresses were not present. The arthritic patients' inability to express anger may make some situations more stressful to them than these same situations would be to other people. Similar situations may be differentially stressful to different individuals because of their particular personality characteristics.

In an attempt to overcome the objection that observed personality traits might be induced by the disease or when reported as existing prior to disease might represent retrospective distortions, we attempted to correlate personality variables with a physiological variable, rheumatoid factor, that may be predisposing towards rheumatoid disease (Lawrence, 1963). Rheumatoid factor is a macromolecular anti-gamma globulin auto-antibody that itself is a gamma globulin (IgM). We utilized the MMPI, analysing 12 basic and 66 special scales in a group of relatives of rheumatoid patients deemed physically healthy on the basis of medical history, physical examinations and x-rays. Twenty-one FII (rheumatoid factor) positive female relatives were compared with 21 FII-negative female relatives (Solomon and Moos, 1965).

The responses of the subjects on 16 of the 88 MMPI scales showed statistically significant differences between the two groups. The FII-*positive* relatives scored significantly higher on scales reflecting inhibition of aggression (impulse control), concern about the social desirability of actions and about socio-economic status, and ego strength (indicative of capacity for successful psychological defence, coping, mastery, and integration). They also scored higher on an ulcer scale, the items of which reflect compliance, shyness, conscientiousness, religiosity, and moralism.

The FII-*negative* relatives scored higher on the standard psychasthenia scale, essentially indicative of the obsessive–compulsive syndrome consisting of rumination and rituals, abnormal fears, worrying, difficulties in concentrating, guilt feelings, excessive vacillation in making decisions, excessively high personal standards, self-critical feelings, and aloofness. Interestingly, the FII-negative relatives had more somatic complaints; showed more psychoneuroticism and less ego mastery, with defective inhibition of impulses; and tended more readily to admit psychiatric symptoms, to lack self-acceptance, and to feel both self and social alienation. Self-concept and ideal self are seen as relatively disparate in the FII-negative group. The FII-negative groups also tended more frequently to dissimulate, to attempt deliberately to appear less healthy. This group more often demonstrated evidence of failure of psychological defences, as reflected in scores on the judged-anxiety scale and inner-maladjustment scales, indices of emotional illness. Consistent with these elevations, the FII-negative group had higher dependency scores. Their relative elevation on the ethnocentrism scale implies rigidity and inflexibility of emotional attitudes, which may be related to poor prognosis in psychotherapy. It should be recalled that the ego strength scale, the criterion for the development of which was response to psychotherapy, was higher in the FII-positive group. The FII-negative group also scored higher on the paranoid schizophrenia scale, which serves well in separating new schizophrenics from other general psychiatric cases and which, as might be expected, contains a great number of unfavourable items.

Both scale score and specific item differences showed that apparently healthy relatives of rheumatoid arthritic patients who had rheumatoid factor in their sera tended to have well-functioning psychological defences and to be essentially psychiatrically asymptomatic. On the other hand, psychoneurosis and even more serious mental disturbances with failure of psychic homeostasis—anxiety, alienation, lack of control, fear, guilt, low self-esteem—were relatively much more common in those relatives lacking rheumatoid factor. A reasonable hypothesis based upon these data would seem to be that, given a genetic or constitutional predisposition to rheumatoid disease, expressed in some individuals by the presence of rheumatoid factor, only those individuals with significant emotional conflict and psychological distress go on to the development of diesase, the rate of progression of which may be related to the degree of psychic turmoil (Moos and Solomon, 1964b). Thus, individuals with rheumatoid factor but without manifest rheumatoid disease must be in good psychological equilibrium; if they were not, they might be expected to become physically ill. In this regard, a recent study of eight sets of monozygotic twins discordant for rheumatoid arthritis documented stress preceding onset of disease (Meyerowitz, Jacox and Hess, 1968).

Although the presence of rheumatoid factor in a healthy individual seems to be related to well-functioning psychological defences, it seems that the *kind* of adaptations of FII-positive relatives are similar to those in persons with rheumatoid arthritis, but that they are working better, either as a result of greater ego strength or of less environmental stress. The inhibition of aggression, concern about appearances, and similarity to another psychosomatic group seen in the FII-positive relatives have been found in patients with rheumatoid arthritis when compared with a group of healthy relatives without regard to their FII status. Thus, a propensity to formation of rheumatoid factor might be linked to psychological mechanisms but still needs to be coupled with some degree of emotional decompensation to lead to disease. The possible physiological mechanism for emotional influence on production of rheumatoid factor, especially if not tied to the concept of psychological distress, which I shall try to relate to dysfunction of the immunological system, is unclear. Genetic or constitutional factors might be integrated with a psychological theory by the assumptions that the biological *capacity for* production of rheumatoid factor is present in some or all individuals; that actual rheumatoid factor production is triggered in some cases by the physiological consequences of certain types of psychological conditions and is accompanied by *disease* in the presence of other or more intense psychological factors.

PSYCHOLOGICAL FACTORS IN OTHER AUTO-IMMUNE DISEASES

Psychosomatic studies of other diseases with auto-immune features reveal findings similar to ours and others' studies of patients with rheumatoid arthritis. Engel's (1955) classical review and study of psychological processes in ulcerative colitis, a disease often associated with anti-colon antibodies, refers to obsessive–compulsive character traits of neatness, indecision, conscientiousness, worrying, rigid morality and conformity. Engel's colitis patients, likewise, generally had difficulty directly expressing hostility, were concerned with appearance and others' opinions and had significant conflicts over dependency. Colitis patients' mothers were controlling and had a propensity to assume the role of a martyr, again as arthritics' mothers have been described (Cleveland and Fisher, 1954; Alexander, 1956). The hyperthyroidism and exophthalmos of Graves' disease result from the action of long-acting thyroid stimulator

(LATS), a unique anti-thyroid auto-antibody with physiological activity (Kriss, 1968). Mandelbrote and Wittkower (1955) state about female Graves' disease patients, 'Hidden behind their bustling activities and their constant emphasis on independence and self-sufficiency lie the same outdated needs for maternal love . . .' These authors found *chronic* stress generally preceded onset of hyper-thyroidism.

Stress, especially loss of a significant relationship or fear of loss of love, can be documented as preceding the onset of systemic lupus erythematosus, a serious disease associated with a variety of anti-nuclear globulins (McClary, Meyer and Weitzman, 1955). These authors' lupus patients showed compulsive traits and an unusual need for activity and independence, interpreted as a defensive denial of guilt-provoking wishes for maternal affection. Childhood emotional deprivation and stress prior to onset of illness were more common in a group of women with systemic lupus erythematosus than in a group of matched controls with accidental haemorrhage in pregnancy (Otto and Mackay, 1967).

Grinker and Robbins (1954) state about patients with multiple sclerosis, which some feel may be an immune disease analogous to experimental allergic encephalomyelitis, 'The multiple sclerotics seem to have an excessive need for love and affection, which was not gratified in childhood. The resulting frustration evokes anger which must be repressed in order to preserve whatever gratification was available. As a result, the external personality is happy-go-lucky with a paramount desire to please and be appreciated.'

These similarities among personality factors in various diseases with immunological aberration raise serious questions about any symbolic psychological significance of the physical symptoms *per se*. As good a case can be made for 'anality' among arthritics as for motility conflicts among colitis patients, for example. Even considering involvement of the autonomic nervous system, it is hard to make a case for the psychological defence mechanism of conversion in auto-immune diseases which have such disparate manifestations (Engel, 1968).

Incidence of disease or of serological abnormalities in certain groups may also be linked to personality factors. Rheumatoid arthritis, like systemic lupus erythematosus and thyroid disease, occurs more commonly in females. Some auto-antibodies are more common in symptom-free females than males (Hill, 1961; Goodman *et al.*, 1963). Earlier, the question was raised whether psychosomatic disease at times emerges when psychological defences fail. In the context of the personality trait structure described for patients who develop diseases associated with immunological dysfunction, the possibility presents itself that males are better able to ward off anxiety and depression by physical activity, busyness, and hyper-independence than are females, whose social role involves need for greater submissiveness and allows for less mobility. Also, the apparently crucial role of the mother may have greater impact on the female child, for whom mother is not only a source of nurturance but also a subsequent figure for identification. As has been said, the doing sort of psychological defence is prone to failure in old age. Auto-antibodies, like clinical depression, are more commonly found in the elderly.

POSSIBLE PATHOGENIC MECHANISMS

The pathogenic modes by which specific personality characteristics, conflicts or emotions might be related to the production of auto-antibodies and/or auto-immune diseases will now be considered. How might their specific physiological concomitants make development of disease more likely?

Peripheral Mechanisms

In the case of rheumatoid arthritis, argument can be made for a peripheral mechanism. It has been suggested that chronically inhibited rage may lead to higher muscle tension, which may, in turn, lead to increased internal joint pressure with consequent inflammation and pain. Joint pain produces immobility, which in some individuals may lead to anxiety and greater muscle tension. Arthritics have higher muscle tension in muscles traversing symptomatic joints than do hypertensives in corresponding muscles, and arthritics react to stress with greater muscle tension increases than do hypertensives (Moos and Engel, 1962). Anxious individuals respond to an auditory stimulus with greater muscle tension than do non-anxious subjects, and this response is related to personality characteristics, which include impulsivity, a hurried pace in most activities, and high responsiveness to the environment (Balshan, 1962). In this connection, the possibility that the auto-antibodies found in rheumatoid arthritics are 'secondary', i.e. that they constitute a response to tissue change, should be raised. Damaged tissue might be so altered as to 'fool' the normal self-recognition system. Milgrom (1965) suggests that the formation of rheumatoid factor is stimulated by the patient's own γ-globulin that has been altered in the course of the disease. Proteolytic (plasmin) activity may be increased in conditions of mental stress (Macfarlane and Biggs, 1948). Experimentally, partially denatured protein can 'break' acquired immunological tolerance (Weigle, 1965). Thus, *in vivo* protein damage might alter natural self-tolerance. Holman (1962) mentions the possibility that once tissue damage has been initiated, the reaction of anti-tissue antibodies with constituents of damaged cells helps to perpetuate the tissue injury.

Central Mechanisms

Immunological mechanisms, which may be influenced by emotions and stress via central nervous system mediation, may provide the pathogenic link between psychological factors and auto-immune diseases, which appear to be associated with clinical and experimental states of immunological deficiency (Fudenberg, 1968). Auto-immune diseases are relatively frequent in patients with hypo- or agammaglobulinaemia and with malignancies of immunological cells (lymphomas). Thymic and lymphoid dysfunction may underlie immunological deficiency, auto-immunity and lymphomas. There are several lines of evidence to support this concept. For example, neonatally thymectomized animals, which have deficient delayed hypersensitivity and graft rejection (cellular immunity), develop a wasting disease and have a high evidence of auto-immune phenomena. NZB mice, which develop a spontaneous auto-immune disease, have an abnormal thymus and poor immunological responses and frequently also develop lymphomas.

Several mechanisms might account for the association of immunological deficiency and auto-immunity. Every individual may have some auto-antibody forming cells, any 'excess' antibody forming cells directed against self-constituents being destroyed or inactivated by a normal immunological apparatus. Or self-reactive immunologically competent cells could arise via somatic mutation and fail to be eliminated by a deficient immunological apparatus. Alternatively, an infectious agent, such as a slow-virus, which an inadequate immunological defence might fail to eliminate, could alter the genetic make-up of an immunological cell to render it self-reactive. Analogous mechanisms have been proposed in the case of cancer. A mutant cell, whether arising spontaneously by somatic mutation or induced by virus, radiation or chemical carcinogen, may be able to thrive only under conditions of relative failure of immunological resistance (Habel, 1963; Prehn, 1963). (It has even been suggested that cellular immunity may have been developed phylogenetically as a protection against neoplasia.) Although to pursue this area would lead us afield, it is noteworthy that psychological mechanisms not too different from those described in auto-immune disease have been proposed in patients with cancer (Leshan and Worthington, 1956; Bahnson, 1969).

Auto-immune tissue change can be regarded as arising from the action of immunologically competent cells, specific auto-antibodies (less likely) or non-specific antigen–antibody complexes (Mackay, 1964). Circulating antigen–antibody complexes occur when antibody appears in an environment of moderate antigen excess (relatively little antibody in comparison to antigen) and their persistence can be related to relative immunological incompetence (Dixon, Feldman and Vasquez, 1961). These complexes occur transiently in serum sickness, the pathology of which has a resemblance to rheumatoid arthritis, systemic lupus erythematosus, glomerulonephritis and periarteritis nodosa. In an attempt to produce chronic disease, Dixon, Feldman and Vasquez (1961) injected daily small amounts of purified serum proteins into rabbits. Animals responded in one of three ways: by making large amounts of antibody, thus rapidly eliminating the antigen after each injection; by making no detectable antibody whatsoever, allowing the injected antigen to circulate; and by making small amounts of antibody insufficient to remove the antigen from circulation but capable of forming soluble antigen–antibody complexes, which would persist in the circulation for most of the interval between antigen injections. Animals making an excess of antibody passed through a phase of acute serum sickness; those making no antibody suffered no adverse effects. Those animals making a small amount of antibody developed a chronic glomerulonephritis with deposits of antigen, host globulin, and host complement in the glomerular basement membranes. Dixon states that these results show that individuals making relatively small antibody responses can be prone to develop certain diseases, in contrast to the usual anaphylactic type of hypersensitivity reaction in which the best antibody producers are usually the most susceptible. Dixon's findings also demonstrate that immunological complexes can produce chronic degenerative tissue change and that the injured tissue needs no immunological relationship to the antigen involved. His work suggests that immunological complexes might augment injury produced by anti-tissue antibody, infective, physical, or chemical agents. Also, antigen–antibody complexes themselves might act as new antigens, inducing the formation of further antibody. In this regard, it has been shown that rheumatoid factor seems to have a greater affinity for antigen–antibody complexes than for native human γ-globulin (Aho and Simons, 1963). Hyperimmunized rabbits, which might be expected to have circulating antigen–antibody complexes, produce both anti-γ-globulin factors (analogous to rheumatoid factor) and anti-DNA antibody (analogous to lupus factor) (Christian, De Simone and Abruzzo, 1963).

Effects of adrenocortical steroids upon antibody formation are complex (McMaster and Franzl, 1961). Corticosteroids markedly depress antibody formation in some animals (possibly via lympholysis, interference with maturation of plasma cells or plasma protein catabolism), but this effect seems less striking in humans (Raffel, 1961). Many animal studies employed non-physiological doses of steroids or non-naturally occurring compounds, and there are few studies of prolonged administration. Inhibition of antibody formation by corticoids is dependent upon the dose of the antigen, the nature and dose of the hormone, and the time of administration of the hormone in relation to the injection of the antigen. There is considerable evidence that ACTH and adrenocortical steroids given prior to and accompanying injection of antigen suppress circulating antibody.

Plasma hydrocortisone increases under conditions of emotional stress. Hamburg (1962) cites data from two dozen different studies showing that there is a significant elevation of adrenal hormones under conditions of personal threat, sustained tension and intense distress. Particularly high hydrocortisone levels occur in the presence of disintegrative anxiety. Prolonged periods of increased hydrocortisone levels occur in clinical depressive disorders and can be correlated with severity of the clinical syndrome. Consistent corticosteroid elevations occur in situations characterized by high degrees of novelty and ambiguity (Wadeson *et al.*, 1963). In monkeys, both conditioned fear and conditioned avoidance situations were associated with increases in plasma hydrocortisone levels as great as those following injection of a large dose of corticotropin (Mason *et al.*, 1961). Whether such psychogenic increases in plasma hydrocortisone are immunosuppressive is open to question. Duration as well as degree of elevation of corticosteroids may be important.

STRESS AND IMMUNE RESPONSE

There is indirect and, more recently, direct experimental evidence that stress may be immunosuppressive. Avoidance learning and restraint leads to increased susceptibility to herpes simplex virus in mice (Rasmussen, Spencer and Marsh, 1957). Although neither stress nor Coxsackie B virus alone is sufficient to produce disease in mice, the combination results in a loss of body weight (Friedman, Ader and Glasgow, 1965). Disappearance of vesicular stomatitis virus from the site of inoculation is retarded in stressed mice

(Yamada, Jensen and Rasmussen, 1964). Wild mice housed in groups show increased susceptibility to trichinosis over singly housed animals (Davis and Read, 1958). Male mice crowded before or after inoculation with a low dose of tubercle bacilli show less resistance to chronic infection, while female mice under the same conditions show increased resistance (Tobach and Bloch, 1956). Male and female mice crowded before and housed singly after a large inoculum of bacilli are more resistant to acute tuberculosis than mice housed singly before and crowded after infection. Overcrowding stress and ACTH both were noted to reactivate rabies virus in guinea-pigs (Soave, 1964, 1964). Previously isolated mice were placed in groups of six for four hours a day and were injected with beef serum on the fifth day of stress (Vessey, 1964). Grouped mice developed significantly less precipitating antibody and had heavier adrenals.

Monkeys subject to various 'psychological' stresses such as noise, light, or loss of support after immunization with bovine serum albumin showed delayed antibody formation, and the antibodies rose to a lower level than in a control group (Hill, Greer and Felsenfeld, 1967). Overcrowding stress but not the stress of apprehension–electric shock administered for a week prior to immunization with a potent bacterial antigen, flagellin, and continued during the course of observation significantly reduced both primary and secondary antibody response in inbred male rats (Solomon, 1969). The stress of remaining on a platform over a pan of water significantly reduced primary but not secondary response.

That some stresses can be immunosuppressive in animals seems clear, though mediating mechanisms, immune dynamics and significance for human diseases associated with immunological deficiency remain to be clarified.

The immunological responsivity of the adult seems to be modified by early experience (Solomon, Levine and Kraft, 1968). The antibody response to flagellin of mature inbred rats, which had been handled in infancy by simply being picked up and removed from the nest for three minutes from birth until weaning (21 days), was higher in every case after primary and secondary immunization in handled than in unhandled animals. Initial 19S (IgM) response of handled animals was double that of unhandled. Secondary response titre dropped off more quickly in unhandled animals. Mechanisms of this effect can only be speculated upon. Environmentally responsive hormones may effect thymic function, which is important in the establishment of immunological competence (Miller, Osoba and Dukor, 1965). These data might be interpreted as supporting evidence, to be described, that the hypothalamus has a regulatory role in immunity because other physiological parameters modified by early experiences are thought to have hypothalamic mediation (Levine, 1966).

THE CENTRAL NERVOUS SYSTEM AND IMMUNITY

Several lines of evidence point to a direct role of the central nervous system in control of immunogenesis. Mental stress has been reported to produce a rise in 19S gamma globulin (Fessel, 1962). Electrical stimulation of the lateral hypothalamus of rats altered gamma globulin levels (Fessel and Forsyth, 1963). Soviet workers in questionable work have for a long time claimed to be able to condition antibody response, to obtain anamnestic antibody increase by a conditioned stimulus without antigen (Luk'yanenko, 1961). Soviet workers also claim that denervation of the site of antigen deposition diminishes antibody response and nervous stimulation in conjunction with antigen administration enhances response (Gordienko, 1958).

Most interestingly and of potentially great significance is the work I recently observed of Elena A. Korneva at the Institute of Experimental Medicine, Leningrad, on hypothalamic control of immunogenesis. A small destructive lesion in the nucleus hypothalamus posterior markedly suppressed both humoral and cellular immunity. Primary antibody response of the rabbit to foreign serum proteins as measured by complement fixation was virtually eliminated and secondary response diminished for three months post-surgery (Korneva and Khai, 1963). Homografts were retained indefinitely in lesioned mice. Plasma cells were decreased in spleen and nodes in animals with this specific lesion, and immunofluorescence of sensitized splenic cells induced by fluorescein-tagged antigen were reduced, presumably reflecting lowered immunological activity. The relationship of CNS-induced immunosuppression to autosensitization disease is unclear and, of course, deserves study. Kidney and heart damage due to streptococcal antigens did not occur in lesioned animals, but they developed worse experimental polyneuritis (induced by myelin plus adjuvant) than controls.

In even more provocative work, Korneva (1967) claims to enhance antibody response by electrical stimulation of the hypothalamic region by passing direct current between electrodes 'straddling' the nucleus. Five minutes of daily stimulation beginning five or six days before administration of antigen and continued for 15 or 16 days resulted in one or more of three types of increase in immunological activity: (1) earlier onset of antibody response; (2) higher maximum titre; and (3) prolonged elevation of titre.

It remains unclear if there is hormonal mediation of these CNS effects. In a pilot study, Korneva blocked immunosuppression induced by ablation of the hypothalamic nucleus with growth hormone. The immunological deficiency of hypopituitary dwarf mice can be overcome by somatotropic hormone and thyroxin (Pierpaoli *et al.*, 1969), and animals handled in infancy have higher growth hormone levels (Reichlin, 1968). Thus, CNS-regulated changes in growth hormone might be more relevant to immune function than adrenal hormone levels.

If central nervous system regulation of immunological function can be confirmed, there is a basis on which to develop basic understanding of pathogenesis to support clinical and experimental observations on effects of stress and emotions on the onset and course of auto-immune diseases and diseases with immunological resistance, both infectious and neoplastic.

SUMMARY

Personality factors seem to predispose to the development of rheumatoid arthritis and other auto-immune diseases, and stress events and/or decompensation of psychological defences and adaptations to be related to onset of disease. In comparison with their healthy sisters, female patients with rheumatoid arthritis show more masochism, self-sacrifice, denial of hostility, compliance–subservience, depression and sensitivity to anger and are described as always having been nervous, tense, worried, highly strung, moody individuals. Physically healthy relatives of rheumatoid patients *with* rheumatoid factor in their sera are psychologically more healthy than those relatives lacking this auto-antibody, implying combination of physical predisposition and psychological decompensation lead to manifest disease. Personality data similar to those in rheumatoid arthritis have been reported for patients with other auto-immune diseases. Physiologically, auto-immunity appears to be related to relative immunological incompetence. There is evidence that stress may be immunosuppressive, possibly via elevation of adrenal cortical hormones. There is also some experimental evidence for regulation of immune response by the hypothalamus. Thus, central nervous system mediated alteration in immunological responsivity might represent the pathogenic link among stress events, emotions and diseases associated with immunological dysfunction.

ACKNOWLEDGEMENTS

I am very grateful for the invaluable collaboration in all my studies of rheumatoid arthritis of Rudolf H. Moos, Ph.D., Associate Professor of Psychiatry (Psychology), Stanford University School of Medicine. This chapter borrows heavily from Dr. Moos' excellent review. Alfred A. Amkraut, Ph.D., Assistant Professor of Medical Microbiology, Stanford University School of Medicine, is my co-investigator in research on stress and immunity. Our clinical studies were primarily carried out in conjunction with the Rheumatic Disease Group, University of California Medical Center, San Francisco.

REFERENCES

Aho, K. and Simons, K. (1963). 'Studies of the Nature of Rheumatoid Factor: Reaction to Rheumatoid Factor with Human Specific Precipitates and with Native Human Gamma Globulin.' *Arthritis Rheum.*, **6,** 676.

Alexander, F. (1956). *Psychosomatic Medicine.* New York: Norton.

Bahnson, C. B. (Ed.) (1969). 'Second Conference on Psychophysiological Aspects of Cancer.' *Ann. N.Y. Acad. Sci.*, **164,** 307.

Balshan, J. D. (1962). 'Muscle Tension and Personality in Women: Factoral Study.' *Archs gen. Psychiat.*, **7,** 436.

Booth, G. C. (1937). 'Personality and Chronic Arthritis.' *J. nerv. ment. Dis.*, **85,** 637.

— and Klopfer, B. (1936). 'Personality Studies in Chronic Arthritis.' *Rors. Res. Exch.*, **1,** 40.

Christian, D. L., DeSimone, A. P. and Abruzzo, J. L. (1963). 'Anti-DNA Antibodies in Hyperimmunized Rabbits' (Abstract). *Arthritis Rheum.*, **6,** 766.

Cleveland, S. E. and Fisher, S. (1954). 'Behavior and Unconscious Fantasies of Patients with Rheumatoid Arthritis.' *Psychosom. Med.*, **16,** 327.

— — (1960). 'A Comparison of Psychological Characteristics and Physiological Reactivity in Ulcer and Rheumatoid Arthritic Groups: I. Psychological Measures.' *Psychosom. Med.*, **22,** 283.

Cobb, S., Miller, M. and Wieland, M. (1959). 'On the Relationship between Divorce and Rheumatoid Arthritis.' *Arthritis Rheum.*, **2,** 414.

Cohen, D. (1949). 'Psychological Concomitants of Chronic Illness: A Study of Emotional Correlates of Pulmonary Tuberculosis, Peptic Ulcer, the Arthritides, and Cardiac Disease.' Doctoral Dissertation, University of Pittsburgh.

Cormier, B. M., Wittkower, E. D., Marcotte, V. and Forget, F. (1957). 'Psychological Aspects of Rheumatoid Arthritis.' *Can. med. Ass. J.*, **77,** 533.

Davis, D. E. and Read, C. P. (1958). 'Effect of Behavior on Development of Resistance in Trichinosis.' *Proc. Soc. expl. Biol. Med.*, **99,** 269.

Dixon, F. J., Feldman, J. and Vasquez, J. (1961). 'Experimental Glomerulonephritis.' *J. expl. Med.*, **113,** 899.

Ellman, P. and Mitchell, S. D. (1936). 'The Psychological Aspects of Chronic Rheumatic Joint Disease.' In *Reports on Chronic Rheumatic Diseases*, Ed. by C. W. Buckley. New York: Macmillan.

Empire Rheumatism Council (1950). 'A Controlled Investigation into the Aetiology and Clinical Features of Rheumatoid Arthritis.' *Br. med. J.* **1,** 799.

Engel, G. L. (1955). 'Studies of Ulcerative Colitis. III. The Nature of the Psychologic Processes.' *Am. J. Med.*, **19,** 231.

— (1968). 'A Reconsideration of the Role of Conversion in Somatic Diseases.' *Comp. Psychiat.*, **9,** 316.

Fessel, W. J. (1962). 'Mental Stress, Blood Proteins, and the Hypothalamus: Experimental Results Showing Effect of Mental Stress upon 4S and 19S Proteins: Speculation that Functional Behavior Disturbances may be Expressions of a General Metabolic Disorder.' *Archs gen. Psychiat.*, **7,** 427.

— and Forsyth, R. P. (1963). 'Hypothalamic Role in Control of Gamma Globulin Levels.' (Abstract). *Arthritis Rheum.*, **6,** 770.

Friedman, S. B., Ader, R. and Glasgow, L. A. (1965). 'Effects of Psychological Stress in Adult Mice Inoculated with Coxsackie B Viruses.' *Psychosom. Med.*, **27,** 361.

Fudenberg, H. H. (1968). 'Are Autoimmune Diseases Immunologic Deficiency States?' *Hosp. Pract.*, **3,** 43.

Goodman, M., Rosenblatt, M., Gottlieb, J. S. Miller, J. and Chen, C. H. (1963). 'Effect of Age, Sex and Schizophrenia on Thyroid Autoantibody Production.' *Archs gen. Psychiat.*, **8,** 518.

Gordienko, A. N. (1958). 'Control of Immunogenesis by the Nervous System.' U.S. Dept. of Commerce Translation TT60–51069.

Gregg, D. (1939). 'The Paucity of Arthritis among Psychotic Patients.' *Am. J. Psychiat.*, **95,** 853.

Grinker, R. R., Jr. and Robbins, F. P. (1954). *Psychosomatic Case Book.* New York: Blakeston.

Habel, K. (1963). 'Immunologic Aspects of Oncogenesis by Polyoma Virus.' In *Conceptual Advances in Immunology and Oncology.* New York: Hoeber.

Halliday, J. L. (1942). 'Psychological Aspects of Rheumatoid Arthritis.' *Proc. R. Soc. Med.*, **35,** 455.

Hamburg, D. A. (1962). 'Plasma and Urinary Corticosteroid Levels in Naturally Occurring Psychologic Stresses.' *Res. Publ. Ass. Res. nerv. ment. Dis.*, **40,** 406.

Hill, C. W., Greer, W. E. and Felsenfeld, O. (1967). 'Psychological Stress, Early Response to Foreign Protein, and Blood Cortisol in Monkeys.' *Psychosom. Med.*, **29,** 279.

Hill, O. W. (1961). 'Thyroglobulin Antibodies in 1,297 without Thyroid Disease.' *Br. med. J.*, **1,** 1793.

Holman, H. R. (1962). 'Clinical and Immunological Evidence for Predisposition to Rheumatic Disease in Certain Families.' *Progr. med. Genet.*, **2,** 210.

Johnson, A., Shapiro, L. and Alexander, F. (1947). 'Preliminary Report on a Psychosomatic Study of Rheumatoid Arthritis.' *Psychosom. Med.*, **9,** 295.

Korneva, E. A. (1967). 'The Effect of Stimulating Different Mesencephalic Structures on Protective Immune Response Patterns.' *Fizio. Zh. SSR. Sechenov*, **53,** 42.

— and Khai, L. M. (1963). 'Effect of Destruction of Hypothalamic Areas on Immunogenesis.' *Fizio. Zh. SRR. Sechenov*, **49,** 42.

Kriss, J. P. (1968). 'The Long-acting Thyroid Stimulator.' *Calif. Med.*, **109,** 202.

Lawrence, J. S. (1963). 'Epidemiology of Rheumatoid Arthritis.' *Arthritis Rheum.*, **6,** 166.

Leshan, L. L. and Worthington, R. E. (1956). 'Personality as Factor in Pathogenesis of Cancer: Review of Literature.' *Br. J. med. Psychol.*, **29,** 49.

Levine, S. (1966). 'Endocrines and the Central Nervous System.' *Res. Publ. Ass. Res. nerv. ment. Dis.*, **13,** 280.

Ludwig, A. O. (1955). 'Psychiatric Considerations in Rheumatoid Arthritis.' *Med. Clins. N.Am.*, **39,** 477.

Luk'yanenko, V. I. (1961). 'The Problem of Conditioned Reflex Regulation of Immunobiological Reactions.' *Vspekhi Sovremmenoy Biologii*, **51,** 170.

McClary, A. R., Meyer, E. and Weitzman, D. J. (1955). 'Observations on Role of Mechanism of Depression in some Patients with Disseminated Lupus Erythematosus.' *Psychosom. Med.*, **17,** 311.

Macfarlane, G. G. and Biggs, R. (1948). 'Fibrinolysis: Its Mechanisms and Significance.' *Blood*, **32,** 1167.

Mackay, I. R. (1964). 'A Survey of Autoimmunity.' *Postgrad. Med.*, **35,** 7.

McMaster, P. D. and Franzl, R. E. (1961). 'The Effects of Adrenocortical Steroids upon Antibody Formation.' *Metabolism*, **10,** 990.

Mandelbrote, B. M. and Wittkower, E. D. (1955). 'Emotional Factors in Graves' Disease.' *Psychosom. Med.*, **17**, 109.

Mason, J. W. *et al.* (1961). 'Concurrent Measurement of 17-Hydroxycorticosteroid, Epinephrine, and Norepinephrine Responses to Conditioned Emotional Stimuli in Monkeys.' *Psychosom. Med.*, **23,** 344.

Meyerowitz, S., Jacox, R. F. and Hess, D. W. (1968). 'Monozygotic Twins Discordant for Rheumatoid Arthritis: A Genetic, Clinical and Psychological Study of 8 Sets.' *Arthritis Rheum.*, **11,** 1.

Milgrom, F. (1965). 'Response to Altered Autologous Antigens.' (In Autoimmunity—Experimental and Clinical Aspects.) *Ann. N.Y. Acad. Sci.*, **124,** 118.

Miller, J. F. A. P., Osoba, D. and Dukor, P. (1965). 'A Humoral Thymus Mechanism Responsible for Immunologic Maturation.' (In Autoimmunity—Experimental and Clinical Aspects.) *Ann. N.Y. Acad. Sci.*, **124,** 95.

Moos, R. H. (1963). 'Personality Factors Associated with Rheumatoid Arthritis: A Review.' *J. chron. Dis.*, **17,** 41.

— and Engel, B. T. (1962). 'Psychological Reactions in Hypertensive and Arthritic Patients.' *J. psychosom. Res.*, **6,** 227.

— and Solomon, G. F. (1964a). 'Minnesota Multiphasic Personality Inventory Response Patterns in Patients with Rheumatoid Arthritis.' *J. Psychosom. Res.*, **8,** 17.

Moss, R. H. and Solomon, G. F. (1964b). 'Personality Correlates of the Rapidity of Progression of Rheumatoid Arthritis.' *Ann. rheum. Dis.*, **23,** 145.

— —(1965a). 'Psychologic Comparisons between Women with Rheumatoid Arthritis and their Nonarthritic Sisters. I. Personality Test and Interview Rating Data.' *Psychosom. Med.*, **27,** 135.

— — (1965b). 'Psychologic Comparisons between Women with Rheumatoid Arthritis and their Nonarthritic Sisters. II. Content Analysis of Interviews.' *Psychosom. Med.*, **27,** 150.

Mueller, A. D. and Lefkovitz, A. M. (1956). 'Personality Structure and Dynamics of Patients with Rheumatoid Arthritis.' *J. clin. Psychol.*, **12,** 143.

— — Bryant, J. E. and Marshall, M. L. (1961). 'Some Psychosocial Factors in Patients with Rheumatoid Arthritis.' *Arthritis Rheum.*, **4,** 275.

Nissen, H. A. and Spencer, K. A. (1936). 'The Psychogenic Problem (Endocrinal and Metabolic) in Chronic Arthritis.' *New Engl. J. Med.*, **214,** 756.

Otto, R. and Mackay, I. (1967). 'Psychosocial and Emotional Disturbance in Systemic Lupus Erythematosus.' *Med. J. Aust.*, **2,** 488.

Paterson, P. Y., Jacobs, A. F. and Coia, E. M. (1965). 'Complement-Fixing Antibrain Antibodies and Allergic Encephalomyelitis II. Further Studies Concerning their Protective Role.' (In Autoimmunity—Experimental and Clinical Aspects.) *Ann. N.Y. Acad. Sci.*, **124,** 292.

Pierpaoli, W., Baroni, C., Fabris, M. and Sorkin, E. (1969). 'Hormones and Immunologic Capacity. II. Reconstitution of Antibody Production in Hormonally Deficient Mice by Somatotropic Hormone, Thyrotropic Hormone and Thyroxin.' *Immunology*, **16,** 217.

Pilkington, T. L. (1956). 'The Coincidence of Rheumatoid Arthritis and Schizophrenia.' *J. nerv. ment. Dis.*, **124,** 604.

Prehn, R. T. (1963). 'The Role of Immune Mechanisms in the Biology of Chemically and Physically Induced Tumors.' In *Conceptual Advances in Immunology and Oncology*. New York: Hoeber.

Raffel, S. (1961). *Immunity*, 2nd ed. New York: Appleton-Century-Crofts.

Rasmussen, A. F., Jr., Spencer, E. S. and Marsh, J. T. (1957).' Increased Susceptibility to Herpes Simplex in Mice Subjected to Avoidance-Learning Stress or Restraint.' *Proc. Soc. expl. Biol. Med.*, **96,** 183.

Reichlin, S. (1968). 'Hypothalamic Control of Growth Hormone Secretion and Response to Stress.' In *Endocrinology and Human Behavior.* Oxford University Press.

Rimón, R. (1969). 'A Psychosomatic Approach to Rheumatoid Arthritis: A Clinical Study of 100 Female Patients.' *Acta rheum. scand.*, Suppl. No. 13.

Robinson, C. E. (1957). 'Emotional Factors in Rheumatoid Arthritis,' *Can. med. Ass. J.*, **77,** 344.

Rothermilch, N. O. and Philips, V. K. (1963). 'Rheumatoid Arthritis in Criminal and Mentally Ill Populations.' *Arthritis Rheum.*, **6,** 639.

Salk, J. (1962). 'Biological Basis of Disease and Behavior.' *Perspect. Biol. Med.*, **5,** 198.

Samter, M. and Alexander, H. L. (Eds.) (1965). *Immunological Diseases.* Boston: Little, Brown.

Soave, O. A. (1962). 'Reactivation of Rabies Virus Infection in a Guinea Pig with ACTH.' *J. infect. Dis.*, **110,** 129.

— (1964). 'Reactivation of a Rabies Virus in the Guinea Pig Due to the Stress of Crowding.' *Am. J. vet. Res.*, **25,** 268.

Solomon, G. F. (1969). 'Stress and Antibody Response in Rats.' *Int. Archs Allergy*, **35,** 97.

— Levine, S. and Kraft, J. (1968). 'Early Experience and Immunity.' *Nature*, **220,** 821.

— and Moos, R. H. (1964). 'Emotions, Immunity and Disease: A Speculative Theoretical Integration.' *Archs gen. Psychiat.*, **11,** 657.

— — (1965). 'The Relationship of Personality to the Presence of Rheumatoid Factor in Asymptomatic Relatives of Patients with Rheumatoid Arthritis.' *Psychosom. Med.*, **27,** 350.

Tobach, E. and Bloch, H. (1956). 'Effect of Stress by Crowding Prior to and Following Tuberculosis Infection.' *Am. J. Physiol.*, **187,** 399.

Trevathan, R. D. and Tatum, J. C. (1954). 'Rarity of Occurrence of Psychosis and Rheumatoid Arthritis in Individual Patients.' *J. nerv. ment. Dis.*, **120,** 83.

Vaughn, J. H. (1965). 'Diseases with Immunological Features.' In *Immunological Diseases*, Ed. by M. Samter and H. L. Alexander. Boston: Little, Brown.

Vessey, S. H. (1964). 'Effects of Grouping on Levels of Circulating Antibodies in Mice.' *Proc. Soc. expl. Biol. Med.*, **115,** 252.

Wadeson, R. W. *et al.* (1963). 'Plasma and Urinary 17-OHCS Responses to Motion Pictures.' *Archs gen. Psychiat.*, **9,** 146.

Weigle, W. O. (1965). 'The Antibody Response in Rabbits to Previously Tolerated Antigens.' (In Autoimmunity—Experimental and Clinical Aspects.) *Ann. N.Y. Acad. Sci.* **124,** 133.

Wiener, D. (1952). 'Personality Characteristics of Selected Disability Groups.' *Genet. Psychol. Monogr.*, **45,** 175.

Yamada, A., Jensen, M. M. and Rasmussen, A. F., Jr. (1964). 'Stress and Susceptibility to Viral Infections. III. Antibody Response and Viral Retention During Avoidance-Learning Stress.' *Proc. Soc. expl. Biol. Med.*, **116,** 677.

CHAPTER 13

THE SIGNIFICANCE OF EMOTIONS IN THE COURSE OF RHEUMATOID ARTHRITIS

HARVEY MOLDOFSKY

INTRODUCTION

Rheumatoid arthritis, as commonly accepted, is a widespread systemic connective tissue disease that particularly ravages the peripheral joints. It is a disease of unknown aetiology. Yet, while the quest continues for clearly aetiologically significant biological factors, the role of emotional issues has been less certain.

Biological hypotheses come and go following a current wave of biological interest. For example, at one time, approximately one hundred years ago, it was thought that the basis for the joint lesions of rheumatoid arthritis lay in spinal irritation. Then, with the discovery of infective micro-organisms, the theory of the cryptic septic focus came into vogue. Subsequently, the chain of theories have implicated endocrinopathic, virological, immunological and biochemical issues. Unfortunately, relatively little in the way of solid confirmatory biological evidence has appeared to dispel the mystery of this disease and the treatment remains empirical.

Nevertheless, in spite of the shifting preoccupations with essentially biological conceptual models, throughout, the psychosomatic hypothesis has stood vaguely in the background, periodically capturing some fleeting attention. Over the years, psychiatrists or psychologists have reported on some emotional, personality, psychodynamic, interpersonal, or social factor or factors alleged to be significant to the disease. But, unfortunately, as has been pointed out in a recent critique (Scotch and Geiger, 1962), very few of the studies have met even minimal criteria for scientific evidence or inference. This relative inadequacy of objective evidence, in turn, allows for the continued questioning by rheumatologists of the relative importance of these psychical phenomena (Folley, 1965).

It is the purpose of this section to examine the possible factors involved in the persistent uncertainty as to the significance of emotional issues in rheumatoid arthritis. Then, recent endeavours, at studying the influences of emotional issues in the ongoing course of rheumatoid disease, will be reviewed.

SOME DIFFICULTIES IN DEMONSTRATING THE PSYCHOSOMATIC LINK IN RHEUMATOID ARTHRITIS

Particularly since the early 1930s, at a time of growing medical interest in the association of certain disturbed emotional states or personality patterns with physical diseases, psychiatrists and psychologists have mounted statistical evidence for the psychosomatic hypothesis. A survey of this psychosomatic literature attests to some important psychological or psychosocial variable presumably highly significant in the genesis or course of rheumatoid arthritis. Solomon reviews this aspect of the work in this volume. But the research for so-called emotionally stressful situations, faulty personality character traits, or insoluble conflictual difficulties had tended to leave investigators in the psychosomatic field in the indefensible position of retrospective bias and inadequate or poor controls (Scotch and Geiger, 1962). These glaring deficiencies have perpetuated the emphasis on somatic concerns while demeaning the importance of emotional factors. As an example of this, one rheumatologist (West, 1965) has deprecatingly commented: 'The hypothesis still being pressed in some quarters is that rheumatoid arthritis is a psychosomatic disease—that is a disease caused by something called "emotional conflict" which exists in a region of the mind of which the subject is not normally aware. Have we any clinical knowledge that this might be so, and that it deserves study? Research funds have been given to psychiatrists who favour the hypothesis so that they would seek evidence in its favour but no evidence has been forthcoming. Needless to say, in the British National Health Service, psychiatrists do not expect to be sent patients with rheumatoid arthritis unless they are psychologically disturbed. In the author's experience, surprisingly few need to be seen.' This attitude has been further bolstered by the conclusions of a survey analysis carried out by the Empire Rheumatism Council in 1950. With regard to judged past precipitant emotionally stressful events, this study affirmed the lack of significant differences between rheumatoids and controls.

Again, there are those investigators who might acknowledge the so-called 'somato-psychic' view, and claim that emotional disturbances might possibly arise as a consequence to the disease but have little bearing in its genesis or course of activity. Their evidence has been the 'natural' or common experiences of the resultant state of unhappiness of the physically ill.

A resolution of the controversy is essential. For one cannot lightly dismiss the evidence of various investigators and their reports of 5,000 patients with the nihilistic view that emotions have little to do with the disease.

There are three key sources to the controversy:

First of all, the fact of disturbed emotional states or stress might be misrepresented, either by the patient, or secondly, by the investigator. The patient might be biased in looking for some reason for his disease and might focus on some issue within his past that might be reasonably acceptable to him. Just to amplify on this point, soon after the diagnosis of rheumatoid arthritis is made, the patient, generally, is not offered very much in the way of prospects for a cure, perhaps relief from discomfort and hopefully prevention against progressive deformities. The afflicted person must come to face a most fearful uncertain void; somehow he must come to terms with the disease. Commonly, there is the dilemma of whether to deny the dependency and restrictions fostered by the disease, or to accept and submit, but, then, how is one to accept a disorder that is seen as ego-alien, that is viewed with fear, and coloured by misinformation, or despair following the failure of hopeful ready cures? Often, the question arises, why did this dreadful thing happen to me? The patient, grappling with the insecurity of the unknown, and alien, searches out and might focus upon some earlier possibly stressful situation. Or, on the other hand, even if something emotionally threatening may have elapsed, the patient, particularly as is commonly found, who is troubled by a difficulty in readily expressing feelings, might very well repress the incident. Consequently, the event would not be readily available for discussion within the context of a more superficial enquiry.

Another major source of potential bias, of course, stems from the attitude of the investigator or practitioner. His enquiry might be prejudiced in either direction. That is, anything that might be evaluated as to be the least bit disturbing, just prior to the onset of the disease activity, might be heavily weighted as the precipitating factor. Or, on the other hand, the enquiring physician, who has personal difficulty grappling with patient's sensitivities, might selectively exclude enquiry into what might be construed as private and considered unimportant psychological or social issues.

Finally, there is a third, and perhaps less obvious problem area; that is, the nature of the disease itself. It might very well be characteristic of the ill-defined nature of this disease that serves as a stumbling block to satisfactory clinical investigation. As in most disease phenomena, there is a hard core area of general agreement. Clinically there are symptoms and/or signs that are absolutely valid, reliable and explicitly formulated. Now, only as recently as 1956 following upon a documentation meeting of the American Rheumatism Association, was there a consensus as to appropriate diagnostic criteria for rheumatoid arthritis. Some of the criteria are still considered unsatisfactory. The quest continues for stricter formulation of standard, more reliable methods of examination and appraisal. Therefore, if the practitioner can *see*, and *measure* the characteristic distribution of deformities, the swellings, the subcutaneous nodules, the radiological and serological indicators, the diagnosis of rheumatoid arthritis is readily established. However, the greatest difficulties arise in assessing both the very early relatively quiescent cases, and once more, the ongoing quantity of the disease. The basis for these difficulties lay within the context of such relatively subjective, poorly quantifiable criteria as pain, morning stiffness, loss of strength and fatigue. In most clinical studies, it is these latter criteria that may be naturally selected and weighted in determining the severity of the disease state. To this date, very little in the way has been done to devise satisfactory instruments that could indicate to what degree the disease is in a flaring or receding state. Therefore, if the patient persistently complains of much joint and muscle pain, stiffness, and in addition, a general malaise, and ready fatigability, he is alleged to be experiencing an increment in disease activity. But, similarly, if the patient feels little pain and stiffness and displays more energy and activity, this disease is said to be 'under control' or quiescent. So the diagnostic impression hinges on two general issues: The first matter is largely 'hard' data, that is, objective, structural, and readily quantifiable, e.g. the number and size of joints involved; the second matter is largely 'soft' data for the clinical material is primarily of a subjective nature, functional, and less readily quantifiable, e.g. intensity of pain, stiffness or fatigue. To sum up, in the first instance, the issue bears somatic implications, and in the second instance, the issue bears psychological implications, the presence, then, of the relatively less well-defined psychological parameter, within the structural disease state cannot be safely ignored, but, in spite of the deprecations of some more somatically biased rheumatologists, continues to demand investigation.

THE PROSPECTIVE STUDY OF THE RELATIONSHIP OF SYMPTOMS TO EMOTIONAL CONFLICT IN RHEUMATOID ARTHRITIS

One possible solution to this psyche-soma controversy results within the concept of the prospective study. For in such a study the temporal relationship between psychological or environmental events and the disease state would then come under close scrutiny. Not until recently have suitable valid and reliable techniques become available to more clearly characterize rheumatoid disease (Lansbury, 1966) and psychological state.

As an example of one recent prospective objective approach (Moldofsky and Chester, 1970), attention was directed to the examination of the relationship between emotion and disease activity by correlating mood with joint tenderness. Here, 16 randomly selected patients who suitably fulfilled the American Rheumatism Association criteria for definite or classical rheumatoid arthritis, all in an acute early stage, were involved in a longitudinal psychosomatic study during their course of stay on a rheumatic diseases unit of a general hospital. Twice daily mood and pain ratings were conducted by a single observer employing an adjective check list of varied emotional states, and a dolorimeter (McCarty and Gatter, 1965) applied to all peripheral joints to derive a quantifiable index to joint inflammation. At the termination of the patient's stay in hospital, each of a mean forty-day duration, the raw data was mathematically analysed such that standardized specific mood parameters derived from factor analysis, were then correlated to the quantified dimensions of joint tenderness.

A review of studies of pain perception or reaction and emotion (Merskey and Spear, 1967) had indicated that anxiety is the main factor thought to lower pain thresholds. More specifically, restrictive expression of hostile impulses and anxiety with increased muscle tension have been broadly implicated in flares of joint pain (Cobb, 1959; Moos, 1964). Contrary to this popularly held view that painful experience is heightened in the presence of disturbed feelings, this ongoing study of day-to-day changes in mood and pain indicated that the relationship of intensity of pain and emotional reactivity was much more complex. Two characteristic pain–mood patterns emerged from this investigation. In the first instance eight patients were discovered to have a pattern of pain–mood association, termed a 'synchronous' state; that is, the altered mood either preceded by one day or was simultaneously directly associated with changing dolorimetric readings. Generally, the characteristic mood posture in this group ranged through a bipolar continuum from degrees of overt hostility or anxiety to degrees of calmness. In other words, associated with an increase in manifest anger or anxiety, there was a coincident flare in joint pain. On the other hand, in a second group of eight patients another pattern, termed 'asynchronous' or 'paradoxical' state was found. In this latter group, an inverse relationship existed between the intensity of mood disturbance and the quantified pain experience. Generally, their mood constellation tended to be characterized by a bipolar construct ranging from degrees of hopelessness through degrees of confidence. Here, although an amelioration in the pain dimension of their disease took place, the emotional state displayed a mounting sense of despair about their immediate state and pessimism about their future. Similarly, in the context of an intensification of their joint pain, they appear paradoxically calm and optimistic. Presumably, then, even though their joint pain had subsided, these people were in no way free of ill health. Neither age, sex and social status of the patient, nor medication, duration and stage of disease, had any bearing on these patterns.

In a two-year follow-up study of these same patients, those within the 'paradoxical' group encountered more medical complications, required further admissions to hospital usually for prolonged time intervals, and invariably were subjected to more hazardous forms of treatment, e.g. immunosuppressant drug treatment and joint surgery. Furthermore, they generally adapted poorly not only to their disease but as well within their socio-economic network. This was in total contradistinction to those of the 'synchronous' group who expressed calmness, confidence and hope with decrement in their joint pain. These people appeared to adapt much more easily, require less medical attention, and were able to carry on reasonably well with their life.

Other follow-up studies have suggested a similar disparity between the capabilities of the rheumatoid and objective clinical findings relevant to their disease state. The overall consensus is that psychological and social issues contribute significantly to the mode of adjustment. As has been suggested by one author (Lowman, 1954), those who achieve a successful rehabilitation and a more favourable prognosis are able to rely upon such psychological and social resources that permit an attitude of confidence, hope and trust to prevail. This author points out that unsuccessfully rehabilitated cases make little or no attempt at self-care and independence, whereas those successfully rehabilitated have a strong desire for pleasure that outweighs their depression. In another follow-up study (Moos and

Solomon, 1965), the personality characteristics of rheumatoids who had managed well as opposed to those who had faired poorly, have been discerned. The authors studied two groups of arthritic patients with equivalent duration and stage of illness but where differences lay only in the degree of functional incapacity relative to objective disease findings. The patients within the group exhibiting greater functional incapacity reflected more depression, apathy, and lack of motivation. Moreover, these rheumatoids tended to be more complaintive, more emotionally disturbed, more unstable, and more socially withdrawn than those with favourable functional capacity.

To summarize briefly this section, some of the factors involved in the persistent uncertainty of the significance of the psychosomatic viewpoint as applied to rheumatoid arthritis have been examined. Then, current studies, directed at clarifying the role of emotions within the ongoing clinical course of rheumatoid disease, were reviewed.

REFERENCES

Cobb, S. (1959). 'Contained Hostility in Rheumatoid Arthritis.' *Arthritis Rheum.*, **2,** 419.

Empire Rheumatism Council, Scientific Advisory Committee. (1950). *Br. med. J.*, **1,** 799.

Folley, H. F. (1965). 'Presidential Address to the American Rheumatism Association.' *Arthritis Rheum.*, **4,** 581.

Lansbury, J. (1966). 'Methods for Evaluating Rheumatoid Arthritis.' In *Arthritis and Allied Conditions, Textbook of Rheumatology*, 7th Ed., p. 269, Ed. by J. L. Hollander. Philadelphia: Lea & Febiger.

Lowman, E. W., Miller, S., Lee, P. R., Stein, H., King, R. and Heald, L. (1954). 'Psycho-social Factors in Rehabilitation of the Chronic Rheumatoid Arthritic.' *Ann. rheum. Dis.*, **13,** 312.

McCarty, D. J. and Gatter, A. (1965). 'A Dolorimeter for Quantification of Articular Tenderness.' *Arthritis Rheum.*, **8,** 551.

Merskey, H. and Spear, F. G. (1967). *Pain, Psychological and Psychiatric Aspects*, p. 150, London: Baillière, Tindall & Cassell.

Moldofsky, H. and Chester, W. J. (1970) 'Pain and Mood Patterns in Rheumatoid Arthritis.' (Abstract of paper delivered at the Annual Meeting of the American Psychosomatic Society, March 1969) *Psychosom. Med.* In press.

Moos, R. H. (1963). 'Personality Factors Associated with Rheumatoid Arthritis: A Review.' *J. chron. Dis.*, **17,** 41.

— and Solomon, G. F. (1965). 'Personality Correlates of the Degree of Functional Incapacity of Patients with Physical Disease.' *J. chron. Dis.*, **18,** 1019.

Scotch, N. and Geiger, H. J. (1962). 'The Epidemiology of Rheumatoid Arthritis: A Review with Special Attention to Social Factors.' *J. chron. Dis.*, **15,** 1037.

West, H. P. (1967). 'Rheumatoid Arthritis: The Relevance of Clinical Knowledge to Research Activities.' *Abstr. World Med.*, **41,** 401.

CHAPTER 14

CHRONIC PAIN

A STUDY OF SOME GENERAL FEATURES WHICH PLAY A ROLE IN MAINTAINING A STATE OF CHRONIC PAIN AFTER AMPUTATION

F. S. MORGENSTERN

INTRODUCTION

Reactions to chronic pain vary widely among different patients, and there are some differences in clinical response which cannot be adequately explained in terms of pathology or local tissue changes. A whole range of general reactions appears to be involved. Many of these have been studied extensively and a large body of the relevant literature was recently assembled by Merskey and Spear (1967). There are still, however, a number of questions and problems concerning this general aspect of the response to trauma which have been incompletely answered, and the following account is based on an investigation of some of the outstanding issues.

The particular form of chronic pain examined in these studies is that which follows amputation. The investigation was confined in this way so that an effective control group could be obtained to separate out effects due to chronic pain from others which are specific to a given lesion. All the subjects who took part in the study had therefore undergone amputation, and they were assigned to experimental and control groups according to the presence or absence of chronic pain among their symptoms. Differences between general reactions observed in these groups can therefore be attributed to chronic pain with some degree of confidence.

Objections may be raised to such a study, as it only deals with one form of chronic pain. It could be argued that post-amputation pain is highly specific, being notorious for its resistance to treatment and persisting in some cases even when all afferent pathways from the site of the lesion have been interrupted by neurosurgery. The circumstantial accounts of their pain which patients have recorded are equally familiar—they even feature in the early account given by Ambroise Paré (English translation, 1634). More cogently, perhaps, it could be opposed that pain from visceral lesions differs from pain in the extremities, and that there are numerous aches and pains met in clinical practice which cannot be traced to any known pathology, least of all to a major trauma like amputation. While some of these objections cannot be met by a restricted study, the features of post-amputation pain are so varied and embracing that a brief account may serve to justify its use as a basis for a general discussion.

POST-AMPUTATION PAIN

Most studies of post-amputation pain have been concerned with pain referred to a phantom limb and with the special sensations which these embody. They are extensively reviewed by Bradley (1955). The term 'phantom limb' was coined by Weir Mitchell in 1872: 'Nearly every man who loses a limb carries about with him a constant or inconstant phantom of the missing member, a sensory ghost of that much of himself, and sometimes a most inconvenient presence, faintly felt at times, but ready to be called up to his perception by a blow, a touch or a change of wind.' The most complete account of phantom limb sensations comes from Riddoch (1944). In his article on 'phantom limbs and body shape', he describes painless and painful phantom limbs in detail, enumerates some other conditions apart from amputation in which phantom sensations have been reported, and discusses the basis of these sensations. He points out that if there is pain, the sensations change in character—they are more persistent, and also lose the power of independent 'movement' which may be present in a painless phantom. He also details conditions which alter the character of the sensations in painful cases, and these include various manipulations of the stump, as well as a series of general conditions: yawning, micturition or defaecation, fatigue, sleeplessness or persistent worry. In a later section he mentions that the patient's general health can influence the strength of the phantom limb sensations; for example, during a febrile attack the phantom may become faint, and after the fever has passed become clear once more. Riddoch concludes from his observations that 'Emotional instability, in varying degrees, is therefore an inevitable complication, as in all disorders in which severe incessant pain is a prominent symptom'.

The incidence of chronic post-amputation pain varies in different series, but a figure of 3 per cent, taken from Solonen's (1962) study of one thousand Finnish War Veterans may be taken as representative. The incidence varies for different age groups, becoming more common with advancing age (Solonen, 1962; Jalavisto, 1950;

Cronholm, 1951), and Simmel (1958) has pointed out that phantom limb sensations are unknown in children operated before the age of five years.

In some cases the pain can be traced to recognizable, local pathologies in the stump. Such conditions are listed by Gillis (1954). The most common is a painful neuroma; others are local infections, foreign bodies, a variety of vascular malformations (*see also* Leriche, 1949; Erikson, 1965), and pain has also been ascribed to the muscles of the stump with traction on the periosteum; occasionally pain is referred to an amputation stump from a distant lesion, e.g. from a coronary lesion or a gastro-intestinal ulcer.

But these conditions do not account for all cases of post-amputation pain. Since the studies of Head and Holmes (1911), cases have been described in which all the afferent pathways from the stump have been severed without abolishing phantom pain. Irrespective of the level at which the afferent pathway is interrupted—peripheral nerves or limb plexus (Riddoch, 1944; Gillis, 1954), spinothalamic tract (Falconer and Lindsay, 1946; Leriche, 1949), thalamus (Hecaen *et al.*, 1949), or cerebral cortex (Lewin and Phillips, 1952; Pertuiset *et al.*, 1959; Torok, 1960; Constans, 1960)—there is no guarantee that pain will not return in time. Once a state of chronic pain is established, a self-perpetuating cycle seems to develop, which operates as a special condition and interferes with the response to treatment. A distinction is therefore drawn between the initial cause of the pain, and a secondary reaction which maintains a state of chronic pain. This does not apply equally to all patients, as reflected in the figure of 3 per cent quoted above for the incidence of chronic intractable post-amputation pain. In the following investigation an attempt is made to find some reasons for these differences in individual response in the medical histories and clinical findings of patients who had undergone amputation.

The selection of patients and the standards for the assessment of pain are described in some detail to establish the nature of the study, and the adequacy of the control group. There is no simple objective standard for judging chronic pain, and a working definition had to be obtained. Arbitrary standards are difficult to assemble, because of the variety of influences which can alter the judgment of pain, even if this is experimentally induced, and rated by trained observers. Beecher (1957), for instance, lists 27 ways in which the reaction to pain may be altered: race, sex, age, autonomic activity, circulatory change, skin temperature, sweating, elevation of carbon dioxide tension, hyperalgesia, other forms of trauma, nausea, fatigue, anxiety, fear, training, bias, adaptation, distraction and inattention, lethargy, judgment impaired by drugs, suggestion and emotion, diurnal variation, the passage of time—as well as a group of miscellaneous factors which might include personality characteristics and mental disorder. If the judgment of acute pain under controlled conditions is vulnerable to so many influences, this would render judgments of the intensity of chronic pain even more uncertain.

For these reasons, a practical definition of chronic pain was sought from physicians who had extensive experience of this problem. It is reported in some detail, because the meaning of 'chronic pain' as used by this study is derived from a specific investigation, and must be interpreted accordingly.

METHODS

Subjects

All the subjects who took part in this investigation were patients who attended the Ministry of Pensions Limb Fitting Centre, Roehampton. The source from which the names were drawn was the list of out-patient attendances at the Limb Fitting Centre, attendance having taken place for the purpose of limb fitting, or for the adjustment of prostheses. This rendered participation in the study independent of other medical complaints or treatments which might have biased selection. Attendance during the months of October and November were chosen as being less likely to be affected by holidays, intercurrent illnesses and transport difficulties than other months. All patients had undergone amputation at least two years before the time of attendance, so that chronic pain should not be confused with acute, self-limiting pain in the post-operative phase. The total population from which the sample was drawn was 3,000 patients.

A second list of patients was obtained from attendances at a special clinic for patients suffering from 'intractable pain'. This clinic had been especially designed to study and treat the problem of pain in amputees. Although some patients ultimately included in the 'high pain' group (the experimental group) came from the first list of subjects, most were obtained from the second list.

Selection Procedure

The selection procedure was to enter a table of random numbers, the *n*th patient following the one previously chosen being taken from the sample (where *n* represents the successive numbers in the random table). Wherever this could be ascertained from the notes, a name was discarded if the patient was attending for the fitting of a congenital limb dysplasia.

Criteria for Group Selection

The criteria used to assign patients to the experimental and control groups were clinical, and based on the practical judgments of physicians who were regularly concerned with the treatment of chronic pain. A pain scale was devised so that selection should be consistent; each patient could thus be given a 'pain score' which decided if he should be in the high pain (I), intermediate (II) or no pain (III) group.

Physician's Ratings

Seven physicians were invited to list their criteria for judging the intensity of pain suffered by patients. Each had extensive experience of the practical problems of chronic pain, as this was a regular feature of their out-patient clinics at the Limb Fitting Centre. All of them were aware of the nature of this study and had been of the greatest help in discussing the problems which were being investigated. The following questionnaire was given to them, some of the questions being formulated to take account of the special circumstances of amputation, since this was the common condition of all the patients.

Questionnaire for Doctors

For the survey it is necessary to classify patients into 'pain' and 'no pain' groups. To do this we need adequate criteria for including a patient in either of the groups.

(1) Would you agree that there is a certain type of post-amputation pain which is a problem because there is no known cause and no treatment which is completely satisfactory?

(2) From the doctor's point of view, what would the main characteristics of this particular pain be (e.g. duration, intensity, time since amputation etc.)?

(3) What features in the patient's account of his pain or in his history would lead you to make this diagnosis (e.g. affecting sleep, work, etc.)?

(4) Do you take the personality of the patient into account when you make this diagnosis?—Why? (Doctor to rate his statements.)

(5) Would you make your diagnosis on the basis of any one of these characteristics alone?

(6) Which would you consider to be adequate for the diagnosis? (*a*) Doctor. (*b*) Patient.

(7) Would you reject the complaints of pain made by certain patients? (That is, do you simply accept the patient's account of

his disability or do you relate it to your own personal criteria before assessing the extent of the pain?)

(8) What would lead you to reject the complaints of certain patients?

(9) When you make the diagnosis of intractable phantom or stump pain do you use the same criteria for both diagnoses?

(10) If not which would you exclude? (*a*) Phantom. (*b*) Stump.

The Pain Scale

The replies to these questions provide a basis from which a pain scale can be constructed for the use of a study of chronic pain. After doing a frequency analysis of the replies a short scale was constructed, and was based on the following 12 most common statements:

(1) Chronic pain is of such intensity that it interferes with sleep, work, and wearing the prosthesis.

(2) When really severe it affects the general condition of the patient.

(3) If not continuous, it is at least present during 24 hours.

(4) Treatment has been sought, but failed to give relief.

(5) Pain has been present since the time of the amputation.

(6) Pain is localized in the stump or in a phantom limb.

(7) Pain is not relieved by wearing a prosthesis.

(8) There is continuous pain with exacerbations in the form of jactitations.

(9) The description of the pain is in dramatic terms.

(10) If amputation was preceded by injury, pain is centred around the site of the injury.

The maximum score on this scale is 54 and the minimum 0. An arbitrary cut-off point of 32 was used to categorize the experimental group (high pain). Patients with scores between 0 and 32 formed the intermediate group, while a score of 0 implied that the subjects had not had or could not remember having any pain since the time of amputation, and they comprised the control (no pain) group.

Medical History and Clinical Examination

The medical history was elicited in the routine manner; it dealt with the circumstances of the amputation, its consequences, medically as well as more generally, for the patient; standard medical and psychiatric enquiries were made. Physical examination was similarly conducted along routine lines, but included a careful examination of the amputation stump. Standard clinical assessment of sensory changes in the stump were used in view of the general experience that special methods for the determination of sensory thresholds require special training on the part of the subject. Such training was out of the question in the setting of this study.

Examination of the Amputation Stump

In examining the stump, particular attention was paid to the length of the stump, its shape, the state of the musculature, the scars of the incisions and any sensory changes in the stump compared with the proximal part of the same limb, and an equivalent area of the normal limb (in unilateral amputees). The presence of adherence of skin and underlying tissues was noted, the subjective difference of temperature between the stump and the normal limb, and pallor or cyanosis if these were present. Attention was directed to the pulsations of superficial arteries, but this was only assessed by palpation. The degree of mobility of the remaining joints of the limb as well as those of the other side and of the spine were recorded. Assessment of the stump allowed a scheme of classification to be developed to describe the final result. Stumps were rated according to this scheme, using the following categories:

Stump Ratings

0 = Square end of stump, excellent scar, warm to touch, full muscle power and movements at all joints.
1 = Conical stump, good scar, fair muscle power, full movement at all joints, cool, but not cold to touch.
2 = Irregular end of stump, puckered scars non-adherent to bone, cold extremity of stump, muscle wasting, some limitation of movement of proximal joint.
3 = Irregular stump, scar adherent to bone, cold to touch, wasting of muscles, limitation of movements at proximal joints.

RESULTS

(1) Age

The composition of the three groups (I = high pain, II = intermediate, III = no pain) is shown in Table 1.

No patients were suffering from severe, chronic pain in age groups below 34.

The analysis of variance, Table 1a, indicates that the age distribution of the three groups does not differ significantly in other respects, so that this difference can be attributed to the presence of chronic pain.

TABLE 1
Age Distribution of Patients Classified by Intensity of Pain

Age	*Group* I	II	III	*Total*
15–25	0	4	3	7
25–34	0	4	8	12
35–44	6	12	6	24
45–54	17	19	8	44
55–64	10	8	7	25
65–74	16	18	6	40
75–84	5	3	2	10
85–94	1	0	1	2
95+	0	0	0	0
Total	55	68	41	164

(chi^2 35 – : 35+ = 16·6)

Note: While 201 patients were examined, the above is the distribution for that group of patients who completed all the forms of enquiry.

TABLE 1a
Analysis of Variance of Age Distributions (Table 1)

	d.f.	*S.S.*	*V.R.*	*F-ratio*	*Sig.*
Due to pain grouping	2	15·58	7·79	0·52	n.s.
Due to age grouping	7	557·33	79·62	5·31	0·01
Total variance	23	783·33			
Residual	14	210·42	15·03		

There is a significant interaction between age and liability to chronic pain.

(2) Sex

The composition of the groups in terms of the patients' sex is shown in Table 2. Differences in the sex distribution of the groups were not significant (chi^2 groups I : III = 0·69, n.s.).

TABLE 2
Sex Distribution of the Sample

	Group I	II	III	*Total*
Male	51	59	36	146
Female	4	9	5	18

(3) Marital Status

The marital status of the patients is shown in Table 3. There was no significant difference in the marital status of the three groups.

TABLE 3
Marital Status of Patients in the Three Groups

	Group I	Group II	Group III	Total
Single	6	6	10	22 (chi² n.s.)
Married	45	51	29	125 (,,)
Separated	0	1	0	1 (,,)
Divorced	3	5	2	10 (,,)
Widowed	1	5	0	6 (,,)

(4) *Medical Authority*

While the Limb Fitting Centre was established to deal with casualties from World War I, the number of patients attending in consequence of civil injuries has increased during the years.

The incidence of chronic pain was significantly higher among war pensioners than among civilian casualties ($chi^2 = 10{\cdot}06$, $p = 0{\cdot}01$).

TABLE 4
Medical Authority Responsible for the Patients

	Group I	Group II	Group III	Total
War pensioners	39	37	16	92
National Health Service	16	31	25	72

(5) *Occupational Status*

Significantly more patients with chronic pain had retired from active work than patients in the control groups.

TABLE 5
Occupational Status of the Patients

	Group I	Group II	Group III	Total
(1) Professional	1	5	1	7
(2) Intermediate	2	7	9	18
(3) Skilled	21	22	19	62
(4) Partly skilled	4	1	0	5
(5) Unskilled	4	2	3	9
(6) Retired	22	23	8	53
(7) Housewife	1	6	1	8
(8) Student	0	2	0	2

(chi^2 for retired: active $= 4{\cdot}55$, $p = 0{\cdot}05$)

(6) Limb Amputated

The distribution of the amputations is shown in Table 6. There was no significant difference between the incidence of pain in upper and lower limb amputations.

Differences between the lateralization of the amputations were highly significant. Patients with left-sided amputations are significantly more prone to suffer from chronic pain than patients with right-sided lesions.

TABLE 6
Distribution of Limb Amputations

	Group			*Total*
	I	II	III	
Left leg	29	26	13	68
Right leg	15	29	23	67
Left arm	5	3	0	8
Right arm	2	1	1	4
Both legs	4	9	4	17
Total left	38	38	17	93
Total right	21	39	27	87

(chi² left: right = 5·74, p = 0·02; the bilateral amputations are included in both left and right totals)

(7) Site of Amputation

Table 7 shows the differences in distribution of proximal and distal lesions within the groups. Patients with proximal lesions suffered from chronic pain significantly more commonly than patients with distal lesions.

TABLE 7
Distribution of the Site of Amputation

	Group			*Total*
	I	II	III	
Disarticulation at hip	3	5	0	8
Above knee	30	35	12	77
Through knee	1	33	3	7
Below knee	14	17	24	55
Disarticulation at shoulder	1	1	0	2
Above elbow	4	3	0	7
Through elbow	0	0	0	0
Below elbow	2	0	0	2
One above knee + one below knee	0	4	1	5
Total proximal	39	51	16	106
Total distal	16	21	25	62

(chi² proximal : distal = 17·95, p = 0·001)

N.B. In calculating the total proximal and total distal amputations the five above knee and below knee amputations appear in both groups.

(*8*) *Cause of Amputation*

The distribution of causes for the amputation is shown in Table 8.

There was no significant difference between the incidence of pain following traumatic amputation and operations undertaken because of disease.

TABLE 8

Causes of Amputation

	Group			*Total*
	I	II	III	
Trauma	47	52	30	129
Disease	8	16	9	33
Congenital	0	0	2	2

(chi^2 congenital : disease = 2·60, p = n.s.)

In the following comparisons, data are only given for the high pain and no pain groups (I and III respectively).

(*9*) *Incidence of Chronic Pain and Final State of the Stump*

The distribution of qualitative results in the stumps in these two groups is shown in Table 9 (using the method of assessment described above). There was no association between chronic pain and the final state of the stump, either when comparing scores of 0 and 1 with scores of 2 and 3, or when comparing all four groups with each other.

TABLE 9

Qualitative Distribution of Amputation Stumps

Classification of stump	*Group*	
	I	III
0	17	14
1	27	17
2	13	12
3	3	1

(chi^2 (0+1):(2+3), =0·41, n.s.)

(*10*) *Abnormalities of Cutaneous Sensation and Chronic Pain*

The incidence of areas of cutaneous anaesthesia and hyperaesthesia on the stumps is shown in Table 10. There was a significant association of areas of cutaneous anaesthesia and chronic pain. There was no association between areas of hyperaesthesia on the stump and chronic pain.

TABLE 10

Abnormalities of Cutaneous Sensations of the Stump and Chronic Pain

Cutaneous	*Group* I	III
Anaesthesia	12	1 (chi^2 = 7·66 p 0·01)
Hyperaesthesia	6	1 (chi^2 = 2·57 p n.s.)
Total with sensory change	18	2 (chi^2 = 11·17 p 0·01)

(11) Abnormalities of Deep Sensation and Chronic Pain

Table 11 shows the distribution of findings of tender spots and neuromata in the two groups. There was a significant association between the presence of tender spots and neuromata, and chronic pain.

TABLE 11

	Group I	III
Tender spot + tender neuroma	39	11 (chi^2 = 17·75, p 0·01)

(12) Limitation of Movement at Joints Proximal to the Amputation Stump

There was gross limitation of movement (by 15 degrees or more) of the proximal joints in 9 cases of group I and 11 cases of group III. There was no significant relationship between limitation of movement at proximal joints, and chronic pain.

(13) Association Between Other Pathological Conditions and Chronic Pain

Clinical data from the case histories and physical examinations were analysed for possible associations with chronic pain. For brevity, these are only presented in summary form in Table 12. It will be noted that three items stand out in which there are significant differences between groups I and III. Patients who suffered from chronic pain had also undergone more operations for other disorders than patients free from pain. Chronic pain was significantly associated with amputations which had been preceded by acute osteomyelitis. The incidence of recurrent depressive illnesses was significantly higher among patients with chronic pain than in the control group. There were no other significant differences between the groups in respect of any other previous illnesses, or contemporary pathological conditions found on physical examination.

While the total number of disorders encountered in patients of the high pain group is greater than that in the no pain group, the difference in numbers is not statistically significant.

TABLE 12

Summary of Past and Present Illnesses of Patients in Groups I and III

	Group	
		III
Surgical operations (other than amputation)	24	5
Cardiovascular	24	27
Respiratory tract	21	14
Gastro-intestinal (unoperated)	6	5
Uro-genital (unoperated)	5	3
Central nervous	7	3
Orthopaedic (unoperated)	17	13
Endocrine	1	2
Vitamin deficiency	1	0
Infectious and tropical	16	4
Osteomyelitis (acute and chronic)	12	5
Dermatological	1	5
Psychiatric	18	10
(recurrent depressive states)	15	4
Other	2	6
Total	155	109

DISCUSSION

(1) Patients are Significantly More Liable to Suffer from Chronic Pain after the Age of 35

This observation is in agreement with the findings of Henderson and Smyth (1948); it is also consistent with the studies of Cronholm (1951), Jalavisto (1950) and Solonen (1962), all of whom noted that phantom sensations in general become more frequently noted with advancing age; while Simmel (1958) states that phantom limbs do not develop if amputation takes place before the age of five years. A progressive change in response to trauma as the patient grows older is the kind of general reaction to chronic pain which was sought in this study. In this sample the change was not due to the healing properties of tissues, as the lesions had often existed for years before the onset of chronic pain. In patients who are free from pain for a long period of time after the amputation and only experience chronic pain late in life, it must be supposed that there are either chronic, progressive tissue changes at the site of the lesion, or that there is a general reaction of personality to disability which only becomes apparent with increasing age.

(2) Patients who had been Injured during Military Service were More Prone to Suffer from Chronic Pain than Those Injured as Civilians

This cannot be due to the traumatic causes for amputation which apply to military service, since it was found that chronic pain was no more common after amputations due to traumatic injury than when the amputation was necessary for medical reasons (Table 8). General attitudes towards disability would seem to be involved (and this is supported by an unpublished study).

(3) Left-sided Lesions were More Liable to Cause Chronic Pain than Right-sided Lesions

A difference in lateral effects of the amputation cannot be due to local responses to injury. Some more general psychological or neurological response is implicated. The non-dominant side is more prone to be painful after injury, and this side is less highly trained in general sensorimotor skills. It may be that the selective practice of skills of the dominant side also facilitates its adaptation to trauma. If this applies to the adaptation to a change in sensation and to pain, sensory skills like motor skills would seem to be influenced by laterality, and therefore related at a high level of neurological integration.

(4) Proximal Lesions Lead to Chronic Pain More Often than Distal Lesions

Cronholm has pointed out that phantom limb sensations are more persistent in proximal than in distal amputations. This also appears to be true for chronic pain. It is tempting to ascribe such a difference to a more intensive cortical representation of the distal parts of the limbs—especially the hands—but this is clearly speculative. All that can be deduced from the simple observation is that a distal amputation leaves more of the nervous afferent supply from the limb intact than a proximal amputation, and that there is a relationship between the extent of the damage to the peripheral afferent supply and the development of chronic pain.

(5) Areas of Local Anaesthesia at the Site of Injury are Associated with Chronic Pain

Any amputation interferes with local cutaneous innervation. Weddell has shown that unpleasant painful sensations are associated with isolated nerve nets in which there is no overlap with adjacent innervation. In the present instances there was effective cutaneous anaesthesia in the area around the scar and on the stump. A local source for chronic pain would indicate the presence of hyperaesthetic regions, but these were not associated (in the skin) with chronic pain. As in the case of proximal lesions, this relationship between local cutaneous anaesthesia and chronic pain involves reduction of sensations and not an excess of painful stimuli. In the case of chronic pain, therefore, diminution of sensibility needs to be considered, as well as active sources of pain, as in the next section.

(6) Tender Spots and Neuromata are Associated with Chronic Pain

This does not need much discussion as a general cause of pain. Since pain from a neuroma is increased by mechanical irritation, it would be expected to contribute to chronic as well as acute states of pain.

(7) Patients with Chronic Pain had Undergone More Operations for Other Causes than Patients Free from Pain

This may be part of a general personality response to chronic pain. The kinds of operation which accounted for the difference between the groups were operations in which pressure from the patient is likely to influence the choice of treatment—e.g. operations for gastro-duodenal ulcer, for hernias, for haemorrhoids, etc. Other investigators have also commented that patients with non-specific pains appear to undergo operation more readily than those free from pain (as discussed by Merskey and Spear, 1967). Once more, this is a general reaction to chronic pain, and not one due to local features of injury.

(8) Amputations Performed Because of Acute Osteomyelitis were Liable to be Followed by Chronic Pain

The data from this investigation is not sufficient to follow up this observation. It could be that this is due to areas of cutaneous anaesthesia around the sinuses which were noted in these cases. Gangrene was not a cause of later pain, so that this is not an association between bone destruction and pain; possibly vascularization in acute osteomyelitis is a contributing cause.

(9) Recurrent Depressions were More Common Among Patients in Chronic Pain than Among Patients Free from Pain

This investigation does not permit a distinction between depressive states which appeared for the first time after amputation, and others which had already featured earlier in the life of the patients. It should be mentioned, however, that although the patients tended to trace their depression to the amputation, relief from a depressive state has no influence on pain, and that on some occasions, pain is relieved, without changing a depressive mood.

(10) To Recapitulate the Negative Findings

There were no associations between the groups in respect of:
Sex
Marital status
Arm versus leg amputations
Causes of amputation
Final result as regards the stump
Past medical disorders or present physical disorders.

PSYCHOSOCIAL FACTORS

While the above discussion is confined to medical features which are relevant to a state of chronic pain, some other aspects of this problem were also studied. The same populations of patients were approached for these data which relate to psychological and social circumstances, rather than to medical findings.

The first of these studies was concerned with an attempt to modify chronic, severe post-amputation pain, by training the patient to ignore a variety of prolonged sensory distractions: visual, auditory, tactile and deep-pressure sensations were used. While exposed to these distractions, the patient was engaged in very difficult tasks which required intense concentration on a motor skill. The details of the experiment are described elsewhere (Morgenstern, 1964). The following summary is taken from that and other studies:

(1) Intersensory distraction, combined with the distraction of intense concentration on task performance, can effectively abolish chronic, pathological pain.

(2) The repeated exposure to such distraction has a cumulative effect in reducing, and sometimes permanently relieving, chronic pain.

(3) Such pain relief is achieved in the absence of any interference with the stump or its afferent nervous pathways.

(4) Accompanying the relief from pain, there is a rapid shrinking of the phantom limb, with regression into the stump.

(5) Once the phantom has regressed into the stump, even a recurrence of pain is not accompanied by lengthening of the phantom limb.

(6) Changes in bilateral phantom limbs are not identical in time course or perceptual content.

(7) In one patient with unilateral thalamotomy for the treatment of post-herpetic neuralgia, and in another with bilateral thalamotomy for the treatment of causalgia, the effects of distraction were more limited in extent and duration.

(8) Two patients, who were known to have produced hysterical conversion symptoms at other times, made an initial response to distraction, but failed to maintain their concentration or to co-operate with the experiment.

The point to be emphasized in these observations is that a state of chronic pain was relieved for prolonged periods without recourse to drugs, and without altering the state of the stump—the traumatized area—in any way. It also became apparent how much less chance there is for training after extensive high level surgery of the central nervous system. The resistance of hysterical patients to treatment is also well known, and it may be important that the two patients known to have produced conversion symptoms in the past resisted the treatment, although they responded to training.

The second study, summarized below, was directed towards personality and social reactions of the patients; it has not yet been reported elsewhere. Three questionnaires were used: The Eysenck Personality Inventory (E.P.I., Eysenck, 1964), and the Cornell Medical Index (C.M.I., Brodman *et al.*, 1951), as well as a specially constructed questionnaire dictated by the requirements of this study. The latter was first subjected to a multiple correlation analysis, and then 57 items were selected for further factorial studies.

(1) Patients from the high pain group scored significantly higher than patients from the no pain group on:

Neuroticism scales (E.P.I. and C.M.I.).

Symptoms scale (C.M.I.), i.e. irrespective of the generally similar medical histories of these groups, they differed greatly in their reports of symptoms of medical disorders.

Psychosomatic (C.M.I.) scale.

(2) Sporadic pain in the low pain group was more common in arm amputations; was more common in cases of multiple amputation than single amputation; if caused by wearing the prosthesis, had the same effects on the habits, mood, and social life of the patients, as stump or phantom limb pain; was more common in patients who had always lived with their parents; was more common if the parents had divorced or separated; was more common among patients who had other siblings, and if the patient had left home for economic reasons.

(3) Treatment was sought if pain interfered with sleep or work, and if the prosthesis caused pain.

(4) The incidence of pain was not related to social habits, even where transport represented a problem.

(5) Phantom limb sensations were commonly evoked by autonomic reflexes, and if the phantom sensations were altered by such reflexes, the patients were more liable to suffer from sporadic pain. Such autonomic effects seemed to be confined to patients who had experienced phantom sensations immediately after amputation. Patients who had required drugs for pain relief after amputation were more prone to the persistence of phantom sensations at a later date.

(6) The clarity of the phantom sensation is related to the incidence of sporadic pain.

(7) All patients in the low pain group had experienced shortening of the phantom limb.

(8) In the high pain group, patients who had undergone further operations on the stump continued to suffer from pain, and were disinclined to go out into company. Treatment was more often undergone by patients who had left home for economic reasons. Shortening of the phantom depended on the pain score; the experience of a phantom limb immediately after amputation, was related to the time spent in hospital after the amputation.

(9) No other single items of family circumstances, school life, work or social events had different loadings in the two groups.

(10) From the factorial study, three orders of factors were obtained, and the three third order factors describe:

(*a*) The events at the time of amputation which should alert the physician that a given patient is liable to suffer from chronic post-amputation pain.

(*b*) The differences in the constellation of present social circumstances and habits of patients in the high pain and no pain groups.

(*c*) Differences between the experiences after the amputation, personality characteristics, and personal criteria on which judgments of pain (by the patient) are based.

(11) Items of work, occupation during the day, stability at work, effects of the amputation on the ability to work, financial problems, and civilian compensation received for amputation, are no different among patients in the high pain and the no pain groups.

CONCLUSION

On a number of counts, this investigation confirms that there are general features of injury and of the personality of the patients which play a role in maintaining a state of chronic pain. This aspect, of maintaining the state of pain, was inferred from the uncertain response of patients to neurosurgery, and additional reasons are traced in these results. At best, neurosurgery reduces sensations in order to remove pain. It was found, however, that chronic pain is selectively more common when there is less sensation from the stump so that what is gained by interrupting afferent pathways of painful sensations, may be lost by increasing vulnerability to chronic pain from a secondary mechanism in a general response.

In respect of the post-operative management of amputations, there is a practical implication. The longer the stump is kept immobilized and isolated from stimulation, the more it is liable to later pain. Passive movements, where active ones are contra-indicated, may therefore be of greater help in the post-operative management than analgesics, and an intensive regime of occupational therapy can help at a general level to involve the patient and prevent his preoccupation with the stump and amputation. The most intensive, active demands are therefore required if post-operative management is to be used as a prophylactic against chronic pain.

SUMMARY

An investigation of general features which perpetuate a state of chronic pain is reported, using chronic intractable post-amputation pain as the experimental condition. The findings were:

(1) Patients are significantly more liable to suffer from chronic pain after the age of 35.

(2) Patients who had been injured during National Service were more prone to suffer from chronic pain than civilians.

(3) Left-sided lesions were more liable to cause chronic pain than right-sided lesions.

(4) Proximal lesions lead to chronic pain more commonly than distal lesions.

(5) Areas of local anaesthesia at the site of injury are selectively associated with chronic pain.

(6) Tender spots and neuromata are associated with chronic pain.

(7) Patients with chronic pain had undergone more operations for other causes than patients free from pain.

(8) Amputations performed because of acute osteomyelitis were especially likely to be followed by chronic pain.

(9) Patients suffering from chronic pain suffered from recurrent depressive states more often than patients free from pain.

There were no significant group differences in respect of the following:

Sex
Marital status
Arm versus leg amputations
Causes of amputation
Final result as regards the stump
Other past or present physical disorders.

ACKNOWLEDGEMENTS

This investigation was made possible by a special grant from the Ministry of Health, and undertaken at the Limb Fitting Centre, Roehampton. The special gratitude of the author is due to Dr. M. Vitali, Miss R. Green field and Dr. I. H. M. Curwen, without whose active help the work would have been impossible, and to Prof. W. Ritchie Russell, from whom the concept of such a study was derived.

REFERENCES

Beecher, H. K. (1957). 'The Measurement of Pain.' *Pharmac. Rev.*, **9,** 59.

Bradley, K. C. (1955). 'The Sequelae of Amputation.' The Trustees of the Services Canteens Trust Fund, Australia.

Brodman, K., Erdmann, A. J., Lorge, I., Wolff, H. G. and Broadbent, T. H. (1951). 'The CMI-Health Questionnaire.' *J. Am. med. Ass.*, **145,** 152.

Constans, J. P. (1960). 'Chirurgie de la Douleur.' *Acta neurochir.*, **8,** 251.

Cronholm, B. (1951). 'Phantom Limbs in Amputees: a Study of Changes in the Integration of Centripetal Impulses with Special Reference to Referred Sensations.' *Acta. psychiat. neurol. scand.*, Suppl. 72.

Erikson, U. (1965). 'Circulation in Traumatic Amputation Stumps: an Angiographic and Physiological Investigation.' *Acta radiol. (diagn.) Stockh.*, Suppl. 238.

Eysenck, H. J. (1964). 'Eysenck Personality Inventory: The Measurement of Personality: A New Inventory.' *J. Indian Acad. Psychol.*, **1,** 1.

Falconer, M. A. and Lindsay, J. S. B. (1946). 'Painful Phantom Limb Treated by High Cervical Cordotomy.' *Br. med. J.*, **33,** 301.

Gillis, L. (1954). *Amputations*. London: Heinemann.

Head, H. and Holmes, G. (1911). 'Sensory Disturbances from Cerebral Lesions.' *Brain*, **34,** 102.

Hecaen, H., Talairach, J., David, M. and Dell, M. B. (1949). 'Coagulations Limitees du Thalamus dans les Algies du Syndrome Thalamique.' *Rev. Neurol.*, **81,** 917.

Henderson, W. R. and Smyth, G. E. (1948). 'Phantom Limbs.' *J. Neurol. Neurosurg. Psychiat.*, **11,** 88.

Jalavisto, E. (1950). 'Adaptation in the Phantom Limb Phenomena as Influenced by the Age of the Amputee.' *J. Gerontol.*, **5,** 339.

Leriche, R. (1949). 'De l'arteriographic dans les Moignons Pathologiques du Role de la Circulation Arterielle dans la Genese des Troubles Trophiques.' *Presse med.*, **57,** 23.

Lewin, W. and Phillips, C. G. (1952). 'Observations on Partial Removal of the Post-central Gyrus for Pain.' *J. Neurol. Neurosurg. Psychiat.*, **15,** 143.

Merskey, H. and Spear, F. G. (1967). *Pain: Psychological and Psychiatric Aspects*. London: Baillière, Tindall and Cassell.

Mitchell, S. W. (1872). 'Injuries of Nerves.' In *Neural Maladies of Stumps*. Philadelphia.

Morgenstern, F. S. (1964). 'Effects of Sensory Input and Concentration on Post-amputation Phantom Limb Pain.' *J. Neurol Neurosurg. Psychiat.*, **27,** 58.

Parè, A. (1634). In *The Works of That Famous Chirugion Ambroise Parey*, Ch. XIII, pp. 456 and 457. London: T. Cotes and R. Young.

Pertuiset, B., Hirsch, J., Valvet, J. and Lefrano, E. (1959). 'Cortical and Subcortical Evocation of a Painful Phantom Extremity.' *Rev. Neurol.*, **101,** 140.

Riddoch, G. (1944). 'Phantom Limbs and Body Shape.' *Brain*, **64,** 197.

Simmel, S. M. L. (1958). 'The Conditions of Occurrence of Phantom Limbs.' *Proc. Am. Phil. Soc.*, **102,** 492.

Solonen, K. A. (1962). 'The Phantom Phenomenon in Amputated Finnish War Veterans.' *Acta orthop. scand.*, Suppl. 54.

Torok, P. (1960). 'Parietal Topectomy in Phantom Pain: Therapeutic Result and Psychopathological Significance.' *Acta neurochir.* (*Wein*), **8,** 293.

CHAPTER 15

DISORDERS OF SEXUAL POTENCY

J. BANCROFT

INTRODUCTION

A man's potency can be defined as his ability to achieve satisfactory vaginal intercourse with a woman. Disorders of potency may involve (*a*) the inability to produce or sustain an adequate erection (erectile impotence); (*b*) the inability to delay ejaculation long enough for satisfactory intercourse to result (premature ejaculation); and (*c*) the inability to terminate intercourse with ejaculation (delayed or absent ejaculation or ejaculatory impotence). The clinical importance of these disorders needs no emphasis, and although a great deal has been written on the subject there is little certain knowledge about aetiology or treatment and systematic studies have only just started (Johnson, 1968; Cooper, 1968).

It is appropriate that this topic should be included in a book on psychosomatic medicine; it is difficult to think of an area of bodily function in which the psyche and soma are both so much in evidence, and where the subject has so little control over them. Until recently, however, the aetiology of these disorders has been clearly divided into 'psychic' (an abnormal psyche finding expression through a normal soma) or 'somatic' (a normal psyche trying to find expression through a soma disturbed by disease or trauma). Both Johnson (1968) and Cooper (1968) stressed the importance of constitutional factors in many cases of disordered potency, and the possibility of a specific physiological vulnerability to psychic influences requires a re-appraisal of the relationship between psyche and soma in this particular area of function. This chapter attempts to do just that. An evaluation of the treatment of these disorders is beyond the scope of this review but it can be said that systematic enquiry into treatment is so far minimal. Recent accounts of treatment have been given by Hastings (1963), Wolpe and Lazarus (1966), Masters and Johnson (1966), Johnson (1968), Cooper (1968) and Friedman (1968).

What do we know of the physiological mechanisms necessary for normal sexual function in the male? In what way and to what extent are these mechanisms affected by psychic influences such as anxiety?

And to what extent can the clinical states of disordered potency be explained in terms of these mind–body relationships? These three questions will be dealt with in turn. In answering the first two questions a certain amount of evidence is available. In dealing with the third question, one is confined to speculation and the hope that future research will put the hypotheses to the test.

Attention will be confined to those parts of the process on which coitus ultimately depends. These can be listed as follows: (*a*) the development of erection; (*b*) emission, ejaculation and orgasm.

PHYSIOLOGICAL MECHANISMS

At the physiological level two systems are mainly involved: the nervous system and the endocrine system.

Role of the Nervous System

Most writers on the subject have presented a simple account of the neurophysiological mechanisms involved using a dualistic concept of the autonomic nervous system. Erection, it would be suggested, results from parasympathetically induced vasodilatation, whereas emission and ejaculation together with the subsequent vasoconstriction and detumescence are functions of the sympathetic nervous system. In this scheme premature ejaculation and impaired erection could be accounted for by overactivity of the sympathetic nervous system and, in view of the apparent association between central anxiety and peripheral sympathetic activity, the role of anxiety in inhibiting sexual potency seemed clear.

However, as in most situations where this dual antagonism of the autonomic system has been invoked, the attractive simplicity of the concept belies the complexity of the real evidence.

The evidence that we have comes from three main sources: (1) animal experiments (François-Franck, 1895; Bacq, 1931; Henderson and Roepke, 1933; Semans and Langworthy, 1938; Root and Bard, 1947; Bors and Comarr, 1960); (2) human clinical evidence—studies of spinal cord injury, or peripheral nerve injury and also results of surgical procedures on the cord, sympathetic chain or peripheral nerves (Bors and Comarr, 1960; Kuhn, 1950; Whitelaw and Smithwick, 1951; Rose, 1953; Talbot, 1955); (3) effects of drugs on human sexual response (Freyhan, 1961; Singh, 1961; Money and Yankowitz, 1967; Pritchard *et al.*, 1968). There is a further source—human experiments (Masters and Johnson, 1966; Freund, 1963; Bancroft, Jones and Pullan, 1966). The evidence can be summarized as follows.

Erection

Mechanisms involved are of two main types: (*a*) reflexive, and (*b*) psychic. Reflexive erections depend on lower spinal pathways only. The efferent pathway is from the erotogenic zones, in particular the skin of the fraenum of the penis via the pudendal nerves. The efferent pathway involves the parasympathetic sacral outflow from spinal levels S.1, 2 and 3, via the nervi erigentes. Stimulation of these nerves produces erection as a result of arterial vasodilatation. Thus, innocuous stimulation of the penis will produce an erection even in spinal man where the cord is transected above the sacral outflow, and where there is complete anaesthesia of the lower body. That this reflexive pathway is normally inhibited by higher centres is shown by the fact that in spinal man these reflexive erections usually have a much lower threshold.

The psychic erection is rather more complicated. It has been shown in cats that psychic erection still occurs in spite of complete extirpation of the sacral outflow providing that the sympathetic chain is intact. But if this is removed also erection will cease altogether (Root and Bard, 1947). There is comparable evidence in man (Kuhn, 1950; Bors and Comarr, 1960).

Some of the effects of sympathectomy in man are also consistent with these results. Whitelaw and Smithwick (1951) reported disturbances in sexual function in a large series of sympathectomies. Removal of the thoracic part of the chain mainly affected erection, whilst removal of the lumbar part was more consistently followed by impaired emission. Such effects of sympathectomy are obviously very inconsistent as other workers have reported different results, with even emission being unaffected in some cases (Rose, 1953), and it is likely that individuals vary in the importance that the sympathetic chain plays in these mechanisms.

Thus, it can be concluded that in some men and animals, if not all, erection can be mediated by the sympathetic system as well as the parasympathetic, that it is mainly in psychic erections that the sympathetic nervous system plays a part, and that it is the thoracic part of the sympathetic chain which is involved, the lumbar part being more clearly related to vasoconstriction and emission.

The mechanism involved in sympathetically induced erection remains uncertain, but a possible explanation is given by the findings of Deysach (1939), who examined the vascular anatomy of the penises of various mammals. In those without an os penis, such as man, he described various channels with thick artery-like walls, which, by constriction, could direct blood into the erectile tissues and prevent its draining into the venous system. He called these sluice channels.

Thus, erection could result not only from arterial vasodilatation and increased blood flow, but also from the venous shunting and stasis following closure of these 'sluice channels'. This latter process provides a mechanism by which adrenergic stimulation could produce erection.

Evidence concerning central mechanisms involved in erection is limited. Recently MacLean and Ploog (1962) reported interesting results from intracerebral stimulation studies in monkeys. They mapped out areas in the limbic system, very similar in position to the positive reinforcement system of Olds and Milner (1954), the stimulation of which results in erection.

Orgasm

The main features of the orgasm are a climax of intensified erotic sensation accompanying spasmodic muscle contraction, sometimes confined to the perineum and sometimes involving the whole body (Masters and Johnson, 1966; Money, 1961b; Kinsey *et al.*, 1953).

Although the sensations resulting from emission and ejaculation form a characteristic part of the male orgasmic experience it is clear that neither ejaculation nor emission is an essential part of the orgasm. Pre-adolescent boys not uncommonly experience orgasm without ejaculation (Kinsey, Pomeroy and Martin, 1948) and cases of 'dry-run' orgasm (i.e. with no emission or ejaculation) occur as a result of adrenergic blocking drugs in some cases (Money and Yankowitz, 1967).

The neurophysiological mechanisms underlying the orgasm remain obscure, but from the available evidence one can postulate that central excitation in the spinal centre builds up in such a way and to such a level that a spread of excitation occurs involving emission and the muscular contraction accompanying it. The speed at which the critical level is reached and the degree to which the excitation spreads presumably depends to a large extent on excitatory or inhibitory influences from higher centres as well as individual differences in reactivity at the spinal level.

Emission and Ejaculation

Contraction of the smooth muscles of the vas deferens resulting from sympathetic stimulation produces emission of semen into the posterior urethra. This acts as a trigger stimulus to rhythmic contractions of the ischio- and bulbo-cavernosus muscles leading to spurts of semen or ejaculation. These rhythmic muscular contractions are mediated by the parasympathetic or sacral outflow (Semans and Langworthy, 1938).

Role of the Endocrine System

It is now generally agreed that the hormones principally concerned with sexual behaviour in the male are the androgens, in particular testosterone. It is also becoming apparent that the ways in which testosterone may affect sexual behaviour are complex. In the first place there are relatively irreversible effects on maturation which androgens exert, probably at critical periods of development; secondly, there are direct effects which the hormone exerts on the mature animal and which depend on the continued presence of the hormone (Harris, 1964; Goy, 1968).

The questions which concern us here are: (*a*) how necessary is testosterone to the production of erection and emission; and (*b*) if it is necessary, what relevance has it to first reflexive and second psychic erections.

The occurrence of erections throughout childhood in normal males indicates that erection can occur without adult levels of testosterone.

With the gradual increase in androgens before puberty and the marked increase at puberty (Hamburg and Lunde, 1967) there is an accompanying increase of sexual arousability. The penis enlarges and probably becomes more susceptible to tactile stimulation. In other words the threshold for reflexive erection is lowered. In addition, however, psychic erections become increasingly prevalent. Ramsey (1943) showed that boys between the ages of 10 and 20 showed erections to a wide range of erotic psychic stimuli. An additional finding of great interest was that the boys aged 10 to 12 reported erections to a wide range of non-erotic stimuli, mainly situations involving excitement of a frightening or pleasant but non-sexual kind (e.g. being chased by police or riding in an aeroplane). Reports of this kind decreased rapidly after 12 and apparently these experiences are rarely recalled by adults.

Considerable variation also occurs between individuals in the degree of responsiveness to erotic psychic stimuli (Kinsey *et al.*, 1953; Gebhard *et al.*, 1965) and it is reasonable to account for at least part of this variation in terms of androgen effects, either in level of androgen or in 'target-organ' sensitivity. Reports of hypogonadism in the male indicate that the sexual responsiveness is less affected, and can be more easily corrected by replacement therapy, in cases where the deficiency started following puberty rather than preceding puberty. This suggests that one of the effects of increased androgens at puberty is to determine the degree of 'target-organ' sensitivity thereafter.

The need for the maintenance effect of testosterone is shown by the fall in sexual responsiveness when replacement therapy lapses (Money, 1961a). Additional evidence comes from recent work with a specific anti-androgen Cyproterone, which is considered to act by blocking the effects of testosterone. Preliminary findings suggest that it reduces the libido in males although its use has been confined so far to sexual offenders (Laschet and Laschet, 1967).

A convincing demonstration of the effect of testosterone on psychic erections was shown in a case report by Beaumont *et al.* (1969). A man with an XXY genetic constitution complained of a complete lack of sexual interest. He had had a moderately satisfactory sexual relationship in the past, but his libido had completely disappeared following an attack of orchitis. Reflexive erections were still possible but emission was not. On investigation he had an abnormally low urinary testosterone level (11·4 μg./24 hours; normal value 40–64·5 μg.). Psychophysiological testing at this stage showed no erections or sexual interest in response to slides of nude women or erotic fantasies. He was then given placebo tablets with the advice that they were male hormones which would restore his sexual interest. After one week on the placebo he was tested again with the same negative results as previously. He was then given sub-lingual methyl testosterone 25 mg. daily and when tested a week later he showed strong erections and moderate sexual interest in response to the same slides, though not to the erotic fantasies. After a further six weeks on testosterone his responses on testing were even stronger and he was now producing erections to fantasies as well (*Figure 1*). In this case although reflexive erections were no doubt facilitated his erectile responses to psychic stimuli were greatly enhanced and continued to improve during the first six weeks of treatment.

The extent to which the waning sexual responsiveness which accompanies advancing age can be explained by reduction in the maintenance effect of testosterone is not certain. The findings of Heller and Myers (1944) of some cases of so-called 'male climacteric' with high gonadatrophin levels and impotence reversible by androtherapy, suggests that some cases may be accounted for in this way.

It has been widely assumed (Money, 1961a) that although testosterone is necessary for the normal male libido, increasing the level beyond a certain point has no further effect and it is only when the level is initially lower than the postulated norm that sexual behaviour will be affected by additional androgens. Evidence from the literature is conflicting, however, and it remains a possibility that some individuals with apparently normal levels of androgens may respond to additional androgen with increased sexual arousability.

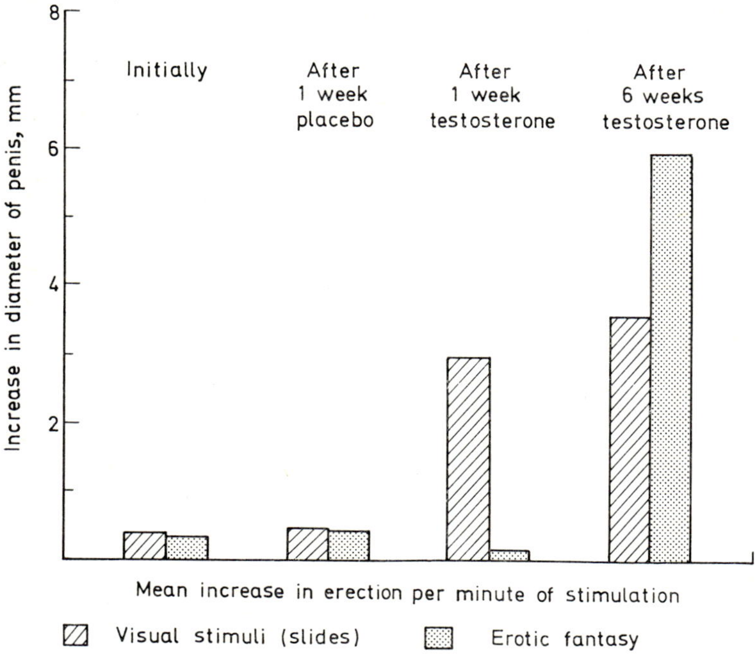

Figure 1. Change in psychic erections following testosterone replacement therapy (man with XXY constitution)

THE RELATIONSHIP BETWEEN MENTAL STATE AND PHYSIOLOGICAL FUNCTION

Psychodynamic mechanisms that have been suggested to explain potency disorders are varied but in most of them two basic assumptions are implicit. First, that anxiety, particularly that provoked by sexual situations, will interfere with normal potency; and secondly that if anxiety is not manifest, inhibition of the sexual mechanisms may result from unconscious processes. These two basic assumptions require closer examination. To do so it is first necessary to consider the relationship between erection, general arousal and subjective anxiety.

General Arousal

Erection has usually been considered part of a generalized sexual arousal response. Kinsey *et al.* (1953) emphasized this point, commenting that cardiovascular and respiratory responses amongst others 'appear to develop simultaneously, sometimes within a fraction of a second, as soon as the animal is stimulated and begins to respond'. Erection, therefore, would presumably be associated with other evidence of autonomic arousal.

Recent evidence has cast doubts on this assumption. MacLean and Ploog (1962), in their cerebral stimulation experiments in monkeys, found that in one-quarter of erection-producing sites erection was the only observable response. In the remainder other responses were also observed, the commonest being micturition, but evidence of generalized arousal in these cases was frequently lacking and in some cases cardiac deceleration or states of increased calm were observed in association with the erection. Thus, erection and arousal can certainly be separated at this level. Levy (1968) has shown that catecholamine secretion is increased in males looking at pornographic films although the range is considerable. The findings suggest that autonomic arousal occurred in most subjects. Wenger, Averill and Smith (1968) recorded various autonomic measures in males who were reading pornographic literature. There were significant increases in blood pressure and skin conductance but not heart rate, respiration rate or finger pulse volume. Unfortunately in neither of these experimental situations was it possible to assess the relationship between the autonomic arousal observed and penile erection as no measurement of erection was available. The relationship between psychic erections and other autonomic measures of arousal has been investigated in normal subjects, however, by Bancroft and Mathews (1967, 1970). Recordings of erection, skin conductance, pulse rate and forearm blood flow were taken during the presentation of erotic visual stimuli and fantasies. In ten subjects correlations were computed between erectile change and change in the other autonomic measures, during presentation of both erotic and neutral stimuli or fantasies. All but two of the subjects produced at least one obvious erection during the testing. Six (60 per cent) showed significant positive correlations between changes in erection and changes in at least one of the autonomic measures. One (10 per cent) showed significantly negative correlations and three showed no significant correlations, although in one of these a negative correlation approached significance. Thus, although in most cases erection was associated with increased autonomic arousal as reflected in these variables this was not always so, as in some a decrease in arousal occurred.

Further evidence has resulted from psychophysiological monitoring of behaviour therapy for sexual disorders such as homosexuality (Bancroft, 1970). *Figure 2* shows erectile and skin conductance traces in one subject imagining heterosexual fantasies whilst in a state of induced relaxation. On one occasion erection developed with no evidence of arousal as reflected by skin conductance changes; on the other occasion there was a clear-cut arousal response. In several patients erections to heretosexual fantasies occurred more readily when in a state of induced relaxation than when in a state of normal arousal, whereas in others the reverse was the case.

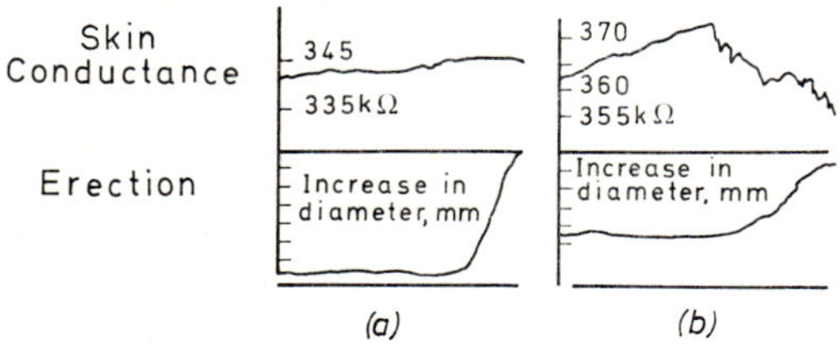

Figure 2. Erectile response during desensitization: (a) with no increase in arousal (skin conductance); (b) with increased arousal (skin conductance)

These preliminary findings demonstrate that erection, although frequently associated with autonomic arousal, is not invariably so. They also support the hypothesis that in a proportion of males erection will usually be associated with a reduction in arousal, or will depend on an optimum level of arousal which is relatively low. If this is so, then development of erection would be inhibited in situations where arousal is increased, e.g. excitement or anxiety.

Anxiety

The fact that anxiety may inhibit erection in some situations is beyond dispute but whether it invariably does so or how it does so is far from clear. The peripheral autonomic changes accompanying anxiety are more or less indistinguishable from those accompanying other higher arousal states such as excitement or anger (Lader, 1969). The fact that ejaculation occurs more rapidly in states of heightened excitement (Schapiro, 1943) does make it feasible that anxiety may act to speed ejaculation. On the other hand, we know that arousal usually if not invariably accompanies erection. It would be surprising, therefore, if the presence of anxiety inhibited erection simply because of the peripheral autonomic activity accompanying it, although this is commonly held to be so. If anxiety is associated with inhibition of erection it must be presumably due to: (*a*) a specific inhibition of the erectile mechanism; (*b*) a non-specific interference with central processes leading to erection; or (*c*) an idiosyncratic negative association between arousal and erection such as has been postulated above.

Gantt (1944), in his experiments with dogs, showed that in some animals the experimentally-induced anxiety-provoking conflict situation was associated consistently with spontaneous and rapid erection, whereas in other animals this did not happen; instead the anxiety inhibited sexual responses to normal sexual stimuli. There are also animals in whom naturally-produced sexual arousal (i.e. by presenting a bitch in heat) resulted in inhibition of the anxiety produced by the experimental conflict situation. Thus, he demonstrated three different types of relationship between anxiety and sexual response; first where anxiety is associated with a sexual response, second where anxiety inhibits sexual response, and third where sexual response inhibits anxiety. These different relationships are probably found in man and it may be that because of the individual's particular 'response-specificity' he will be predisposed to show one relationship rather than another.

The association of anxiety with sexual response can be accounted for in two ways. First, anxiety has a sexually stimulating effect by simply producing a state of heightened arousal. This would explain the erections to non-erotic frightening situations reported by Ramsey (1943) in pre-adolescent boys. Secondly, sexual response or erection itself might provoke anxiety due to guilt or fear of the consequences.

The author has been using a form of electric aversion therapy in the treatment of sexual deviations (Bancroft, 1970). This method depends on associating a painful shock with the first sign of an erection in response to deviant stimuli. In this situation one would naturally expect the development of erection to provoke anxiety and frequently this was the case. The surprising thing was that in several cases erection continued to develop in spite of this. One such patient reported having experienced erection since early adolescence in various frightening or exciting but non-sexual situations (as described by Ramsey, 1943) and he experienced a similar effect during treatment as though the erections developed 'automatically' in response to the anxiety. Such evidence is hardly unequivocal but it does support the possibility that in certain individuals and in certain situations anxiety can facilitate erection.

A frequent observation in plethysmographic recordings of erections is a 'rebound' erection occurring as soon as any effort to produce the erection ceases. This is most striking when the threat of shock is involved as in aversion but it also occurs in non-aversive situations. The impression is that the excitatory effect of the erotic stimulus or fantasy is counteracted by an inhibitory process which may be sufficient to cancel it out, but that when the stimulation ceases there is a 'rebound' effect in the Sherringtonian sense with the excitatory effect briefly outlasting the inhibitory. This once again limited evidence does suggest that specific inhibitory forces may operate to counteract excitatory erectile ones, and if sufficient will prevent erection from developing. Such inhibition would be beyond the subject's awareness and would not depend on the presence of manifest anxiety.

To return to the two initial assumptions it can now be tentatively concluded that specific inhibition of erection at an unconscious level is clearly a possibility and may or may not co-exist with subjective anxiety. Anxiety *per se* is unlikely to inhibit erection because of its peripheral 'sympathetic' effects, but may do so by increasing arousal above the optimum level, which in some individuals may be relatively low. Anxiety by increasing arousal is likely directly to affect the speed of ejaculation.

DISORDERS OF POTENCY IN PSYCHOPHYSIOLOGICAL TERMS

Finally, on the basis of the preceding psychophysiological evidence some tentative hypotheses can be suggested to account for some of the variety of potency disorders.

Erectile Impotence

The following types of erectile difficulty may occur:

(1) Total erectile impotence, in which neither psychic nor reflexive erections have ever occurred since puberty or at the most only partial erections have ever occurred. Such cases are probably uncommon and little is known about them.

(2) 'Primary' acute onset erectile impotence, in which erections may have occurred during erotic fantasies, masturbation, or on waking but which failed to occur at first and subsequent attempts at intercourse.

(3) 'Secondary' acute onset erectile impotence, in which following a period of normal potency impotence occurs in relation to some traumatic event.

(4) Gradual onset erectile impotence in which after a period of relatively normal potency there is a falling off in interest and increasingly frequent erectile failure.

The findings of Cooper (1968) suggest that cases of both 'primary' and 'secondary' acute onset type involve anxiety in the sexual situation although they are not generally more anxious or neurotic than other groups. Anxiety may produce impotence by increasing arousal above the optimum level in people in whom this level is low or who show a negative correlation between arousal and erection. Secondly, the anxiety may co-exist with specific inhibition of erection, both stemming from an appraisal of threat in the sexual situation. In addition, both mechanisms may be involved.

If the first mechanism predominated then the potency should be improved by measures which simply lower the anxious over-arousal (e.g. drugs or alcohol). With the second mechanism predominating treatment would need to remove the threat from the sexual situation, and here psychotherapeutic or behavioural techniques would be indicated. In gradual onset impotence anxiety is less obviously involved and when present is more frequently a reaction to the impotence itself (Cooper, 1968). The natural history of this group is different to the acute onset groups. To start with, the age group involved is usually older (Cooper, 1968) and the previous histories of such cases show that interest in sexual intercourse has been waning for some time, the impotence being the culmination. It was noticeable in Cooper's findings that most of these patients sought treatment at the wife's instigation.

Here the basic fault appears to be fall-off in sexual arousability in the first instance. In such a situation psychic erections would not develop and the male would be less likely to seek physical contact in which reflexive erections might occur. This in itself would not explain why eventually even reflexive erections become impossible, but it is feasible that the hostility and anxiety that the lack of interest would provoke in the marital relationship would be associated with inhibition of the reflexive erections as well.

It is in such cases that the possibility of endocrine deficiency should be considered. Availability of new and better methods of estimating androgens now makes renewed investigation of these cases worthwhile and it is likely that a proportion of them would benefit from testosterone.

Premature Ejaculation

Schapiro (1943) divided a large series of cases of premature ejaculation into two groups: (1) those in whom sexual arousal and excitement was high and in whom the rapid ejaculation appeared to be a symptom of a general sexual hyperexcitability; and (2) those in whom there was a general sexual hypoexcitability and frequently impaired erection, as well. Johnson (1968) has suggested that the morbidity lies in a failure to learn to delay ejaculation.

Anxiety would be expected to speed ejaculation by its generally arousing effect although the relationship between level of arousal and ejaculation is likely to vary from individual to individual. Thus, as in Schapiro's first type, where this mechanism is probably the predominant one, arousal-reducing drugs should delay orgasm. To some extent Schapiro's findings support this suggestion. In other cases where anxiety does not appear to play such a primary role, Johnson's mechanism of failure to learn delay may be operating. It is at such cases that Semans' technique (Semans, 1956) is clearly aimed. In this the patient repeatedly stimulates himself to the point just short of orgasm, allowing excitation to subside before resuming the stimulation. Eventually his partner stimulates him in the same way. When effective this technique results in gradually increasing control over the ejaculation process. There are many cases, however, who respond to neither of these approaches and in whom the precise mechanism involved is not clear, although it is likely that some physiological vulnerability is involved.

Although premature ejaculation and erectile impotence are considered to be distinct entities (Johnson, 1968) they not infrequently co-exist. This could be due to vulnerabilities affecting both systems or it may result from one deficiency being secondary to the anxiety engendered by the other.

Delayed or Absent Ejaculation

Much of the writing on this condition has been confusing because it has not always been made clear whether both orgasm and ejaculation are involved. The presence or absence of orgasm determines two types of disorder:

(1) 'Dry-run' orgasm, in which a relatively normal orgasm occurs but without the sensation of emission and ejaculation. Most commonly this is a side effect of drugs, in particular hypotensive or phenothiazine drugs (Money and Yankowitz, 1967). It may be due to intravesical ejaculation which can follow prostatectomy. Cases in which it occurs for no such reason are certainly rare (Kinsey, Pomeroy and Martin, 1948).

(2) Delayed orgasm, in which both orgasm and ejaculation are delayed. This is much more common (Cooper, 1968) and can be of varying severity. In some cases it may result from insufficient excitation and arousal, as in some sexual deviants who require specific types of stimulation. In others it appears to be associated with anxiety. Why anxiety should cause precipitate orgasm in some and delayed orgasm in others is obscure.

Cooper (1968) considered that these cases were similar in many ways to 'gradual onset impotence' cases, both showing generally low sexual arousability throughout their lives. Certainly some cases may be explained by insufficient arousability, but in others the evidence suggests that a selective inhibition of orgasm is occurring leaving erection unaffected.

CONCLUSIONS

It will have been apparent that our knowledge in this area is still limited and there is relatively little recent work to review. With the recent introduction of new techniques and a less inhibited attitude to research into sexual behaviour, there is now considerable scope for solving many of the outstanding problems.

The available evidence does justify one important conclusion: that the complexity of the physiological mechanisms involved in establishing potency is sufficient to allow considerable variation from individual to individual. This variation is such that with a given psychodynamic problem and a given amount of anxiety, the effects on the individual's sexual potency will vary also. In one individual with major sexual conflicts and accompanying anxiety, potency may remain intact; in another with trivial problems impotence may result.

There is no longer justification for the assumption that if erection occurs at any time then the physiological mechanisms must be normal and the problem must be entirely psychological. There may well be optimum physiological as well as psychological conditions for sexual effectiveness, and these physiological conditions as well as the psychological, may vary considerably from one individual to another. This variation is entirely consistent with the concept of 'response specificity' which is gaining increasing recognition in the general field of autonomic responses. Not only is this of theoretical importance, it has implications in the sphere of treatment as well.

REFERENCES

Bacq, Z. M. (1931). 'Impotence of the Male Rodent after Sympathetic Denervation of the Genital Organs.' *Am. J. Physiol.*, **96,** 321.

Bancroft, J. H. J. (1970). 'A Comparative Study of Aversion Therapy and Desensitisation in the Treatment of Homosexuality.' Proceedings of Symposium *Behaviour Therapy in the 1970s,* Rochdale, October 1969. Bristol: John Wright. (In Press.)

— Jones, H. G. and Pullan B. R. (1966). 'A Simple Transducer for Measuring Penile Erection, with Comments on its use in the Treatment of Sexual Disorders.' *Behav. Res. Ther.*, **4,** 239.

— and Mathews, A. (1967). 'Penis Plethysmography; its Physiological Basis and Clinical Application.' (Proceedings of 7th European Conference on Psychosomatic Research, Rome). *Acta med. psychosomat.*, 475.

Beaumont, P. J. V., Bancroft, J. H. J., Russell, G. F. M. and Beardwood, C. J. (1969). 'Behavioural Changes Following Replacement Treatment with Testosterone—a Case Report.' Paper read at Royal Society of Medicine, June 10th, 1969.

Bors, E. and Comarr, E. (1960). 'Neurological Disturbances of Sexual Function with Special Reference to 529 Patients with Spinal Cord Injury.' *Urol. Surv.*, **10,** 191.

Cooper, A. J. (1968). 'A Factual Study of Male Potency Disorders.' *Br. J. Psychiat.*, **114,** 719.

Deysach, L. J. (1939). 'The Comparative Morphology of the Erectile Tissue of the Penis with Especial Emphasis on the Probable Mechanism of Erection.' *Am. J. Anat.*, **64,** 111.

François-Franck, M. (1895). 'L'Innervation Vaso-motrice du Penis.' *Arch. Phys. norm. path.*, **5,** 122.

Freund, K. (1963). 'A Laboratory Method for Diagnosing Predominance of Homo- or Hetero-erotic Interest in the Male.' *Behav. Res. Ther.*, **4,** 301.

Freyhan, F. A. (1961). 'Loss of Ejaculation During Melleril Treatment.' *Am. J. Psychiat.*, **118,** 171.

Friedman, D. (1968). 'The Treatment of Impotence by Brietal Relaxation Therapy.' *Behav. Res. Ther.*, **6,** 257.

Gantt, H. (1944). *The Experimental Basis of Neurotic Behaviour.* New York: Hoeber.

Gebhard, P. H., Gagnon, J. H., Pomeroy, W. B. and Christenson, C. V. (1965). *Sex Offenders.* New York: Harper & Row.

Goy, R. N. (1968). 'Organising Effects of Androgen on the Behaviour of Rhesus Monkeys.' In *Endocrinology and Human Behaviour*, Ed. by R. P. Michael. Oxford University Press.

Hamburg, D. A. and Lunde, D. T. (1967). In *The Development of Sex Differences*, Ed. by E. E. Maccoby. London: Tavistock.

Harris, G. W. (1964). 'Sex Hormones, Brain Development and Brain Function.' *Endocrinology*, **75,** 627.

Hastings, D. W. (1963). *Impotence and Frigidity.* London: Churchill.

Heller, C. G. and Myers, G. B. (1944). 'Male Climacteric. *J. Am. med. Ass.*, **126,** 472

Henderson, V. E. and Roepke, M. H. (1933). 'On the Mechanism of Erection.' *Am. J. Physiol.*, **106,** 441.

Johnson, J. (1968). *Disorders of Sexual Potency in the Male.* Oxford: Pergamon.

Kinsey, A. C., Pomeroy, W. B. and Martin, C. E. (1948). *Sexual Behaviour in the Human Male.* Philadelphia and London: Saunders.

— — — and Gebhard, P. H. (1953). *Sexual Behaviour in the Human Female.* Philadelphia and London: Saunders.

Kuhn, R. A. (1950). 'Functional Capacity of the Isolated Human Spinal Cord.' *Brain*, **73,** 1.

Lader, M. H. (1969). 'Psychophysiology of Anxiety.' In *Studies of Anxiety*, Ed. by M. H. Lader. *British Journal of Psychiatry* Special Publication No. 3.

Laschet, V. and Laschet, L. (1967). 'Anti-androgen Therapy of Pathologically Increased or Abnormal Sexuality in Men.' *Klin. Wschr.*, **45,** 324.

Levy, L. (1968). 'Sympatho-adrenomedullary Activity, Diuresis and Emotional Reaction during Visual Sexual Stimulation in Females and Males.' Reports from Laboratory for Clinical Stress Research, Karolinska Sjukhuset, Stockholm, Number 3.

MacLean, P. D. and Ploog, D. W. (1962). 'Cerebral Representation of Penile Erection.' *J. Neurophysiol.*, **25,** 29.

Masters, W. H. and Johnson, V. E. (1966). *Human Sexual Response.* London: Churchill.

Money, J. (1961a). 'Components of Eroticism in Man. I. The Hormones in Relation to Sexual Morphology and Sexual Desire.' *J. nerv. ment. Dis.*, **132,** 239.

— (1961b). 'Components of Eroticism in Man. II. The Orgasm and Genital Somesthesia.' *J. nerv. ment. Dis.*, **132,** 289.

— and Yankowitz, R. (1967). 'The Sympathetic-inhibiting Effects of the Drug Ismelin on Human Male Eroticism, with a Note on Melleril.' *J. Sex. Research* **3,** 69.

Olds, J. and Milner, P. (1954). 'Positive Reinforcement Produced by Electrical Stimulation of Septal Area and other Regions of Rat Brain.' *J. comp. Physiol. Psychol.*, **47,** 419.

Pritchard, B. N. C., Johnston, A. N., Hill, I. D. and Rosenheim, M. L. (1968). 'Bethanidine, Guanethidine and Methyldopa in Treatment of Hypertension—a Within-patient Comparison.' *Br. med. J.*, **1,** 135.

Ramsey, G. V. (1943). 'The Sexual Development of Boys.' *Am. J. Psychol.*, **56,** 217.

Root, W. S. and Bard, P. (1947). 'The Mediation of Feline Erection through Sympathetic Pathways with Some Remarks on Sexual Behaviour after Deafferentation of the Genitalia.' *Am. J. Physiol.*, **151,** 80.

Rose, S. S. (1953). 'An Investigation into Sterility after Lumbar Ganglionectomy.' *Br. med. J.*, **1,** 247.

Schapiro, B. (1943). 'Premature Ejaculation. A Review of 1130 Cases.' *J. Urol.*, **50,** 374.

Semans, J. H. (1956). 'Premature Ejaculation: a New Approach.' *J. Urol.*, **40,** 836.

— and Langworthy, O. R. (1938). 'Observations on the Neurophysiology of the Sexual Function in the Male Cat.' *J. Urol.*, **40,** 836.

Singh, H. (1961). 'A Case of Inhibition of Ejaculation as a Side Effect of Melleril.' *Am. J. Psychiat.*, **117,** 1041.

Talbot, H. S. (1955). 'The Sexual Function in Paraplegia.' *J. Urol.*, **73,** 91.

Wenger, M. A., Averill, J. A. and Smith, D. D. B. (1968). 'Autonomic Activity during Sexual Arousal.' *Psychophysiology*, **4,** 468.

Whitelaw, G. P. and Smithwick, R. H. (1951). 'Some Secondary Effects of Sympathectomy—with Particular Reference to Disturbance of Sexual Function.' *New Engl. J. Med.*, **245,** 121.

Wolpe, J. and Lazarus, A. A. (1966). *Behaviour Therapy Techniques.* Oxford: Pergamon.

CHAPTER 16

BEHAVIOUR THERAPY AND PSYCHOSOMATIC ILLNESS

EDWARD CHESSER and VICTOR MEYER

INTRODUCTION

Much has been written concerning the historical, philosophical and semantic status of psychosomatic medicine (Lewis, 1954). In common usage, 'psychosomatic' has two meanings (W.H.O., 1964). The first is a wider one referring to a basic approach in which the patient is considered as a unique person in whom psychological and social factors will influence any illness or disorder he may develop or suffer from. The second meaning is more specific and refers to demonstrable and sustained or intense disorders of the structure or function of part of the body in which psychological factors may play a major role in causation, aggravation or maintenance. Peptic ulcer and bronchial asthma are two commonly accepted examples of psychosomatic disorders. In considering whether or not a disorder is 'psychosomatic', there are two aspects to be taken into account. First the evidence for psychogenic aetiological factors; and secondly the evidence of significant structural or functional disorder of part of the body. Clearly there may be great difficulty in assessing both of these aspects. Classification is for convenience, and is therefore inconsistent, reflecting both the purposes for which it is intended and the personal inclination of the classifier. However, there is general agreement that somatic symptoms, sometimes accompanied by evidence of functional or structural pathology, may be found in association with a variety of psycho-social stresses and psychiatric disorders. Many clinicians adopt a classification of these conditions on the basis of the known or presumed pathways by which the interaction between the psychological and somatic processes are mediated. One category would include somatic illnesses facilitated by conscious behaviour patterns, for example cirrhosis in the alcoholic, septicaemia in a mainline heroin addict, deliberate self-poisoning or injury. Accident proneness, obesity and anorexia nervosa might also sometimes come within this category. A second broad category is formed by conditions in which a clearly defined psychiatric disorder, for example depressive or anxiety states, are accompanied by somatic symptoms such as constipation or tachycardia. A third category (less easily delineated) is conversion hysteria, in which symptoms of somatic illness such as paralysis or anaesthesia appear as part of an attempt, never fully conscious, by the patient to obtain relief from intolerable stress. The symptoms adopted may have some symbolic relationship to the stress or conflict and may also be influenced by the patient's own concept of illness which may be based in part on his previous experience of illness and imitation. The fourth category comprise psychophysiological reactions in which somatic reactions such as bronchospasm or gastric hypersecretion are a somatic component of an affective response of fear or anger. Prolonged or intense psychophysiological reactions may lead to structural damage as may be found in bronchial asthma and duodenal ulcer. The term psychosomatic illness is often restricted to this last category.

Although this clinical classification is of some value, it is at times somewhat arbitrary. In considering the application of behaviour therapy in psychosomatic disorders, it would seem useful to discuss the ways in which learning principles and other experimental psychological findings may lead to an understanding of their acquisition, maintenance and methods of modification. In a short review we can only give some illustrations, and we have chosen conditions which lend themselves to a behavioural analysis or have already been shown to be susceptible to behaviour therapy techniques, rather than restricting discussion to the narrowly defined psychosomatic disease group.

It is a truism to state that behaviour, and therefore psychosomatic disorders and indeed all illnesses, are multi-factorially determined and involve the interaction between genetic and constitutional factors with the total environment of the subject, physical, psychological and social. A behavioural analysis alone would therefore never completely account for the genesis of psychosomatic disorders. It is important to bear this in mind in the subsequent discussion which will obviously be focused on those aspects of psychosomatic conditions in which learning and other psychophysiological processes seem relevant. There is no need to cite the large literature dealing with the genetic, epidemiological and laboratory human and animal studies which demonstrate the importance of factors other than learning. As the pathogenesis of bronchial asthma and peptic ulcer will be discussed further, however, it would be appropriate at least to emphasize initially the importance of genetic factors, as shown for instance by the field study of asthma by Leigh and Marley (1967) and the relation between genetically determined blood group and the incidence of peptic ulcer. A final preliminary point worth making in discussing the pathogenesis of psychosomatic conditions is that earlier views that specific psychosomatic disorders are related to a characteristic personality profile confronted by a particular type of stress have not received consistent experimental support and are no longer widely held. On the other hand, in a more qualified form they cannot be dismissed entirely.

THE BEHAVIOURAL APPROACH

The behaviour therapist, in his initial assessment of a psychosomatic disorder, might construct a formulation along the following lines. An unconditioned aversive stimulus evokes an unconditioned response which may include autonomic, skeletal, endocrine and overt behavioural components. Adopting the commonly accepted two-factor learning theory, the following situations could result from either intense single trial learning or the additive effects of multiple trial learning. By classical conditioning, contiguous neutral stimuli might become conditioned aversive stimuli evoking a conditioned emotional response (C.E.R.) in which a particular neuro-endocrine component such as raised blood pressure or cortisol secretion is prominent. This initial selectivity in the components of the C.E.R. could be determined by genetic factors or previous somatic illness or learning experiences. However, the subsequent development of a particular neuro-endocrine component of the response will be influenced by instrumental conditioning according to the subsequent reinforcements experienced. Relevant here are the reduction in anxiety which may follow the performance of the C.E.R., and the reinforcement which may occur if performance of the C.E.R. is followed by food, water, sex or social reinforcement. Obviously such instrumental conditioning could lead to the establishment of a neuro-endocrine response which was not necessarily an original component of a C.E.R.

As already stated, the constituents of the initial C.E.R. may be determined by genetic or environmental factors. The work of Lacey *et al.* (1963) suggests that there are marked individual differences in patterns of autonomic reactivity to stress as well as differences within each individual according to the type of stress experienced and that some patterns of response may be fixed by the age of six. There is some evidence that there is a relationship between the patient's pattern of autonomic reactivity and his psychosomatic symptoms (Malmo and Shagass, 1949; Malmo, Shagass and Davis,

1950; Sainsbury and Gibson, 1954; Hahn and Clark, 1967). Social factors may be of supreme importance in the subsequent instrumental learning of any somatic response, whether or not autonomic. The types of illness, child-rearing practices and cultural attitudes prevalent within the community may influence the initial probability of emission of a somatic response and its subsequent shaping and reinforcement.

By adopting two-factor learning theory and taking into account the accumulating evidence that autonomic as well as skeletal responses can be acquired by instrumental conditioning (e.g. Miller, 1969), the experimental psychologist's analysis of psychosomatic 'symptoms' would tend to fall into two broad categories. The first would be responses evoked by anxiety or accompanied by anxiety reduction, or both: the second operant responses reinforced by primary or secondary rewards other than anxiety reduction. There is only a very rough correspondence between these two categories and the clinical classification of psychophysiological reactions and somatic conversion reactions. The experimental psychologist's formulation may lead to a rational selection of behaviour therapy techniques and be capable of experimental refutation. However, it is only fair to add a word of caution. Hereditary differences, classical and instrumental learning, stimulus generalization, higher order conditioning, and the vicissitudes of the subject's lifetime environmental experiences and reinforcement history are all possible relevant variables. This gives it wide explanatory power which is not necessarily indicative either of its validity or pragmatic value in choice of therapy.

It must be emphasized that we are not adopting a primitive stimulus–response paradigm. Organismic variables and mediational processes must be involved. 'Internal' processes, whether peripheral (involving interoceptive or proprioceptive cues and visceral or skeletal responses undetectable by ordinary external observation) or central processes of thought and fantasy may be an essential factor in the initiation or maintenance of somatic responses (Hefferline, 1962). The perception of many of the somatic components of a conditioned emotional response, for example intestinal colic or tachycardia, may themselves be unconditioned aversive stimuli or become conditioned aversive stimuli. Similarly, thought and fantasies may become conditioned aversive stimuli. Schachter (1964) has demonstrated the importance of environmental factors in the subject's cognitive appraisal and labelling of his perceived bodily state. Taylor (1966) has offered a speculative but plausible account of the interaction between the patient's cognitive experiences and somatic responses in the transition of a hypochondriacal fear into a conviction and finally the manifest somatic dysfunction.

It is obvious that the behavioural paradigm outlined above is both deficient as an account of psychosomatic conditions with sustained structural damage and not fully satisfactory as an account of psychophysiological reactions. To take the second point first, the main difficulty in accounting, for example, for recurrent migraine or 'nervous diarrhoea' is the same as that posed by a persistent phobic reaction. If they are conditioned emotional responses, why are they not extinguished? Experimental findings illustrate that aversive classical and instrumental conditioning can lead to the acquisition of responses which are very resistant to extinction, and may actually increase without further exposure to the unconditioned stimulus (U.C.S.). Theoretical formulations of this phenomenon have been put forward by writers such as Solomon and Wynne (1954) and Eysenck (1968).

The second issue, the deficiency of the model as an explanation of psychosomatic disorders, is that it accounts for psychophysiological *reactions* rather than *disorders*. There is convincing evidence that psychogenic stimuli may evoke a rise in blood pressure or gastric secretion and hyperaemia. But whether or not as a result of the intensity, duration and frequency of such stimulation, this may in turn lead to sustained hypertension or peptic ulceration is a more complex issue. Until recently, the psychosomatic hypothesis rested on the theoretical assumption that persistent tissue changes could occur as a result of intense or prolonged neuro-endocrine response to stress. However, we now have experimental support for this. Peptic ulceration has been induced in monkeys (Brady *et al.*, 1958) and rats (Sawrey, Conger and Turrell, 1956), sustained hypertension in dogs (Napalkov, 1963), cats (Schunk, 1954), and rats and mice (Henry, Meehan and Stephens, 1967). Although even enthusiastic exponents of psychosomatic disease are aware that 'all that wheezes is not asthma' (Redlich and Freedman, 1966), 'asthma-like behaviour' has been induced experimentally in dogs (Gantt, 1944), monkeys (Massermann and Pechtel, 1953) and humans (Dekker, Pelser and Groen, 1957). A final point worth reiterating in any discussion of 'functional' as opposed to 'structural' changes and the ability of psychogenic stimuli to induce them, is that it is a continuum rather than a disjunctive categorization. Stanley Cobb has emphasized this very forcibly on theoretical grounds. That it may also be misleading in terms of prognosis is shown by the occasional cerebral infarction and death due to migraine.

We will now attempt to illustrate the application of a learning approach to the understanding and treatment of some specific psychosomatic conditions.

BRONCHIAL ASTHMA

It is generally accepted that genetic, allergic, infective, olfactory and emotional factors are relevant variables in bronchial asthma and these may interact in such a fashion that they may be positively or negatively correlated in an individual patient (Rees, 1956; Block, 1968). There is no compelling evidence that asthma occurs only in a particular personality type or in response to a particular type of stress or conflict.

Franks and Leigh (1959) formulated a conditioning model which could account for some attacks of asthma. Turnbull (1962) has put forward a detailed and sophisticated theoretical model to account for the pathogenetic factors in asthma which are learnt. He points out that asthma-like responses may first occur as unconditioned responses to allergens and then become conditioned responses to neutral stimuli by the ordinary process of classical conditioning. Suggestive evidence of such conditioning has been provided in clinical histories and laboratory studies. Dekker and Groen (1956) reproduced asthmatic attacks in a proportion of asthmatic patients by exposure to symbolic cues such as photographs or models of scenes or objects (whether emotionally significant or allergic) which had seemed to precipitate previous attacks. This could be an example of stimulus generalization. Dekker, Pelser and Groen (1957) succeeded in evoking asthmatic attacks in two patients by the inhalation of neutral solvent or oxygen, and by the introduction of the mouthpiece alone, after these had been paired with inhalation of allergen (U.C.S.). Similar experimental studies in guinea-pigs have been reported by Ottenberg *et al.* (1958). Respiratory responses have also been elicited in animals with aversive rather than allergic stimuli as the U.C.S. Liddell (1951) states that respiratory responses are commonly found in 'experimental neurosis'. Gantt (1944) induced a respiratory disturbance in a dog, and Massermann and Pechtel (1953) conditioned similar responses in monkeys.

It seems that asthma-like behaviour or respiratory changes can be induced by emotionally disturbing material, allergens or aversive stimuli and can then be conditioned to previously neutral stimuli. However, it must be pointed out that when allergic U.C.S. are employed, only a proportion of subjects can be conditioned and extinction is usually rapid (with the notable exception of the two patients of Dekker, Pelser and Groen). When noxious stimuli have been employed, a large proportion of animals develop respiratory responses and their resistance to extinction is greater, but their similarity to clinical asthma is less obvious. Turnbull therefore next considers the possible ways in which asthma-like behaviour conditioned by allergic stimuli may become more resistant to extinction, and how respiratory responses to painful stimuli may come to resemble asthma more closely. Two possible learning processes immediately suggest themselves. It is well known that avoidance responses are very resistant to extinction. If the performance of an asthma-like response is followed by reduction or avoidance of pain or anxiety, it may become very resistant to extinction and also a characteristic response of the individual to other aversive stimuli. Turnbull suggests that the fact that asthma-like responses are usually only gradually learnt in experimental neurosis experiments supports the hypothesis that it is an avoidance response rather than an innate component of an emotional response.

The second learning process suggested by Turnbull to account for the development of asthmatic responses from respiratory responses is by the shaping that can occur in operant conditioning. If crying or other respiratory responses emitted by the child are not effectively rewarded, for example by comfort and attention from mother, he is likely to perform slightly different responses (Hullian response hierarchy) to obtain reinforcement and asthmatic breathing may become a more effective method of obtaining reward. If this occurs, asthmatic breathing may become a frequent operant response emitted both to obtain positive reward or anxiety reduction. Operant conditioning could therefore account for the development of asthma behaviour in subjects in whom allergic stimuli do not elicit asthma.

Two other types of experimental induction of asthma may be relevant to pathogenesis and treatment. The studies of Treuting and Ripley (1948) demonstrated the additive effect of exposure to allergen and discussion of the patient's life problems in the induction of wheezing, while the work of Luparello *et al.* (1968) illustrates the possible role of suggestion; 12 out of 40 asthmatics developed clinical attacks when inhaling a neutral solvent, having been told it was an irritant or an allergen. (Suggestion may also have played a significant role in one of the patients described above in the experiment of Dekker, Pelser and Groen.)

In summarizing the possible learning processes involved in asthma, the behaviour therapist would consider the extent to which it might be an innate emotional or allergic response which is also being evoked by conditioned stimuli (C.S.) as a result of classical conditioning, the extent to which it is an operant response reinforced by anxiety reduction or positive reward, and the extent to which any mild subjective experience of respiratory difficulty is acting as an anxiety stimulus and precipitating a full-blown asthmatic attack.

Patients whose asthmatic attacks appear to be conditioned anxiety, allergic or avoidance responses are likely to be suitable for a counter-conditioning technique, in which the patient is desensitized to the C.S. which evoke attacks. The most commonly used method is systematic desensitization in imagination (Wolpe, 1958) and a controlled trial of this technique has been carried out by Moore (1965). In a balanced incomplete block design, 12 consecutive asthmatic patients referred to a chest clinic each received two of three different methods of treatment, consisting of muscular relaxation, relaxation with suggestion, and systematic desensitization in imagination. Each treatment was given for half an hour each week for two months. Progress was rated by subjective report and maximum peak flow before and after isoprenaline inhalation. Patients were desensitized to three graduated hierarchies of possible asthma-evoking stimuli, one based on the actual asthmatic attack, the second on any relevant infective and allergic situations, and the third on potential key psychological stresses. All treatments resulted in subjective improvement initially, but there was a tendency for this to be better maintained in the desensitization group. Only in systematic desensitization was there significant objective improvement. For fuller details Moore's paper should be studied. However, it seems fair to conclude that a worthwhile clinical improvement can be achieved in a sample of asthmatic patients who have not been specifically selected as suitable for this technique.

Another example of counter-conditioning is provided in a single case study by Walton (1960) in which behavioural analysis suggested that asthmatic attacks tended to occur in interpersonal situations, involving meeting strangers, having to give a ruling or criticism, or feeling resentment and not expressing it. In these situations he had frequent recourse to his 'pump'. Desensitization was carried out using assertive responses to inhibit anxiety (Wolpe, 1958). In addition, a practical re-training procedure, described by Walton as a generalization technique, was adopted to reduce the patient's dependency on his 'pump'. He first had to leave the pump at home when he was going to be exposed to the least disturbing situations, and then in progressively more stressful situations. After eight treatment sessions and during an eight-month follow-up, no asthmatic attacks occurred and his occupational and social adjustment improved.

In patients whose asthmatic attacks do not appear to be mediated or are no longer mediated by anxiety or allergic stimuli, but are maintained by positive reinforcement such as increased attention, or treats, an operant technique might be applicable. It may be found that parents or teachers are giving inappropriate reinforcement to the asthmatic child by neglecting or rejecting him when social approval and attention should be forthcoming and only giving them when the child wheezes. In such a case the reinforcement contingencies should be altered so that non-asthmatic behaviour is suitably rewarded more than asthmatic behaviour. Obviously, it would not be safe to withhold all attention or actually punish asthmatic behaviour which is potentially lethal. The degree to which positive reinforcement may be withheld will be a matter of fine judgment in which the potential danger of the treatment must be weighed against the predicted course of the disorder without such treatment. Successful treatment by operant techniques of disorders such as temper tantrums, crying spells and self-mutilating acts have been described (Williams, 1959; Hart *et al.*, 1964), and afford a possible example of how it may be incorporated in the behaviour modification of asthma.

For the sake of completeness it should be remembered that hypnosis alone has been found to have a therapeutic effect in asthma (Research Committee of the British Tuberculosis Association, 1968). Hypnosis and suggestion can be conceptualized within a learning framework and have been considered as behaviour therapy techniques by some theorists (Eysenck, 1964; Krasner and Ullmann, 1965). However, Moore's study described above suggests that systematic desensitization is more effective than hypnosis.

NERVOUS DIARRHOEA AND VOMITING

In any anxiety or phobic anxiety reaction, specific autonomic responses may be the major or the only component. Patients who display symptoms such as diarrhoea or vomiting in response to anxiety or other conditioned stimuli could therefore be treated by systematic desensitization to both the situations in which the response occurs and the actual subjective experience of the symptom which may act as an anxiety cue maintaining the response. Cohen and Reed (1968) have described the treatment of six patients, two with nausea and vomiting when eating in public places, two with frequency of defaecation and one with frequency of micturition when travelling, and one with excessive sweating in company. All had had symptoms for between three and twelve years and three had already received prolonged psychiatric treatment without benefit. All patients received systematic desensitization in imagination under methohexitone or muscle relaxation, and one patient had practical re-training in addition. Progress was rated in two ways: first the frequency of the symptom per day rated by the patient; and secondly a rating of degree of change in freedom of activity. All patients improved (number of treatment sessions ranged from 6 to 19). Two patients became free of symptoms after desensitization to the situation hierarchy alone. One patient who had improved considerably broke off treatment after 12 sessions in order to have a lumbar sympathectomy which cured the residual sweating of her feet. At six-month follow-up of the patients there had been 'continued improvement' and no evidence of symptom substitution.

Although this is a very small series of patients the clinical improvement is impressive. That some patients responded to desensitization to the anxiety-evoking situations alone suggests that their disorder is similar to phobic anxiety reactions with less prominent or isolated autonomic components. However, it is of possibly greater significance that in three patients desensitization to the situation produced little or no improvement, but persistent and marked improvement after desensitization to the symptom. One could speculate that this difference in therapeutic response implies that the autonomic response is less contingent upon the external phobic situation, and had developed some autonomy. If this were the case, the differential therapeutic response may be discriminating between phobic anxiety reactions and psychosomatic reactions.

INVOLUNTARY MOVEMENTS

Learning theory formulations and behaviour therapy techniques have been employed in various motor disorders such as tics, writer's cramp and torticollis. Yates (1958) has suggested that some tics may be drive-reducing conditioned avoidance responses originally evoked in a traumatic situation and reinforced because they were followed by or led to reduction of anxiety. Conditioned avoidance responses are very resistant to extinction and by means of stimulus generalization the tic may be evoked in other anxiety situations. Yates considered that a tic may be a learned habit which had achieved maximum habit strength and that it should be extinguished by massed non-reinforced practice, in other words its repeated performance without subsequent anxiety reduction. Treatment sessions consist of the patient having to perform his tic as accurately and rapidly as possible. Yates' experimental study of the patient's disorder led him to hypothesize that prolonged periods of practice and prolonged rest period would be the most effective method of producing extinction.

Jones (1960) described the further treatment of Yates' patient for 34 weeks, during which she had 33 sessions at hospital. At 17-month follow-up her tics were less frequent and caused less social embarrassment and restriction of activities. Other case reports employing similar and adjunctive procedures have been published by Lazarus (1961), Rafi (1962) and Walton (1961, 1964), while Barrett (1962) employed an operant conditioning paradigm. Clark (1966) has described the successful treatment of two out of three patients with Gilles de la Tourette syndrome by means of negative practice. The idea that repetitive habits could be eliminated by making the patient perform them has been in existence for many years (Dunlap, 1932; Lehner, 1954).

There is more published evidence available on the treatment of writer's cramp by behavioural methods. Crisp and Moldofsky (1965) have reviewed the syndrome of writer's cramp, including historical, physiological and psychological aspects, and describe a broad spectrum treatment programme applied to seven patients, which included muscular relaxation and practical re-training. Liversedge and Sylvester (1955) treated 39 out of 56 patients with a behavioural technique. They considered that the disorder had two components, tremor and spasm. To deal with the tremor, the patient was required to insert a stylus into a series of progressively smaller holes and received an electric shock if the stylus touched the edge of the hole. In the next stage the patient had to trace straight, curved and zigzag lines on a metal plate, and any deviation resulted in a shock. To treat the component of muscle spasm, the patients had to write with a special pen, designed so that excessive thumb pressure led to electric shock. Initial improvement after 3–6 weeks' treatment was obtained in 29 out of 39 patients. At follow-up (5–54 months after treatment), 24 patients had maintained significant improvement (Sylvester and Liversedge, 1960). Beech (1960) was unable to match these results in four patients who probably had more personality disturbance than those treated by Liversedge and Sylvester. He points out that in patients in whom the cramp is still evoked by anxiety, presentation of aversive stimuli may serve only to strengthen the response.

Brierley (1967) has reported the treatment of two patients with spasmodic torticollis by means of traumatic avoidance learning. In these two patients the symptom was thought to be a conditioned avoidance response which was now a maladaptive habit rather than a manifestation of an extrapyramidal lesion. The patients each had 12 treatment sessions in which they wore a headgear arranged so that a mild electric shock was delivered to the wrist if improved posture of the head was not maintained. One patient was symptom-free after the fourth session and was well at follow-up one year after the start of treatment. The second patient responded more slowly but was symptom-free after the tenth session. She started work six months after the end of treatment but had two short relapses in the next eight months when under severe external stress. As both patients had been ill for two years before behaviour treatment, one can conclude that traumatic avoidance learning can be a useful therapeutic technique in some types of torticollis.

OTHER DISORDERS

There is a large literature on the experimental and therapeutic aspects of disorders such as nocturnal enuresis and stammering, in which behaviour therapy has been of value. For further information, the reader is referred to the monographs of Lovibond (1964) and Beech and Fransella (1968), and the papers by Turner and Young (1966), Young and Turner (1965) and Werry and Cohrssen (1965). Some reference to behavioural methods employed in sexual and feeding disorders will be found in the relevant chapters in this volume.

DISCUSSION

In a short space we have been able only to outline how learning principles and behaviour therapy techniques may provide an approach to the understanding and treatment of psychosomatic disorders. Although a multi-factorial aetiology is accepted, learning processes are always involved in their development and maintenance. Because of this, learning processes may also be capable of modifying or eliminating them. Treatment of psychosomatic conditions should be designed on the basis of a careful analysis of the behaviour disorder. For example, it would be important to know the extent to which they are being maintained by anxiety or positive reward. A broad approach to the management of psychosomatic patients is necessary because physical, psychological and social variables may be involved. The disorders are usually complex and a combination of physical and behavioural methods will usually be required. At the present time, there is evidence that behaviour therapy, including the non-specific processes associated with its administration (Meyer and Chesser, 1970) may be a useful form of treatment in asthma, nervous vomiting and diarrhoea, and some motor disorders. So far there has been very little experimental research designed to test theoretical formulations, the selection of patients and the type of treatment in psychosomatic disorders. Exciting therapeutic advances may lie ahead if it is found that conditioned autonomic responses can be extinguished by counter-conditioning methods or brought under operant control. If a subject can be taught to lower his blood pressure by operant conditioning or to reduce the number of situations which evoke a rise in blood pressure, it is quite possible that he may reduce his risk of developing hypertension or cardiovascular disease. The potential advantage of operant control is that it may influence responses of varied causation and not necessarily evoked by emotional stimuli. The successful operant control of temporal lobe epilepsy described by Efron (1957) could offer a paradigm for the treatment of 'psychosomatic' or 'physical' diseases.

REFERENCES

Barrett, B. H. (1962). 'Reduction in Rate of Multiple Tics by Free Operant Conditioning Methods.' *J. nerv. ment. Dis.*, **135,** 187.

Beech, H. R. (1960). 'The Symptomatic Treatment of Writer's Cramp.' In *Behaviour Therapy and the Neuroses,* Ed. by H. J. Eysenck. Oxford: Pergamon Press.

— and Fransella, F. (1968). *Research and Experiment in Stuttering.* Oxford: Pergamon Press.

Block, J. (1968). 'Further Consideration of Psychosomatic Predisposing Factors in Allergy.' *Psychosom. Med.*, **30,** 202.

Brady, J. V., Porter, R. W., Conrad, D. G. and Mason, J. W. (1958). 'Avoidance Behaviour and the Development of Gastroduodenal Ulcers.' *J. expl. Anal. Behav.*, **1,** 69.

Brierley, H. (1967). 'The Treatment of Hysterical Spasmodic Torticollis by Behaviour Therapy.' *Behav. Res. Ther.*, **5,** 139.

Clark, D. F. (1966). 'Behaviour Therapy of Gilles de la Tourette's Syndrome.' *Br. J. Psychiat.*, **112,** 771.

Cohen, S. I. and Reed, J. L. (1968). 'The Treatment of "Nervous Diarrhoea" and Other Conditioned Autonomic Disorders by Desensitization.' *Br. J. Psychiat.*, **114,** 1275.

Crisp, A. H. and Moldofsky, H. (1965). 'Psychosomatic Study of Writer's Cramp.' *Br. J. Psychiat.*, **111,** 841.

Dekker, E. and Groen, J. (1956). 'Reproducible Psychogenic Attacks of Asthma. A Laboratory Study.' *J. Psychosom. Res.*, **1,** 58.

— Pelser, H. E. and Groen, J. (1957). 'Conditioning as a Cause of Asthma.' *J. Psychosom. Res.*, **2,** 97.

Dunlap, K. (1932). *Habits, Their Making and Unmaking.* New York: Liveright.

Efron, R. (1957). 'The Conditioned Inhibition of Uncinate Fits.' *Brain,* **80,** 251.

Eysenck, H. J. (Ed.) (1964). *Experiments in Behaviour Therapy.* Oxford: Pergamon Press.

Eysenck, H. J. (1968). 'A Theory of the Incubation of Anxiety/Fear Responses.' *Behav. Res. Ther.*, **6,** 309.

Franks, C. M. and Leigh, D. (1959). 'Theoretical and Experimental Application of a Conditioning Model to Bronchial Asthma in Man.' *J. Psychosom. Res.*, **4,** 88.

Gantt, W. H. (1944). 'Experimental Basis for Neurotic Behaviour.' *Psychosom. Monogr.*, **3,** Nos. 3 and 4.

Hahn, H. W. and Clark, J. A. (1967). 'Psychophysiological Reactivity of Asthmatic Children.' *Psychosom. Med.*, **29,** 526.

Hart, B. M., Allen, K. E., Buell, J. S., Harris, F. R. and Wolf, M. M. (1964). 'Effects of Social Reinforcement on Operant Crying.' *J. expl. Child Psychol.*, **1,** 145.

Hefferline, R. F. (1962). 'Learning Theory and Clinical Psychology—an Eventual Symbiosis?' In *Experimental Foundations of Clinical Psychology*, Ed. by A. J. Bachrach. New York: Basic Books.

Henry, J. P., Meehan, J. P. and Stephens, P. M. (1967). 'The Use of Psychosocial Stimuli to Induce Prolonged Systolic Hypertension in Mice.' *Psychosom. Med.*, **29,** 408.

Jones, H. G. (1960). 'Continuation of Yates' Treatment of a Tiqueur.' In *Behaviour Therapy and the Neuroses*, Ed. by H. J. Eysenck. Oxford: Pergamon Press.

Krasner, L. and Ullmann, L. P. (Eds.) (1965). *Research in Behaviour Modification.* New York: Holt, Rinehart & Winston.

Lacey, J. I., Kagan, J., Lacey, B. L. and Moss, H. A. (1963). 'The Visceral Level. Situational Determinants and Behavioural Correlates of Autonomic Response Patterns.' In *Expressions of the Emotions in Man*, Ed. by P. H. Knapp. New York: International University Press.

Lazarus, A. A. (1961). 'Objective Psychotherapy in the Treatment of Dysphemia.' *J. Sth. Afri. Logopedic Soc.*, page 8.

Lehner, G. F. J. (1954). 'Negative Practice as a Psychotherapeutic Technique.' *J. gen. Psychol.*, **51,** 68.

Leigh, D. and Marley, E. (1967). *Bronchial Asthma. A Genetic, Population, and Psychiatric Study.* Oxford: Pergamon Press.

Lewis, A. J. (1954). 'Aspects of Psychosomatic Medicine.' *Rec. Progr. Medicina*, **16,** 434.

Liddell, H. (1951). 'Influence of Experimental Neuroses on Respiratory Function.' In *Somatic and Psychiatric Treatment of Asthma*, Ed. by H. A. Abrahamson. Baltimore: Williams & Wilkins.

Liversedge, L. A. and Sylvester, J. D. (1955). 'Conditioning Techniques in the Treatment of Writer's Cramp.' *Lancet*, **1,** 1147.

Lovibond, S. H. (1964). *Conditioning and Enuresis.* Oxford: Pergamon Press.

Luparello, T., Lyons, H. A., Bleecker, E. R. and McFadden, E. R. (1968). 'Influences of suggestion on Airway Reactivity in Asthmatic Subjects.' *Psychosom. Med.*, **30,** 819.

Malmo, R. B. and Shagass, C. (1949). 'Physiologic Study of Symptom Mechanisms in Psychiatric Patients Under Stress.' *Psychosom. Med.*, **11,** 25.

Malmo, R. B., Shagass, C. and Davis, J. F. (1950). 'Symptom Specificity and Bodily Reactions During Psychiatric Interview.' *Psychosom. Med.*, **12,** 362.

Massermann, J. H. and Pechtel, C. (1953). 'Neuroses in Monkeys. A Preliminary Report of Experimental Observations.' *Ann. N.Y. Acad. Sci.*, **56,** 253.

Meyer, V. and Chesser, E. S. (1970). *Behaviour Therapy in Clinical Psychiatry.* Harmondsworth: Penguin Education.

Miller, N. E. (1969). 'Learning of Visceral and Glandular Responses.' *Science*, **163,** 434.

Moore, N. (1965). 'Behaviour Therapy in Bronchial Asthma: A Controlled Study.' *J. psychosom. Res.*, **9,** 257.

Napalkov, A. V. (1963). 'Information Process of the Brain.' In *Progress in Brain Research*, Ed. by N. Wiener and J. P. Schade, Vol. 2. Nerve, Brain and Memory Models. Amsterdam: Elsevier.

Ottenberg, P., Stein, M., Lewis, J. and Hamilton, C. (1958). 'Learned Asthma in the Guinea Pig.' *Psychosom. Med.*, **20,** 395.

Rafi, A. A. (1962). 'Learning Theory and the Treatment of Tics.' *J. psychosom. Res.*, **6,** 71.

Redlich, F. C. and Freedman, D. X. (1966). *The Theory and Practice of Psychiatry.* New York: Basic Books.

Rees, L. (1965). 'The Role of the Autonomic Nervous System in Asthma and Allied Disorders.' *J. psychosom. Res.*, **9,** 149.

Research Committee of the British Tuberculosis Association (1968). 'Hypnosis for Asthma—a Controlled Trial.' *Br. med. J.*, **4,** 71.

Sainsbury, P., and Gibson, J. G. (1954). 'Symptoms of Anxiety and the Accompanying Physiological Changes in the Muscular System.' *J. Neurol. Neurosurg. Psychiat.*, **17,** 216.

Sawrey, W. L., Conger, J. J. and Turrell, E. S. (1956). 'Experimental Investigation of Role of Psychological Factors in Production of Gastric Ulcers in Rats.' *J. comp. Physiol. Psychol.*, **49,** 457.

Schachter, S. (1964). 'The Interaction of Cognitive and Physiological Determinants of Emotional State.' In *Advances in Experimental Social Psychology*, Vol. II, Ed. by L. Berkowitz. New York: Academic Press.

Schunk, J. (1954). 'Emotionale Faktoren in der Pathogenese der Essentiellen Hypertonie.' *Z. klin. Med.*, **152,** 251. (Quoted by Henry *et al.*, 1967.)

Solomon, R. L. and Wynne, L. C. (1954). 'Traumatic Avoidance Learning: the Principle of Anxiety Conservation and Partial Irreversibility.' *Psychol. Rev.*, **81,** 353.

Sylvester, J. D. and Liversedge, L. A. (1960). 'Conditioning and the Occupational Cramp.' In *Behaviour Therapy and the Neuroses*, Ed. by H. J. Eysenck. Oxford: Pergamon Press.

Taylor, F. Kraupl (1966). *Psychopathology: Its Causes and Symptoms.* London: Butterworths.

Treuting, T. F. and Ripley, H. S. (1948). 'Life Situations, Emotions and Bronchial Asthma.' *J. nerv. ment. Dis.*, **108,** 380.

Turnbull, J. W. (1962). 'Asthma Conceived as a Learned Response.' *J. psychosom. Res.*, **6,** 59.

Turner, R. K. and Young, G. C. (1966). 'C.N.S. Stimulant Drugs and Conditioning Treatment of Nocturnal Enuresis: A Long Term Follow-up Study.' *Behav. Res. Ther.*, **4,** 225.

Walton, D. (1960). 'The Application of Learning Theory to the Treatment of a Case of Bronchial Asthma.' In *Behaviour and the Neuroses*, Ed. by H. J. Eysenck. Oxford: Pergamon Press.

— (1961). 'Experimental Psychology and the Treatment of a Ticquer.' *J. child. Psychol.*, **2,** 148.

— (1964). 'Massed Practice and Simultaneous Reduction in Drive Level—Further Evidence of the Efficacy of this Approach to the Treatment of Tics.' In *Experiments in Behaviour Therapy*, Ed. by H. J. Eysenck. Oxford: Pergamon Press.

Werry, J. S. and Cohrssen, J. (1965). 'Enuresis—an Etiologic and Therapeutic Study.' *J. Pediat.*, **67,** 423.

Williams, C. D. (1959). 'The Elimination of Tantrum Behaviour by Extinction Procedures.' *J. abnorm. soc. Psychol.*, **59,** 269.

Wolpe, J. (1958). *Psychotherapy by Reciprocal Inhibition.* Stanford: University Press.

World Health Organization (1964). 'Psychosomatic Disorders.' *Wld Hlth Org. techn. Rep. Ser.*, 275.

Yates, A. J. (1958). 'The Application of Learning Theory to the Treatment of Tics.' *J. aborm. soc. Psychol.*, **56,** 175.

Young, G. C. and Turner, R. K. (1965). 'C.N.S. Stimulant Drugs and Conditioning Treatment of Nocturnal Enuresis.' *Behav. Res. Ther.*, **3,** 93.

CHAPTER 17

THE PSYCHOLOGICAL PROBLEMS OF RENAL DIALYSIS AND TRANSPLANTATION

W. A. CRAMOND

INTRODUCTION

Since 1960 the treatment of chronic renal failure has undergone dramatic and far-reaching change; two techniques, one medical and the other surgical, have made this possible. Although the feasibility of haemodialysis had been established by Kolff in 1946, it was not until the introduction of the arteriovenous shunt by Scribner *et al.* (1960a) that regular, repeated haemodialysis became possible. As a result, in many centres throughout the world people who would otherwise have died in uraemic coma have been enabled to prolong their lives.

Kidney transplantation had been attempted in animals in the early years of the century but, because of host rejection, failure was the rule until 1954 when it was shown that grafts between identical twins were possible; then in 1962 the discovery that the immuno-suppressive drug, azathioprine when given along with prednisolone, largely prevented host rejection, made this surgical technique available for many more patients in terminal renal failure. While many technical and clinical problems still remain unsolved, it is nevertheless true to state that the quality of living allowed many patients by these developments, has improved in recent years. In at least half the cases, life approximating to the pre-morbid state can be resumed; it is not uncommon now to find patients whose effective life span has been extended by three or four years because of these therapeutic advances.

As many workers have noted, excessive cost and scarcity of trained personnel remain the major deterrents to broadening the application of haemodialysis to an estimated 40,000 uraemic patients in the United States alone by 1973 (Bluemle, 1968). It has been estimated from a variety of world sources that one organ transplantation and renal unit per two million of population is advisable to meet an incidence of 30 per million of population per annum requiring such treatment (N.H. and M.R.C. of Australia, 1969). Cost reduction, through home dialysis, continued technical improvements and more adequate financing arrangements, consistent with current concepts of comprehensive health care, offer realistic hope that this valuable product of clinical research will be available to those in need. On the one hand it is important that the established units are provided with sufficient funds, facilities and staff to meet society's demands so that duplication of effort in many hospitals does not lead to a fall of standards due to rising costs. On the other hand the disruption of life to the patient and his family in moving house and home to be near a large experienced renal unit in a regional centre must be kept in mind and a balance struck between realistic economy and the psychosocial rights of the individual. Nor must it be forgotten that money and effort must be available for basic research into the preventive aspects of renal disease.

The psychological problems raised by chronic haemodialysis and by renal homotransplantation are both old and new. The old problems are those associated with any acute and/or chronic illness. For example, episodes of psychotic decompensation, whether due to raised levels of urea nitrogen in the blood or to acute panic or to both, are seen but are relatively uncommon. The style of psychotic breakdown is, as would be expected, determined by personality and constitutional factors. All patients, faced with the crisis of a potentially lethal and certainly permanent illness, show an initial reactive depression. Defences against anxiety, as bodily and psychic integrity is threatened, are mobilized. The patient has to make a fundamental re-assessment of his life situation and his family members are required to re-orientate themselves to a changed and suddenly insecure environment. The more brittle and vulnerable the patient's and the family's resources, the more likely it is that the protracted crisis of illness will test the ability to survive.

The new psychological problems are seen in relation to the actual technical advances themselves—the patient becoming dependent on an impersonal machine and its technicians. While early anxieties were concerned with such simple issues as the operation of the mechanical pump in the artificial kidney, later anxieties have developed from the practice of home haemodialysis with the spouse responsible for the technique. Certainly, in the early days of dialysis the patient often saw his role as that of an experimental animal. 'What I'm going through will, I hope, help others after me.' Among the new psychological problems the psychodynamics of living donor motivation must be mentioned, as must the effect of giving permission for the taking of a cadaveric kidney on the bereavement process of close relatives. The anxiety from all these sources, intra- and extra-psychic, old and new, have been intensified by the very real ethical and moral issues raised in particular by renal homotransplantation, by the need to refine the interpretation of the definition of death and by the problems of selection for the few places on overcrowded dialysis programmes. The fact that all this has taken place in the fierce glare of the public spotlight has had psychological implications for patient and staff alike.

The psychological problems have been old and new for the staffs of the rapidly developing and expanding renal units. Nurses, social workers, biochemical technicians, surgeons and physicians have been required to work closely together in a very interdependent team relationship and to pool their resources and skills. The old problems include the fact that chronic illness is never easy for the medical attendant to bear. There are the problems of dealing with the anxiety and anger of helplessness when the new techniques fail; the problems of an unrecognized 'transference' situation and the subtle interprofessional rivalries with which to contend. New problems include the uncertainty experienced as new techniques are mastered and refined, as new unexpected side effects appear, as new team relationships are hammered out and new methods of communication within the therapeutic group are explored—sometimes deliberately, more often intuitively.

Clearly, the manifest anxieties of the patient, his family and of the staff, individually and in groups have to be defended against. Denial, withdrawal, depression, acting out, regression, displacement of affect, rationalization, counterphobia, exaggerated attempts at obsessional control and less frequently projection, are all seen and are important to identify and understand. The issue of the patient selection for a place on the programme is at the back of everyone's mind. Is selection to be based on some value judgment according to medical criteria, or to moral standards based on value to the community, or is it to be a simple case of first come, first served? Again, the overall picture of decision making is affected by the different professional training, goals and attitudes of the physician, surgeon, nurse, social worker, psychiatrist and technician.

To this must be added the pressure of personal and team ambition to be in the lead in a new and significant international medical advance, the 'breakthrough phenomenon' with its attendant mass media publicity.

The Chinese word for crisis derives from two other words meaning danger and opportunity. The quality of the team in its own intragroup relationship is vital if a patient and family in crisis is to be helped to grow psychologically from the frightening experience. Only if the treatment team is stable and well integrated will there be an optimal psychological climate with emotional as well as physical care which will give opportunities for greater self-realization.

To date, much of the research work carried out in this field by psychiatrists has been descriptive and phenomenological. This is largely due to the need to give direct, practical help in a new clinical situation. The actual role of ancillary helpers has had to be defined, especially those of the psychiatrist and the social worker. It is not always easy to communicate across disciplinary boundaries; consequently many of the early papers in the literature describe the physical disposition of staff and the roles attempted but the picture is rapidly changing as new and more economical aids to therapy evolve. No sooner had dialysis units been planned for general hospitals than home dialysis became a reality with a host of new psychological clinical problems. Because of this, basic psychosomatic issues, for example the role of anxiety in graft rejection, have yet to be studied in depth by the few psychiatrists available for work in this field. For the purposes of this review, the psychological problems will be looked at from the points of view of the recipient to dialysis and to transplantation, the recipient's family, the living donor and his family, the family of the cadaver donor and the renal unit team.

THE PATIENT ON HAEMODIALYSIS

The problems facing the patient depend on the speed of onset of the condition causing the renal failure. If the condition has been slowly developing over months and years, the patient will have become more or less adjusted to the situation. Problems of easy fatiguability and of diet have been worked out. As a result, when the time comes to consider haemodialysis the patient is usually well briefed and in good control of the situation. When the onset of the illness is sudden the psychological sequence of events is rather different. Denial is the most commonly used ego defence. There are fantasies that the doctor has made a mistake in diagnosis; this is particularly prominent when there has been in fact some delay in discovering the kidney lesion. Anger against medical failure is experienced but seldom is expressed because of the dependence on the physician. Following the period of denial the patient will experience a period of grief reactive to the loss of health, status and security. In predisposed patients there may be a period of confusion with or without ill-systematized delusions, this break with reality ranging aetiologically from the purely toxic to the purely functional. During the period of depression the patient is assessed for inclusion into the haemodialysis programme. To keep him going he may have required a small number of peritoneal dialyses, which are frequently reported by the patient as being very painful. From observation it appears clear that the patient's high anxiety level and toxic disinhibition lowers the pain threshold.

On chronic haemodialysis, once the permanently indwelling Teflon cannulae are in position, the patient is generally treated once every 4–6 days according to need for continuous periods of from 7 to 14 hours, depending on the type of dialyser used. Removal of toxic substances is by diffusive transport across a semi-permeable cellulose membrane according to individual concentration gradients between blood and dialysing fluid. The patient during this time lies in bed, dozes or reads, listens to the radio or talks to other patients or to staff. Most of the early accounts of psychological factors on recurrent dialysis referred to the difficulties briefly and in a relatively superficial way. For example, Scribner *et al.* (1960b) commented that one of their patients lacked stamina, felt fine as long as he was sedentary, but was easily fatigued. Gutch, Stevens and Watkins (1964) mentioned that their patient on periodic peritoneal dialysis had good morale and was active and alert out of hospital. Barber *et al.* (1963) emphasized the optimism and co-operation of their patients and noted the difficulties in evaluating other psychological factors. Walker Brown *et al.* (1962) commented on the variety of psychiatric disturbances observed and noted that the mental, emotional and personality upsets may be due to uraemia, to the provocation of a chronic debilitating disease or to the repeated technical procedures of dialysis. Wright (1966) followed eleven patients on chronic dialysis for between 6 and 34 months and mentions a number of stresses affecting his patients such as the unpredictability of feeling well, the tensions arising in the marriage situation from guilt and anger, the effect of separation on families and financial anxieties.

Shea *et al.* (1965) reported their experience with nine patients on haemodialysis who had been seen regularly over 2½ years. The patient's reactions occurring before dialysis consisted mainly of irritability, fear and insomnia while during dialysis the anxiety was related to the efficiency of the machine and there was some reactive depression. Following dialysis the main response was relief. They briefly discuss the patient's reaction to dietary restrictions. Sand, Livingstone and Wright (1966) and Retan and Lewis (1966), in accounts of the psychological assessment of candidates for haemodialysis programmes and experiences of working on such a programme, agreed that successful adjustment appears to depend on higher intelligence, free admission of anxiety or emotional difficulty and avoidance of emotional defences that involve the use of physical symptoms such as hypochondriasis and hysteria; of importance too is strong emotional support from family members.

In most cases such stresses as faced by these patients were handled by denial and projection. They were supported through identification in group treatment and open discussion with interested family members and with members of the team. Without such opportunity for discussion or in the absence of strong motivation for good self-care, depression and continuous ongoing complications can be expected. Cramond, Knight and Lawrence (1967) describe a group of 21 patients who were observed before, during and after dialysis as part of a research programme. They describe a sequence of psychological reactions beginning with denial followed by grief and mourning which was seen in the majority of their cases. Regression, acting out and projection were all observed in different patients from time to time, and the psychiatrist's role in this team was that of acting as a mediator between patient and staff so that staff members could understand the meaning of the patient's behaviour in dynamic terms. They agreed with Scribner *et al.* (1965) that there is continuing improvement in well being by each year that the patient's life is prolonged.

Few children have been treated by chronic dialysis and one of the most thought-provoking papers is by Salisbury (1968). He described a nine-year-old child with severe glomerulonephritis who was maintained for three weeks on peritoneal dialysis after complete anuria. From this the child then had haemodialysis for six months on a twice-weekly basis, dying 17 days after a transplant from an unrelated human donor. With a pre-dialysis blood urea nitrogen of 150 mg. per cent, the child was lethargic, slow, irritable, showed lability of mood and was quite intolerant of fluid reduction in the diet. Post-dialysis the blood urea nitrogen became 25 mg. per cent and the child showed mentally an alertness, improved concentration and was less demanding. However, over the nine-month period of treatment there was a slow, general mental deterioration. She became depressed, demanding of everyone and indulged in tantrums if frustrated; she was attention-seeking and used the care of her shunt and regular epistaxis to control her environment; towards the end there was massive regression. Salisbury's views, based on this case, were that very few hospitals can provide the psychological help to allow the young child to cope and he noted the emotional toll that this one case took on staff and parents.

Abram (1968) makes the point that the stress of chronic haemodialysis may arouse emotional conflicts in the patient that lead him into open rebellion against the medical regime upon which his life depends. This author stresses the importance of psychiatric selection and the meaning of prolongation of life to the patient including resolution of the dependency/independency conflicts. Abram in general follows Scribner's criteria for guidance of selection for haemodialysis. Scribner in 1963 proposed the following guidelines:

(1) Self-supporting adult under the age of 45.

(2) Stability and maturity of the patient.

(3) Absence of heart disease, strokes and other complications of long standing.

(4) Admitted willingness to co-operate.

(5) The patient's renal function should be stable or deteriorating slowly.

(6) Children and young adults not potentially self-supporting except for research purposes, have been excluded up to this time.

The reasons for rejection in the programme with which Abram was connected were either mental deficiency or pre-existing psychosis in the patient. Of interest is his note that the physicians very often became angry with him because they saw the psychiatrist as 'stirring up the patient and the patient's problems'.

Meldrum, Wolfram and Rubini (1968), discussing the impact of chronic haemodialysis upon the socio-economics of a veteran patient group consider that the principal condition for selection should be a potential for complete rehabilitation and full-time gainful occupation. As a result of their experience with 24 patients, they consider that an emotionally stable home environment and a high degree of motivation towards a specific goal are essential pre-requisites for successful adaptation to chronic haemodialysis. The rehabilitation process is more difficult if the patient has had no college training.

They also noted that age under 40 and more than one child in the family increase optimum rehabilitation. Norris (1967), discussing personality factors in the performance of dialysis patients, describes 15 patients as giving one of three main types of response:

(1) Conformist—that is to say, passive, dependent.

(2) Masculine—by this he means individualistic and independent, reactive.

(3) Adaptive type—successful, realistic and because of this such patients will show early anxiety and depression.

Only the extreme conformist and masculine types were unsuitable for treatment. Two social workers, Goodey and Kelly (1967) have looked at the problems of a socially unselected group of 24 patients on dialysis between 1963 and 1966 in the United Kingdom; 10 of these patients had been on treatment for longer than one year; 16 of the 24 were married and 11 had families. Patients in the poorer socio-economic groups had the most noticeable drop in income; 10 thought the diet cost more since being ill; only 2 were working full time and 1 part time and all of these 3 were either in social classes I or II. The main difficulties in obtaining employment were not only the illness, but the distance from therapy and day-time dialysis. Only 2 of the patients from the 11 families with children reported that the children were unaffected by the patient's illness; 10 of the 14 noted a big difference in sexual libido. MacNamara (1967, 1968) has given valuable accounts of the anxiety occasioned by socio-economic factors affecting the patient and his family in the crisis of terminal renal failure. Of particular interest is her description of her counselling role to these families.

Tiller *et al.* (1969), reporting on 31 patients over a fifteen-month period in a newly established unit, commented briefly that most patients showed some anxiety early in the course of dialysis but that this lessened as they became used to the procedure. Intravenous diazepam in doses of 10 to 20 mg. gave symptomatic relief without the undesirable hypotension noted when phenothiazines were used. Menzies and Stewart (1968), in a review of seven dialysis patients over a nine-month period, noted that all their patients showed emotional symptoms reactive to stress. Intermittent delirious or sub-delirious reactions were seen and the patients often showed evidence of increased cerebral dysfunction during or just after dialysis. They thought that assessment of mental status and previous personality was of value in understanding the responses to the illness and its treatment.

Cooper in 1967 described one case of hypomanic psychosis precipitated by haemodialysis. The content of the psychosis appeared related to the patient's contemporary conflicts. Kaplan De-Nour, Schaltiel and Czaczkes (1968) described a group of nine patients whom they intensively studied for a year. As with other workers they noted the uniform defences of denial, displacement, isolation, reaction formation and projection. No matter the background of the patient these defences, while adaptive in one sense, led to marked ego restriction. They believe that the main stress of chronic haemodialysis is the dependency on the machine, the staff and the aggression resulting from the dependency. Some of their clinical manifestations also suggest brain dysfunction and this was supported by psychological testing and E.E.G. studies.

In the past two years there has been a great deal of interest in home dialysis and several interesting papers have been produced relating to this topic. Shaldon (1968) stated that home haemodialysis will only succeed if the patient can be truly independent of the hospital and the spouse. The equipment must be as used in the hospital and reliable so that confidence can be built up. Selection includes age, severity of illness, intelligence and likelihood of full rehabilitation. Instruction is oral and by demonstration rather than by manual assistance. The requirements from the patient's point of view are stoicism, self-control and an average intelligence. A high intelligence, Shaldon found, was often related with over-anxiety and a low intelligence with irresponsibility; he thought that manual labourers should be excluded. Leg cannulae seemed most successful so that the patient can cope with a reasonable daily round.

Smith *et al.* (1969) noted that by October 1968, 464 patients were supported in England and Wales by the National Health Service on maintenance dialysis, of whom 132 were on home dialysis. Like Hampers, Merrill and Cameron (1965) and Shambaugh *et al.* (1967), they too were struck by the fact that the stress of home dialysis was felt more by the spouse than by the patient. Of the 12 patients who had gone home, a significant problem had occurred in 7 spouses. Three of them had required psychiatric help for agitated depression and a common problem was fatigue. Shambaugh and Kanter in 1969, in an excellent article on group meetings with spouses of patients on haemodialysis, show how the group progressed from an initial state of panic and denial to one of more openness and interaction among members. The most striking accomplishment of the group was the spouses' progressively increasing sense of emotional separateness from their partners as they lessened their reliance on the defence of denial. The stress on the spouse is enormous and there is clear potential for serious regression and disastrous loss of control. They believe that the spouse should operate the artificial kidney machine only if he or she has passed careful psychiatric screening and is provided with appropriate emotional support. Group discussions, they thought, were one such therapeutic possibility and they believed that their supportive, non-interpretative technique was effective, although it was very demanding on the leader and difficult to sustain. If psychiatric screening and support are not feasible, and this is more likely to be the case in most centres than not, they believe that the spouse should not undertake the responsibility for the dialysis procedure. Shambaugh and Kanter detail the dynamic struggles which all 18 of the spouses under review shared. They had to cope with many stresses including their marital partner's severe illness, possible death and regressive behaviour. In response to this they reacted with intense feelings of deprivation and primitive urges towards psychological closeness to their partners, with enormous hostility which often gave rise to great guilt. Those who operated the artificial kidney machine had a fear that they might destroy their 'patient' partner. This led them to massive denial which was often supported by blind faith in renal transplantation.

It is difficult to obtain overall figures of the success of chronic haemodialysis but Bluemle (1968) considers that it is not unreasonable to anticipate that about half of the patients now undergoing chronic dialysis at qualified American centres will be alive in seven years. His review of the literature, including papers by Gottschalk (1967), Drukker *et al.* (1966), Comty *et al.* (1966) and Pendras and Erikson (1966), suggests that the majority of patients undergoing long-term dialysis in well-established programmes can be expected to resume relatively useful, productive lives. It is clear that chronic haemodialysis, whether conducted in the home or in the hospital, has moved from the tentative experimental stage to the practical clinical stage during the period under review in this chapter. While occasionally patients who do not wish to accept life on the restrictive terms of dependence on an artificial kidney and its operators are still met, the great majority make sound adaptations over an average period of a year to the new situation. Most patients see the period of haemodialysis as a time of waiting until transplantation can free them of much of their dependence on hospital, and the general restrictiveness of their lives. Some few prefer to remain on dialysis and this is particularly so if they are aware of the death of fellow patients following transplantation. Patients themselves in a unit develop their own sources of information and, from this, their own standards and criteria of the effectiveness of therapy. While the availability of places on a dialysis programme depends in part on the number of transplantations successfully done, the wish of the individual patient to settle for adjustment to living on dialysis alone must be remembered and respected.

THE LIVING KIDNEY DONOR AND HIS FAMILY

A review of the literature shows that the psychological, moral and ethical problems of renal homotransplantation using a living volunteer donor have demanded more attention and concern than those facing the recipient; for this reason they will be first considered. It is of significance that over the years fewer living donors are used as sources of transplantation kidneys. This appears to be due partly to improved results from cadaver kidneys following on better immunosuppressive techniques and partly to the realization of the possible adverse psychological interaction between donor and recipient following transplantation.

The first human renal homotransplantation was performed in 1936 and by now more than a thousand human kidney transplants have been performed, some 60 per cent from living donors. In 1965 the Transplantation Registry reported the percentage survival of recipients at the end of one year with donors being a monozygotic twin as 89 per cent, a related living donor 53 per cent, a cadaver 21 per cent and unrelated donors only 12 per cent. By 1969 Shiel *et al.* in Sydney showed that of 75 renal transplants after a period of 18 months, 25 had died, 6 had had a second transplant, with a further 4 awaiting retransplantation. From Melbourne Marshall *et al.* (1968) reported a 60 per cent success rate from predominantly cadaveric donor kidneys. Scribner (1964) in his Presidential Address to the American Society for Artificial Internal Organs proposed that a new code of ethics was required to meet the problem of transplantation. He pointed out that the surgeon involved in this work has to decide which patient will be chosen and also whether the homografts should be obtained from a family or a friend, from an anonymous volunteer or from a cadaver or from publicly maintained organ banks. Leake (1964), in a thoughtful paper on the moral problems of organ transplantation, states that these are not the exclusive responsibility of physicians, nor of biomedical scientists involved in this work, nor of the prospective recipients or donors. He believes society intelligently informed, must make the final decision for the attainment of maximum social welfare. Hamburger, Crosnier and Dormont (1964) make two points about the living donor. First, the doctor must respect the desire of one person to risk his or her life for another; and secondly he must be sure that the risk is very much less than the probability of success for the recipient. The two dangers to be avoided are the exertion of undue pressure on the potential donor who must be healthy, emotionally stable and a genuine volunteer. Woodruff (1964), discussing the ethical problems in organ transplantation, sees the donation of a kidney as a purely voluntary act; but to cover the doctor, the necessary conditions, although he doubts whether they are sufficient conditions, are to establish beyond reasonable doubt, that the patient has gross renal failure which it is not possible to manage by other methods; the donor must be in good health; consent which must be entirely voluntary must also be the result of an informed opinion and the chances of success must be good.

Ayd (1964) reported a case where a woman who was profoundly depressed volunteered to be a donor in the hope that during the operation she would die and thus indirectly commit suicide. Even before transplantation is mentioned by the treatment team, it is often noted that the possibility has been discussed by the family who have selected likely donors. Those who refuse to co-operate run the risk of being rejected by the family and are made to feel guilty. The end result is family quarrelling and estrangement. An Editorial (1964) quotes the case of one family torn apart as the result of the mother giving a kidney to her child against the wishes of the husband and father. Holmes (1964) observed that situations of familial ostracism can be created unless care is taken to avoid donor coercion, while Dunea *et al.* (1965), reporting their experiences of renal homotransplantation in 24 patients, note that close blood relatives served as living donors and an unrelated living donor, a brother-in-law, was used only once. They note that donors with young children or having family responsibilities are to be avoided. Evans (1969) states that renal transplantation is morally justifiable provided it conferred a proportionate benefit on the recipient without exposing the donor to great risk of life or depriving him completely of an important function. What was 'proportionate benefit' and 'risk of life' can only depend on the expert judgment of the surgeons and physicians working and experienced in this field.

Kemph (1966) was impressed by the unconscious resentment of donors to recipients, a finding which was confirmed by Cramond, Knight and Lawrence (1967). Fellner and Marshall in 1968 interviewed 12 renal homotransplantation donors in depth between five weeks and 18 months after surgery. They found, unexpectedly, that the decision-making process about donorship did not at all follow a pattern compatible with the concept of informed consent but occurred as an instantaneous, irrational response which subsequently was justified and maintained with the aid of a number of defensive techniques. They did not agree with Kemph's findings that a period of depression beginning three to five days after surgery and lasting for various lengths of time occurred. All Fellner and Marshall's donors reported that the event had been a very meaningful experience in their lives, of substantial impact on them and that it had brought about internal psychic changes which they felt were beneficial. The forces on the donor in a positive direction came from several sources. First, their belief in the good they were doing for the recipient—saving a life; secondly, their positive relationship with their physician both actual and symbolic; thirdly, the positive emotional reinforcement from the recipient and family; and fourthly, the considerable attention paid to them by friends, acquaintances, news media and other means of support.

Cramond (1968), in a review of the psychiatrist's contribution to a renal unit, states that psychological understanding of the motives of volunteering and of the family dynamics is essential in helping to determine 'when a volunteer is not a volunteer'. The apparently well-motivated donor may in an interview in depth indicate in all manner of subtle and indirect ways, his dislike of his possible sacrifice. It is important to screen out those whose relationships with the recipient contain an excess of negative feelings. A follow-up of donors confirmed that intense feelings of obligation develop between donor and recipient, between the one who gives, and the one who receives a gift, that can never be repaid. Where the pre-existing relationship at all levels of interaction has been relatively harmonious, the problem of obligation is not of great significance, but when the relationship has been ambivalent to a marked degree, the post-transplant situation exaggerates the hostile, unhappy interdependency.

If no undue ambivalence exists and the potential donor is acceptable on all counts, this author agrees with Fellner and Marshall that such a person should be allowed to perform a heroic act as this can be a psychologically rewarding experience for the donor.

Colomb and Hamburger (1967) report on 22 donors psychiatrically assessed prior to nephrectomy. They consider that the most suitable donor is affectionate, has had a secure childhood with easy social adjustment and relationships and whose anxiety is slight and well tolerated. These workers, however, did not explore the psychodynamic interactions of donor and recipient; 20 per cent of their donors presented with a limited degree of anxiety after transplantation.

In Cramond's series of eight living donors followed up over a two-year period, only one showed deterioration. He was unrelated to the recipient, was drinking alcohol in an uncontrolled way and had somatic symptoms of discomfort related to the nephrectomy scar. Dynamically this appeared to relate to his suppressed resentment to the recipient.

Contrary to that which might have been expected, no aesthetic objections from recipients to the grafting and implantation of cadaver kidneys have been reported. The general feelings expressed by recipients is that there is less sense of obligation and therefore less guilt.

A short follow-up study (Cramond, 1968) of four relatives who had given permission for a deceased family member's kidneys to be removed for transplantation purposes showed that all were warm, outgoing and giving people who felt that this act was consonant with the personality of the deceased person. The decision did not appear to have any effect on reducing the time of the mourning period nor of altering its character in any way.

PSYCHOLOGICAL PROBLEMS OF THE RECIPIENT

Following transplantation patients are nursed in isolation with access to their room guarded by air locks and ultra-violet light to reduce the risk of infection; nursing and medical requirements are delivered through two-way closets, the room being entered by medical and nursing personnel to a minimum degree; conversation with relatives is by means of a two-way radio system, a situation that does not permit the communication of doubts and anxieties; a patient who is prone to a phobic anxiety state may find this type of situation frightening and stressful. Once the immediate post-operative phase is over, the recipient meets a variety of socially critical situations. The new organ, which is very often palpable in the iliac fossa, has to be integrated into the body schema. Patients tend initially to be very aware of its presence and to protect it from harm; sexual intercourse presents a conflict situation with fear that the thrusting of the coital act will damage the kidney and fear that the marital partner will find continued abstinence unduly difficult. This anxiety, together with the loss of libido that occurs during the intensive treatment phase, resolves over a period of approximately six months following operation.

Other disturbances of body image noted include the cushingoid syndrome which follows the exhibition of cortisone and which can be quite disturbing, particularly for the younger woman who may find the alteration of her facial appearance extremely threatening. In general, recipients have reported that the operation has given them a symbolic rebirth and a second chance in life. Many believe that they have some special task or role to carry out and life becomes more meaningful and yet more simple.

Kemph (1966), in his follow-up of recipients, noted periods of severe depression concerned with body damage, particularly a fear that the operation might have produced sexual change. Post-operative depression, however, was not noted by Cramond (1967) but he drew attention to the possibility of a conflict situation arising where a patient unsure of his sexual identity receives a kidney from the opposite sex. Periods of acute anxiety for recipients occur during episodes of graft rejection and many are aware that second transplantation operations may be required and express fear lest there be no place for them to be re-admitted to a dialysis programme. There is a general awareness among patients of the hazards of the immunosuppressive therapy with associated risks of infection. A potentially traumatic situation exists when the recipient is brought into hospital to await the death of a donor, particularly if the waiting period is prolonged. Great care is required to keep the recipient completely separated from the dying donor and to keep nursing staff separated. It is important to note that no recipient need be rejected on psychiatric grounds alone and it has been interesting to find successful outcomes achieved with patients who would appear to be unsuitable due to personal immaturity, mild socio-pathic tendencies or low intelligence. The most important factor in avoiding psychiatric problems is to have staff with the ability and the time to provide the social and psychological support necessary.

THE PROBLEMS OF A RENAL UNIT TEAM

Patients' relationships with the medical team create particular problems in dialysis and transplantation units. This is in part due to the degree of dependence of the patient on the team, coupled with his knowledge that he has no choice of treatment if he is to live, other than that given by the team members; he cannot, without risk to his life, change to another doctor. The close association with other patients creates an awareness of the doubtful long-term prognosis for the individual patient—a situation which requires a high degree of understanding on the part of the team members and in particular the medical leaders. The information obtained in a full psychiatric history to assess a patient's style of life, his handling of stress, anxiety and anger, his present family role and the role he played in his original nuclear family, should all be made available to the members of the team. This provides a guide on the handling of the needs of a particular patient; regular group meetings of the team to discuss these matters are important. It has been noted that a patient normally chooses one person in a team as the point of contact, and this may be a relatively junior nurse, a resident doctor or the senior physician. It is important that this key person is regularly able to communicate information to the rest of the team members and to obtain advice and interpretation of the needs and management of that patient at the particular time.

Kaplan De-Nour and Czaczkes in 1968 looked at the emotional problems and reactions of a medical team in a chronic haemodialysis unit. After a two-year study of the emotional problems of the medical team, they consider the main reactions were feelings of guilt, possessiveness, over-protectiveness and withdrawal from the patients. The reactions of the physicians including the psychiatrist, were mostly of guilt and withdrawal while over-protectiveness and possessiveness was seen mostly in the nurses. A major source of stress for the physician is the problem of selection. The physician tries to alleviate some of his problems by developing as objective medical, psychological and social criteria as possible to ensure a scientific selection; this constant stress may create anxiety followed by guilt feelings. Guilt, too, is stirred up by the unconscious wish to be omnipotent and to enjoy the feeling of power; each patient who does well proves the correctness of the physician's selection. Below the over-protectiveness of the nurses lay hostility and unconscious aggression; the patients, they thought, received all the attention but rarely implied by word or action any gratitude and often complained and demanded more attention. This paper brought forth considerable emotional response in the correspondence columns in the succeeding issues of the *Lancet*. However, because of his training the psychiatrist can play a useful part helping the treatment team to deal with transference and counter-transference problems. These have to be brought to notice tactfully and it appears essential to do so if valid clinical appraisals are to be made, and the patient who irritates and annoys or whose unco-operative behaviour we do not wish to understand is really to be helped.

THE PSYCHOLOGICAL PROBLEMS OF THE FAMILY OF THE RECIPIENT

Of great importance for the future is an understanding of the impact of this illness and its treatment over a prolonged period of time on the family. The stress of having the wage-earner ill, or of having the mothering figure incapacitated, alters family relationships; children have been reported as requiring treatment for anxiety and depression. Marriages have broken up; parents have required psychotherapy for help with guilt feelings over their handling of a son with renal disease. The association of chronic illness with disruption of family life, often with financial hardship, leads to feelings of fear, insecurity, unhappiness and depression, and those families least well prepared to cope show clear signs of stress and decompensation leading to recognizable clinical disorder. This observation suggests that the renal unit must link up with family doctors and social agencies and develop a community side to its work.

Living with haemodialysis or with a transplanted kidney is difficult and the relative merits of the two approaches may not be determined for several years to come. The duration of life following these medical and surgical interventions, has in general not been sufficiently long to enable the person living to enjoy a sense of deep and lasting security. All the patients are aware that they use borrowed time and, as an Editorial in the *Journal of the American Medical Association* stated in 1966, 'the man who lives on borrowed time lives uneasily, and the latest medicosurgical creations of borrowed time must eventually be questioned in terms of their moral result, as well as their physical result. They may be creating nothing, except something of that which philosopher Unamuno called the "too long" life.'

Those patients who have adapted well to therapy and for whom the procedures have worked smoothly are well satisfied and many report emotional growth as a result of this prolonged grim crisis in their life. With the psychological insights reported in the literature workers in this field should be able to aid and speed up the processes of adjustment for all patients in need.

REFERENCES

Abram, H. S. (1968). 'The Psychiatrist, the Treatment of Chronic Renal Failure and the Prolongation of Life. I.' *Am. J. Psychiat.*, **124,** 1351.

Ayd, F. (1964). Personal Communication.

Barber, N. D., Nakamoto, S., McCormack, L. J. and Kolff, W. J. (1963). 'Pathologic Anatomy of 13 patients after Prolonged Periodic Haemodialyses.' *Tr. Am. Soc. artif. int. Organs*, **9,** 21.

Bluemle, L. W., Jr. (1968). 'Current Status of Chronic Haemodialysis.' *Am. J. Med.*, **44,** 749.

Colomb, G. and Hamburger, J. (1967). 'Psychological and Moral Problems of Renal Transplantation.' In *Psychological Aspects of Surgery*, p. 157. Boston: Little, Brown.

Comty, C. M., Baillod, R. A., Crockett, R. and Shaldon, S. (1966). 'Forty Months' Experience with a Nurse-Patient Operated Chronic Dialysis Unit.' *Proc. European Dialysis and Transplant Assoc.*, **3,** 98.

Cooper, A. J. (1967). 'Hypomanic Psychosis Precipitated by Haemodialysis.' *Comp. Psychiat.*, **8,** 168.

Cramond, W. A. (1967). 'Renal Homotransplantation—Some Observations on Recipients and Donors.' *Br. J. Psychiat.*, **113,** 1223.

— (1968). 'Medical, Moral and Legal Aspects of Organ Transplantation and Long-Term Resuscitative Measures. Psychological, Social and Community Aspects.' *Med. J. Aust.*, **2,** 622.

— Knight, P. R. and Lawrence, J. R. (1967). 'The Psychiatric Contribution to a Renal Unit Undertaking Chronic Haemodialysis and Renal Homotransplantation.' *Br. J. Psychiat.*, **113,** 1201.

Drukker, W., Alberts, C., Ode, A., Roozendaal, K. J. and Wilnink, G. (1966). 'Report on Regular Dialysis Treatment in Europe. II.' *Proc. European Dialysis and Transplant Assoc.*, **3,** 90.

Dunea, G., Nakamoto, S., Strafforn, R. A., Figueroa, J. E., Versaci, A. A., Schibagaki, M. and Kolff, W. J. (1965). 'Renal Homotransplantation in 24 patients.' *Br. med. J.*, **1,** 7.

Editorial (1964). *Ann. int. Med.*, **60,** 309.

Editorial (1966). *J. Am. med. Ass.*, **195,** 1146.

Evans, C. P. (1969). Personal Communication.

Fellner, C. H. and Marshall, J. R. (1968). 'Twelve Kidney Donors.' *J. Am. med. Ass.*, **206,** 2703.

Goodey, J. and Kelly, J. (1967). 'Social and Economic Effects of Regular Dialysis.' *Lancet*, **2,** 147.

Gottschalk, C. W. (1967). 'Report of the Committee on Chronic Renal Disease.' Bureau of the Budget, U.S.A.

Gutch, C. F., Stevens, S. C. and Watkins, F. L. (1964). 'Periodic Peritoneal Dialysis in Chronic Renal Insufficiency.' *Ann. int. Med.*, **60,** 289.

Hamburger, J., Crosnier, J. and Dormont, J. (1964). 'Problèmes Moraux Posés par les Méthodes de Suppléance et de Transplantation d'Organes.' *Rev. franc. Etudes clin. biol.*, **9,** 587.

Hampers, C. L., Merrill, J. P. and Cameron, E. (1965). *Tr. Am. Soc. artif. int. Organs*, **11,** 3.

Holmes, J. H. (1964). In *Experience in Renal Transplantation*, Ed. by T. Starzl. Philadelphia: Saunders.

Kaplan De-Nour, A., Schaltiel, J. and Czaczkes, J. W. (1968). 'Emotional Reactions of Patients on Chronic Haemodialysis.' *Psychosom. Med.*, **30,** 521.

— and Czaczkes, J. W. (1968). 'Emotional Problems and Reactions of the Medical Team in a Chronic Haemodialysis Unit.' *Lancet*, **2,** 987.

Kemph, J. P. (1966). 'Renal Failure, Artificial Kidney and Kidney Transplant.' *Am. J. Psychiat.*, **122,** 1270.

Kolff, W. J. (1947). *New Ways of Treating Uraemia*. London: Churchill.

Leake, C. D. (1964). In *Experience in Renal Transplantation*, Ed. by T. Starzl. Philadelphia: Saunders.

MacNamara, F. M. (1967). 'Psychosocial Problems in a Renal Unit.' *Br. J. Psychiat.*, **113,** 1231.

— (1968). 'The Crisis of Dialysis and Renal Homotransplantation: A Team Approach to Patients and Families.' *Br. J. Psychiat.*, **9,** 193.

Marshall, V., Kincaid-Smith, P., Morris, P. J., Saker, B. and Eremin, J. (1968). 'Cadaveric Renal Transplantation.' *Lancet*, **2,** 927.

Meldrum, M. W., Wolfram, J. G. and Rubini, M. E. (1968). 'The Impact of Chronic Haemodialysis upon the Socio-economics of a Veteran Patient Group.' *J. chron. Dis.*, **21,** 37.

Menzies, I. C. and Stewart, W. K. (1968). 'Psychiatric Observations on Patients Receiving Regular Dialysis Treatment.' *Br. med. J.*, **1,** 544.

Murray, J. E., Gleason, R. and Bartholomay, A. (1965). 'Fourth Report of the Human Kidney Transplant Registry: 16th Sept. 1964–15th March, 1965.' *Transplantation*, **3,** 684.

National Health and Medical Research Council of Australia (1969). Report on Organ Transplantation and Renal Dialysis, p. 3.

Norris, A. S. (1968). 'The Performance of Dialysis Patients.' *J. Iowa med. Soc.*, **58,** 671.

Pendras, J. P. and Erickson, R. V. (1966). 'Haemodialysis: a Successful Therapy for Chronic Uremia.' *Ann. int. Med.*, **64,** 293.

Retan, J. W. and Lewis, H. Y. (1966). 'Repeated Dialysis of Indigent Patients for Chronic Renal Failure.' *Ann. int. Med.*, **64,** 284.

Salisbury, R. E. (1968). 'Behavioural Responses of a nine-year-old-child on Chronic Dialysis.' *J. Am. Acad. child Psychiat.*, **7,** 282.

Sand, P., Livingston, G. and Wright, R. G. (1966). 'Psychological Assessment of Candidates for a Haemodialysis Program.' *Ann. int. Med.*, **64,** 602.

Scribner, B. H. (1963). Proceedings of Conference to Consider the Treatment of Patients with Chronic Kidney Disease with Uremia. New York.

— (1964). 'Presidential Address: Ethical Problems of using Artificial Organs to Sustain Human Life.' *Tr. Am. Soc. artif. int. Organs*, **10,** 209.

— Buri, R., Caner, J. E. Z., Hegstrom, R. and Bumell, J. M. (1960a). 'The Treatment of Chronic Uremia by Means of Intermittent Hemodialysis: a Preliminary Report.' *Tr. Am. Soc. artif. int. Organs*, **6,** 114.

— Caner, J. E. Z., Buri, R. and Quinton, W. (1960b). 'The Technique of Continuous Hemodialysis.' *Tr. Am. Soc. artif. int. Organs*, **6,** 88.

— Fergus, E. B., Boen, S. T. and Thomas, E. D. (1965). 'Some Therapeutic Approaches to Chronic Renal Insufficiency.' *Ann. rev. Med.*, **16,** 285.

Shaldon, S. (1968). 'Independence in Maintenance Haemodialysis.' *Lancet*, **1,** 520.

Shambaugh, P. W., Hampers, C. L., Bailey, G. L., Snyder, D. and Merrill, J. P. (1967). 'Haemodialysis in the Home—Emotional Impact on the Spouse.' *Tr. Am. Soc. artif. int. Organs*, **13,** 41.

— and Kanter, S. S. (1969). 'Spouses under Stress: Group Meetings with Spouses of Patients on Haemodialysis.' *Am. J. Psychiat.*, **125,** 928.

Shea, E. J., Bogdan, D. F., Freeman, R. B. and Schreiner, G. E. (1965). 'Haemodialysis for Chronic Renal Failure IV—Psychological Considerations.' *Ann. int. Med.*, **62,** 558.

Shiel, A. G. R., Stewart, J. H., May, J., Johnson, J., Tiller, D. J., George, C. R. P., Rogers, J. H., Storey, B. J., Mani, M. K., Gibson, G. R., Sharp, A., Wyatt, K. M., Sands, J. R. and Loewenthal, J. (1968). 'Renal Transplantation from Cadaver Donors.' *Med. J. Aust.*, **2,** 1079.

Smith, E. K. M., Curtis, J. R., McDonald, S. J. and De Wardener, H. E. (1969). 'Haemodialysis in the Home. Problems and Frustrations.' *Lancet*, **1,** 614.

Tiller, D. J., Johnson, J. R., May, J. and Sands, J. (1969). 'Fifteen Months' Experience in a New Haemodialysis Unit.' *Med. J. Aust.*, **1,** 1231.

Walker Brown, H., Maher, J. F., Lapierre, L., Bledsoe, F. H. and Schreiner, G. E. (1962). 'Clinical Problems Related to the Prolonged Artificial Maintenance of Life by Haemodialysis in Chronic Renal Failure.' *Tr. Am. Soc. artif. int. Organs*, **8,** 281.

Woodruff, M. F. A. (1964). 'Ethical Problems in Organ Transplantation.' *Br. med. J.*, **1**, 1457.

Wright, R. G., Sand, P. and Livingston, G. (1966). 'Psychological Stress during Haemodialysis for Chronic Renal Failure.' *Ann. int. Med.*, **64**, 611.

CHAPTER 18

PRACTICE AND TEACHING OF PSYCHOSOMATIC MEDICINE IN GENERAL HOSPITALS

HEINZ H. WOLFF

CONTRIBUTIONS OF PSYCHOSOMATIC MEDICINE

Interest in psychosomatic medicine in hospital practice has increased considerably since the introduction of psychiatric units into general hospitals, especially in Great Britain and the United States (Hill, 1969a). By making it easier for psychiatrists to co-operate with their non-psychiatric colleagues, this development has led to greater awareness of the psychological aspects of medical practice and to research into the interaction between biological, psychological and social factors in health and illness.

In spite of this, hospital specialists differ considerably in the degree to which they are interested in the psychosomatic approach. This is, of course, largely due to the fact that the scientific advances in the biological aspects of medicine have led to an increasing degree of specialization so that the interest of specialists tends to become restricted to the detailed understanding of the mechanisms of illness in their particular specialty. While we owe to this development the rapid progress in physical diagnosis and treatment of organic disease, the patient as a whole and the fact that emotional experience can act as an important factor among others in influencing the onset and course of a disease process, tends to be overlooked or even denied. Some specialists do, of course, combine with their particular expert knowledge a natural interest in the emotional aspects of illness but others either lack such interest or the training required to elicit and handle the emotional factors relevant to their patients' condition. Family doctors tend to be more aware of these aspects (Hopkins, 1955), although there are many exceptions in either direction. Studies by Walton *et al.* (1963, 1964) and by Balint *et al.* (1966) have also shown that the personalities of medical students and doctors differ with regard to their interest and skill in dealing with the psychological aspects of medical practice.

There are, therefore, good reasons why there is a need in hospitals for doctors with special interest in psychosomatic medicine. One of their main contributions will be to practise and teach the psychosomatic approach, not by over-emphasizing the psychological aspects but by stressing the interaction of biological, psychological and social factors. Besides carrying out this general function they will have special contributions to make by virtue of their own specialist training and experience in psychosomatic medicine.

These will include especially their knowledge of psychodynamics and psychopathology and their skill in applying dynamic interviewing techniques in diagnosis and treatment; and their ability to evaluate the relation of the patient's personality and life experience to his illness. They will also contribute their special knowledge of social and cultural factors concerned with the maintenance of health and development of disease. To this must be added the important contributions arising out of the increasing body of scientific knowledge and research concerned with the interaction of mental and physical phenomena in health and illness. These include the interrelationship between cerebral function and psychological processes, and the influence of emotional experience on endocrine and other physiological functions, as well as the study of pathways and mechanisms involved in these psychophysiological relationships. Such research requires a combination of biological and psychological methods of investigation (Crisp, 1968).

Psychosomatic medicine, although it draws attention to the need to understand and treat patients as whole persons, therefore, accepts the fact that mental and physical phenomena require different methods of study and observation. This has been pointed out by Wolff (1968) and also by Lipowski (1968) from whom the following conclusion may be quoted: 'Both the psychic and somatic phenomena are aspects (or modes of abstraction) of persons. A person is and responds as a unity, but limitations of man as an investigator necessitate the breakdown of the unity for the purpose of observation, description and study of relationships among selected variables. Whatever the merits of the holistic conception as a theoretical construct, the study of the person-as-a-whole is a wishful fiction.'

Lastly, as Engel (1967a) has pointed out, these various contributions of psychosomatic medicine are no longer restricted to a limited group of illnesses, the so-called psychosomatic disorders in whose origin and course psychological factors are likely to be particularly important. The majority of diseases are multi-factorial in origin and psychological and somatic aspects and their mutual interaction need to be taken into consideration in every patient who is ill.

THE PSYCHOSOMATIC CONSULTATION

Although most doctors on the staff of general hospitals will, themselves, be paying a greater or lesser degree of attention to the psychosocial problems of their patients, depending on their personal interest and experience, specialists in psychosomatic problems will exert their influence mainly by being called in for consultation by their colleagues. The nature and function of such consultations has been discussed by several authors (Rosenbaum and Reiser, 1958; Meyer and Mendelson, 1961; Wolfe, 1966).

As Lipowski (1967a) has pointed out in a recent review, three types of such consultations can be distinguished: (1) a patient-oriented consultation where advice is requested on the patient's condition, especially on differential diagnosis and on the relative importance of psychological and physical factors, and on the patient's treatment; (2) a consultee-oriented consultation where the referring doctor asks for help on account of his own difficulties in relation to his patient; and (3) a situation-oriented consultation where assistance is asked for because the patient's attitude and behaviour, and sometimes that of his relatives, is causing disturbance and disruption among the clinical team responsible for his treatment. In practice all three functions are likely to play a part to varying degrees whenever a psychosomatic consultation is requested.

The success of all such consultations will depend on a number of factors. Foremost among these is the consultant's ability to elicit the relevant information from the patient, his relatives, the doctors, nurses and social workers. He will have to use his skill at conducting dynamic interviews and his knowledge of psychodynamics to assess the patient's personality, the influence of his present life situation and past experience, as well as the psychological mechanisms he adopts in response to emotional stress and conflict; he will have to be versed in the handling of inter-personal relationships and in psychotherapy; and in addition, he will have to be experienced in the diagnosis and treatment of medical and psychiatric illness related to stress.

Although there are by now a number of general physicians with special interest in psychosomatic medicine, psychiatrists who are interested and experienced in both the biological and the psychodynamic aspects of their subject, are the ones most likely to combine these various skills. Psychiatrists whose main interest lies in the organic and descriptive aspects of their subject and in the major psychoses often lack the necessary interest in personality disorders, intrapsychic processes and the details of inter-personal relationships to be much help in the diagnosis and psychotherapeutic management of minor and major stress disorders; pure psycho-analysts, on the other hand, frequently lack the necessary knowledge and interest in the biological aspects of medicine and psychiatry to be able to give sound and practical advice when invited by their colleagues to advise on medical and surgical patients.

Fortunately, this unnecessary and harmful division between organically and analytically oriented psychiatrists is gradually being overcome. Psychiatrists who combine a biological and social with a psychodynamic orientation, and who recognize the importance of biological and social phenomena as well as of inner and subjective human experience, including unconscious mental processes, are most likely to be of real practical help to their colleagues during psychosomatic consultations.

It must be stressed also that the consulting psychiatrist must have learnt to give his verbal or written opinion in a form which is easily understandable by his non-psychiatric colleagues; complicated dynamic formulations and especially the use of technical psychoanalytic or other psychiatric terms are best avoided. Instead, what is required is a detailed factual account of the patient's past and present experience, of conflicts and stresses in his inter-personal relationships and his reactions to them in as far as these are relevant to his condition. Only in this way can the referring physicians and surgeons be helped to appreciate the significance of dynamic and social factors.

When the reason for referral arises out of difficulties in the doctor–patient relationship or the patient's or his relatives' attitudes to the clinical team, the consultant must direct his attention to an understanding of the whole interactional situation and avoid siding with one or more of the members involved against the rest of them. His task will be to make the patient feel that he understands his problems and is there to help him with his difficulties while, at the same time, making him gradually more aware of how his attitude and behaviour make the staff react to him as they do; similarly, he must help the staff to understand how the patient feels and help them to tolerate better the disturbed behaviour of, say, a patient who, perhaps as a result of prolonged illness and personal problems, has regressed to an attitude of demandingness and hostility. Apart from helping to resolve crisis situations of this kind, he must be prepared to continue to play an active part himself by seeing the patient and members of the staff or relatives regularly over a longer period. Dynamic psychiatrists who are used to handling similar situations on psychiatric wards and in therapeutic communities are likely to be particularly helpful in situation-oriented consultations of this kind.

DEMAND FOR PSYCHOSOMATIC CONSULTATIONS

This will largely depend on the conditions which prevail at each individual hospital and especially on the size of the psychiatric department, on whether or not the psychiatrists are experienced and interested in psychosomatic problems, and also on the attitude of the non-psychiatric staff of the hospital (Lipowski, 1967b). These are, of course, not independent variables; in a hospital in which there is only a small psychiatric department and where its members are only, or mainly, interested in formal psychiatric illness, they are unlikely to be consulted by their colleagues to give advice on psychosomatic problems. If, on the other hand, the psychiatrists are interested in psychosomatic medicine, their colleagues will soon learn to appreciate the help they can give them, and the interest in psychosomatic medicine and the number of requests for consultations will increase correspondingly. This applies particularly to teaching hospitals, in as far as residents who, during their own training, were shown the importance of the psychosomatic approach, are likely to detect many more patients who could benefit from a psychosomatic consultation than residents who did not receive such training in their student days (Kaufman, 1953; Wolff, 1967); as time goes on, an increasing proportion of the non-psychiatric staff on medical, surgical, obstetric, gynaecological and paediatric units will develop an interest in these problems; they will therefore deal with some of these themselves, while calling in their psychosomatically-oriented psychiatric colleagues if the problem is more complicated or time consuming and appears to demand more expert help. This has certainly been our experience at University College Hospital in London (Tredgold, 1962; Wolff, 1966) and similar observations have been reported from other centres (Lipowski, 1967a).

In terms of actual figures, Shepherd, Davies and Culpan (1960) report that in a general hospital in which a psychiatric consultation service had only recently been introduced, 1·34 per cent of all medical, surgical and gynaecological in-patients and 3·4 per cent of all new out-patients were referred; a psychiatric and psychosomatic morbidity study of 200 newly referred out-patients at the same hospital showed that psychosocial factors were, in fact, of practical importance in 36 per cent of the patients; over ten times as many were referred for a psychiatric opinion. Rud (1953) reports from a hospital in Norway that 4·8 per cent of medical in-patients were referred to the psychiatric department; Helsberg (1958), on the other hand, found that in another medical department, out of 500 patients 22 per cent were suffering from illnesses which were primarily psychiatric or psychosomatic. Querido (1959), in a medical and sociological study at a general hospital in Amsterdam, showed that in about 50 per cent of patients, psychological and/or social stresses had a significant influence on the progress of the disease, and diminished the chances of recovery with physical treatment alone. Lipowski (1967b) states that the percentage of medical and surgical in-patients referred for psychiatric opinion in a number of American hospitals varied from 4 to 13 per cent.

These various figures suggest that psychosocial factors are of practical importance in from 20 to 50 per cent of all in- and out-patients of general hospitals, but that only a small proportion of these are referred to psychiatrists with an interest in psychosomatic medicine. It is not suggested, of course, that all of them should be so referred but it seems likely that a higher referral rate would benefit a number of patients.

ORGANIZATION OF THE CONSULTATION SERVICE

It follows that special attention should be paid to the organization of psychosomatic consultation services in all general hospitals. This can take a number of different forms. In the majority of cases where the psychiatric department is relatively small, it may not be possible to provide more than one or two dynamically oriented psychiatrists with interest in psychosomatics who are available for consultation. At the other extreme are some special units such as the medical-psychiatric liaison group at the University of Rochester School of Medicine (Romano, 1961; Kehoe, 1961; Engel, 1967b) which consists not only of psychiatrists but also of general physicians, paediatricians, obstetricians and general practitioners, with special training in psychosomatic medicine. The majority of large general hospitals provide intermediate services; if the psychiatric department is large enough, one member of its staff can be attached to each of the various non-psychiatric units. Thus at University College Hospital, London, one or more psychiatrists work in liaison with each of the separate medical firms, and also in the paediatric and obstetric departments; a psychiatrist is also attached to certain special units such as the asthma clinic and the dermatological department. Clearly there is room for further expansion of the service, especially on surgical firms, and in the emergency and accident, and intensive-care units. Hackett and Weisman (1960) have described how psychiatrists can co-operate with their surgical colleagues in evaluating and handling the complications which may arise in surgical patients pre-operatively, post-operatively and during the convalescent period; Kornfeld (1969) has emphasized the need to pay attention to the psychiatric aspects of patients undergoing cardiac surgery and patients in intensive-care units; similarly, Cramond in this present volume describes the psychological complications of patients undergoing haemodialysis, and the reactions of the staff working in a dialysis unit. In fact, greater awareness of the psychological aspects in these and other units could lead to improved design and management so that psychiatric complications could be prevented rather than having to be treated after they have developed. Details of consultation services of this kind have also been reported from a number of hospitals in Canada and North America: by Lipowski (1967b) at the Royal Victoria Hospital in Montreal; by Kaufman (1957) at the Mount Sinai Hospital, in New York; by Beigler *et al.* (1959) at the Michael Reese Hospital in Chicago; and by Zinberg (1964) at the Beth-Israel Hospital in Boston.

TREATMENT

If a psychiatrist who is called in for consultation on psychosomatic problems is to provide a useful service it is essential that, in addition to his consultative role, he must be able to provide the necessary psychiatric services required for treatment.

The first essential is that any therapy he may advise must be based on realistic expectations. In patients who have developed structural lesions, it is often no longer possible to rely on psychological treatment methods only, even if emotional factors were important in their causation, as the organic lesions or disturbances of function may have reached a stage when medical or surgical treatment is essential and sometimes urgently required to save life; this applies, for example, to patients with chronic peptic ulceration, long-standing ulcerative colitis or severe attacks of asthma. Unrealistic advice which ignores the need for physical treatment will rightly make the referring doctor mistrust the psychiatrist's opinion.

However, in many cases a combination of physical and psycho-social treatment methods may be needed. Once attention has been drawn to the relevant psychological and social factors, this can often be carried out by the referring doctor or his staff or, after discharge, by the patient's general practitioner, with or without the help of social workers. If the junior hospital staff and social workers are going to provide the necessary supportive psychotherapy and case-work, the psychiatrist should remain available to them for advice, if needed. Organized supervisory seminars for the junior staff and social workers, run by psychotherapists along the lines of seminars introduced by Balint (1964) for general practitioners, may be of great help here.

In other cases, however, the psychiatrist may have to take over the patient for treatment in his own department. This does, of course, apply particularly if the patient is suffering from a severe psychiatric illness, such as an organic psychiatric syndrome, severe depressive illnesses or intractable conversion symptoms; in some cases transfer to a psychiatric ward may therefore be needed. Most other patients with psychosomatic symptoms can continue to be treated on general wards, provided there is sufficient psychiatric staff available to see the patient regularly and to assist the medical staff.

In some cases the question will arise whether the patient should be taken on, usually as an out-patient, for formal psychotherapy (Wolff, 1962). Patients with somatic symptoms are, of course, often particularly resistant to the idea that their illness might be partly of psychological origin, and not infrequently this defensive attitude will have been strengthened by prolonged physical investigation and treatment. Many patients will be found to be unsuitable for formal psychotherapy, especially those who are defending against a serious and possibly psychotic breakdown; in such cases it will be safer to respect these defences and to restrict oneself to a combination of supportive psychotherapy and physical treatment.

In others the first task will be to help the patients gradually to overcome their resistances. If this can be achieved, and in those who from the beginning were more strongly motivated towards insight-directed psychotherapy, and who are thought to be capable of using a psychotherapeutic experience constructively, formal psychotherapy may be indicated. Sufficient psychotherapists should, therefore, be available on the hospital staff for such patients to be taken on, usually as out-patients, for individual or group psychotherapy. It must be realized, too, that although psycho-analytical principles and especially understanding and interpretation of transference phenomena will form the basis of such psychotherapeutic procedures, formal analysis is frequently not the treatment of choice, quite apart from the fact that it is unlikely to be available, except for a small proportion of patients. A more flexible psychotherapeutic approach is usually needed in patients with psychosomatic disorders (Wolff, 1962, 1968), and in many cases psychotherapy will have to be combined not only with continued physical treatment but also with social measures involving the patient and his relatives.

TEACHING PSYCHOSOMATIC MEDICINE

It will be clear from what has been said about the practice of psychosomatic medicine in general hospitals that such practice, properly conducted, will by itself have an educational influence on the rest of the staff and students, and should lead to an increased awareness of the psychosomatic aspects of medicine. However, an organized training programme is necessary if the principles of psychosomatic medicine are to be taught properly. This will next be considered in relation to medical students, junior non-psychiatric staff and postgraduate students of psychiatry.

Medical Students

The teaching of the basic facts concerning psychophysical relationships does not differ essentially from the teaching of other aspects of the biological basis of medicine, but it is important that during the pre-clinical and clinical years students are taught how psychological processes affect physiological function, and *vice versa*, both in health and disease.

The real problem, however, is how to make students sensitive to the fact that their patients' life experience, both past and present, may be of significance to their illness; they must be taught how to interview patients and to relate to them in such a manner that they can elicit the relevant information from them; at the same time they will have to learn that this cannot be done properly without becoming aware of their own emotional reactions in the interview situation. It is in this respect that the teaching of the psychosomatic approach differs most from what students are used to in their scientific training (Thomae and Turquet, 1964; Wolff, 1966; Woodmansey, 1967).

Details of training programmes and teaching methods have been described among others by Engel *et al.* (1957) and Romano (1961) from the Liaison Service in Rochester, and by Tredgold (1962) and Wolff (1966) from University College Hospital, London. It is important that students should be introduced early on in their training, through lectures and in small discussion groups, to an understanding of psychological processes in man, of personality development and family interaction, and their relation to stress and illness. In Great Britain the Report of the Royal Commission on Medical Education (1968) has stressed the need for teaching the behavioural sciences during the pre-clinical years; but in planning such courses the emphasis must be placed on human psychological experience and on the influence of inter-personal relationships and of the social environment, rather than on theoretical psychological, psycho-analytical or sociological concepts, or experimental psychology much of which is irrelevant to the practice of medicine; any over-emphasis in these directions is likely to diminish the students' interest in the psychological aspects of medicine. On the other hand, a well-planned course in the behavioural sciences (Hooper and Humphrey, 1968) can serve as a valuable preparation for the practice of psychosomatic medicine, especially if much of the teaching is done by clinicians interested in psychological, psychosomatic and social medicine.

As soon as students start their clinical work they should be taught, alongside their scientific and clinical studies, how to interview patients and to evaluate the significance of emotional factors in their patients. At University College Hospital, for example, while students are working on medical firms for six months, they meet the psychiatrist attached to their firm each week on the medical wards, in small groups of four to six; whenever possible a medical patient is interviewed in front of the group, either by the psychiatrist or, better still, by one of the students themselves; subsequently the group discusses the interview and the student–patient or doctor–patient relationship, and the significance of what has come to light. When relevant to the particular patient, details of psychophysiological and psychosocial aspects are discussed as well, and so is the question of what can be done to help the patient. Similar teaching sessions can be held for students on obstetric, paediatric and surgical firms.

While students are doing their psychiatric clerkship, these skills and attitudes can be developed further in relation to patients with psychiatric illnesses and those with psychosomatic symptoms referred to the department. Again, the learning process depends on letting students conduct interviews themselves and on providing ample time for discussion in small seminars (Wolff, 1966, 1967). At this stage students can begin to appreciate that psychosomatic concepts are relevant also to psychiatry proper and that the brain itself can be looked upon as a target organ responding to emotional stress; for example, the biochemical changes accompanying severe depressive illnesses may be the result of stressful experience acting on a person constitutionally predisposed to depression; the same may apply to the development of a schizophrenic illness.

The result of integrated medical–psychiatric training programmes of this kind (Tredgold, 1962) is that some students may develop a special interest in the psychosomatic and psychotherapeutic aspects of medicine. How such students can be taught more about the doctor–patient relationship in Balint-type seminars, has been described by Balint (1957); and how senior students can be given the opportunity of taking on a patient with psychosomatic or psychiatric symptoms for regular psychotherapy under supervision, has been described by Ball and Wolff (1963) from University College Hospital and by Heine (1962) from the University of Chicago School of Medicine.

Lastly, at some time during their training all students should be attached to a general practitioner in order to gain first-hand experience of the importance of psychological and social aspects of illness, as seen in the general practitioner's surgery and during visits to the patient's home and family.

Junior Non-psychiatric Staff

It would clearly be valuable if the junior staff on non-psychiatric firms could also attend seminars in which the psychosomatic and psychotherapeutic aspects of their patients are discussed. However, in most hospitals these postgraduate students are necessarily so involved in the further study of their own chosen specialty and in routine work that they are rarely willing or able to take part in seminars of this kind. In practice one therefore has to rely mainly on trying to teach them more about the psychosomatic aspects of medicine by contact with them during consultations and day-to-day discussion of problems concerning their own patients; at University College Hospital a few of them take part in the weekly liaison teaching sessions for medical students on medical wards; those who do can gain a great deal themselves from this experience. However, the need to extend the teaching of psychosomatic medicine to these postgraduate students is a challenge that still needs to be met.

Postgraduate Psychiatric Students

As most future psychiatrists will be spending at least part of their time in general hospitals, all of them should during their training have gained some experience in psychosomatic consultative work and in the management of psychosomatic disorders. This is best achieved by ensuring that all postgraduate psychiatric students also spend some time in a psychiatric unit of a general hospital. While doing so they should themselves do consultative work on patients with psychosomatic problems. As always, they will learn most by doing the work themselves, but the more time is available for staff meetings and discussion of psychosomatic aspects of medicine and for supervision of their own psychotherapeutic work, the more successful is their training in psychosomatic medicine likely to be.

THE HOSPITAL AND THE COMMUNITY

Although this chapter has been concerned with work in hospitals, these are, of course, intimately related to the community they serve. Close contact between the hospital staff and general practitioners and social workers is therefore essential for the proper interchange of knowledge and practice of psychosomatic medicine. This can be achieved through postgraduate courses on psychosomatic medicine for general practitioners organized by the psychiatric and other hospital departments, and by holding weekly Balint-type seminars for general practitioners run by the psychiatric staff of the hospital (Balint, 1964). But at least as important are regular and informal contacts and discussions between the hospital staff and general practitioners. These can take place during domiciliary visits but also by giving them ready access to the hospital so that they can discuss with their hospital colleagues the many psychosomatic aspects of their patients' illnesses.

REFERENCES

Balint, M. (1957). 'Training Medical Students in Psychotherapy.' *Lancet*, **2,** 1015.

— (1964). *The Doctor, His Patient and the Illness*. London: Pitman.

— Balint, E., Gosling, R. and Hildebrand, P. (1966). *A Study of Doctors*. London: Tavistock Publications.

Ball, D. H. and Wolff, H. H. (1963), 'An Experiment in the Teaching of Psychotherapy to Medical Students.' *Lancet*, **1,** 214.

Beigler, J. S., Robbins, F. P., Lane, E. W., Miller, A. A. and Samelson, C. (1959). 'Report on Liaison Psychiatry at Michael Reese Hospital, 1950–1958.' *Archs Neurol. Psychiat.*, **81,** 733.

Crisp, A. H. (1968). 'Some Approaches to Psychosomatic Clinical Research.' *Br. J. med. Psychol.*, **41,** 323.

Engel, G. L. (1967a). 'The Concept of Psychosomatic Disorder.' *J. Psychosom. Res.*, **11,** 3.

— (1967b). 'Medical Education and the Psychosomatic Approach. A Report on the Rochester Experience 1946–1966.' *J. Psychosom. Res.*, **11,** 77.

— Greene, W. A., Reichsmann, F., Schmale, A. H. and Ashenburg, N. (1957). 'A Graduate and Undergraduate Teaching Programme in the Psychological Aspects of Medicine.' *J. med. Educ.*, **32,** 859.

Hackett, T. P. and Weisman, A. D. (1960). 'Psychiatric Management of Operative Syndromes.' *Psychosom. Med.*, **22,** 267 and 365.

Heine, R. W. (1962). *The Student Physician as Psychotherapist*. University of Chicago Press.

Helsberg, H. C. (1958). 'Psychiatric Investigations of Patients in a Medical Department.' *Acta psychiat. scand.*, **33,** 303.

Hill, Sir Denis (1969a). 'Psychiatric Education During a Period of Social Change.' *Br. med. J.*, **1,** 205.

— (1969b). 'Educational Objectives. Conference on Postgraduate Psychiatric Education. The Training of Psychiatrists.' *Br. J. Psychiat.* In Press.

Hooper, D. and Humphrey, M. (1968). 'Behavioural Science for Medical Students.' *Lancet*, **2,** 1293.

Hopkins, P. (1955). 'The General Practitioner and the Psychosomatic Approach.' In *Modern Trends in Psychosomatic Medicine—1*, p. 1. Ed. by D. O'Neill. London: Butterworths.

Kaufman, R. M. (1953). 'The Role of the Psychiatrist in a General Hospital.' *Psychiat. Quart.*, **27,** 367.

— (1957). 'A Psychiatric Unit in a General Hospital.' *J. Mt. Sinai Hosp.*, **24,** 572.

Kehoe, M. (1961). 'The Rochester Scheme: a Medical-Psychiatric Liaison Service.' *Lancet*, **2,** 145.

Kornfeld, D. S. (1969). 'Psychiatric View of the Intensive Care Unit.' *Br. med. J.*, **1,** 108.

Lipowski, Z. J. (1967a). 'Review of Consultation Psychiatry and Psychosomatic Medicine. I. General Principles.' *Psychosom. Med.*, **29,** 153.

— (1967b). 'Review of Consultation Psychiatry and Psychosomatic Medicine. II. Clinical Aspects.' *Psychosom. Med.*, **29,** 201.

— (1968). 'Review of Consultation Psychiatry and Psychosomatic Medicine. III. Theoretical Issues.' *Psychosom. Med.*, **30,** 395.

Meyer, E. and Mendelson, M. (1961). 'Psychiatric Consultations with Patients on Medical and Surgical Wards: Patterns and Processes.' *Psychiatry*, **24,** 197.

Querido, A. (1959). 'Forecast and Follow-up. An Investigation into the Clinical, Social and Mental Factors affecting the Result of Hospital Treatment.' *Br. J. prev. soc. Med.*, **13,** 33.

Romano, J. (1961). 'Teaching of Psychiatry to Medical Students.' *Lancet*, **2,** 93.

Rosenbaum, M. and Reiser, M. F. (1958). 'Principles of Management of Psychosomatic Disorders.' *Med. Clins N. Am.*, **42,** 769.

Royal Commission on Medical Education (1968). London: H.M.S.O.

Rud, F. (1953). 'Psychiatric Activities and Instruction at a General Hospital.' *J. clin. exp. Psychopath.*, **14,** 139.

Shepherd, M., Davies, B. and Culpan, R. (1960). 'Psychiatric Illness in the General Hospital.' *Acta psychiat. neurol. scand.*, **35,** 518.

Thomae, H. and Turquet, P. M. (1964). 'Training in Psychosomatic Medicine. A Critical Review.' In *Advances in Psychosomatic Medicine*, p. 167. Basel/New York: Karger.

Tredgold, R. F. (1962). 'The Integration of Psychiatric Teaching into the Curriculum.' *Lancet*, **1,** 344.

Walton, H. J., Drewery, J. and Carstairs, G. M. (1963). 'Interest of Graduating Medical Students in Social and Emotional Aspects of Illness.' *Br. med. J.*, **2,** 588.

Walton, H. J. Drewery, J. and Philip, A. E. (1964). 'Typical Medical Students.' *Br. med. J.*, **2,** 744.

Wolfe, H. E. (1966). 'Consultation: Role, Function and Process.' *Ment. Hyg.*, **50,** 132.

Wolff, H. H. (1962). 'The Psychotherapeutic Approach.' In *The Principles of Treatments of Psychosomatic Disorders*, Ed. by P. Hopkins and H. H. Wolff, p. 83. Oxford: Pergamon Press.

— (1966). 'Teaching Psychodynamic Aspects of Psychiatry to Medical Students.' *Br. J. med. Educ.* **1,** 43.

— (1967). 'Influencing Students' Attitudes Towards the Emotional Aspects of Illness.' *J. Psychosom. Res.*, **11,** 87.

— (1968). 'The Psychodynamic Approach to Psychosomatic Disorders: Contributions and Limitations of Psychoanalysis.' *Br. J. med. Psychol.*, **41,** 343.

Woodmansey, A. C. (1967). 'Neglected Fundamentals in Undergraduate Psychiatric Education.' *Br. J. med. Educ.*, **1,** 183.

Zinberg, N. E. (Ed.) (1964). *Psychiatry and Medical Practice in a General Hospital.* New York: International Universities Press.

INDEX